Annual Musical Instrument Auction Price Guide

1991 Edition

From The String Letter Press,
Publishers of *Strings* and
Acoustic Guitar Magazines.

The Publishers wish to thank Frances Gillham and Frederick Oster of Christie's; Sarah Hamill and Kerry Keane of Skinner; and Graham Wells of Sotheby's, for their kind assistance in providing photographs for this Guide.

Special thanks to Dennie Mehocich, David M. Brin, and Joel Murach for careful editorial work in the preparation of this Guide.

Cover design by Ken Piekny.

ISBN 0-9626081-1-4

Photographs on Front Cover: Important Violin, "The Dancla," by Antonio Stradivari, offered at Sotheby's, London, November 22, 1990, Lot 127; Guitar by Hermann Hauser, offered at Sotheby's, London, November 22, 1990, Lot 162. Back Cover: Very Fine and Important Two-Manual Harpsichord by Jacob & Abraham Kirkman, offered at Sotheby's, London, November 22, 1990, Lot 150.

The String Letter Press
412 Red Hill Avenue
San Anselmo, California 94960
(415) 485-6946

Table of Contents

Introduction

This guide offers descriptions and prices in U.S. dollars, Deutsche marks, pounds sterling, and yen of musical instruments and bows offered at auction by identifiable maker at 16 sales held in the United States, Great Britain, and Germany during 1990. [For a complete list of sales, see next page.]

It is emphatically not a guide to the playing qualities of these instruments, nor to their physical condition. Nor does the guide generally reflect "retail prices," since many items bought at auction are subsequently resold.

The guide is divided into two sections. The first section is an "Item by Item Listing." It provides the details on each item: Where it was offered, lot number, where and when made, low and high estimated prices, the specifics of the most recent certificate, if any, with which the item was offered, and the actual selling price shown in four currencies. The first currency is U.S. dollars, followed by pounds sterling, Deutsche marks, and yen. The order of currencies is fixed, regardless of the currency in which the sale was conducted.

The second section contains four "Summaries by Item and Maker" which briefly encapsulate the offerings of the year, each in a different currency. Each summary is subdivided alphabetically by item, from Accordion to Xylophone. Within each, you will find an alphabetical list of makers whose work appeared at auction, along with the barest of facts: How many items by that maker were offered, how many sold, what were the lowest, highest, and average selling prices. If no items were sold, you will find no price information. If no items were *offered* by a particular maker, you will simply not find that maker's name.

Please note that all the basic information in this guide was supplied by the auction houses themselves, and it mirrors whatever inconsistencies or ambiguities you will find in the catalogues and the salerooms. To cite one such example, you will find bows stamped "A. Vigneron," with no attempt to lump them with bows by (Joseph) Arthur Vigneron nor his son, Andre. While authorities may tell us that it was the father who used this stamp, while his son used a stamp reading "Andre Vigneron," we are not prepared to second-guess the auction houses who offered these bows under the sobriquet "A. Vigneron."

At the same time, we have attempted to clear up merely stylistic inconsistencies. These include standardizing Latinate into Italian forms of proper names. Thus, a violin by Amati, Girolamo (II) is summarized with one by Amati, Hieronymus (II).

Let the reader then be wary. When in doubt, first refer, if possible, to the catalogue of the auction house itself. If the catalogue is unavailable to you, contact the auction house directly, using the directory of names and addresses on Page vi of this guide, and request further clarification. ✳

Sales Included in This Guide

The bracketed code is shorthand which consists of a letter denoting the auction house followed by a two-digit number for the month in which the sale took place. You will find these codes used throughout the detailed item-by-item listings later in the guide.

House	*Place*	*Date*	*Code*
Phillips	London	02–08–90	[P02]
Sotheby's	London	03–27–90	[S03]
Christie's	London	03–28–90	[C03]
Phillips	London	03–29–90	[P03]
Bongartz	Koln	04–30–90	[B04]
Christie's	London	06–13–90	[C06]
Sotheby's	London	06–14–90	[S06]
Phillips	London	06–21–90	[P06]
Phillips	London	07–26–90	[P07]
Phillips	London	09–13–90	[P09]
Phillips	London	10–18–90	[P10]
Skinner	Boston	11–11–90	[Sk11]
Phillips	London	11–15–90	[P11]
Christie's	London	11–21–90	[C11]
Sotheby's	London	11–22–90	[S11]

Directory of Auction Houses

These are the firms in the United States, Great Britain, and Germany who regularly conduct sales of musical instruments, particularly stringed instruments and bows.

Bongartz
Am Chorusberg 57
D-5100 Aachen, Germany
Telephone 02-41-69090

Christie's
8 King Street, St. James's
London SW1Y 6QT, England
Telephone 71 839-9060
Fax 71 839-1611
Specialists: Frances Gillham, Venetia Brudenell

Christie's (New York)
502 Park Avenue
New York, NY 10022
Telephone (212) 546-1000
Fax (212) 980-8163
Specialist: Frederick Oster

Phillips
101 New Bond Street
London W1Y 0AS 6UA, England
Telephone 71 629-6602
Fax 71 629-8876
Specialists: Edward Stollar, Philip Scott, Jennifer Harris

Phillips (New York)
406 East 79th Street
New York, NY 10021
Telephone (212) 570-4830
Fax (212) 570-2207

Skinner
357 Main Street
Bolton, MA 01740
Telephone (508) 779-6241
Fax (508) 779-5144
Expert: Kerry K. Keane [in New York, (212) 678-0391]

Sotheby's
34-35 New Bond Street
London W1A 2AA, England
Telephone 71 493-8080
Fax 71 409-3100
Experts: Graham Wells, Andrew Hooker, Adam Watson

Sotheby's (New York)
1334 York Avenue
New York, New York 10021
Telephone (212) 606-7000
Fax (212) 606-7107
Expert: Leah Ramirez

How to Read Summaries by Item by Maker

Beginning on Page 75, you will find four Summaries by Item by Maker. They differ only in the currencies used to express monetary values: Dollars, Deutsche marks, pounds sterling, and yen.

This section summarizes the more detailed data found in the first part of the Guide, the Item by Item Listings. Here, you will find a brief overview of the items offered during 1990, arranged alphabetically first by item—violin, viola, cello, etc.—and then by maker.

In the left-hand column is the name of the maker. Items that have been offered as being "attributed to" or "ascribed to" a particular maker are shown separately from those identified as "by" that maker. [You may find inconsistencies in the way names have been given—a first initial in one case, a full name in the next. These problems have been raised and discussed in the general Introduction to the Guide.]

In the next column, you find a numeric count of the items by that maker which were offered at auction during 1990. To the immediate right is the count of those items which were actually sold. If none were sold, you will see a zero here. (If you are looking for information on a particular maker and cannot find the name, it is because no items by that maker were offered at auction during 1990.)

In the next three columns are monetary values. First is the lowest price of an item by that maker, then the highest, and finally the average. If only one item was sold, you will find the same number in all three columns. Please use extreme caution in assessing these monetary values. From a purely statistical point of view, they are almost completely unreliable. Nonetheless, they can be construed, within narrow limits, as reflective of the current market. This is also a good place to repeat what was said earlier: The guide does not reflect upon the playing qualities or the physical condition of the items offered at auction. The only way to assess these factors is through personal experience. ✳

A Key to the Item by Item Listings

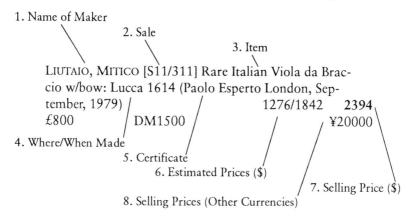

1. Name of Maker

2. Sale

3. Item

LIUTAIO, MITICO [S11/311] Rare Italian Viola da Braccio w/bow: Lucca 1614 (Paolo Esperto London, September, 1979) 1276/1842 **2394**
£800 DM1500 ¥20000

4. Where/When Made

5. Certificate

6. Estimated Prices ($)

7. Selling Price ($)

8. Selling Prices (Other Currencies)

1. Name of Maker. An "attributed" work signals an attribution made, or agreed to, by the auction house; when "ascribed," a traditional ascription is acknowledged but not necessarily agreed with.
2. The Lot Number assigned by the auctioneer is preceded by an initial to identify the house (B Bongartz; C Christie's; P Phillips; S Sotheby's; Sk Skinner) followed by a number for the month of the sale.
3. A description of the item as it appears in the sale catalog. When the item is sold with accessories or when additional items are part of the same lot, a brief itemization appears here. This is also the place where defects or repairs, as reported in the sale catalog, are noted.
4. Place and date, if known, of manufacture.
5. If sold with a certificate attesting to its provenance or identity, the most recent issuer is indicated in parentheses, along with the place and date of issuance.
6. Low and high estimated prices are separated by a slash (/). This is the price range within which the item was expected to sell, in the opinion of the auctioneers. On occasion, no estimate is made—most often involving an important instrument by a famous maker.
7. The actual selling price appears in bold. This includes the buyer's premium, now uniformly 10% at the major auction houses. Prices are given in US dollars converted from local currency at their value on the day sold. An unsold item is recorded "**NS**." These listings do not provide details on size, weight, color, etc. which often help to identify or distinguish particular items. You are advised to consult the catalogs published prior to the sales, which may be obtained directly from the auctioneers.
8. You may determine the country in which the sale took place from the "Sale" information in "2" above. The currency of that country has then been converted to three others as a convenience to readers in different countries.

ACCORDION

Horne, Edgar [P03/54] Rosewood Accordion w/case, excellent condition: Nottingham, late 19th C. 164/329 **307**
£187 DM519 ¥47835

AEOLA

Wheatstone & Co., C. [S11/132] Sixty-Four Button English Aeola w/case: London, c. 1923 982/1376 **1124**
£572 DM1671 ¥143286

BAGPIPES

MacDougall, D. [S11/137] Great Highland Bagpipes w/box: Breadalbane, c. 1880 1965/2948 **NS**

BANJO

Bacon Banjo Co. [Sk11/8] Gold Plated American Tenor Banjo: Groton, c. 1925 400/600 **990**
£505 DM1475 ¥127710

Fairbanks Co., A. C. [Sk11/7] American Five String Banjo w/case: late 19th C. 400/600 **715**
£365 DM1065 ¥92235

Fiesta [P06/44] Good Four-String Tenor Banjo w/case 104/259 **171**
£99 DM287 ¥26374

Libby Bros. [Sk11/9] Rare American Five String Banjo w/case: North Gorham 250/350 **303**
£154 DM451 ¥39023

BASS

Cole, James [S06/332] Double Bass w/cover: Manchester, c. 1870 10260/13680 **11286**
£6600 DM19058 ¥1737120

Derazey, Justin [S03/184] French Double Bass w/cover: Mirecourt, c. 1880 5130/6840 **5643**
£3300 DM9141 ¥836220

Jacquot Family (member of) [Sk11/53] French Double Bass w/case, bow: Nancy 2000/3000 **1760**
£898 DM2622 ¥227040

Panormo, Vincenzo (ascribed to) [S03/185] English Double Bass: London, early 19th C. 6840/10260 **9029**
£5280 DM14626 ¥1337952

BASS BOW

Alvey, Brian [S03/258] Silver Double Bass Bow 1026/1368 **NS**

Bailey, G. E. [P03/301] Silver Double Bass Bow Bottesini pattern 247/493 **995**
£605 DM1678 ¥154759

Dotschkail, R. [P11/260] Nickel Dragonneti Double Bass Bow 295/393 **696**
£354 DM1022 ¥89648

Mettal, O. [P11/262] Nickel Dragonneti Double Bass Bow 236/354 **547**
£278 DM803 ¥70438

Mettal, Walter [P11/258] Gold Dragonneti Double Bass Bow w/case 393/590 **1044**
£531 DM1533 ¥134472

Morizot, Louis [P11/268] Nickel Double Bass Bow w/case 393/590 **374**
£190 DM549 ¥48165

Morizot, Louis [S11/226] Silver Double Bass Bow: Mirecourt, c. 1930 2358/3537 **NS**

Morizot, Louis [S03/249] Silver Double Bass Bow: Mirecourt, c. 1930 3078/3762 **NS**

Paulus, Johannes O. [P11/259] Gold Dragonneti Double Bass Bow w/case 393/590 **945**
£481 DM1387 ¥121665

Paulus, Johannes O. [P11/261] Gold Dragonneti Double Bass Bow 295/491 **994**
£506 DM1460 ¥128069

Riedl, Alfons [P11/263] Dragonneti Double Bass Bow w/bow 393/590 **795**
£405 DM1168 ¥102455

Riedl, Alfons [P11/266] Silver Bottesini Double Bass Bow w/case 491/688 **424**
£216 DM622 ¥54568

Riedl, Alfons [P11/267] Silver Bottesini Double Bass Bow w/case 491/688 **746**
£380 DM1095 ¥96051

Vickers, J. E. [P03/303] Good Silver Double Bass Bow 247/411 **344**
£209 DM580 ¥53462

Vickers, J. E. [P09/235] Nickel Double Bass Bow 224/337 **206**
£110 DM326 ¥28281

Vickers, J. E. [P11/254] Nickel Double Bass Bow 295/590 **238**
£121 DM349 ¥30625

Winkler, Franz [P03/302] Silver Double Bass Bow Bottesini pattern 329/493 **723**
£440 DM1220 ¥112552

BASSOON

Bilton, Richard [S06/169] Six-Keyed Pearwood Bassoon w/touchpiece, 2 crooks: London, c. 1830 1197/1710 **1317**
£770 DM2223 ¥202664

Bocchia, Bono [Sk11/14] Twenty-Three Keyed Cocuswood Bassoon: Milan 350/450 **495**
£252 DM738 ¥63855

Buffet [Sk11/28] Twenty-One Keyed Cocuswood Bassoon w/case: Paris 600/800 **330**
£168 DM492 ¥42570

Buffet-Crampon & Co. [P06/37] Bassoon w/2 cases, 2 mouthpieces: Paris 345/518 **361**
£209 DM605 ¥55678

GOULDING, WOOD & CO. [S11/129] Six-Keyed Bassoon: London, c. 1815 1572/2358 **NS**

GRENSER, JOHANN HEINRICH [S06/166] Eight-Keyed Maple Bassoon: Dresden, c. 1810 6840/8550 **12227**
£7150 DM20646 ¥1881880

HECKEL [S11/130] Bassoon w/crook, case: Biebrich-am-Rhein, c. 1929 3930/5895 **NS**

HECKEL [S11/131] B-flat Bassoon w/case: Biebrich-am-Rhein, c. 1907 11790/23580 **10375**
£5280 DM15428 ¥1322640

HECKEL, WILHELM [S06/164] Bassoon w/case, crook, crutch: Biebrich, c. 1900 3420/5130 **NS**

MILHOUSE, WILLIAM [P07/7] Bassoon w/bassoon, case: London, c. 1800 546/910 **NS**

MILHOUSE, WILLIAM [S06/162] Six-Keyed Maple Bassoon w/touchpiece: London, first quarter, 19th C. 1368/2052 **NS**

MILHOUSE, WILLIAM [S06/167] Eight-Keyed Pearwood Bassoon w/case: London, first quarter, 19th C. 1710/3420 **NS**

ZIMMERMANN, JULIUS HEINRICH [Sk11/29] Eighteen-Keyed Maple Bassoon w/case: Leipzig 100/200 **358**
£182 DM533 ¥46118

BUGLE

ASTOR & CO., GEROCK [P06/43] Keyed Copper and Brass Bugle w/extension and mouthpiece: London, c. 1821-1827 173/345 **608**
£352 DM1019 ¥93773

PACE, CHARLES [P06/26] Keyed Bugle w/case: Westminster, mid 19th C. 345/518 **1672**
£968 DM2802 ¥257875

CITHERN

PRESTON [P11/26] English Cithern: London, c. 1800 590/786 **562**
£286 DM825 ¥72387

CLARINET

BILTON, RICHARD [S06/154] Fourteen-Keyed Boxwood Clarinet w/clarinet, mouthpiece: London, c. 1850 1112/1539 **1693**
£990 DM2859 ¥260568

BILTON, RICHARD [S06/160] Ten-Keyed Ebony Clarinet w/mouthpiece: London, c. 1840 1197/1539 **1317**
£770 DM2223 ¥202664

CRAMER [C03/4] Five-Keyed Boxwood Clarinet w/2 flageolets, incomplete 651/977 **681**
£418 DM1164 ¥107468

DARCHE [P03/45] Ivory Boxwood Clarinet: Paris, c. 1860 411/575 **543**
£330 DM915 ¥84414

FLORIO, PIETRO GRASSI [S06/155] Five-Keyed Boxwood Clarinet: London, late 18th C. 684/855 **1129**
£660 DM1906 ¥173712

GOULDING & CO. [P06/29] Ivory and Boxwood Clarinet w/mouthpiece: London, c. 1820 345/518 **361**
£209 DM605 ¥55678

KLEMM [C11/2] Five-Keyed Boxwood Clarinet w/mouthpiece: Philadelphia 493/690 **758**
£385 DM1117 ¥96481

LOT, ISADORE [P11/54] Ivory and Boxwood Clarinet w/case: c. 1867-1886 393/590 **389**
£198 DM571 ¥50114

MARTIN BROS. [P03/50] Ivory and Boxwood Clarinet w/mouthpiece: Paris 411/575 **434**
£264 DM732 ¥67531

METZLER [Sk11/16] Five-Keyed Boxwood Clarinet: London 400/500 **440**
£224 DM656 ¥56760

OTTEN, JOHN [P07/10] Ivory Boxwood Clarinet minus ivory bell ring: London, c. 1810 182/364 **280**
£154 DM452 ¥41903

WOLF & CO., ROBERT [P03/48] Ivory and Boxwood Clarinet w/mouthpiece: London 329/493 **344**
£209 DM580 ¥53462

WOOD & IVY [P03/47] Ivory and Boxwood Clarinet w/mouthpiece: London, c. 1840 329/493 **398**
£242 DM671 ¥61904

CONN, C. G. [P06/38] Pair Boehm-System Clarinets w/case: Elkhart 173/345 **171**
£99 DM287 ¥26374

SELMER [P06/39] Pair Clarinets w/case: Paris 138/207 **209**
£121 DM350 ¥32234

CLAVICHORD

GOFF, THOMAS [S03/386] Unfretted Clavichord bichordal throughout: London, c. 1971 2565/4275 **NS**

LINDHOLM, PEHR [S11/145] Swedish Bunfrei Clavichord: Stockholm, 1792 11790/15720 **NS**

CONCERTINA

CRABB & SON, H. [P11/48] Good Concertina w/case, excellent condition: London 786/1572 **778**
£396 DM1142 ¥100228

CRABB, HENRY [C06/11] Anglo Concertina w/case 688/1032 **NS**

JEFFRIES BROS. [P11/50] Concertina w/box: London 393/590 **303**
£154 DM444 ¥38977

JEFFRIES, CHARLES [S11/133] Two Concertinas w/2 cases: London, late 19th C. (Maker's, March 16, 1894) 982/1376 **3675**
£1870 DM5464 ¥468435

LACHENAL & CO. [P09/30] Concertina: London 281/467 **782**
£418 DM1237 ¥107468

LACHENAL & CO. [P09/31] Concertina w/case: London 467/655 **NS**

LACHENAL & CO. [S06/186] Forty-Eight Button English Concertina w/case: London 941/1454 **1279**
£748 DM2160 ¥196874

WHEATSTONE & CO., C. [P03/55] Concertina w/box: London, c. 1925 658/822 **1302**
£792 DM2196 ¥202594

WHEATSTONE & CO., C. [P03/56] Miniature Concertina w/case: London, c. 1924 132/247 **506**
£308 DM854 ¥78786

WHEATSTONE & CO., C. [P09/29] Concertina: London 655/842 **1070**
£572 DM1693 ¥147061

WHEATSTONE & CO., C. [P09/32] Duet Concertina: London 467/655 **494**
£264 DM781 ¥67874

WHEATSTONE & CO., C. [P09/33] Concertina 374/561 **905**
£484 DM1433 ¥124436

WHEATSTONE & CO., C. [P11/49] Concertina w/case, good condition: London 491/786 **NS**

COR ANGLAIS

LOREE, FRANCOIS [C06/21] Rosewood Cor Anglais w/case 1376/2064 **3595**
£2090 DM6040 ¥550861

CORNOPEAN

KOHLER, JOHN [S06/171] Silver Cornopean w/case, 3 valves, shank, crooks, tuning bit, 2 mouthpieces: London, mid 19th C. 1368/2052 **3950**
£2310 DM6670 ¥607992

CORONET

CONN, C. G. [Sk11/25] Three-Keyed Coronet w/case, extensions: Elkhart 300/400 **303**
£154 DM451 ¥39023

PEPPER, J. W. [Sk11/26] Three-Keyed Coronet: Philadelphia 100/200 **385**
£196 DM574 ¥49665

ENGLISH HORN

FORNARI [S06/159] Fine Curved Three-Keyed English Horn: Venice, c. 1800 6840/10260 **NS**

FLAGEOLET

BAINBRIDGE [C06/1] Boxwood Flageolet 172/258 **227**
£132 DM381 ¥34791

HASTRICK [P03/49] Rosewood and Ivory Flageolet w/box, C# key missing: London, c. 1840 164/263 **398**
£242 DM671 ¥61904

PELOUBET, C. [Sk11/22] One-Keyed Boxwood Flagolet w/mouthpiece, 2 clarinets, flagolet, piccolo: Bloomfield 300/400 **550**
£280 DM820 ¥70950

FLUTE

BOEHM & MENDLER [C06/3] Fine Cocuswood Boehm-system Flute w/case 2580/3440 **NS**

CAHUSAC, THOMAS [P09/28] Ivory Flute minus top and bottom silver collars: last quarter, 18th C. 561/748 **617**
£330 DM977 ¥84843

CAHUSAC [C11/1] One-Keyed Boxwood Flute: London 394/788 **607**
£308 DM894 ¥77185

CAHUSAC, THOMAS [C06/4] One-keyed Boxwood Flute 516/860 **NS**

CAHUSAC, THOMAS [C06/7] Good Six-keyed Ivory Flute 1376/2064 **NS**

CARTE, RUDALL & CO. [P03/46] Silver and Rosewood Flute w/case, cleaning rod: London, c. 1870 164/247 **2080**
£1265 DM3508 ¥323587

CARTE, RUDALL & CO. [P06/32] Rosewood Flute: London **247**
£143 DM414 ¥38095

CARTE, RUDALL & CO. [P07/12] Rosewood Flute w/case: London, c. 1900 146/218 **NS**

CARTE, RUDALL & CO. [P10/2] Rosewood Flute w/case: London, c. 1900 78/118 **119**
£61 DM179 ¥14847

CLEMENTI & CO. [P06/28] Silver and Rosewood Flute minus top cap: London, c. 1820 259/432 **380**
£220 DM637 ¥58608

CLINTON & CO. [P06/33] Rosewood Flute w/case: London, c. 1850 259/432 **988**
£572 DM1656 ¥152381

CROSBY, W. [Sk11/17] Eight-Keyed Cocuswood Flute w/case, flute, accordion: Boston 200/300 **523**
£266 DM779 ¥67403

FLORIO, PIETRO GRASSI [S11/143] One-Keyed Boxwood Flute: London, c. 1775 1965/2948 **NS**

FLORIO, PIETRO GRASSI [S06/149] Six-Keyed Boxwood Flute w/case: London, 1771 2565/3420 **6019**
£3520 DM10164 ¥926464

GOULDING & CO. [P02/10] Ivory and Boxwood Flute minus ivory cap and button collar: London, c. 1800 170/255 **187**
£110 DM309 ¥27005

GOULDING & D'ALMAINE [P03/51] Good Ivory and Boxwood Flute: London, c. 1830 411/658 **NS**

GOULDING & D'ALMAINE [P06/35] Good Ivory and Boxwood Flute: London, c. 1830 259/432 **361**
£209 DM605 ¥55678

GRAVES, SAMUEL [Sk11/15] American One-Keyed Fruitwood Flute 100/200 **385**
£196 DM574 ¥49665

GRENSER, AUGUSTE [S11/138] Fine One-Keyed Boxwood Flute: Dresden, c. 1800 3537/4323 **18373**
£9350 DM27321 ¥2342175

HALE, JOHN [P07/8] Good Ivory Boxwood Flute: London 273/546 **260**
£143 DM420 ¥38910

HAMMIG, PHILIPP [C03/3] Silver Flute w/case: Markneukirchen 488/651 **860**
£528 DM1470 ¥135749

HAYNES CO., WILLIAM S. [Sk11/23] Silver Boehm-System Flute w/case: Boston 1400/1600 **935**
£477 DM1393 ¥120615

HOLTZAPFFLER [C11/6] Four-Keyed Ebony Flute: Paris 1970/2955 **NS**

LAFLEUR [P06/34] Dark Rosewood Flute w/case: France 173/345 **171**
£99 DM287 ¥26374

LAURENT, CLAUDE [S11/128] Fine Glass Flute w/case: Paris, 1834 5895/9825 **NS**

LAURENT, CLAUDE [S06/148] Fine Four-Keyed Glass Flute: Paris, 1805 11970/17100 **NS**

LAURENT, CLAUDE [C11/7] Six-Keyed Glass Flute: Paris, 1819 7880/11820 **11919**
£6050 DM17557 ¥1516130

LOT, LOUIS [S06/147] Silver Boehm-System Flute: Paris 1710/2052 **941**
£550 DM1588 ¥144760

LOT, LOUIS [S06/163] Silver Boehm-System Flute w/case: Paris 1368/1710 **1505**
£880 DM2541 ¥231616

LOT, LOUIS [C03/1] Silver Plated Flute w/case: Paris 977/1465 **NS**

MAKER'S GUILD NO. 168 [P11/52] Presentation Silver Flute w/case, Boehm system 1965/2948 **NS**

METZLER, VALENTIN [P07/11] Stained Boxwood Flute w/flute, lower head joint with 4 open cracks: London, c. 1800 182/364 **NS**

METZLER, VALENTIN [P10/3] Stained Boxwood Flute w/flute: London, c. 1800 157/196 **172**
£88 DM260 ¥21595

MIYAZAWA & CO. [P06/30] Fine Solid Silver Boehm-System Flute w/case: Asaka 1209/1727 **1235**
£715 DM2070 ¥190476

MONZANI [S11/139] Seven-Keyed Ivory Flute w/case: London, c. 1820 2948/3930 **3242**
£1650 DM4821 ¥413325

POTTER, WILLIAM HENRY [P09/27] Ivory Flute: London, c. 1800 281/374 **494**
£264 DM781 ¥67874

POTTER, WILLIAM HENRY [S06/158] Six-Keyed Boxwood Flute: London, c. 1815 599/770 **NS**

PROWSE, THOMAS [P03/52] Silver and Rosewood Flute: London, c. 1840 329/493 **995**
£605 DM1678 ¥154759

REDE, H. W. [Sk11/19] One-Keyed Boxwood Flute w/fife, piccolo: London 200/400 **358**
£182 DM533 ¥46118

RUDALL, GEORGE [S06/146] Fine Eight-Keyed Cocuswood Flute w/case: London, c. 1820 684/1026 **1505**
£880 DM2541 ¥231616

MILLIGAN [C06/6] Four-keyed Flute in F 172/344 **NS**

FRENCH HORN

HAWKES & SON [P06/41] Brass French Horn w/case: Manchester 173/345 **570**
£330 DM955 ¥87912

GUITAR

BOUCHET, ROBERT [S11/170] Concert Guitar w/case: Paris, 1961 (Maker's, July 11, 1961) 17685/19650 **19454**
£9900 DM28928 ¥2479950

BOUCHET, ROBERT [S06/174] Concert Guitar w/case: Paris, 1964 13680/20520 **26334**
£15400 DM44467 ¥4053280

CONTRERAS, MANUEL [S11/164] Concert Guitar w/case: Madrid, 1970 1572/2358 **NS**

EPIPHONE GUITAR CO. [Sk11/6] American Electric Arch Top Guitar w/case: New York 400/600 **660**
£337 DM983 ¥85140

GIBSON CO. [Sk11/1] Rare American Arch Top Guitar w/case: Kalamazoo, 1914 1500/2500 **2640**
£1346 DM3934 ¥340560

GIBSON CO. [Sk11/3] Arch Top Guitar w/case: Kalamazoo, c. 1935 800/1200 **2310**
£1178 DM3442 ¥297990

GIBSON CO. [Sk11/5] American Guitar w/case: Kalamazoo, c. 1965 500/700 **1210**
£617 DM1803 ¥156090

GUTIERREZ, MANUEL [C06/13] Rare Spanish Guitar: Seville, 1837 3440/4300 **NS**

HAUSER, HERMANN [S11/162] Six-String Guitar w/case, adjuster key: Munich, 1928 3930/5895 **4323**
£2200 DM6428 ¥551100

HAUSER, HERMANN [S11/163] Double-Necked Contra Guitar w/case, adjuster key: Munich, 1924 6877/9825 **NS**

KOHNO, MASARU [S06/173] Concert Guitar w/case: Tokyo, 1978 5985/6840 **NS**

KOHNO, MASARU [S06/177] Concert Guitar w/case: Tokyo, 1964 1368/2052 **2257**
£1320 DM3811 ¥347424

LACOTE, RENE [S11/165] Guitar w/case: Paris, 1837 1965/3930 **4323**
£2200 DM6428 ¥551100

MARTIN CO., C. F. [Sk11/2] Good American Guitar: Nazareth, 1957 800/1000 **1760**
£898 DM2622 ¥227040

MAUCHANT BROS. [S06/178] Guitar w/case: Paris, c. 1840 2565/3420 **2822**
£1650 DM4764 ¥434280

PANORMO, LOUIS [P03/37] English Guitar restoration required on back, table: London, 1827 328/492 **1345**
£820 DM2271 ¥209756

PANORMO, LOUIS [S06/181] Guitar w/case: London, 1831 1197/1710 **2633**
£1540 DM4447 ¥405328

RAMIREZ, JOSE (III) [S11/169] Concert Guitar: Madrid, 1980 1965/2948 **1945**
£990 DM2893 ¥247995

RINALDI, MARENGO ROMANUS [P03/40] Guitar w/cover: Turin, 1894 575/822 **NS**

RINALDI, MARENGO ROMANUS [P06/47] Guitar w/cover: Turin, 1894 432/605 **NS**

ROMANILLOS, JOSE [S11/166] Concert Guitar w/case: Semley, 1972 5895/6877 **6268**
£3190 DM9321 ¥799095

ROMANILLOS, JOSE [S06/175] Concert Guitar w/case: Semley, 1985 6840/8550 **15989**
£9350 DM26998 ¥2460920

HAND HORN

RAOUX, MARCEL-AUGUSTE [S11/134] Hand Horn w/case, detachable valves: c. 1865 1965/2948 **NS**

HARP

BRIGGS [P09/35] Celtic Harp: Glasgow, c. 1930 561/748 **1131**
£605 DM1791 ¥155545

DELVEAU, J. [C03/6] Double-Action Harp 1140/1628 **1791**
£1100 DM3063 ¥282810

ERARD, SEBASTIAN [P03/43] Grecian Harp minus shutter pedal and shutters: London, first quarter, 19th C. 822/1151 **NS**

ERARD, SEBASTIAN [S06/183] Double-Action Pedal Harp: London, c. 1860 855/1197 **1505**
£880 DM2541 ¥231616

ERARD, SEBASTIAN [S06/184] Double-Action Gothic Pedal Harp w/cover: London, mid 19th C. 2565/3420 **4514**
£2640 DM7623 ¥694848

ERARD, SEBASTIAN & PIERRE [P03/44] Gothic Harp minus shutters: London, c. 1850 986/1480 **995**
£605 DM1678 ¥154759

ERARD [P03/42] Grecian Harp: London 986/1315 **995**
£605 DM1678 ¥154759

ERARD, SEBASTIAN & PIERRE [S11/157] Double-Action Gothic Pedal Harp: London, c. 1850 4913/5895 **3026**
£1540 DM4500 ¥385770

ERARD, SEBASTIAN & PIERRE [S11/158] Double-Action Gothic Pedal Harp w/cover: London, c. 1850 1572/2358 **1837**
£935 DM2732 ¥234218

ERARD, SEBASTIAN & PIERRE [S11/159] Double-Action Pedal Harp: London, c. 1835 1179/1572 **2594**
£1320 DM3857 ¥330660

ERARD, SEBASTIAN & PIERRE [S11/160] Double-Action Gothic Pedal Harp: London, third quarter, 19th C. 1572/1965 **2162**
£1100 DM3214 ¥275550

LIGHT, EDWARD [P11/28] Fine Dital Harp w/case: London, c. 1790 **2270**
£1155 DM3332 ¥292331

NADERMANN, HENRY [S06/185] French Pedal Harp: Paris, c. 1790 11970/14535 **NS**

HARPSICHORD

DE BLAISE, WILLIAM [C06/15] Modern Two-Manual Harpsichord w/case 1032/1376 **2081**
£1210 DM3497 ¥318920

DULKEN, JOHAN DANIEL [S03/394] Important Flemish Single Manual Harpsichord: Antwerp, 1755 **127908**
£74800 DM207196 ¥18954320

KIRKMAN, JACOB & ABRAHAM [S11/150] Very Fine and Important Two-Manual Harpsichord original state of preservation: London, 1785 78600/117900 **99429**
£50600 DM147853 ¥12675300

HORN

WHITE, H. N. & CO. [Sk11/24] Three-Keyed Horn w/case: Cleveland 200/300 **110**
£56 DM164 ¥14190

HURDY GURDY

COLSON [P11/30] Hurdy Gurdy: Mirecourt, mid 19th C. 786/1179 **1729**
£880 DM2539 ¥222728

LUTE

ROMANILLOS, JOSE [S11/168] Lute w/case: Semley, 1974 4913/5895 **NS**

RUBIO, DAVID [S11/167] Lute w/case: Semley, 1967 7860/9825 **NS**

RUBIO, DAVID [S06/179] Theorbo Lute: Semley, 1968 3420/5130 **NS**

RUBIO, DAVID [S06/180] Lute w/case: Semley, c. 1967 3420/5130 **6395**
£3740 DM10799 ¥984368

BARRY [P11/27] Lute-Guitar: London, c. 1800 295/590 **389**
£198 DM571 ¥50114

JOHN BETTS
English Violoncello: London, c. 1800
Sotheby's, London, November 22, 1990, Lot 324

LYRA GUITAR

MOZZANI, LUIGI [P06/45] Lyra Guitar: Bologna, 1920 **NS**

MOZZANI, LUIGI [P11/29] Lyra Guitar: Bologna, c. 1920 590/982 **973**
£495 DM1428 ¥125285

BARRY [C11/10] Lyre-Guitar: London 788/1182 **2600**
£1320 DM3831 ¥330792

MANDOLA

MARATEA, MICHELE [P09/34] Italian Mandola w/case: Naples, 1890 187/374 **185**
£99 DM293 ¥25453

MANDOLIN

CECCHERINI, UMBERTO [P07/35] Mandolin w/case: Naples 273/455 **NS**

EMBERGHER, LUIGI [P11/23] Fine Mandolin w/case: Rome, 1920 590/786 **1772**
£902 DM2602 ¥228296

GIBSON CO. [Sk11/4] American Mandolin w/case: Kalamazoo, 1926 1000/1500 **2090**
£1066 DM3114 ¥269610

GIBSON CO. [Sk11/11] Banjo Mandolin w/banjo: Kalamazoo, early 20th C. 50/100 **165**
£84 DM246 ¥21285

SALSEDO, LUIGI [P03/39] Mandolin restoration required to table edge: Naples, c. 1860 411/658 **687**
£418 DM1159 ¥106924

VINACCIA FAMILY (MEMBER OF) (attributed to) [P11/21] Handsome Mandolin 1179/1572 **2810**
£1430 DM4126 ¥361933

VINACCIA, GENNARO & ALLE [P11/22] Fine Mandolin w/case: Naples, 1893 688/982 **908**
£462 DM1333 ¥116932

OBOE

BOOSEY & HAWKES [P02/7] Modern Oboe w/case: London 170/255 **224**
£132 DM371 ¥32406

CABART [P02/8] Blackwood Oboe w/case: Paris 102/170 **103**
£61 DM170 ¥14853

DOELLING [S06/157] Eleven-Keyed Stained Boxwood Oboe: Potsdam, c. 1850 599/855 **1279**
£748 DM2160 ¥196874

HANKEN, GERHARD [C03/5] Twelve-Keyed Boxwood Oboe: Rotterdam 977/1628 **1433**
£880 DM2451 ¥226248

LOREE, FRANCOIS [C11/5] Rosewood Oboe w/case: Paris 985/1379 **NS**

LOREE, FRANCOIS [C06/17] Grenadilla Oboe w/case 860/1204 **4352**
£2530 DM7312 ¥666832

LOUIS [C06/18] Grenadilla Oboe w/case 1032/1720 **3027**
£1760 DM5086 ¥463883

MILHOUSE, WILLIAM [S06/150] Two-Keyed Boxwood Oboe: London, c. 1800 2052/2565 **2633**
£1540 DM4447 ¥405328

MILHOUSE, WILLIAM [S06/168] Two-Keyed Boxwood Oboe w/touchpiece: London, c. 1800 1710/2565 **1693**
£990 DM2859 ¥260568

NONON, JACQUES [S11/140] Ten-Keyed Boxwood Oboe: Paris, c. 1860 3537/4323 **NS**

OBOE D'AMORE

LOREE, FRANCOIS [C06/19] Rosewood Oboe d'Amore w/case 1032/1548 **3027**
£1760 DM5086 ¥463883

LOUIS [C06/20] Grenadilla Oboe d'Amore w/case 2064/2752 **7190**
£4180 DM12080 ¥1101723

OPHICLEIDE

SMITH, HENRY [P06/24] Brass Ophicleide w/case: Wolverhampton, c. 1818-1884 864/1209 **912**
£528 DM1529 ¥140659

PIANO

BALL, JACOB [S11/153] Square Piano: London, c. 1810 1572/2358 **2053**
£1045 DM3053 ¥261773

BATES & CO. [S03/387] Square Piano: London, 1798 1197/1710 **1035**
£605 DM1676 ¥153307

BELL, S. [S03/391] Unusual Upright Piano in regency style: York, c. 1870 3420/4275 **NS**

BEYER, ADAM [S06/187] Square Piano: London, 1793 1710/2565 **1787**
£1045 DM3017 ¥275044

BROADWOOD, JOHN [S11/148] Square Piano: London, 1786 1376/1965 **1772**
£902 DM2636 ¥225951

BROADWOOD, JOHN & SONS [S11/147] Square Piano: London, c. 1830 590/982 **1167**
£594 DM1736 ¥148797

BROADWOOD, JOHN & SONS [S03/392] Square Piano: London, 1804 1710/2565 **3574**
£2090 DM5789 ¥529606

FROSCHLE, GEORGE [S03/385] Square Piano: London, 1776 1026/1710 **4703**
£2750 DM7617 ¥696850

KIRKMAN, JACOB & ABRAHAM [S03/393] Good Square Piano: London, 1775 3420/5130 **8088**
£4730 DM13102 ¥1198582

ATUNES, MANUEL [S11/146] Very Rare Portuguese Grand Pianoforte: last quarter, 18th C. 98250/137550 **134013**
£68200 DM199280 ¥17084100

BROADWOOD, JOHN & SONS [S11/149] Fine Grand Pianoforte: London, 1803 13755/19650 **14698**
£7480 DM21857 ¥1873740

BROADWOOD, JOHN & SONS [S11/155] Grand Pianoforte: London, 1814 11790/15720 **NS**

BROADWOOD, JOHN & SONS [S03/389] Grand Pianoforte: London, 1814 17100/25650 **NS**

BROADWOOD, JOHN & SONS [C06/16] Square Pianoforte: c. 1805 860/1376 **1230**
£715 DM2066 ¥188453

BUNTLEBART, GABRIEL [C03/10] Square Pianoforte: London, 1791 651/1302 **2865**
£1760 DM4902 ¥452496

CLEMENTI, MUZIO [C03/11] Square Pianoforte: London, c. 1800 1140/1628 **2865**
£1760 DM4902 ¥452496

MOTT, J. H. R. [C03/9] Regency Square Pianoforte: London, c. 1815 326/651 **985**
£605 DM1685 ¥155545

ROLFE & CO., WILLIAM [C03/8] Regency Square Pianoforte: London 814/1302 **3044**
£1870 DM5208 ¥480777

PICCOLO

BONNEVILLE [P06/31] Blackwood Piccolo w/case: Paris **1368**
£792 DM2293 ¥210989

LOT, LOUIS [S06/151] Boehm-System Piccolo w/case: Paris 1368/2052 **2445**
£1430 DM4129 ¥376376

PIPES

BURLEIGH, DAVID [C06/2] Northumbrian Small Pipes w/case 516/688 **530**
£308 DM890 ¥81180

REID, ROBERT & JAMES [S06/170] Good Set of Northumbrian Small Pipes w/case: North Shields, c. 1835 3420/5130 **NS**

POCHETTE

JAY, HENRY (attributed to) [P09/157] Fine Pochette 2805/4675 **2880**
£1540 DM4558 ¥395934

TOBIN, RICHARD [P09/158] Fine Pochette: c. 1815 3740/5610 **3908**
£2090 DM6186 ¥537339

QUINTON

SALOMON, JEAN BAPTISTE DESHAYES [S06/282] Quinton set up as a viola: Paris, mid 18th C. 1710/2565 **2069**
£1210 DM3494 ¥318472

WAMSLEY, PETER [S06/283] Quinton: London, c. 1740 1710/2565 **2069**
£1210 DM3494 ¥318472

RECORDER

EICHENTOPF, JOHANN HEINRICH [C06/8] Boxwood Alto Recorder 2580/4300 **2081**
£1210 DM3497 ¥318920

GOBLE, ROBERT [P02/9] Baroque Bass Recorder 170/340 **NS**

DOLMETSCH, ARNOLD [S06/165] Three Recorders w/box: Haslemere, c. 1935 257/342 **489**
£286 DM826 ¥75275

SAXOPHONE

GUINOT, RENE [P11/53] Straight Soprano Saxophone w/case: Paris 197/393 **NS**

SERPENT

METZLER [S06/172] Three-Keyed English Serpent w/crook, mouthpiece: London, c. 1825 1368/2052 **2257**
£1320 DM3811 ¥347424

SPINET

BARTON, THOMAS [S11/156] Spinet: London, 1719 19650/29475 **21615**
£11000 DM32142 ¥2755500

HARRIS, BAKER [S11/151] Spinet: London, c. 1765 11790/17685 **NS**

SLADE, BENJAMIN [S11/144] English Spinet: London, c. 1700 13755/19650 **11240**
£5720 DM16714 ¥1432860

SLADE, BENJAMIN [S03/390] English Spinet: London, c. 1700 11970/17100 **NS**

TAROGATO

STOWASSER, JANOS [S06/161] Rosewood Tarogato w/case: Budapest, c. 1900 1368/2052 **2916**
£1705 DM4923 ¥448756

TROMBONE

COURTOIS, ANTOINE [Sk11/27] One-Keyed Silver Trombone w/case, original mouthpiece: Paris 200/300 **303**
£154 DM451 ¥39023

PEPPER, J. W. [Sk11/30] Trombone w/case: Philadelphia 100/200 **33**
£17 DM49 ¥4257

TRUMPET

GISBORNE [P06/25] Two-Keyed Trumpet w/case: Birmingham, mid 19th C. 259/432 **2565**
£1485 DM4299 ¥395604

VIHUELA

ROMANILLOS, JOSE [S06/176] Vihuela w/case: Semley, 1979 2565/3420 **2633**
£1540 DM4447 ¥405328

VIOL

HEALE, MICHAEL [S06/289] Tenor Viol w/case, bow: Guildford, 1977 2565/4275 NS

HINTZ, FREDERICK [S06/290] Tenor Viola da Gamba w/case, bow: London, c. 1760 10260/13680 **10346**
£6050 DM17469 ¥1592360

NORMAN, BARAK [S06/287] Fine and Important Viol w/case: London, 1692 51300/68400 **52668**
£30800 DM88935 ¥8106560

STEBER, ERNST [S06/288] Bass Viol da Gamba w/cover, bow: Tubingen, 1958 1368/2052 NS

VIOLA

ALBANELLI, FRANCO [S06/280] Italian Viola w/case: Bologna, 1970 6840/10260 NS

ATKINSON, WILLIAM [P03/209] Handsome Viola w/case, bow: Tottenham, 1906 3288/4932 **3255**
£1980 DM5491 ¥506484

ATKINSON, WILLIAM [S06/267] Viola w/case: Tottenham, 1908 4275/5985 NS

BARBIERI, BRUNO [C06/157] Italian Viola: Mantua, 1968 2580/3440 **4541**
£2640 DM7630 ¥695825

BISIACH, LEANDRO (JR.) [S06/269] Italian Viola: Milan, 1973 (Mario Gadda, Porto Mantovano, August 9, 1988) 13680/17100 NS

BOOTH, WILLIAM [P03/146] Good Viola w/case, almost mint condition: Leeds, 1851 1151/1480 **2532**
£1540 DM4270 ¥393932

BOURGUIGNON, MAURICE [S11/278] Viola: Brussels, 1925 3537/4913 **3891**
£1980 DM5786 ¥495990

BUCHNER, RUDOLF [S03/127] Viola: Erlangen/Eltersdorf, 1975 855/1197 **1693**
£990 DM2742 ¥250866

CAPELA, ANTONIO [P06/218] Fine Viola w/case: Espino, 1976 6046/8637 NS

CAPELA, ANTONIO [B04/361] Fine Viola in perfect condition: (Maker's) 3570/5950 **3689**
£2256 DM6200 ¥587399

CARLETTI, GENUZIO [Sk11/33] Italian Viola w/case: Pieve 3800/4200 NS

CARLETTI, GENUZIO [S03/144] Fine Italian Viola: Pieve di Cento, 1948 5985/7695 NS

CHANOT, GEORGE ADOLPH [S11/279] Viola w/case: Manchester, 1898 6877/9825 NS

CHANOT, GEORGE ANTHONY [P11/72] Viola w/case, bow: Manchester, 1898 2948/4913 **6485**
£3300 DM9521 ¥835230

CHAPPUY, NICOLAS AUGUSTIN [P09/80] French Viola w/case: Paris, c. 1770 1496/2244 **3908**
£2090 DM6186 ¥537339

CHARDON & FILS [S11/289] French Viola w/case: Paris, 1906 5895/7860 **6052**
£3080 DM9000 ¥771540

CHEVRIER, ANDRE [S11/291] Viola w/case: Paris, 1959 1670/1965 NS

CLAUDOT, AUGUSTIN [B04/150] Fine French Violin in very good condition: Mirecourt, first half, 19th C. 2975/3570 **1190**
£728 DM2000 ¥189484

CLAUDOT, PIERRE [B04/48] French Viola in perfect condition: Marseilles, c. 1930 3273/3868 **2499**
£1528 DM4200 ¥397916

COCKER, LAWRENCE [S03/136] English Viola w/case: Derby, 1955 3420/5130 **3574**
£2090 DM5789 ¥529606

COCKER, LAWRENCE [S06/273] English Viola: Derby, 1957 1710/2565 **1693**
£990 DM2859 ¥260568

COLIN, JEAN BAPTISTE [P06/215] Viola minus pegs and tailpiece: Mirecourt, 1888 1037/1382 **3040**
£1760 DM5095 ¥468864

COLIN, JEAN BAPTISTE [S06/266] Viola w/case: Mirecourt, 1871 2565/3420 **3198**
£1870 DM5400 ¥492184

CONIA, STEFANO [C06/158] Italian Viola: Cremona, 1976 3096/4300 **3595**
£2090 DM6040 ¥550861

CRASKE, GEORGE [S11/293] English Viola w/case, bow: Stockport 3930/5895 **5404**
£2750 DM8035 ¥688875

CUYPERS, JOHANNES THEODORUS [S03/145] Viola: The Hague, 1770 25650/34200 **28215**
£16500 DM45705 ¥4181100

DEGANI, EUGENIO [S03/141] Viola: Venice, c. 1895 13680/20520 NS

DESIDERI, PIETRO PAOLO [S03/126] Interesting Italian Viola: Riphaeus, late 18th C. (W. E. Hill & Sons, London, October 25, 1945) 34200/51300 NS

DIEUDONNE, AMEDEE [B04/148] Attractive French Viola in excellent condition: Mirecourt, 1942 2975/4165 **3451**
£2111 DM5800 ¥549502

DUKE, RICHARD [P03/245] Small Viola w/case: London, 1776 1644/3288 **5425**
£3300 DM9151 ¥844140

DUKE, RICHARD [S06/279] Viola w/case, bow: London, c. 1770 4275/5985 **4138**
£2420 DM6988 ¥636944

ENDERS, F. & R. [P09/176] Good Modern German Viola: Fertiggestellt, 1973 748/935 **741**
£396 DM1172 ¥101812

EPENEEL, R. V. [P06/111] Russian Viola w/case, bow: 1979 864/1209 NS

ESPOSTI, PIERGIUSEPPE [P03/220] Viola: Cremona, 1975 (Leslie Sheppard, 1977) 1644/1973 **3255**
£1980 DM5491 ¥506484

FENDT, BERNARD [S06/275] Viola w/case: London, 1833 (W. E. Hill & Sons, London, September 9, 1980) 13680/20520 **15989**
£9350 DM26998 ¥2460920

FORSTER, WILLIAM [S03/134] English Viola w/case: London, early 19th C. (J. & A. Beare, London, April 3, 1963) 3420/6840 **NS**

FORSTER, WILLIAM [C06/160] English Viola w/case: London 6020/7740 **6622**
£3850 DM11126 ¥1014745

FORSTER, WILLIAM (II) [S03/121] English Viola: London, 1807 6840/10260 **6190**
£3620 DM10027 ¥917308

FORSTER, WILLIAM (II) [S06/278] Viola w/case, bow: London, c. 1800 5130/8550 **NS**

GABRIELLI, GIOVANNI BATTISTA [C03/209] Good Italian Viola w/case: Florence, 1757 24420/32560 **34025**
£20900 DM58206 ¥5373390

GADDA, GAETANO [S03/120] Viola w/case: Mantua, 1953 5130/8550 **5079**
£2970 DM8227 ¥752598

GADDA, MARIO [S03/123] Viola: Porto Mantovano, 1975 (Maker's, September 12, 1978) 5130/8550 **5267**
£3080 DM8532 ¥780472

GAND & BERNARDEL [C11/79] Good French Viola w/case: Paris, 1884 19700/23640 **23837**
£12100 DM35114 ¥3032260

GARONNAIRE, CHRISTIAN [P03/109] Good Viola w/case: Cremona, 1978 2466/4110 **6149**
£3740 DM10371 ¥956692

GIBSON [P06/98] Viola good condition: Kalamazoo, c. 1910 605/777 **760**
£440 DM1274 ¥117216

GILBERT, JEFFERY J. [C03/208] English Viola w/case, bow: Peterborough, 1919 3256/4070 **3940**
£2420 DM6740 ¥622182

GIRAUD, FRANCO [S03/132] Viola: London, 1976 3078/4275 **NS**

GLAESEL & HERWIG [P10/36] Good Viola w/case, 2 bows, violin, fingerboard loose: Markneukirchen, c. 1880 882/1274 **1682**
£858 DM2537 ¥210553

GOZALAN, MESUT [P06/117] Viola w/case: 1984 864/1382 **874**
£506 DM1465 ¥134798

GUADAGNINI, GAETANO (attributed to) [S11/295] Viola w/case: Turin (Guiseppe Ornati, Milan, June 8, 1945) 5895/9825 **18373**
£9350 DM27321 ¥2342175

GUERSAN, LOUIS [C11/78] Fine French Viola w/case, bow: (W. E. Hill & Sons, January 2, 1947) 15760/23640 **28171**
£14300 DM41499 ¥3583580

GUTTER, G. W. [B04/237] German Viola in very good condition: Markneukirchen, 1965 893/1488 **833**
£509 DM1400 ¥132639

HAENEL, FREDERICK EWALD [Sk11/35A] American Viola w/case, bow: New Milford, CT, 1961 2000/3000 **2970**
£1515 DM4425 ¥383130

HAMMOND, JOHN [C11/69] English Viola w/case: West Burton, 1949 1576/2364 **1625**
£825 DM2394 ¥206745

HILL, LOCKEY (attributed to) [P09/162] English Viola w/case: London, c. 1810 (E. R. Voigt & Son, June, 1977) 3740/5610 **6582**
£3520 DM10419 ¥904992

HILL, W. E. & SONS [C11/76] Good Viola: London, 1937 (W. E. Hill & Sons, July 16, 1971) 9850/15760 **NS**

HUDSON, GEORGE WULME [S06/265] English Viola: London, 1930 (Maker's, June 18, 1930) 8550/11970 **8465**
£4950 DM14293 ¥1302840

HYDE, ANDREW [Sk11/32] American Viola w/case, 2 bows: Northhampton 1000/1200 **715**
£365 DM1065 ¥92235

JAIS, JOHANNES (ascribed to) [S03/146] Tyrolese Viola: Bolzano, c. 1775 11970/17100 **11286**
£6600 DM18282 ¥1672440

KEEN, W. [P09/76] English Viola w/case: London, 1796 1122/1496 **1234**
£660 DM1954 ¥169686

KENNEDY, THOMAS [C06/159] English Viola w/case: London 3440/5160 **4541**
£2640 DM7630 ¥695825

KILBURN, WILFRED [C11/67] English Viola w/case: 1982 985/1576 **NS**

KLOZ FAMILY (MEMBER OF) [S06/262] Fine German Viola w/case: Mittenwald, second half, 18th C. 4275/5130 **4138**
£2420 DM6988 ¥636944

KLOZ FAMILY (MEMBER OF) [C11/77] Good German Viola w/case: Mittenwald, 1806 (Emil Herrmann, January 15, 1960) 7880/9850 **NS**

KOBERLING [P07/97] Viola w/case: Mittenwald, 1979 455/728 **841**
£462 DM1357 ¥125710

LAZARE, ROBERT [P06/116] Viola w/case: 1988 345/518 **NS**

LAZARE, ROBERT [P10/201] Viola w/case: London, 1989 196/392 **237**
£121 DM358 ¥29693

LE GOVIC, ALAIN [P07/80] Good French Viola: Aix-en-Provence, 1986 728/910 **721**
£396 DM1163 ¥107752

LE GOVIC, ALAIN [P07/81] Fine French Viola: Cremona, 1984 910/1092 **1281**
£704 DM2068 ¥191558

LEE, PERCY [C11/74] English Viola: London, 1917 5516/6895 **6068**
£3080 DM8938 ¥771848

LITTLEWOOD, GERALD [S11/286] English Viola: Hollingworth-in-Longdendale, 1977 (Maker's, December 8, 1977) 1179/1572 **1189**
£605 DM1768 ¥151553

LUCCI, GIUSEPPE [P03/148] Viola: Rome, 1979 (Maker's, October, 1979) 3288/4932 **6510**
£3960 DM10981 ¥1012968

LUCCI, GIUSEPPE [P03/150] Fine Viola: Rome (Maker's, Rome, November, 1979) 3288/4932 **6872**
£4180 DM11591 ¥1069244

LUFF, WILLIAM H. [P03/157] Fine Viola w/case: London, 1967 6576/8220 **NS**

LUFF, WILLIAM H. [P06/90] Fine Viola w/case: London, 1967 (Maker's) 4319/6046 **6461**
£3740 DM10827 ¥996336

MARTIN, JOHANN GOTTLIEB [S11/275] German Viola w/case: c. 1787 4716/5502 **NS**

MARTIN, JOHANN GOTTLIEB [S06/258] German Viola w/case: c. 1787 6840/8550 **NS**

MEZZADRI, ALESSANDRO (ascribed to) [C06/162] Interesting Viola w/case: 1715 (Dario D'Attili, October 1, 1982) 20640/25800 **24596**
£14300 DM41327 ¥3769051

MOCKEL, OSWALD [S03/131] Viola: Berlin, 1930 1710/2052 **NS**

MOINEL-CHERPITEL [S11/301] French Viola w/case: Paris, 1908 7860/9825 **NS**

MORASSI, GIOVANNI BATTISTA [S03/128] Viola w/case, cover: Cremona, 1973 5130/6840 **6584**
£3850 DM10664 ¥975590

MORRIS, MARTIN [S11/276] English Viola w/case, bow: Hunsonby, 1982 2948/3930 **NS**

MORRIS, MARTIN [S03/137] English Viola w/case, bow: Hunsonby, 1982 4275/5985 **NS**

NAISBY, THOMAS HENRY [S11/273] Viola w/case: Sunderland, 1916 1965/2948 **3458**
£1760 DM5143 ¥440880

NEUNER & HORNSTEINER [P06/181] Viola w/case, bow, bottom rib requires small restoration: Mittenwald, c. 1840 864/1037 **1292**
£748 DM2165 ¥199267

OBBO, MARCUS [S06/260] Italian Viola w/case: Naples, 1801 17100/25650 **NS**

PACHEREL, PIERRE [C06/161] French Viola w/case: Nice 6880/10320 **7568**
£4400 DM12716 ¥1159708

PANORMO, VINCENZO [P11/209] Fine Rare Viola w/case, cover: London, 1791 (W. E. Hill & Sons, London, November, 1933) **NS**

PANORMO, VINCENZO [S11/269] Fine English Viola original neck: London, c. 1800 49125/68775 **54037**
£27500 DM80355 ¥6888750

PARESCHI, GAETANO [P03/169] Good Viola w/case: good condition (Piacenza, 1978) 1151/1973 **1872**
£1139 DM3157 ¥291228

PARESCHI, GAETANO [S11/271] Italian Viola w/case: Ferrara, 1957 11790/15720 **NS**

PEDRAZZINI, GIUSEPPE [S06/281] Viola: Milan, 1947 13680/20520 **NS**

PERRY, JAMES [S06/261] Fine Irish Viola: Kilkenny, 1786 5985/7695 **7524**
£4400 DM12705 ¥1158080

PERRY, L. A. [P03/110] Good Viola w/case, fine condition: Deganwy, 1988 822/1151 **868**
£528 DM1464 ¥135062

PERRY, THOMAS [P11/117] Fine Viola w/case, 2 bows, original neck lengthened at block: Dublin, c. 1780 3930/5895 **9943**
£5060 DM14598 ¥1280686

RESUCHE, CHARLES [P07/129] Viola 1456/2184 **3203**
£1760 DM5171 ¥478896

RESUCHE, CHARLES [S11/300] Viola: Lyons, 1883 5895/9825 **6484**
£3300 DM9643 ¥826650

RICHARDSON, ARTHUR [C11/75] English Viola w/case, Tertis model: Crediton Devon, 1948 1970/2955 **3251**
£1650 DM4788 ¥413490

RICHARDSON, ARTHUR [C06/155] English Viola w/case: Crediton Devon, 1948 2924/3440 **NS**

RINALDI, MARENGO ROMANUS [S03/124] Italian Viola w/case: Turin, 1891 4275/5130 **4138**
£2420 DM6703 ¥613228

ROCCHI, S. [B04/63] Fine Italian Viola in very good condition: Regiensis, 1947 5950/8330 **5058**
£3093 DM8500 ¥805305

ROST, FRANZ GEORGE [S06/264] Viola: London, 1938 3420/5130 **6019**
£3520 DM10164 ¥926464

ROTH, ERNST HEINRICH [P02/40] Good Viola mint condition: Bubenreuth, 1975 850/1360 **1122**
£660 DM1855 ¥162030

ROTH, ERNST HEINRICH [P09/55] Viola w/case, bow: Bubenreuth, 1974 1122/1496 **1440**
£770 DM2279 ¥197967

ROTH, ERNST HEINRICH [C03/205] German Viola: 1956 977/1302 **985**
£605 DM1685 ¥155545

SACCHI, GIORGIO [Sk11/34] Italian Viola w/case: Piacenza, 1970 3000/4000 **NS**

SAUNDERS, WILFRED G. [S06/271] Viola w/case, cover: Nottingham, 1955 1710/2565 **1787**
£1045 DM3017 ¥275044

SCHEINLEIN, M. F. [P11/154] Viola w/case: Langenfelot, mid 18th C. 491/688 **2118**
£1078 DM3110 ¥272842

SCHMIDT, E. R. & CO. [C06/151] German Viola w/case 860/1204 **1324**
£770 DM2225 ¥202949

SCHWARZ, GIOVANNI [S11/287] Italian Viola: Venice, 1939 7860/11790 **8214**
£4180 DM12214 ¥1047090

SCHWARZ, GIOVANNI [S06/256] Italian Viola: Venice, 1939 10260/13680 **NS**

SGARABOTTO, GAETANO [B04/172] Fine Italian Viola in perfect condition: Milan, 1957 10710/13090 **10115**
£6186 DM17000 ¥1610611

SGARABOTTO, GAETANO [S03/138] Viola w/case: Brescia, 1949 8550/10260 **NS**

SGARABOTTO, GAETANO [S06/263] Viola w/case: Brescia, 1949 5985/7695 **7148**
£4180 DM12070 ¥1100176

SILVESTRE, PIERRE [P03/117] Superb Viola w/case, cover, condition near mint: Lyon, 1848 (Dollin & Daines, March, 1969) 41100/57540 **NS**

SIMONAZZI, AMADEO [S11/285] Italian Viola: Santa Vittoria Emilia, 1962 (Lennart Lee, Gothenburg, April 24, 1987) 5895/7860 **NS**

SOLOMON, GIMPEL [S11/292] Viola w/case, cover: St. Ives, c. 1980 8843/10808 **NS**

SOLOMON, GIMPEL [S06/268] Viola w/case, cover: St. Ives, c. 1980 8550/11970 **9969**
£5830 DM16834 ¥1534456

STORIONI, LORENZO (ascribed to) [S06/284] Italian Viola w/case 68400/85500 **63954**
£37400 DM107992 ¥9843680

TENUCCI, EUGEN [S03/133] Viola: Zurich, 1949 1197/1710 **2445**
£1430 DM3961 ¥362362

THIBOUVILLE-LAMY [P11/116] Good French Viola w/case, bow, good condition: c. 1920 884/1277 **1621**
£825 DM2380 ¥208808

THIBOUVILLE-LAMY, J. [S11/302] French Viola w/case, cover: Paris, 1960 (J. Thibouville Lamy Co., Paris, 1960) 2948/3930 **NS**

TOPHAM, CARASS [P06/223] Viola w/case, bow: Abingdon, 1977 691/1123 **836**
£484 DM1401 ¥128938

VETTORI, CARLO [S11/298] Italian Viola w/case: Florence, 1981 3930/5895 **2162**
£1100 DM3214 ¥275550

VICKERS, J. E. [P11/69] Modern Viola w/case, good condition 688/884 **562**
£286 DM825 ¥72387

VOIGT, ARNOLD [P06/167] Good Viola w/case: Markneukirchen, c. 1890 864/1037 **2280**
£1320 DM3821 ¥351648

VOIGT, E. & P. [C03/212] English Viola Tertis model 2930/3582 **NS**

VUILLAUME, JEAN BAPTISTE [C06/165] Fine French Viola: Paris (Max Moller & Son, May 28, 1974) 51600/68800 **NS**

VUILLAUME, NICHOLAS [S11/303] Belgian Viola w/case: Brussels, 1868 23580/29475 **NS**

WALTON, R. [C06/153] English Viola w/case: 1917 1032/1204 **1230**
£715 DM2066 ¥188453

WHITMARSH FAMILY, (MEMBER OF) [P06/248] Good English Viola good condition: London, 1942 1037/1555 **1530**
£886 DM2564 ¥235897

WITHERS, GEORGE [S11/283] Viola w/case, 2 bows: London, c. 1900 2358/3537 **1837**
£935 DM2732 ¥234218

YOUNGSON, ALEXANDER [P03/222] Viola w/case, Tertis model, good condition: Glasgow, 1974 658/986 **NS**

VIOLA BOW

BERNARDEL, LEON [S11/358] Silver and Ivory Viola Bow: Paris 1376/1965 **1513**
£770 DM2250 ¥192885

BRISTOW, STEPHEN [P06/287] Silver Viola Bow 518/691 **912**
£528 DM1529 ¥140659

BRISTOW, STEPHEN [S03/243] Gold English Viola Bow 1368/2052 **1693**
£990 DM2742 ¥250866

BRYANT, PERCIVAL WILFRED [S11/229] Gold and Ivory Viola Bow: Brighton 982/1376 **2378**
£1210 DM3536 ¥303105

COLLIN-MEZIN [S06/339] Silver Viola Bow: Paris 1026/1368 **1881**
£1100 DM3176 ¥289520

DODD [P09/185] Ivory Viola Bow: c. 1790 187/374 **658**
£352 DM1042 ¥90499

DODD [C06/242] Silver Viola Bow 1376/2064 **2838**
£1650 DM4768 ¥434891

DODD, JOHN [P11/211] Silver Viola Bow: c. 1820 1179/1965 **2810**
£1430 DM4126 ¥361933

DODD, JOHN [S03/270] Ivory Viola Bow: Kew, c. 1790 1026/1368 **2633**
£1540 DM4266 ¥390236

DOTSCHKAIL, R. [P07/156] Silver Viola Bow 364/546 **783**
£430 DM1264 ¥117030

DUPUY, PHILIPPE [P03/118] Silver Viola Bow 986/1315 **2351**
£1430 DM3965 ¥365794

FINKEL, JOHANN S. [S03/244] Silver Viola Bow 1197/1710 **1129**
£660 DM1828 ¥167244

FINKEL, JOHANNES [C06/218] Gold and Ivory Viola Bow 1032/1376 **1041**
£605 DM1748 ¥159460

GEIPEL, RICHARD [B04/280] Silver German Viola Bow in very good condition: c. 1960 417/476 **417**
£255 DM700 ¥66319

GEIPEL, RICHARD [S03/103] Silver Viola Bow 855/1197 **NS**

GEROME, ROGER [B04/108] Gold French Viola Bow in very good condition 2678/3273 **1904**
£1164 DM3200 ¥303174

GOHDE, GREGORY [S03/246] Silver Viola Bow: San Diego 1710/2565 **NS**

HILL, W. E. & SONS [P03/149] Fine Silver Viola Bow 1644/2630 **3978**
£2420 DM6711 ¥619036

HILL, W. E. & SONS [P09/102] Silver Viola Bow 1496/2244 **2983**
£1595 DM4721 ¥410074

HILL, W. E. & SONS [P09/152] Good Silver Viola Bow 1122/1683 **2468**
£1320 DM3907 ¥339372

GOFFREDO CAPPA
Violoncello: Saluzzo, late 17th C.
Sotheby's, London, November 22, 1990, Lot 312

HILL, W. E. & SONS [B04/107] Silver French Viola Bow in very good condition: London, c. 1930
2678/3273 **2618**
£1601 DM4400 ¥416864

HILL, W. E. & SONS [S06/144] Silver and Tortoiseshell Viola Bow: London, 1972
3762/4788 **3762**
£2200 DM6352 ¥579040

HILL, W. E. & SONS [S06/244] Silver Viola Bow: London 2565/3420 **NS**

HOYER, OTTO A. [P11/142] Nickel Viola Bow
786/982 **NS**

HUMS, ALBIN [S03/260] Silver Viola Bow: Markneukirchen 855/1197 **NS**

LAMY, ALFRED [S06/145] Silver Viola Bow: Paris (Bernard Millant, Paris, March 15, 1988)
5130/6840 **6395**
£3740 DM10799 ¥984368

MOINEL, AMEDEE [P10/105] Silver and Ivory Viola Bow: Paris, c. 1914 1176/1568 **1736**
£886 DM2618 ¥217302

MULLER, E. K. [S03/261] German Silver Viola Bow
513/855 **451**
£264 DM731 ¥66898

OUCHARD, EMILE [S06/252] Silver Viola Bow: Paris
2052/2565 **NS**

PAJEOT [S11/232] Silver Viola Bow: Mirecourt (William Lewis & Son, Lincolnwood, December 22, 1976) 2948/3930 **2162**
£1100 DM3214 ¥275550

PAJEOT, ETIENNE [S11/359] Silver Viola Bow w/case: Mirecourt, c. 1835 (Bernard Millant, Paris, June 20, 1990) 6877/7860 **NS**

PENZEL [P06/319] Nickel Viola Bow w/bow
207/345 **456**
£264 DM764 ¥70330

PENZEL, K. GERHARD [S06/238] Silver Viola Bow w/2 bows 1710/2052 **NS**

PFRETZSCHNER, H. R. [S06/139] Silver Viola Bow: Markneukirchen 855/1197 **1223**
£715 DM2065 ¥188188

PFRETZSCHNER, H. R. [C03/277] Silver Viola Bow
651/977 **627**
£385 DM1072 ¥98983

PFRETZSCHNER, L. [P09/101] Viola Bow
561/748 **946**
£506 DM1498 ¥130093

RAMEAU, J. S. [P11/156] Gold Viola Bow w/case
1179/1572 **1044**
£531 DM1533 ¥134472

SARTORY, EUGENE [C11/278] Good Silver Viola Bow
5910/6895 **6068**
£3080 DM8938 ¥771848

SCHMIDT, C. HANS CARL [P06/286] Gold Viola Bow 864/1296 **2090**
£1210 DM3503 ¥322344

SCHULLER, OTTO [S03/99] German Silver Viola Bow
684/1026 **527**
£308 DM853 ¥78047

THIBOUVILLE-LAMY [P11/216] Silver Viola Bow
393/590 **NS**

THIBOUVILLE-LAMY, JEROME [P06/224] Silver Viola Bow: Mirecourt 345/605 **912**
£528 DM1529 ¥140659

THIBOUVILLE-LAMY, JEROME [P06/225] Silver Viola Bow: Mirecourt 345/605 **1045**
£605 DM1751 ¥161172

THOMASSIN, CLAUDE [S06/126] Nickel Viola Bow: Paris 1368/1710 **1787**
£1045 DM3017 ¥275044

TUBBS, EDWARD [S03/245] Silver Viola Bow: London 7695/8550 **10346**
£6050 DM16758 ¥1533070

TUBBS, JAMES [P11/210] Good Silver Viola Bow
1965/2948 **4755**
£2420 DM6982 ¥612502

TUBBS, JAMES [S11/356] Silver Viola Bow: London
4913/6877 **7133**
£3630 DM10607 ¥909315

TUNNICLIFFE, BRIAN [P09/191] Gold Viola Bow
935/1122 **1440**
£770 DM2279 ¥197967

VAN DER MEER, KAREL [Sk11/99] Silver Viola Bow: Amsterdam 800/1000 **1100**
£561 DM1639 ¥141900

VAN DER MEER, KAREL [S11/357] Silver Viola Bow: Amsterdam, c. 1910 1572/2358 **1945**
£990 DM2893 ¥247995

WILSON, GARNER [S06/251] Gold and Tortoiseshell Viola Bow: Bury St. Edmunds 1710/2052 **1693**
£990 DM2859 ¥260568

WITHERS, GEORGE & SONS [S11/46] Silver Viola Bow: London 1179/1572 **1470**
£748 DM2186 ¥187374

ZOPHEL, ERNST WILLY [P07/157] Silver Viola Bow 455/637 **645**
£354 DM1041 ¥96378

VIOLA D'AMORE

GUIDANTUS, JOANNES FLORENUS (attributed to) [C11/70] Good Italian Viola D'Amore
9850/13790 **NS**

VIOLETTA

GRANCINO, GIOVANNI (III) [S11/393] Interesting Violetta now converted to a violin: Milan, 1701 1965/3930 **4755**
£2420 DM7071 ¥606210

VIOLIN

ACHNER, PHILIP [S03/16] Violin: Mittenwald, 1774
1368/2052 **2257**
£1320 DM3656 ¥334488

ACOULON, ALFRED (attributed to) [P09/163] Handsome Violin w/case, 2 bows, 2 minor repairs on table: c. 1900 2244/3366 **NS**

ACOULON, ALFRED (attributed to) [P11/155] Good French Violin w/case, 2 bows, 2 minor repairs on table 1572/2358 **2594**
£1320 DM3808 ¥334092

ACOULON, ALFRED (FILS) (ascribed to) [S03/225] French Violin 1368/2052 **1411**
£825 DM2285 ¥209055

ADAMS, HENRY THOMAS [P07/115] Good Violin: Abbeywood, 1913 910/1274 **3339**
£1835 DM5391 ¥499249

ADAMSEN, P. P. [C03/157] Danish Violin: Copenhagen, 1897 3256/4884 **3582**
£2200 DM6127 ¥565620

AIRETON, EDMUND [C03/165] Good English Violin: (J. & A. Beare, March 17, 1971) 11396/14652 **NS**

AIRETON, EDMUND (ascribed to) [S11/96] Fine English Violin w/case 9825/11790 **7349**
£3740 DM10928 ¥936870

AITCHISON, FRANK [P06/462] Violin w/case, bow: Gattonside Melrose, 1939 259/432 **494**
£286 DM828 ¥76190

ALBANELLI, FRANCO (attributed to) [C11/168] Violin w/case 2955/4925 **NS**

ALBANI, JOSEPH (attributed to) [S06/65] Violin w/case: Bolzano, 1712 (Chardon & Fils, Paris, August 28, 1936) 5130/6840 **5643**
£3300 DM9529 ¥868560

ALBERT, CHARLES F. [Sk11/110A] American Violin w/case, bow: Philadelphia, 1883 800/1200 **1650**
£841 DM2459 ¥212850

ALDRIC, JEAN FRANCOIS [S11/90] Fine French Violin w/case, cover: Paris, 1792 19650/29475 **NS**

ALDRIC, JEAN FRANCOIS [B04/272] Fine French Violin in excellent condition: Paris, 1806 11900/17850 **8925**
£5458 DM15000 ¥1421127

ALDRIC, JEAN FRANCOIS [S03/230] Fine French Violin w/case, cover: Paris, 1792 25650/34200 **NS**

ALDRIC, JEAN FRANCOIS [C03/188] Good French Violin: 1820 9768/13024 **16117**
£9900 DM27571 ¥2545290

AMATI, ANTONIO [S06/223] Fine Italian Violin w/case: 1588 (Hart & Son, London, May 22, 1918) 102600/136800 **NS**

AMATI, ANTONIO & GIROLAMO [P11/176] Violin w/case, overall condition good, table by A. Gragnani: Cremona, 1623 (W. E. Hill & Sons, London, October, 1918) **49715**
£25300 DM72991 ¥6403430

AMATI, ANTONIO & GIROLAMO (ascribed to) [S06/384] Violin w/case 17100/25650 **NS**

AMATI, DOM NICOLO [C11/181] Italian Violin 23640/29550 **NS**

AMATI, NICOLO [S11/412] Important Italian Violin: Cremona, 1683 (W. E. Hill & Sons, London, June 8, 1945) 353700/491250 **NS**

AMATI, NICOLO (attributed to) [S03/70] Violin w/case: (Giuseppe Fiorini, Zurich, November 4, 1924) 42750/59850 **47025**
£27500 DM76175 ¥6968500

AMATI FAMILY (MEMBER OF) [B04/143] Interesting Composite Violin: (Jean Frederic Schmitt, April 24, 1980) 2380/2975 **NS**

AMATI FAMILY (MEMBER OF) [C11/179] Fine Italian Violin: W. E. Hill & Sons (March, 1949) 59100/78800 **NS**

ANTONIAZZI, ROMEO [S11/32] Italian Violin w/case: Cremona, 1907 (Dario D'Attili, Dumont, January 9, 1983) 13755/19650 **NS**

ANTONIAZZI, ROMEO [S03/307] Italian Violin w/case: Cremona, 1907 (Dario D'Attili, Dumont, January 9, 1983) 15390/20520 **NS**

ANTONIAZZI, ROMEO (ascribed to) [C06/117] Violin 3440/4300 **5676**
£3300 DM9537 ¥869781

APPARUT, GEORGES [B04/47] Fine French Violin excellent condition: 1942 (Maker's, 1943) 2975/4165 **2856**
£1747 DM4800 ¥454761

ARDERN, JOB [P03/247] Violin w/case, minor repair to scroll volute: c. 1890 1315/1644 **1483**
£902 DM2501 ¥230732

ARDERN, JOB [P06/103] Violin w/case, fine condition: Wilmslow, 1894 1037/1555 **1900**
£1100 DM3184 ¥293040

ARDERN, JOB [P06/247] Good Violin w/case: Wilmslow 1209/1555 **1292**
£748 DM2165 ¥199267

ARDERN, JOB [P09/137] Violin: Wilmslow 1309/1683 **NS**

ARDERN, JOB [P11/99] Violin: Wilmslow 1179/1572 **1124**
£572 DM1650 ¥144773

ASCHAUER, LEO [C11/345] German Violin: Mittenwald, 1970 1970/2955 **1517**
£770 DM2235 ¥192962

ATKINSON, WILLIAM [P06/199] Fine Violin w/case, bow, mint condition: Tottenham, 1904 3455/5182 **4751**
£2750 DM7961 ¥732600

ATKINSON, WILLIAM [S11/385] English Violin: Tottenham, 1903 3930/5895 **NS**

AUBRY, JOSEPH [B04/268] Fine French Violin: Mirecourt, 1924 3570/4760 **3451**
£2111 DM5800 ¥549502

AUBRY, JOSEPH [B04/51] Fine French Violin in perfect condition: Le Havre, 1927 2975/4165 **3094**
£1892 DM5200 ¥492657

AUBRY, JOSEPH [C06/326] French Violin: 1929 3440/5160 **3784**
£2200 DM6358 ¥579854

AUDINOT, NESTOR [B04/174] Fine French Violin in excellent condition: Paris, 1899 8925/11900 **8330**
£5095 DM14000 ¥1326385

AYLOR, ALBERT [Sk11/206] American Violin: Maywood, 1893 200/300 **330**
£168 DM492 ¥42570

AZZOLA, LUIGI (ascribed to) [S03/340] Italian Violin w/case 5985/7695 **6019**
£3520 DM9750 ¥891968

BAADER & CO. [C11/140] German Violin: 1906
985/1576 **NS**

BAADER & CO. [C11/297] German Violin: 1910 (Rudolph Wurlitzer, August 12, 1915)
985/1576 **1300**
£660 DM1915 ¥165396

BAILLY, PAUL [S11/390] French Violin: Paris
4913/5895 **5188**
£2640 DM7714 ¥661320

BAILLY, PAUL [S11/408] French Violin w/case: early 20th C. 2948/3930 **NS**

BAILLY, PAUL [B04/169] Fine French Violin in very good condition: Paris, 1903 (E. Vatelot, Paris, 1983)
7735/8925 **7438**
£4549 DM12500 ¥1184273

BAILLY, PAUL [S03/208] French Violin w/case: early 20th C. 4275/5985 **NS**

BAILLY, PAUL [C11/320] Good Violin w/case, 2 bows: 1890 5910/7880 **9752**
£4950 DM14365 ¥1240470

BAILLY, PAUL [C03/353] French Violin: Paris, 1887 4070/5698 **7521**
£4620 DM12867 ¥1187802

BAILLY, PAUL (ascribed to) [S11/28] Violin w/case, 2 bows 3930/5895 **4107**
£2090 DM6107 ¥523545

BAILLY, PAUL (attributed to) [C06/138] French Violin w/case 5160/6020 **8514**
£4950 DM14305 ¥1304672

BAILLY, R. [B04/34] French Violin in perfect condition: 1929 1785/2380 **1547**
£946 DM2600 ¥246329

BAJONI, LUIGI (ascribed to) [S06/3] Violin w/case 5130/8550 **7524**
£4400 DM12705 ¥1158080

BALESTRIERI, TOMASO [S06/216] Italian Violin w/case, cover, 2 bows: Mantua, 1768 (Fridolin Hamma, Stuttgart, September 17, 1957)
42750/59850 **43263**
£25300 DM73054 ¥6658960

BALESTRIERI, TOMASO [C06/141] Italian Violin w/case: (Henry Werro, November 26, 1946)
51600/60200 **NS**

BALESTRIERI, TOMASO [C03/363] Fine Italian Violin: Mantua, 1778 (W. E. Hill & Sons, October 1, 1946)
89540/105820 **152218**
£93500 DM260397 ¥24038850

BANKS, BENJAMIN [S03/45] Violin: Salisbury, 1779
3078/3420 **3010**
£1760 DM4875 ¥445984

BANKS, JAMES & HENRY (attributed to) [P07/44] Violin w/case, restoration required on two lower ribs 1092/1456 **NS**

BANKS, JAMES & HENRY (attributed to) [P10/58] Violin w/case, 2 bows, restoration required on 2 lower ribs 686/882 **1401**
£715 DM2114 ¥175461

BARBE, F. [B04/36] French Violin in good condition
1190/1785 **1250**
£764 DM2100 ¥198958

BARBE, FRANCOIS [P07/38] Good French Violin: 1896 1001/1274 **1562**
£858 DM2521 ¥233462

BARBIERI, ENZO [S06/80] Violin w/case: Mantua, 1983 2565/3420 **3198**
£1870 DM5400 ¥492184

BARBIERI, PAOLO (ascribed to) [S03/190] Italian Violin 2565/4275 **2633**
£1540 DM4266 ¥390236

BARZONI, FRANCOIS [P03/177] Violin repaired: c. 1880 411/658 **344**
£209 DM580 ¥53462

BASTA, JAN [S03/64] Bohemian Violin w/case, bow: Schonbach, 1898 (Maker's, December 17, 1898)
1197/1710 **NS**

BAUR, MARTIN [P06/164] Good Violin w/case, good condition: 1838 1382/2073 **2850**
£1650 DM4777 ¥439560

BAZIN, C. [C06/268] French Violin w/case, 2 bows
1204/1720 **NS**

BELLOSIO, ANSELMO (attributed to) [S03/15] Italian Violin w/case: (Arthur Dykes, London, May 10, 1955) 10260/13680 **12227**
£7150 DM19805 ¥1811810

BERGONZI, LORENZO [C11/158] Italian Violin: Mantua, 1986 1970/2955 **2167**
£1100 DM3192 ¥275660

BERNARDEL, AUGUST SEBASTIAN [C11/166] French Violin: Paris, 1836 3940/5910 **8235**
£4180 DM12130 ¥1047508

BERNARDEL, AUGUST SEBASTIEN PHILIPPE [B04/177] Fine French Violin in excellent condition: Paris, 1837 20825/23800 **17850**
£10917 DM30000 ¥2842254

BERNARDEL, AUGUST SEBASTIEN PHILIPPE [B04/186] Important French Violin: Paris, 1836
26775/32725 **24990**
£15284 DM42000 ¥3979156

BERNARDEL, AUGUST SEBASTIEN PHILIPPE [S06/199] French Violin w/case: Paris, c. 1835 (Etienne Vatelot, Paris, October 2, 1989) 20520/25650 **24453**
£14300 DM41291 ¥3763760

BERNARDEL, AUGUST SEBASTIAN [Sk11/242] Two French Violins w/4 cases, 4 bows: Paris, 1834 1500/1800 **11000**
£5610 DM16390 ¥1419000

BERNARDEL, GUSTAVE [C06/334] Good French Violin: Paris, 1897 13760/17200 **15136**
£8800 DM25432 ¥2319416

BERNARDEL, GUSTAVE [C03/182] Good French Violin: Paris, 1897 16280/19536 **NS**

BERNARDEL, LEON [C03/347] French Violin: Paris
3256/4070 **3940**
£2420 DM6740 ¥622182

BERTELLI ENZO [S03/339] Italian Violin w/case: Verona, 1978 2565/3420 **2916**
£1705 DM4723 ¥432047

BETTS [P03/353] Violin w/case, bow, body repaired: London, c. 1780 197/362 **796**
£484 DM1342 ¥123807

BETTS, EDWARD (attributed to) [P03/145] Good Violin w/case, good condition 6576/8220 **6510**
£3960 DM10981 ¥1012968

BETTS, EDWARD (attributed to) [P09/87] Good Violin w/case, bow **3703**
£1980 DM5861 ¥509058

BETTS, JOHN [C06/319] Good English Violin: London 6880/8600 **6811**
£3960 DM11444 ¥1043737

BETTS, JOHN [C03/163] English Violin 1628/2442 **2328**
£1430 DM3983 ¥367653

BETTS, JOHN (ascribed to) [C03/166] English Violin w/case: (Max Moller & Son, January 28, 1965) 6512/13024 **16117**
£9900 DM27571 ¥2545290

BETTS, JOHN (attributed to) [P11/75] Good English Violin good condition 1179/1572 **1297**
£660 DM1904 ¥167046

BIGNAMI, OTELLO (ascribed to) [S06/84] Violin: Bologna, 1969 3420/5130 **NS**

BIRD, CHARLES A. EDWARD [P06/193] Good Violin w/case: London, 1891 864/1209 **3040**
£1760 DM5095 ¥468864

BISIACH, LEANDRO [S11/3] Italian Violin w/case: Milan, 1919 (J. & A. Beare, London, March 1, 1962) 19650/29475 **25938**
£13200 DM38570 ¥3306600

BISIACH, LEANDRO [C11/358] Italian Violin w/case: 1910 15760/23640 **18420**
£9350 DM27134 ¥2343110

BISIACH, LEANDRO [C06/333] Fine Italian Violin: Milan, 1924 17200/25800 **20812**
£12100 DM34969 ¥3189197

BISIACH, LEANDRO (JR.) [S11/274] Italian Violin: Milan, 1973 (Mario Gadda, Porto Mantovano, August 9, 1988) 9825/13755 **NS**

BLACKBURN, G. B. [P11/387] Violin w/case, good condition: 1961 393/590 **303**
£154 DM444 ¥38977

BLANCHARD, PAUL [B04/257] Fine French Violin: Lyon, 1882 8925/11900 **8628**
£5277 DM14500 ¥1373756

BLANCHART (ascribed to) [S11/122] French Violin w/case, 2 bows 3537/4323 **NS**

BLANCHART (ascribed to) [S06/72] French Violin w/case, 2 bows: Lyon 4275/5985 **NS**

BLANCHI, ALBERT [B04/161] Fine Italian Violin in perfect condition: Nizza, 1934 (B. Millant, Paris, 1988) 8330/10710 **7140**
£4367 DM12000 ¥1136902

BLANCHI, ALBERT [C03/317] Good Italian Violin: 1924 5698/7326 **7521**
£4620 DM12867 ¥1187802

BLONDELET, EMILE [S03/338] French Violin: Paris, 1927 (Maker's, 1927) 1710/2565 **2069**
£1210 DM3352 ¥306614

BLONDELET, H. E. [S11/84] French Violin: Paris, 1922 1965/2948 **1945**
£990 DM2893 ¥247995

BLONDELET, H. E. [S03/367] Violin: Paris, 1926 1368/2052 **1599**
£935 DM2590 ¥236929

BLYTH, WILLIAMSON [P03/136] Violin w/case, minus tailpiece: Edinburgh, 1895 411/658 **541**
£329 DM912 ¥84133

BOLLINGER, JOSEPH [P02/97] Violin: Steyr, 1823 680/1020 **486**
£286 DM804 ¥70213

BONNEL, JOSEPH (attributed to) [P03/96] Violin w/case, 2 bows: Rennes, c. 1820 986/1480 **995**
£605 DM1678 ¥154759

BOOSEY & HAWKES [P09/57] French Violin: London, 1934 655/935 **823**
£440 DM1302 ¥113124

BOQUAY, JACQUES (attributed to) [C11/175] Fine Violin w/case, bow 11820/15760 **NS**

BORELLI, ANDREA [B04/192] Important Italian Violin in good condition: Parma, 1744 32725/38675 **29750**
£18195 DM50000 ¥4737090

BORLAND, HUGH [P03/357] Violin w/case: 1903 132/296 **957**
£582 DM1614 ¥148850

BOSSI, GIUSEPPE [S06/86] Violin: Stradella, 1922 (Dario D'Attili, Dumont, July 1, 1979) 1026/1368 **NS**

BOULANGEOT, EMILE [S11/213] French Violin: Lyons, 1927 7860/9825 **9727**
£4950 DM14464 ¥1239975

BOULANGEOT, EMILE (workshop of) [C06/310] French Violin w/case: Lyon 860/1376 **1703**
£990 DM2861 ¥260934

BOULLANGIER, CHARLES (attributed to) [P03/155] Good Anglo-French Violin 3288/4932 **5064**
£3080 DM8541 ¥787864

BOURBEAU, E. A. [P11/112] American Violin neck out from block: 1921 590/786 **648**
£330 DM952 ¥83523

BOVIS, FRANCOIS [P11/135] Violin w/case, bow, resin on table and sides requires cleaning: Nice, 1876 (W. E. Hill & Sons, June, 1942) 3930/4913 **13401**
£6820 DM19676 ¥1726142

BRANDINI, JACOPO [S06/410] Italian Violin: Pisa, 1794 2565/3420 **NS**

BRANDINI, JACOPO (attributed to) [C06/144] Interesting Italian Violin w/case 13760/20640 **15136**
£8800 DM25432 ¥2319416

BRAUND, FREDERICK T. [P06/101] Good Violin w/case, good condition: Colchester, 1963 691/1037 **836**
£484 DM1401 ¥128938

BRETON [S11/397] French Violin: Mirecourt 1376/1965 **1081**
£550 DM1607 ¥137775

BRETON, FRANCOIS [P06/86] French Violin w/case: Mirecourt, c. 1830 605/950 **NS**

BRETON, FRANCOIS [P09/180] Violin w/case: Mirecourt, c. 1830 467/561 **520**
£278 DM824 ¥71551

WILLIAM FORSTER
Violoncello, "The Royal George": London, c. 1790
Sotheby's, London, November 22, 1990, Lot 336

Breton, Francois [P09/290] French Violin: Mirecourt, 1892 467/655 **576**
£308 DM912 ¥79187

Breton, Francois [S11/380] French Violin w/case: Mirecourt 1572/2358 **1729**
£880 DM2571 ¥220440

Brierley, Joseph [P06/56] Good Violin w/case, good condition: 1893 777/1123 **1235**
£715 DM2070 ¥190476

Briggs, James William [P11/74] Good Violin w/case, good condition: Glasgow, 1921 1965/2948 **3675**
£1870 DM5395 ¥473297

Briggs, James William [S06/85] Good Violin w/case: Glasgow, 1924 5130/6840 **5267**
£3080 DM8894 ¥810656

Briggs, James William (attributed to) [C11/286] Violin w/case 2955/3940 **NS**

Broughton, Leonard W. [P10/23] Good Violin in good condition: Southampton, 1973 588/980 **NS**

Broughton, Leonard W. [P10/25] Violin in good condition: Southampton, 1977 392/588 **446**
£228 DM673 ¥55878

Brown, James (attributed to) [P06/409] Violin slight old neck and upper back 518/691 **494**
£286 DM828 ¥76190

Browne, John [C11/317] English Violin: London, 1732 3349/3940 **NS**

Bruckner, E. [B04/236] German Violin in very good condition: Steinkirchen, 1927 476/1071 **1250**
£764 DM2100 ¥198958

Brugere, CH. [B04/159] Fine French Violin w/case, in perfect condition: Paris, 1927 6545/8330 **6248**
£3821 DM10500 ¥994789

Brugere, CH. [B04/75] Fine French Violin in perfect condition: Paris, 1910 4760/5950 **4760**
£2911 DM8000 ¥757934

Brugere, Charles Georges [S03/331] Violin: Paris, 1896 1026/1368 **1035**
£605 DM1676 ¥153307

Brugere, Charles Georges [C03/345] Good French Violin: Paris, 1905 4070/5698 **7163**
£4400 DM12254 ¥1131240

Bruni, Mateo [B04/166] Fine Italian Violin in excellent condition: Buenos Aires, 1931 8330/9520 **8330**
£5095 DM14000 ¥1326385

Bryant, Ole H. [Sk11/129] American Violin w/case: Boston, 1932 1000/1500 **2860**
£1459 DM4261 ¥368940

Buthod [P09/133] French Violin w/case: Paris, c. 1885 748/935 **741**
£396 DM1172 ¥101812

Buthod, Charles [C06/95] French Violin w/case 1376/1720 **1892**
£1100 DM3179 ¥289927

Buthod, Charles Louis [S03/354] Violin w/case, bow: Mirecourt, c. 1870 1197/1710 **1693**
£990 DM2742 ¥250866

Buthod, Charles Louis [S03/42] Violin w/case: Paris 1197/1539 **1505**
£880 DM2438 ¥222992

Button & Whitaker [S03/363] English Violin w/case: London, 1807 1026/1368 **NS**

Button & Whitaker [S03/369] English Violin: London, c. 1810 684/1026 **752**
£440 DM1219 ¥111496

Button & Whitaker [S06/221] English Violin w/case: London, 1807 1026/1368 **846**
£495 DM1429 ¥130284

Byrom, John [C11/149] English Violin w/case, bow: Liverpool, 1902 2955/3940 **4551**
£2310 DM6704 ¥578886

Cabasse [P11/80] French Violin: Mirecourt, c. 1810 590/982 **646**
£329 DM949 ¥83245

Cahusac [P06/445] Violin w/violin: London, 1787 518/864 **1140**
£660 DM1911 ¥175824

Calace, Cavaliere Raffaele [Sk11/118] Italian Violin w/case: Naples, 1897 2500/3500 **3410**
£1739 DM5081 ¥439890

Calcagni, Bernardo [P09/160] Violin: Genoa, c. 1740 (J. & A. Beare, London, 1964) 41140/52360 **NS**

Calcagni, Bernardo [S11/36] Violin w/case: Genoa, c. 1740 19650/29475 **49715**
£25300 DM73927 ¥6337650

Calcagni, Bernardo [C03/361] Fine Italian Violin w/case: Genoa, 1751 (W. E. Hill & Sons, June 6, 1921) 24420/32560 **46561**
£28600 DM79651 ¥7353060

Callsen, B. [B04/141] German Violin in very good condition: Zittau, 1924 1190/1785 **1071**
£655 DM1800 ¥170535

Callsen, B. (ascribed to) [C11/355] Italian Violin: (Max Moller & Son, August 30, 1956) 15760/23640 **39006**
£19800 DM57460 ¥4961880

Camilli, Camillus [C06/145] Fine Italian Violin: Mantua, 1742 (W. E. Hill & Sons, August 16, 1961) 68800/86000 **75680**
£44000 DM127160 ¥11597080

Candi, Oreste [C06/147] Italian Violin w/case: Genoa, 1912 6880/8600 **6811**
£3960 DM11444 ¥1043737

Capellini, Virgilio [S03/202] Violin w/case: Cremona, 1977 (Maker's, November 15, 1977) 2565/4275 **3010**
£1760 DM4875 ¥445984

Capicchioni, Marino [S11/378] Violin: Rimini, 1929 3537/4323 **14698**
£7480 DM21857 ¥1873740

Cappa, Goffredo (ascribed to) [C03/358] Interesting Violin: 1684 (Rembert Wurlitzer, August 21, 1959) 19536/24420 **NS**

CARCASSI, LORENZO (ascribed to) [C11/353] Italian Violin w/case: (Ferron & Kroeplin, December 10, 1926) 8865/10835 **8668**
£4400 DM12769 ¥1102640

CARCASSI, LORENZO & TOMASSO [S06/12] Italian Violin w/case: Florence, c. 1785 (W. E. Hill & Sons, Great Missenden, April 3, 1979) 51300/59850 **NS**

CARESSA, ALBERT [S11/368] Violin w/case: Paris, 1933 5895/9825 **6917**
£3520 DM10285 ¥881760

CARESSA & FRANCAIS (attributed to) [P03/194] Fine Violin 1644/3288 **4340**
£2640 DM7321 ¥675312

CARLISLE, JAMES REYNOLD [Sk11/208] American Violin: Cincinnati, early 20th C. 300/400 **248**
£126 DM369 ¥31928

CARNY, V. [B04/154] French Violin in very good condition: Niort, 1868 3570/4165 **2380**
£1456 DM4000 ¥378967

CASTAGNERI, ANDREA (attributed to) [C11/337] Interesting Violin w/case 7880/9850 **NS**

CASTELLO, PAOLO (ascribed to) [C03/356A] Violin w/case, bow: (Dario D'Atili, Dumont, June 14, 1989) 9768/13024 **10745**
£6600 DM18381 ¥1696860

CAVACEPPI, MARIO [Sk11/111] Contemporary Italian Violin: Rome, 1981 2000/3000 **3080**
£1571 DM4589 ¥397320

CAVALLI, ARISTIDE [P03/170] Violin w/case, cover, minus pegs and tailpiece: Cremona, 1920 575/822 **1561**
£949 DM2632 ¥242831

CAVALLI, ARISTIDE [P09/75] Good Violin w/case, 2 repairs lower left table: Cremona, 1923 1403/1777 **1810**
£968 DM2865 ¥248873

CAVALLI, ARISTIDE [S06/211] Violin w/case: Cremona, 1928 1368/2052 **2257**
£1320 DM3811 ¥347424

CAVALLI, ARISTIDE (workshop of) [P09/99] Violin w/case, cover, bow, restorations: Cremona, 1923 748/1122 **1234**
£660 DM1954 ¥169686

CAVANI, GIOVANNI [B04/67] Fine Italian Violin in very good condition: Modena, 1900 5950/8330 **5950**
£3639 DM10000 ¥947418

CERPI, G. [P07/39] Violin w/case: 1906 728/1092 **1161**
£638 DM1874 ¥173600

CERPI, G. [S11/186] Violin: Paris, 1905 1376/1965 **NS**

CERPI, G. [S03/222] Violin w/violin: Paris, 1905 1197/1710 **NS**

CERPI, G. [S03/376] French Violin: Mirecourt, c. 1900 1026/1539 **1035**
£605 DM1676 ¥153307

CERUTI, GIOVANNI MARIA [S11/197] Italian Violin w/case, bow: Cremona, 1923 2751/3144 **3458**
£1760 DM5143 ¥440880

CHAMPION, RENE (ascribed to) [Sk11/136] French Violin w/case 1800/2200 **2090**
£1066 DM3114 ¥269610

CHANOT, FRANCIS [S03/211] Violin w/violin: Paris, c. 1819 1368/1710 **1787**
£1045 DM2895 ¥264803

CHANOT, FREDERICK WILLIAM [P11/148] Violin: London, 1894 982/1376 **2983**
£1518 DM4379 ¥384206

CHANOT, FREDERICK WILLIAM [S11/184] Violin: London, 1893 5895/9825 **8646**
£4400 DM12857 ¥1102200

CHANOT, FREDERICK WILLIAM [S06/386] Violin w/case: London, 1900 5130/8550 **NS**

CHANOT, G. A. [P09/113] Violin good condition: Manchester, 1898 1496/2244 **NS**

CHANOT, G. A. [P11/98] Violin good condition: 1898 1179/1572 **NS**

CHANOT, GEORGE [C03/174] English Violin: London 1628/1954 **1791**
£1100 DM3063 ¥282810

CHANOT, GEORGE ADOLPH [P03/168] Good Violin w/case, cover, bow: Manchester, c. 1880 2466/3288 **2441**
£1485 DM4118 ¥379863

CHANOT, GEORGE ADOLPH [S11/181] English Violin: Manchester, 1887 5895/6877 **8214**
£4180 DM12214 ¥1047090

CHANOT, GEORGE ADOLPH [S03/203] English Violin w/case: Manchester, 1895 4275/5985 **7148**
£4180 DM11579 ¥1059212

CHANOT, GEORGE ADOLPH [S03/233] Violin: Manchester, 1902 3420/5130 **NS**

CHANOT, GEORGE ADOLPH [S03/373] English Violin: Manchester, 1906 5130/6840 **NS**

CHANOT, GEORGES [P11/204] Fine Violin w/case, bow: Paris, 1825 (W. E. Hill & Sons, London, 1942) 9825/15720 **16211**
£8250 DM23801 ¥2088075

CHANOT, GEORGES [S11/37] Patent Violin: Paris, 1818 1572/1965 **NS**

CHANOT, JOSEPH ANTHONY [P11/175] Violin w/case, restoration required on table: London, 1899 982/1572 **1541**
£784 DM2263 ¥198506

CHAPPUY, A. [B04/167] Fine French Violin in excellent condition: Mirecourt, 1775 5950/7140 **5355**
£3275 DM9000 ¥852676

CHAPPUY, A. [B04/252] French Violin needs restoration: Paris, 1787 893/1488 **833**
£509 DM1400 ¥132639

CHAPPUY, N. [B04/40] Old French Violin in good condition: Mirecourt, late 18th C. 1488/2083 **1428**
£873 DM2400 ¥227380

CHAPPUY, NICOLAS AUGUSTIN [P06/207] Violin w/case, bow: Paris, c. 1770 1727/2418 **3040**
£1760 DM5095 ¥468864

CHAPPUY, NICOLAS AUGUSTIN [S06/190] French Violin w/case: Paris, 1779 1368/2052 **2069**
£1210 DM3494 ¥318472

CHAPPUY, NICOLAS AUGUSTIN (ascribed to) [S06/205] Violin w/case, bow: Paris, mid 18th C. 1026/1368 **1129**
£660 DM1906 ¥173712

CHARTREUX, EUGENE [P09/143] Small Size Violin w/case, bow: Lyon, c. 1920 467/748 **NS**

CHARTREUX, EUGENE [P11/386] Small-Size Violin w/case, bow: Lyon, c. 1920 295/491 **648**
£330 DM952 ¥83523

CHIPOT, JEAN BAPTISTE [C06/323] French Violin: 1928 1720/2580 **NS**

CHIPOT-VUILLAUME [P06/102] Good Violin w/case, good condition: Paris, 1893 1037/1382 **3040**
£1760 DM5095 ¥468864

CHIPOT-VUILLAUME [P06/144] Violin w/case, bow: Paris, 1889 691/1037 **1900**
£1100 DM3184 ¥293040

CHIPOT-VUILLAUME [P11/83] Good French Violin good condition: Paris, 1890 1277/1670 **2734**
£1392 DM4014 ¥352189

CHIPOT-VUILLAUME [S03/49] Violin w/case: Paris, 1894 1368/1710 **NS**

CLARK, SAMUEL [Sk11/135] American Violin w/case, bow: Westmoreland, 1866 1000/1200 **550**
£280 DM820 ¥70950

CLAUDOT, CHARLES [S11/88] French Violin: Mirecourt 2948/3930 **NS**

CLAUDOT, CHARLES [B04/37] Fine French Violin in very good condition: Mirecourt, 1849 1488/2380 **1131**
£691 DM1900 ¥180009

CLAUDOT, CHARLES [S03/310] French Violin: Mirecourt 4275/5985 **NS**

CLAUDOT, CHARLES (ascribed to) [S03/365] French Violin 2052/2565 **NS**

CLAUDOT, NICOLAS [P09/90] French Violin: Mirecourt, c. 1840 655/1029 **699**
£374 DM1107 ¥96155

CLOTELLE, H. [P06/216] Violin: Mirecourt, c. 1880 691/950 **950**
£550 DM1592 ¥146520

CLOTELLE, H. [P07/59] Good French Violin w/case: c. 1900 637/1001 **NS**

COLE, JAMES [P03/107] Good Violin w/case, bow, 2 open minor cracks, lower right table: Manchester, 1889 1315/1973 **2622**
£1595 DM4423 ¥408001

COLIN, CLAUDE [P06/63] Violin w/case, minus bridge: Mirecourt, 1910 691/864 **1330**
£770 DM2229 ¥205128

COLIN, CLAUDE [P06/67] French Violin minor table restoration required: 1893 605/950 **NS**

COLIN, JEAN BAPTISTE [P02/28] Good French Violin w/case, bow: 1895 510/680 **1346**
£792 DM2226 ¥194436

COLIN, JEAN BAPTISTE [P06/228] Good Violin w/case: 1892 864/1209 **2404**
£1392 DM4028 ¥370696

COLIN, JEAN BAPTISTE [P07/62] French Violin post repair table, gluing required bottom rib to table, back: 1888 546/910 **901**
£495 DM1454 ¥134690

COLIN, JEAN BAPTISTE [P10/78] French Violin minor table restoration required: 1893 980/1176 **NS**

COLIN, JEAN BAPTISTE [P11/56] Good Violin w/case, 2 bows, good condition: Mirecourt, 1902 786/1179 **1686**
£858 DM2475 ¥217160

COLLENOT, LOUIS [B04/152] French Violin in good condition: Reims, 1911 1488/1785 **1428**
£873 DM2400 ¥227380

COLLIN-MEZIN [S11/375] French Violin: Paris, 1925 1965/2948 **3026**
£1540 DM4500 ¥385770

COLLIN-MEZIN [S03/201] Violin: Paris, 1922 1197/1710 **1223**
£715 DM1981 ¥181181

COLLIN-MEZIN [S03/362] French Violin: Paris, 1922 2565/3420 **2822**
£1650 DM4570 ¥418110

COLLIN-MEZIN [S06/77] Violin w/case: Paris, 1927 1710/2052 **1693**
£990 DM2859 ¥260568

COLLIN-MEZIN, CH. J. B. [P03/100] Violin: Paris, 1936 986/1480 **2261**
£1375 DM3813 ¥351725

COLLIN-MEZIN, CH. J. B. [P06/271] French Violin w/case, minor restorations on table: 1897 1209/1555 **NS**

COLLIN-MEZIN, CH. J. B. [P06/77] Good Violin w/case, minor varnish blemish on back: 1928 1209/1555 **2090**
£1210 DM3503 ¥322344

COLLIN-MEZIN, CH. J. B. [P09/115] Fine Violin w/case, short post restoration on table: c. 1930 1496/2244 **1687**
£902 DM2670 ¥231904

COLLIN-MEZIN, CH. J. B. [P09/139] Good Small-Size Violin w/case, good condition: Paris, 1899 1309/1683 **2160**
£1155 DM3419 ¥296950

COLLIN-MEZIN, CH. J. B. [S11/11] Violin w/case, bow: Paris, 1898 2358/3537 **3675**
£1870 DM5464 ¥468435

COLLIN-MEZIN, CH. J. B. [S11/38] Violin w/case: Paris, 1887 2948/3930 **4323**
£2200 DM6428 ¥551100

COLLIN-MEZIN, CH. J. B. [S11/399] Violin w/case: Paris, 1897 2948/3930 **3458**
£1760 DM5143 ¥440880

COLLIN-MEZIN, CH. J. B. [S11/5] Violin w/case: Paris, 1888 2948/3930 **3675**
£1870 DM5464 ¥468435

COLLIN-MEZIN, CH. J. B. [B04/163] Fine French Violin in perfect condition: Paris, 1896 7140/8330 **6843**
£4185 DM11500 ¥1089531

COLLIN-MEZIN, CH. J. B. [B04/173] Fine French Violin in perfect condition: Paris, 1912 (H. Schicker, Freiburg, 1980) 10710/14875 **10710**
£6550 DM18000 ¥1705352

COLLIN-MEZIN, CH. J. B. [B04/242] French Violin in very good condition: Paris, 1942 1488/1785 **1369**
£837 DM2300 ¥217906

COLLIN-MEZIN, CH. J. B. [S03/46] Violin w/case, bow: Paris, 1889 3078/4275 **3762**
£2200 DM6094 ¥557480

COLLIN-MEZIN, CH. J. B. [S06/68] Violin w/case: Paris, 1892 3078/3762 **3762**
£2200 DM6352 ¥579040

COLLIN-MEZIN, CH. J. B. [C11/143] French Violin w/case, bow: 1951 1182/1576 **672**
£341 DM990 ¥85455

COLLIN-MEZIN, CH. J. B. [C11/287] French Violin w/case 1379/1773 **NS**

COLLIN-MEZIN, CH. J. B. [C11/299] French Violin w/case, 2 bows: 1927 1379/1970 **1409**
£715 DM2075 ¥179179

COLLIN-MEZIN, CH. J. B. [C11/322] French Violin 3546/4334 **4334**
£2200 DM6384 ¥551320

COLLIN-MEZIN, CH. J. B. [C11/335] French Violin: Paris 1970/2955 **4767**
£2420 DM7023 ¥606452

COLLIN-MEZIN, CH. J. B. [C06/304] French Violin w/case, bow: 1882 2580/3440 **2838**
£1650 DM4768 ¥434891

COLLIN-MEZIN, CH. J. B. [C03/150] French Violin w/case, bow 1302/1954 **NS**

COLLIN-MEZIN, CH. J. B. [C03/175] French Violin w/case: 1900 2930/4070 **2686**
£1650 DM4595 ¥424215

COLLIN-MEZIN, CH. J. B. [C03/180] French Violin: 1889 2279/2930 **2686**
£1650 DM4595 ¥424215

COLLIN-MEZIN, CH. J. B. [C03/300] French Violin w/case: 1953 1465/1954 **1612**
£990 DM2757 ¥254529

COLLIN-MEZIN, CH. J. B. [C03/318] French Violin w/case: 1920 1628/2442 **1612**
£990 DM2757 ¥254529

COLLIN-MEZIN, CH. J. B. [C03/336] French Violin w/case, bow: 1890 2930/4070 **5014**
£3080 DM8578 ¥791868

COLLIN-MEZIN, CH. J. B. [C03/342] French Violin: 1889 2442/4070 **2328**
£1430 DM3983 ¥367653

COLLIN-MEZIN, CH. J. B. (FILS) [P06/71] Violin w/case, bow 2591/4319 **3991**
£2310 DM6687 ¥615384

COLLIN-MEZIN, CH. J. B. (FILS) [P07/127] Violin: 1882 (J. & A. Beare, London, September 29, 1950) 1092/1638 **2903**
£1595 DM4686 ¥434000

COLTON, WALTER E. [Sk11/152] Two American Violins w/case, 3 bows: New York, 1911 2000/3000 **1980**
£1010 DM2950 ¥255420

COMUNI, ANTONIO [B04/187] Fine Italian Violin in good condition: Piacenza, c. 1810 (Dario D'Attili, Dumont, 1989) 26775/32725 **21420**
£13100 DM36000 ¥3410705

CONIA, STEFANO [P03/152] Good Violin mint condition: Cremona, 1974 (Maker's) 3288/4110 **5787**
£3520 DM9761 ¥900416

CONIA, STEFANO [S06/193] Italian Violin: Cremona, 1985 (Maker's) 4275/5985 **5455**
£3190 DM9211 ¥839608

CONTI ALDO [C11/159] Italian Violin w/case: Cesena, 1925 3940/4925 **4984**
£2530 DM7342 ¥634018

CONTINO, ALFREDO [Sk11/141] Italian Violin w/case: Naples, early 20th C. 3000/4000 **11550**
£5890 DM17210 ¥1489950

COOPER, HUGH W. [P10/20] Good Scottish Violin in good condition: Glasgow, 1902 686/1078 **1509**
£770 DM2277 ¥188958

COPELLI, MAURIZIO [P06/212] Good Violin: Cremona, 1989 1382/2073 **2660**
£1540 DM4458 ¥410256

COUTURIEUX [P06/406] Violin 432/605 **NS**

COUTURIEUX [P10/185] Violin: Mirecourt, c. 1910 294/392 **647**
£330 DM976 ¥80982

CRASKE, GEORGE [P03/104] Violin w/case, cover: c. 1830 1315/1973 **4159**
£2530 DM7016 ¥647174

CRASKE, GEORGE [P03/205] Violin w/case, 2 bows: London 822/1151 **3255**
£1980 DM5491 ¥506484

CRASKE, GEORGE [P06/230] Violin w/case, 2 bows 1727/3109 **3801**
£2200 DM6369 ¥586080

CRASKE, GEORGE [P11/149] Violin w/case: Manchester, c. 1840 (W. E. Hill & Sons, London, September, 1982) 3930/5895 **6052**
£3080 DM8886 ¥779548

CRASKE, GEORGE [S11/34] English Violin w/case, bow: Stockport, mid 19th C. 2358/3537 **2594**
£1320 DM3857 ¥330660

CRASKE, GEORGE [S03/364] Violin w/case: Stockport, 1850 1368/2052 **1693**
£990 DM2742 ¥250866

CRASKE, GEORGE [S03/47] English Violin w/case: W. E. Hill & Sons (London, February 2, 1971) 2565/3420 **3198**
£1870 DM5180 ¥473858

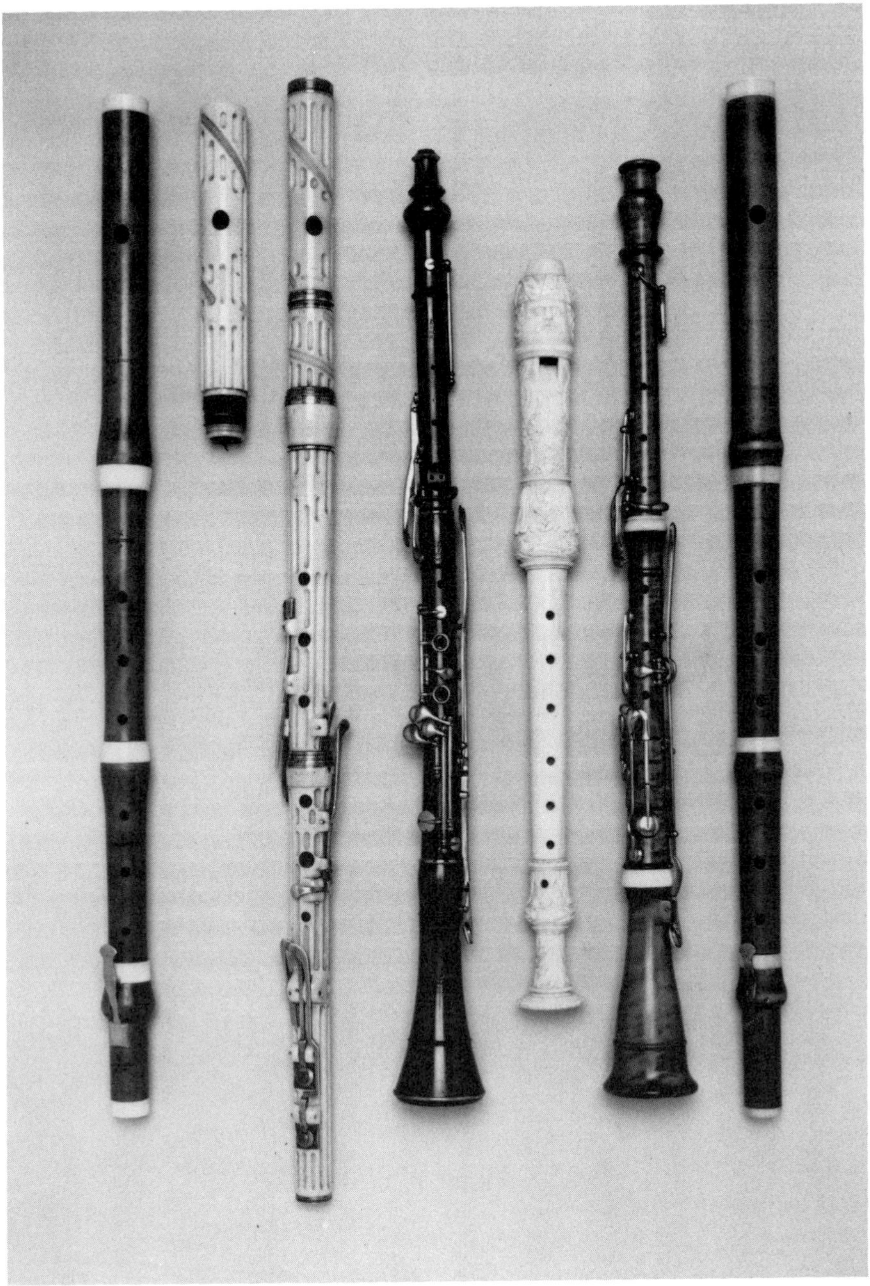

AUGUSTE GRENSER
Fine One-Keyed Boxwood Flute: Dresden, c. 1800 (left)
Sotheby's, London, November 22, 1990, Lot 138

CRASKE, GEORGE [S03/65] Violin: Stockport
2565/3420 **2445**
£1430 DM3961 ¥362362

CRASKE, GEORGE [S06/104] Violin w/case: Stockport, 1856 (W. E. Hill & Sons, January 29, 1942)
3420/5130 **7900**
£4620 DM13340 ¥1215984

CRASKE, GEORGE [C11/340] Good English Violin w/case
4925/6895 **5201**
£2640 DM7661 ¥661584

CRASKE, GEORGE [C03/173] English Violin w/case
3582/4558 **4477**
£2750 DM7659 ¥707025

CRASKE, GEORGE [C03/178] English Violin: 1820
1628/2442 **1701**
£1045 DM2910 ¥268669

CRASKE, GEORGE [C03/297] Good English Violin
3256/4884 **2865**
£1760 DM4902 ¥452496

CRASKE, GEORGE [C03/352] Good English Violin w/case
4884/5698 **NS**

CRASKE, GEORGE (ascribed to) [C03/337] English Violin
1302/1628 **NS**

CRASKE, GEORGE (attributed to) [P11/182] English Violin w/case
1376/1768 **1865**
£949 DM2739 ¥240268

CRASKE, GEORGE (attributed to) [C11/315] English Violin w/case, bow
788/1576 **823**
£418 DM1213 ¥104751

DAL CANTO, GIUSTINO [Sk11/117] Modern Italian Violin: Pisa, 1946
2500/3500 **1870**
£954 DM2786 ¥241230

DALLA COSTA, ANTONIO [S11/210] Violin: Treviso, 1764 (W. E. Hill & Sons, London, January 6, 1965)
58950/68775 **62683**
£31900 DM93212 ¥7990950

DARCHE, HILAIRE [C11/173] Belgian Violin: Brussells, 1926
7880/11820 **11268**
£5720 DM16599 ¥1433432

DARTE, AUGUST (attributed to) [C11/311] French Violin
1970/2955 **3034**
£1540 DM4469 ¥385924

DE RUB, AUGUSTO (ascribed to) [C11/170] Interesting Violin
5910/7880 **NS**

DEARLOVE, MARK WILLIAM [P11/64] Small-Size Violin w/case: Leeds
295/491 **735**
£374 DM1079 ¥94659

DEBLAYE, ALBERT [P02/20] Violin: 1926
510/680 **598**
£352 DM989 ¥86416

DECHANT, G. [Sk11/131] American Violin: Galesburg, 1909
1000/1500 **2090**
£1066 DM3114 ¥269610

DEGANI, (WORKSHOP OF) [C03/187] Italian Violin w/case, bow: Venice, 1895
4884/8140 **19699**
£12100 DM33698 ¥3110910

DEGANI, EUGENIO [P03/206] Violin excellent condition: Venice, 1889
8220/11508 **10850**
£6600 DM18302 ¥1688280

DEGANI, EUGENIO [P06/178] Fine Violin w/case: Venice, 1893
8637/12092 **14822**
£8580 DM24839 ¥2285712

DEGANI, EUGENIO [S03/1] Violin w/case, 2 bows: Venice, 1897
11970/15390 **18810**
£11000 DM30470 ¥2787400

DEGANI, EUGENIO [C11/357] Italian Violin w/case: Venice, 1899
13790/19700 **26004**
£13200 DM38306 ¥3307920

DEGANI, GIULIO [P11/118] Violin w/case, bow, varnish needs attention: Venice, c. 1890
3930/5895 **5188**
£2640 DM7616 ¥668184

DEGANI, GIULIO [S11/111] Violin w/case: Venice, 1924
11790/15720 **12969**
£6600 DM19285 ¥1653300

DEGANI, GIULIO [S03/187] Violin w/case: Venice, 1924
11970/17100 **NS**

DEGANI, GIULIO [S03/224] Italian Violin w/case, bow: Venice, 1902
3078/4275 **15048**
£8800 DM24376 ¥2229920

DEGANI, GIULIO [C06/284] Italian Violin: Venice, 1910
6880/8600 **7568**
£4400 DM12716 ¥1159708

DELANOY, ALEXANDRE [P07/303] French Violin
2730/3640 **3964**
£2178 DM6399 ¥592634

DELANOY, ALEXANDRE [B04/46] Fine French Violin in very good condition: Bordeaux, 1913
2678/3570 **2678**
£1638 DM4500 ¥426338

DELIVET, AUGUSTE [B04/49] Fine French Violin in perfect condition: Paris, 1909
2380/3570 **2618**
£1601 DM4400 ¥416864

DELLA CORTE, ALFONSO (ascribed to) [S06/19] Neapolitan Violin w/case, cover
5130/8550 **14108**
£8250 DM23822 ¥2171400

DEMAY [B04/260] French Violin in very good condition: Lille, c. 1930
2380/3570 **2023**
£1237 DM3400 ¥322122

DERAZEY, HONORE [P03/111] Good Violin w/case, bow, excellent condition: Mirecourt, c. 1870
5754/8220 **10850**
£6600 DM18302 ¥1688280

DERAZEY, HONORE [P03/133] Violin restored: c. 1850
1315/1644 **1664**
£1012 DM2806 ¥258870

DERAZEY, HONORE [S11/114] Violin w/case: Mirecourt, c. 1870
4913/6877 **5620**
£2860 DM8357 ¥716430

DERAZEY, HONORE [S11/379] French Violin w/case: Mirecourt, 1864
7860/11790 **NS**

DERAZEY, HONORE [S03/374] Violin: Mirecourt, c. 1860
3420/5130 **5643**
£3300 DM9141 ¥836220

DERAZEY, HONORE [S06/2] Violin w/case: Mirecourt, c. 1830 (W. E. Hill & Sons, London, January 7, 1902)
2565/3420 **2257**
£1320 DM3811 ¥347424

DERAZEY, HONORE [C11/330] French Violin w/case 1970/2955 **5201**
£2640 DM7661 ¥661584

DERAZEY, HONORE [C11/342] French Violin w/case: Mirecourt 3940/5910 **5201**
£2640 DM7661 ¥661584

DERAZEY, HONORE [C06/325] French Violin 3440/5160 **3595**
£2090 DM6040 ¥550861

DERAZEY, HONORE (attributed to) [P09/94] Good French Violin 1496/2244 **NS**

DERAZEY, JUSTIN [B04/155] French Violin in good condition: Mirecourt, c. 1850 2975/4165 **2975**
£1819 DM5000 ¥473709

DERAZEY, JUSTIN [S06/392] French Violin: Mirecourt 1710/2565 **NS**

DERAZEY, JUSTIN [C03/333] French Violin 1628/2442 **2865**
£1760 DM4902 ¥452496

DEVEAU, JOHN G. [P10/64] Good Violin w/case, cover, good condition: New Rochelle, 1940 980/1372 **1141**
£582 DM1721 ¥142798

DIDIER, MARIUS [B04/243] French Violin in very good condition: Mattaincourt, 1926 1785/2678 **1666**
£1019 DM2800 ¥265277

DIDIER, MARIUS [S06/89] Violin w/case, cover, 2 bows: Mattaincourt, 1929 2565/3420 **2822**
£1650 DM4764 ¥434280

DIEHL, A. [B04/56] German Violin in mint condition: Hamburg, 1889 2975/4165 **2678**
£1638 DM4500 ¥426338

DIEHL, M. [B04/142] Fine German Violin in perfect condition: Hamburg, 1906 2380/3570 **4165**
£2547 DM7000 ¥663193

DIEHL, M. [B04/253] German Violin needs restoration, scroll restored: Mainz, second half, 18th C. 893/1488 **833**
£509 DM1400 ¥132639

DIEUDONNE, AMEDEE [Sk11/108] French Violin: Mirecourt, 1912 1500/2000 **2420**
£1234 DM3606 ¥312180

DIEUDONNE, AMEDEE [Sk11/113] French Violin: Mirecourt, 1955 1800/2200 **2310**
£1178 DM3442 ¥297990

DIEUDONNE, AMEDEE [B04/263] French Violin in very good condition: Mirecourt, c. 1930 3000/3600 **3900**
£2340 DM6500 ¥615810

DIEUDONNE, AMEDEE [S06/391] French Violin: Mirecourt, 1941 2565/3420 **2822**
£1650 DM4764 ¥434280

DIEUDONNE, AMEDEE [C06/106] French Violin 1720/2580 **2838**
£1650 DM4768 ¥434891

DIEUDONNE, AMEDEE [C06/305] French Violin: Mirecourt, 1943 1720/2580 **3027**
£1760 DM5086 ¥463883

DIXON, ALFRED THOMAS [P03/198] Good Violin w/case, good condition: Normanby, 1928 658/986 **796**
£484 DM1342 ¥123807

DOLLENZ, GIOVANNI (ascribed to) [S11/21] Violin: Trieste, 1807 9825/13755 **NS**

DOLLENZ, GIOVANNI (ascribed to) [S03/350] Violin 11970/15390 **NS**

DOLLING, LOUIS (JUN) [P03/223] Good Violin w/case, mint condition: Markneukirchen, 1904 822/1151 **995**
£605 DM1678 ¥154759

DOLLING, LOUIS (JUN) [P06/182] Good Violin: Markneukirchen, 1948 1037/1382 **1520**
£880 DM2548 ¥234432

DOLLING, ROBERT A. [Sk11/176] German Violin w/case: Markneukirchen, early 20th C. 300/400 **825**
£421 DM1229 ¥106425

DROUIN, CHARLES [S03/195] Violin: Mirecourt, 1892 1197/1710 **NS**

DROUIN, CHARLES [S03/326] Violin w/case: Mirecourt, 1896 1710/2565 **NS**

DUERER, WILHELM [P06/414] Violin: Saxony, 1925 345/518 **329**
£190 DM551 ¥50696

DUGADE, AUBRY [S03/351] Violin: Paris, 1910 1026/1368 **1975**
£1155 DM3199 ¥292677

DUGARDE, AUBRY [P10/41] Violin in good condition: Paris, 1925 686/882 **1438**
£734 DM2170 ¥180050

DUKE, RICHARD [P03/244] Violin w/case, 2 bows: London, c. 1770 3288/4932 **5787**
£3520 DM9761 ¥900416

DUKE, RICHARD [P06/73] Violin w/case, bow: London, c. 1770 (L. P. Balmforth & Son, 1988) 2591/4319 **2470**
£1430 DM4140 ¥380952

DUKE, RICHARD [S06/218] English Violin: London, third quarter 18th C. 5130/6840 **NS**

DUKE, RICHARD [C06/134] English Violin w/case: (J. & A. Beare, November 29, 1955) 3440/5160 **5676**
£3300 DM9537 ¥869781

DUPARY, ADOLPHE [C06/84] French Violin w/2 bows 1204/1720 **2270**
£1320 DM3815 ¥347912

EBERLE, TOMASO [C11/178] Italian Violin w/case, 2 bows, reduced in size from a small viola: Naples, 1784 13790/19700 **34672**
£17600 DM51075 ¥4410560

ECKLAND, DONALD [Sk11/126] Good Contemporary American Violin: Miami, 1977 2000/3000 **3410**
£1739 DM5081 ¥439890

ELLIOT, WILLIAM [P06/108] Good Violin w/case, 2 bows: Hawick, 1910 864/1382 **2470**
£1430 DM4140 ¥380952

GIUSEPPE (FILIUS ANDREA) GUARNERI
Important Violin: Cremona, c. 1705
Sotheby's, London, November 22, 1990, Lot 43

ENDERS, F. & R. [C11/341] German Violin w/case: 1924 1970/2955 **3034**
£1540 DM4469 ¥385924

EYLES, CHARLES [P07/52] Violin post repair required on table: Wangford, 1910 728/910 **NS**

FABRICATORE, GENNARO [B04/191] Fine Italian Violin in excellent condition: Naples, 1829 (W. Lindorfer, Weimar, 1967) 26775/32725 **25585**
£15648 DM43000 ¥4073897

FABRICATORE, GIOVANNI BATTISTA [S11/395] Italian Violin: Naples, early 19th C. (Dario D'Attili, Dumont, February 28, 1985) 6877/8843 **6484**
£3300 DM9643 ¥826650

FABRICATORE, GIOVANNI BATTISTA (ascribed to) [S03/191] Italian Violin w/case 10260/15390 **11662**
£6820 DM18891 ¥1728188

FABRIS, LUIGI (ascribed to) [S06/96] Violin 3420/5130 **NS**

FAGNOLA, HANNIBAL [B04/189] Fine Italian Violin in perfect condition: Turin, 1930 23800/29750 **20825**
£12736 DM35000 ¥3315963

FALISSE, A. [B04/149] Fine Violin in perfect condition: Brussels, 1926 3570/4760 **2380**
£1456 DM4000 ¥378967

FALISSE, A. [S03/40] Violin w/case: Brussels, 1932 2565/3420 **3574**
£2090 DM5789 ¥529606

FELICI, ENRICO [P06/213] Good Violin: Rome, 1989 1555/2591 **2850**
£1650 DM4777 ¥439560

FENDT, BERNARD (attributed to) [C11/152] English Violin w/case, bow 2955/3940 **3251**
£1650 DM4788 ¥413490

FENDT, BERNARD (attributed to) [C03/136] English Violin w/case, bow 3256/4070 **NS**

FENT, FRANCOIS [S11/42] Violin: Paris, late 18th C. (Pierre Vidoudez, Geneva, July 3, 1974) 15720/23580 **NS**

FERRARI, GIUSEPPE [S03/302] Violin: Ferrara, 1951 1710/2052 **2069**
£1210 DM3352 ¥306614

FICHTL, M. [B04/160] Fine German Violin in very good condition: Vienna, 1747 (Millant-Deroux, Paris, 1960) 7140/8925 **6843**
£4185 DM11500 ¥/2511089531

FICHTL, MARTIN MATHIAS [Sk11/128] Tyrolian Violin w/case, bow: Vienna, 1799 1500/1800 **NS**

FICKER, C. S. [B04/251] German Violin in good condition: Markneukirchen, 1823 1190/1785 **1071**
£655 DM1800 ¥170535

FICKER, JOHANN CHRISTIAN [P06/251] Violin w/case: 1750 1382/2591 **3325**
£1925 DM5573 ¥512820

FICKER, JOHANN CHRISTIAN [P11/82] Good Violin w/case: 1750 2948/3930 **2810**
£1430 DM4126 ¥361933

FICKER, JOHANN CHRISTIAN [S11/86] Violin w/case: Markneukirchen, 1708 1965/2948 **2378**
£1210 DM3536 ¥303105

FICKER FAMILY (MEMBER OF) [P11/70] Good Violin w/case, old restorations: Markneukirchen, c. 1770 688/1081 **NS**

FILLION, G. [P11/183] Good French Violin w/case, minor old table post repair: 1896 1179/1572 **NS**

FIORINI, RAFFAELE (attributed to) [C11/336] Italian Violin 3940/5910 **4767**
£2420 DM7023 ¥606452

FISCHER, H. A. [P11/107] Good Violin w/case, bow, good condition: Markneukirchen, c. 1910 1572/2358 **3891**
£1980 DM5712 ¥501138

FLAMBEAU, CHARLES [P03/143] Violin: Mirecourt, c. 1780 1315/1973 **NS**

FLEURY, BENOIT [S03/210] Violin: Paris, c. 1780 1026/1368 **1035**
£605 DM1676 ¥153307

FORBES-WHITMORE, ANTHONY [P06/246] Fine Violin: Harrogate 1382/1727 **3420**
£1980 DM5732 ¥527472

FORCELLINI, F. [B04/66] Fine Italian Violin in perfect condition: Mantua, 1968 5355/6545 **4760**
£2911 DM8000 ¥757934

FORD, JACOB (attributed to) [P06/172] Good Violin w/case, overall condition excellent: London, c. 1770 2591/4319 **4941**
£2860 DM8280 ¥761904

FORRESTER, ALEXANDER [P02/60] Violin w/case, bow, good condition 425/595 **785**
£462 DM1298 ¥113421

FORSTER, WILLIAM [Sk11/132] English Violin: London, 18th C. 1500/2000 **1760**
£898 DM2622 ¥227040

FORSTER, WILLIAM (II) [S03/196] Violin w/case, bow: London, 1796 5130/8550 **9405**
£5500 DM15235 ¥1393700

FORSTER, WILLIAM (II) [S03/239] Violin: London, c. 1790 1710/2565 **2822**
£1650 DM4570 ¥418110

FORSTER, WILLIAM (II) [S06/387] Violin w/case: London, c. 1800 2565/3420 **2445**
£1430 DM4129 ¥376376

FUCHS, W. K. [Sk11/224] German Violin w/case, bow: Erlangen, 1925 800/1000 **990**
£505 DM1475 ¥127710

FURBER, JOHN (attributed to) [P03/171] Violin w/case, good condition 2466/4110 **3074**
£1870 DM5186 ¥478346

FURBER, MATTHEW (attributed to) [P07/99] English Violin w/case, bow, back joint proud 546/910 **1041**
£572 DM1681 ¥155641

FURBER FAMILY (MEMBER OF) (attributed to) [P06/229] Good Violin w/case: (J. & A. Beare, London, 1971) 3455/5182 **4371**
£2530 DM7324 ¥673992

GABRIELLI, GIOVANNI BATTISTA [S06/101] Fine Italian Violin w/case: Florence, 1770 (J. & A. Beare, London, January 15, 1971) 51300/59850 **67716**
£39600 DM114345 ¥10422720

GADDA, GAETANO [B04/175] Fine Italian Violin in perfect condition: Mantua, 1915 10710/13090 **12495**
£7642 DM21000 ¥1989578

GADDA, GAETANO [C06/146] Good Italian Violin w/case: Mantua, 1903 6880/8600 **11352**
£6600 DM19074 ¥1739562

GADDA, MARIO [S06/81] Violin: Porto Mantovano (Maker's) 5130/8550 **NS**

GADDA, MARIO [C06/327] Good Italian Violin w/case: Mantua, 1910 6020/7740 **6054**
£3520 DM10173 ¥927766

GAGLIANO, FERDINAND [S11/124] Violin w/case, 2 bows: Naples, c. 1750 58950/68775 **88622**
£45100 DM131782 ¥11297550

GAGLIANO, FERDINAND (attributed to) [C06/321] Neapolitan Violin w/case, bow 10320/17200 **28380**
£16500 DM47685 ¥4348905

GAGLIANO, GENNARO [C06/148] Fine Italian Violin: Naples, 1763 (W. E. Hill & Sons, May 4, 1982) 43000/51600 **56760**
£33000 DM95370 ¥8697810

GAGLIANO, JOSEPH [S03/375] Violin w/case: Naples, c. 1780 51300/68400 **43263**
£25300 DM70081 ¥6411020

GAGLIANO, JOSEPH [S03/38] Child's Violin w/case: Naples, 1785 (W. E. Hill & Sons, Great Missenden, January 19, 1983) 13680/20520 **27275**
£15950 DM44181 ¥4041730

GAGLIANO, JOSEPH [S06/22] Violin w/case, 2 bows: Naples, c. 1783 25650/42750 **NS**

GAGLIANO, JOSEPH & ANTONIO [Sk11/122] Italian Violin w/case: Naples, late 18th C. 16000/18000 **13200**
£6732 DM19668 ¥1702800

GAGLIANO, NICOLO [B04/194] Important Italian Violin w/case, in very good condition: Naples, 1737 107100/130900 **89250**
£54585 DM150000 ¥14211270

GAGLIANO, NICOLO [S03/218] Italian Violin: Naples, third quarter, 18th C. (Dario D'Attili, Dumont, May 15, 1985) 17100/25650 **23513**
£13750 DM38087 ¥3484250

GAGLIANO, NICOLO [S06/98] Fine Italian Violin w/case: Naples, 1733 42750/51300 **65835**
£38500 DM111169 ¥10133200

GAGLIANO, RAFFAELE & ANTONIO [P06/250] Violin w/case: Naples, 1859 27640/31095 **30404**
£17600 DM50952 ¥4688640

GAGLIANO FAMILY (attributed to) [C03/348] Italian Violin 19536/24420 **21490**
£13200 DM36762 ¥3393720

GAIDA, GIOVANNI [P03/167] Good Violin w/case, cover, fine condition: c. 1920 (J. P. Guivier & Co., June, 1971) 8220/9864 **11212**
£6820 DM18912 ¥1744556

GAIDA, GIOVANNI [S03/347] Italian Violin w/case, 2 bows, bow case: Ivrea, 1908 6840/10260 **15048**
£8800 DM24376 ¥2229920

GALEA, ALFREDO G. [P03/192] Good Violin w/case, fine condition: Long Beach, 1970 1315/1973 **1808**
£1100 DM3050 ¥281380

GALLA, ANTON (attributed to) [C06/103] Czechoslovakian Violin: 1948 1032/1376 **NS**

GAND, CHARLES FRANCOIS (ascribed to) [S03/242] Fine French Violin w/case, bow 10260/13680 **26334**
£15400 DM42658 ¥3902360

GARIMBERTI, F. [B04/273] Fine Italian Violin in very good condition: Milan, 1938 (Fa. Machold, Bremen, 1989) 11900/14875 **10710**
£6550 DM18000 ¥1705352

GAVATELLI, ALCIDE [P10/81] Violin w/case, minor right wing repair 1470/1862 **2182**
£1113 DM3292 ¥273179

GAVINIES, FRANCOIS [S03/198] Violin: Paris, 1750 5130/6840 **5267**
£3080 DM8532 ¥780472

GEISSENHOF, FRANZ [C03/351] Good Austrian Violin: Vienna, 18th C. 6512/9768 **10745**
£6600 DM18381 ¥1696860

GEISSENHOF, FRANZ (attributed to) [C11/172] Good Violin: Vienna 7880/11820 **8668**
£4400 DM12769 ¥1102640

GEMUNDER, GEORGE [Sk11/123] Fine American Violin w/case: Astoria, 1907 3000/4000 **4510**
£2300 DM6720 ¥581790

GERARD, GRAND [B04/24] French Violin in very good condition: Mirecourt, 19th C. 595/1190 **833**
£509 DM1400 ¥132639

GERMAIN, EMILE [C11/319] French Violin w/case, bow: Monmartre, 1886 2955/4925 **6501**
£3300 DM9577 ¥826980

GIGLI, GIULIO CESARE [S06/196] Violin w/case: Rome, mid 18th C. 2052/3078 **3010**
£1760 DM5082 ¥463232

GILBERT, JEFFERY J. [S03/235] Violin: Peterborough, 1904 1026/1368 **1317**
£770 DM2133 ¥195118

GILBERT, JEFFERY JAMES [S03/237] Child's English Violin: New Romney, 1884 1026/1368 **1599**
£935 DM2590 ¥236929

GILKS, WILLIAM [C06/273] English Violin w/case, bow 1204/1376 **NS**

GLASEL, ERNST [P02/164] Violin minus tailpiece: Markneukirchen, 1888 340/510 **785**
£462 DM1298 ¥113421

GLASEL, LOUIS [Sk11/196] German Violin w/case: Markneukirchen, c. 1920 400/500 **550**
£280 DM820 ¥70950

GLASEL & MOSSNER (attributed to) [P11/300] Full Size German Violin w/bow 393/590 **562**
£286 DM825 ¥72387

GLASS, JOHANN [P11/128] Good Violin good condition: Leipzig, 1918 786/1179 **1491**
£759 DM2190 ¥192103

GLENISTER, WILLIAM [S11/190] Violin w/case, bow: London, 1905 2358/2948 **3458**
£1760 DM5143 ¥440880

GLENISTER, WILLIAM [S03/66] Violin w/case, bow: London, 1905 3420/5130 **NS**

GOBETTI, FRANCESCO [S06/1] Violin w/case, cover: Venice, c. 1700 10260/13680 **13543**
£7920 DM22869 ¥2084544

GOFFRILLER, FRANCESCO [S06/390] Italian Violin w/case: Udine, first half, 18th C. (Dario D'Attili, Dumont, October 18, 1982) 42750/51300 **41382**
£24200 DM69878 ¥6369440

GOFTON, ROBERT [P03/108] Violin w/case: Whitby, 1880 822/986 **1175**
£715 DM1983 ¥182897

GORDON [P10/59] Violin: Belfast, c. 1850 490/686 **690**
£352 DM1041 ¥86381

GOULDING [P02/99] English Violin w/case, bow, restorations: London, c. 1800 170/340 **374**
£220 DM618 ¥54010

GOULDING (attributed to) [P06/191] Violin 1209/1555 **1520**
£880 DM2548 ¥234432

GOULDING & CO. [S06/411] English Violin w/case: London, c. 1800 1710/2565 **NS**

GRAGNANI, ANTONIO [C11/182] Fine Italian Violin: Liburni, 1783 27580/35460 **34672**
£17600 DM51075 ¥4410560

GRANCINO, FRANCESCO & GIOVANNI [Sk11/153] Italian Violin w/case: Milan, early 18th C. (Hart & Son, London, July 19, 1907) 3000/4000 **8250**
£4207 DM12293 ¥1064250

GRANCINO, GIOVANNI [S03/61] Italian Violin w/case, 2 bows: Milan, 1719 42750/51300 **71478**
£41800 DM115786 ¥10592120

GRANCINO, GEBR. [B04/274] Fine Italian Violin well-restored: Milan, c. 1700 23800/29750 **20825**
£12736 DM35000 ¥3315963

GRAND-GERARD, JEAN BAPTISTE [P06/84] French Violin w/case, bow, restorations: Mirecourt, c. 1800 605/950 **NS**

GRAND-GERARD, JEAN BAPTISTE [P10/47] French Violin w/case, bow, restorations: Mirecourt, c. 1800 490/686 **604**
£308 DM911 ¥75583

GRAND-GERARD, JEAN BAPTISTE [S03/308] Violin: Mirecourt, c. 1810 1197/1710 **6019**
£3520 DM9750 ¥891968

GRANDJON, JULES [S03/345] Travelling Violin w/case, bow: Mirecourt, third quarter, 19th C. 1368/2052 **2445**
£1430 DM3961 ¥362362

GRATER, THOMAS [P02/74] Violin minus tailpiece: c. 1870 1020/1360 **1646**
£968 DM2720 ¥237644

GRIBBEN, P. J. [P03/402] Full Size Violin: Dalmuir, 1926 132/197 **289**
£176 DM488 ¥45021

GRUNER [B04/235] German Violin in very good condition 476/893 **565**
£346 DM950 ¥90005

GUADAGNINI, ANTONIO (attributed to) [B04/275] Fine Italian Violin in excellent condition: (H. Schmidt, Mittenwald, 1973) 23800/29750 **21420**
£13100 DM36000 ¥3410705

GUADAGNINI, FRANCESCO [C03/186] Italian Violin: Turin, 1929 6512/8140 **12536**
£7700 DM21444 ¥1979670

GUADAGNINI, G. B. & PIETRO [S11/403] Italian Violin w/case: Turin, c. 1780 (Benjamin Koodlach, Palm Desert, December 11, 1976) 176850/216150 **NS**

GUADAGNINI, GIOVANNI BATTISTA [S11/218] Fine Violin: Turin, 1772 (Max Moller, Amsterdam, December 2, 1977) 216150/235800 **345840**
£176000 DM514272 ¥44088000

GUADAGNINI, GIOVANNI BATTISTA [S06/23] Fine and Important Violin w/case: Turin, 1780 (W. E. Hill & Sons, London, August 14, 1925) 153900/188100 **244530**
£143000 DM412912 ¥37637600

GUADAGNINI, GIOVANNI BATTISTA [S06/398] Italian Violin: Parma, second half, 18th C. (W. E. Hill & Sons, London, April 22, 1953) 102600/153900 **82764**
£48400 DM139755 ¥12738880

GUADAGNINI, GIOVANNI BATTISTA [C03/190] Italian Violin w/case: Milan, 1752 (Dario D'Attili, Dumont, November 20, 1988) 40700/48840 **44770**
£27500 DM76587 ¥7070250

GUARNERI, ANDREA [S11/214] Italian Violin w/case: Cremona, second half, 17th C. (Frank Passa, San Francisco, March 15, 1977) 35370/43230 **32422**
£16500 DM48213 ¥4133250

GUARNERI, ANDREA [C03/359] Italian Violin w/case: Cremona, 1679 16280/24420 **53724**
£33000 DM91905 ¥8484300

GUARNERI, GIUSEPPE (FILIUS ANDREA) [S11/43] Important Violin w/case: Cremona, c. 1705 275100/314400 **354486**
£180400 DM527129 ¥45190200

GUARNERI, GIUSEPPE (FILIUS ANDREA) (attributed to) [S03/360] Violin: (Hamma & Co., Stuttgart, November 4, 1939) 51300/68400 **60192**
£35200 DM97504 ¥8919680

GUARNERI, JOSEPH (DEL GESU) (attributed to) [S06/400] Interesting Italian Violin w/case, cover, bow: (Hamma & Co., Stuttgart, August 25, 1951) 8550/11970 **31977**
£18700 DM53996 ¥4921840

GUARNERI, PIETRO (OF MANTUA) [S03/67] Fine Italian Violin w/case: Mantua, 1685 (Rembert Wurlitzer, New York, February 21, 1964) 205200/307800 **NS**

GUASTALLA, DANTE [S03/60] Italian Violin: Reggiolo-Emilia, 1939 (Carlo Carfagna, Rome, November 15, 1989) 3420/5130 **6395**
£3740 DM10360 ¥947716

GUASTALLA, DANTE & ALFREDO [Sk11/121] Modern Italian Violin: Reggiolo, 1924 2500/3500 **9900**
£5049 DM14751 ¥1277100

GUASTALLA, DANTE & ALFREDO [S03/12] Violin w/case, 2 bows: Reggio Emilia, 1929
3420/5130 **6019**
£3520 DM9750 ¥891968

GUERRA, E. [B04/76] Fine Italian Violin in perfect condition: Turin, 1938 17850/23800 **18445**
£11281 DM31000 ¥2936996

GUERRA, EVASIO EMILE [S06/62] Fine Violin: Turin, 1939 (Giuseppe Lucci, Rome, August 23, 1983)
13680/17100 **13167**
£7700 DM22234 ¥2026640

GUERSAN, LOUIS [P09/109] French Violin w/case, 2 bows: Paris, 1739 (J. W. Briggs, Glasgow, 1911)
2805/3740 **3188**
£1705 DM5047 ¥438356

GUERSAN, LOUIS [S03/303] Violin: Paris, mid 18th C. 3420/5130 **NS**

GUERSAN, LOUIS (attributed to) [P09/89] French Violin 1029/1403 **NS**

GUERSAN, LOUIS (attributed to) [P11/195] French Violin 786/1179 **908**
£462 DM1333 ¥116932

GUIDANTUS, JOANNES FLORENUS [S06/222] Violin w/case: Bologna, c. 1730 11970/17100 **26334**
£15400 DM44467 ¥4053280

GUIDANTUS, JOANNES FLORENUS [C06/332] Good Italian Violin w/case, 2 bows: 1743 (William Moennig, January 30, 1967) 43000/51600 **NS**

GUIDANTUS, JOANNES FLORENUS (ascribed to) [S03/30] Violin w/case, cover: Bologna, c. 1700
20520/30780 **NS**

GUIDANTUS, JOANNES FLORENUS (ascribed to) [S06/194] Italian Violin w/case, cover
11970/15390 **12227**
£7150 DM20646 ¥1881880

HAMMA & CO. [B04/45] Fine German Violin nearly original condition: Stuttgart, 1940
1785/2975 **1547**
£946 DM2600 ¥246329

HAMMETT, THOMAS [P11/173] Good English Violin good condition: 1924 884/1277 **1254**
£638 DM1841 ¥161478

HAMMIG, M. [B04/43] Fine German Violin in very good condition: Dresden, 1919 (Heinz Hammig, Dresden, 1980) 1785/2380 **4284**
£2620 DM7200 ¥682141

HAMMIG, WILHELM HERMAN [S03/17] Violin w/case: Leipzig, 1885 3420/4275 **4891**
£2860 DM7922 ¥724724

HARDIE, JAMES & SONS [P02/100] Violin: Edinburgh, 1891 510/680 **774**
£455 DM1280 ¥111801

HARDIE, JAMES & SONS [P02/79] Violin: Edinburgh, c. 1870 850/1190 **561**
£330 DM927 ¥81015

HARDIE, MATTHEW [S03/309] Scottish Violin: Edinburgh, 1809 3420/5130 **NS**

HARDIE, THOMAS [S03/238] Violin: Edinburgh, c. 1840 3420/5130 **NS**

HART & SON [P07/128] Good French Violin: London, c. 1890 1456/1820 **3403**
£1870 DM5494 ¥508827

HART & SON [S11/35] Violin w/case, bow: London, 1926 4913/5895 **6052**
£3080 DM9000 ¥771540

HAWKES & SON [P09/175] Good French Violin w/case, bow: London, 1893 748/1122 **1467**
£784 DM2322 ¥201644

HEBERLEIN, HEINRICH TH. [Sk11/202] German Violin w/case, bow: Markneukirchen, 1887
400/500 **495**
£252 DM738 ¥63855

HEBERLEIN, HEINRICH TH. (JUNIOR) [Sk11/201] German Violin w/case: Markneukirchen, 1913 800/1200 **1045**
£533 DM1557 ¥134805

HECKEL, RUDOLF [C03/149] German Violin
2442/3256 **4656**
£2860 DM7965 ¥735306

HEINICKE, MATHIAS [B04/164] Very Attractive Violin in very good condition: Wildstein, c. 1925
4760/5950 **4463**
£2729 DM7500 ¥710564

HEINRICH, THEODORE [Sk11/236] Violin w/case, 2 bows: Markneukirchen, 1921 800/1000 **1045**
£533 DM1557 ¥134805

HEL, JOSEPH [B04/179] Very Attractive Violin in perfect condition: Lille, 1902 17850/20825 **16660**
£10189 DM28000 ¥2652770

HEL, JOSEPH [S03/55] Violin: Lille, 1884
13680/17100 **14108**
£8250 DM22852 ¥2090550

HELD, JOHANN JOSEPH [P09/136] Interesting Violin w/case 2805/4675 **3394**
£1815 DM5372 ¥466637

HERTL, ANTON [P10/17] German Violin: 1928
588/784 **647**
£330 DM976 ¥80982

HESKETH, J. EARL [S11/29] Violin w/case: Manchester, 1892 1965/2948 **2053**
£1045 DM3053 ¥261773

HESKETH, THOMAS EARLE [P03/99] Good Violin mint condition: Manchester, 1929 2466/2959 **4702**
£2860 DM7931 ¥731588

HESKETH, THOMAS EARLE [S06/206] Violin w/case, bow: Manchester, 1932 5130/5985 **4703**
£2750 DM7941 ¥723800

HILL, HENRY LOCKEY [S11/386] Violin: London, 1759 1572/2358 **NS**

HILL, W. E. & SONS [P06/220] Violin w/case, cover, bow: London, 1975 1382/2591 **5131**
£2970 DM8598 ¥791208

HILL, W. E. & SONS [C06/136] Fine English Violin: (W. E. Hill & Sons, January 11, 1967)
9460/11180 **10406**
£6050 DM17484 ¥1594599

HILL, W. E. & SONS [C06/324] English Violin: London, 1910 4300/6020 **5676**
£3300 DM9537 ¥869781

HERMANN HAUSER
Double-Necked Contra Guitar: Munich, 1924
Sotheby's, London, November 22, 1990, Lot 163

Hill, W. E. & Sons [C03/349] English Violin: London, 1933 4884/5698 **5372**
£3300 DM9190 ¥848430

Hill, W. E. & Sons (workshop of) [S11/372] Violin: London, 1925 5895/9825 **NS**

Hoffmann, Eduard [S03/304] Violin: Silesia 2565/4275 **43263**
£25300 DM70081 ¥6411020

Hofmann, Johann Martin [S03/337] Bavarian Violin: Schillingsfurst, c. 1800 855/1197 **2445**
£1430 DM3961 ¥362362

Hofmans, Mathias (ascribed to) [S11/108] Violin 4913/6877 **NS**

Hoing, Clifford A. [P06/72] Violin w/case, good condition: High Wycombe Bucks, 1932 864/1209 **1064**
£616 DM1783 ¥164102

Hopf [P02/202] Violin w/violin, 2 cases: Klingenthal, c. 1840 102/136 **204**
£120 DM337 ¥29435

Hopf [B04/219] German Violin: Markneukirchen, c. 1800 119/298 **298**
£182 DM500 ¥47371

Hopf [B04/25] Fine German Violin w/case, in very good condition: late 18th C. 893/1190 **1131**
£691 DM1900 ¥180009

Hopf, David [P09/300] Violin w/violin: Klingenthal, c. 1800 281/561 **453**
£242 DM716 ¥62218

Hornsteiner, Mathias [B04/52] Fine German Violin in perfect condition: Mittenwald, 1781 4760/7140 **5236**
£3202 DM8800 ¥833728

Hornsteiner, Mathias [S03/348] Bavarian Violin w/case: Mittenwald 1368/2052 **NS**

Hudson, George Wulme [P09/178] Violin: London, c. 1925 5610/7480 **5965**
£3190 DM9442 ¥820149

Hudson, George Wulme [S11/391] Violin: London, second quarter, 20th C. 4913/5895 **4971**
£2530 DM7393 ¥633765

Hudson, George Wulme [C06/97] English Violin w/case: London, 1942 2064/3096 **NS**

Hutton, Adam [P10/202] Violin w/case, bow: 1859 98/196 **162**
£83 DM244 ¥20246

Iarovoi, Denis [P09/81] Russian Violin w/case: Moscow, 1988 935/1309 **NS**

Jacobs, Hendrik [P06/268] Rare Violin w/case, cover: Amsterdam, 1714 (J. & A. Beare, London, January, 1926) 10365/15547 **14822**
£8580 DM24839 ¥2285712

Jacquot, Albert [S03/319] French Violin w/case: Paris, third quarter, 19th C. 6840/8550 **12791**
£7480 DM20720 ¥1895432

Jacquot, Charles [B04/176] Fine French Violin in perfect condition: Nancy, c. 1870 13685/15470 **13090**
£8006 DM22000 ¥2084320

Jacquot, Charles (ascribed to) [S06/10] French Violin w/case 6840/8550 **NS**

Jais, Anton [P02/53] Violin 255/510 **711**
£418 DM1175 ¥102619

Jaura, Wilhelm Thomas [C11/162] Austrian Violin w/case: Vienna, 1899 1576/2955 **NS**

Jaura, Wilhelm Thomas [C03/137] Austrian Violin w/case: Vienna, 1899 2442/3256 **NS**

Jaura, Wilhelm Thomas (ascribed to) [S11/103] Violin 1965/3930 **5404**
£2750 DM8035 ¥688875

Jaura, Wilhelm Thomas (ascribed to) [S03/7] German Violin 5130/6840 **NS**

Jay, Henry [S11/208] Violin w/case, Baroque specification: London, 1766 1572/1965 **1729**
£880 DM2571 ¥220440

Jay, Henry [S06/389] Violin w/case, baroque specification: London, 1766 2565/3420 **NS**

Jay, Henry (attributed to) [P09/156] English Violin original neck 1870/2805 **1193**
£638 DM1888 ¥164030

Jeune, Laurent [B04/39] French Violin in good condition: Mirecourt, late 18th C. 1190/1785 **1250**
£764 DM2100 ¥198958

Johnson, Peter Andreas [Sk11/192] American Violin w/case: Aurora, 1914 300/400 **385**
£196 DM574 ¥49665

Johnston, Thomas [P06/459] Violin w/case, bow: Edinburgh, 1910 173/259 **266**
£154 DM446 ¥41026

Juzek, John [P02/71] Violin good condition: Prague, 1944 1020/1360 **1964**
£1155 DM3246 ¥283553

Juzek, John [P06/263] Fine Violin w/case, fine condition: Prague, 1920 2591/5182 **4181**
£2420 DM7006 ¥644688

Kaul, Paul [B04/72] Excellent Violin in perfect condition: Nantes, 1917 8330/10710 **7438**
£4549 DM12500 ¥1184273

Kaul, Paul [S03/18] Violin w/case: Paris, 1930 3420/5130 **3198**
£1870 DM5180 ¥473858

Keffer, Joannes [B04/32] German Violin w/case, 2 bows, in perfect condition 2083/2678 **2023**
£1237 DM3400 ¥322122

Kennedy, Thomas [S06/388] Violin w/case, bow: London, c. 1850 3420/6840 **6395**
£3740 DM10799 ¥984368

Kloz, Aegidius [S11/99] Violin w/case, bow: Mittenwald, c. 1770 (W. E. Hill & Sons, London, July 16, 1901) 3930/4913 **6917**
£3520 DM10285 ¥881760

Kloz, Aegidius [B04/184] Important Violin: Mittenwald, second half, 18th C. 17850/20825 **13090**
£8006 DM22000 ¥2084320

KLOZ, AEGIDIUS [S03/36] Violin w/case: Mittenwald, 1800 (Erich Lachmann, Berlin, March 10, 1922) 5985/8550 **7148**
£4180 DM11579 ¥1059212

KLOZ, AEGIDIUS [C03/346] German Violin w/case, 2 bows: Mittenwald, 1752 (Joseph Vedral, June 19, 1929) 4070/4884 **3223**
£1980 DM5514 ¥509058

KLOZ, GEORGE [B04/65] Fine German Violin in good condition: Mitttenwald, 1734 4760/5950 **4463**
£2729 DM7500 ¥710564

KLOZ, JOAN CAROL [P06/261] Violin w/case: Mittenwald, 1752 1382/2073 **2660**
£1540 DM4458 ¥410256

KLOZ, JOSEPH [S03/352] Violin w/case: Mittenwald, c. 1780 5130/6840 **6019**
£3520 DM9750 ¥891968

KLOZ, SEBASTIAN [P03/164] Violin good condition: Mittenwald, 1754 (W. E. Hill & Sons, London, 1907) 6576/9864 **NS**

KLOZ, SEBASTIAN (attributed to) [C03/315] German Violin 1628/2442 **3223**
£1980 DM5514 ¥509058

KLOZ, SEBASTIAN (I) [P06/125] Violin good condition: Mittenwald, 1754 (W. E. Hill & Sons, London, 1907) 5182/6910 **6081**
£3520 DM10190 ¥937728

KLOZ FAMILY (MEMBER OF) [Sk11/127] Violin w/case, 2 bows: Mittenwald, 1746 1500/2500 **2640**
£1346 DM3934 ¥340560

KLOZ FAMILY (MEMBER OF) [Sk11/150] Violin w/case: Mittenwald 350/450 **825**
£421 DM1229 ¥106425

KLOZ FAMILY (MEMBER OF) [S11/199] Bavarian Violin w/case: Mittenwald 2358/2948 **3675**
£1870 DM5464 ¥468435

KLOZ FAMILY (MEMBER OF) [S06/17] Bavarian Violin w/case: Mittenwald 4275/5985 **NS**

KLOZ FAMILY (MEMBER OF) [S06/191] Violin w/case: late 18th C. 3420/5130 **NS**

KLOZ FAMILY (MEMBER OF) [S06/64] Bavarian Violin w/case: Mittenwald, late 18th C. 5130/6840 **10346**
£6050 DM17469 ¥1592360

KLOZ FAMILY (MEMBER OF) [C06/135] German Violin w/case, 2 bows 4300/6020 **NS**

KLOZ FAMILY (MEMBER OF) (attributed to) [C06/316] German Violin w/case 1720/3440 **1892**
£1100 DM3179 ¥289927

KNORR, P. [B04/267] Fine German Violin in perfect condition: Markneukirchen, c. 1950 3570/4760 **3927**
£2402 DM6600 ¥625296

KNUPFER, ALBERT [P06/151] Good Violin w/case: Wirnitzgrun, c. 1920 691/1037 **988**
£572 DM1656 ¥152381

KRAFT, PETER [S06/90] Violin w/case: Stockholm, 1767 6840/8550 **NS**

KREUTZINGER, ANTON [S03/29] Violin: Znaim, 1910 855/1197 **1035**
£605 DM1676 ¥153307

KRUG, J. ADOLPH [Sk11/189] American Violin w/case: Detroit, 1903 600/800 **770**
£393 DM1147 ¥99330

KRUSE WILHELM [P03/341] Violin w/case, good condition: Markneukirchen, c. 1920 329/493 **707**
£430 DM1193 ¥110020

KUDANOWSKI, JAN [C06/78] Violin w/case 2064/2580 **2270**
£1320 DM3815 ¥347912

KUNZE, WILHELM PAUL [S11/384] Dutch Violin: 's-Gravenhage, 1927 4913/5895 **NS**

L'ANSON, EDWARD (attributed to) [C11/292] English Violin 1182/1970 **NS**

LABERTE-HUMBERT BROS. [S03/234] French Violin: Mirecourt, 1911 1710/2565 **1881**
£1100 DM3047 ¥278740

LANCASTER [P09/280] Violin w/case, bow: Colne, 1896 187/281 **453**
£242 DM716 ¥62218

LANCINGER, ANTONIN [C11/165] Czechoslovakian Violin: 1931 2364/2955 **2384**
£1210 DM3511 ¥303226

LANDOLFI, PIETRO ANTONIO [S11/40] Fine Violin: Milan, 1761 (W. E. Hill & Sons, London, April 10, 1916) 88425/108075 **95106**
£48400 DM141425 ¥12124200

LANG, J. S. [P03/377] Full Size Violin w/case: Wandsworth, 1897 132/247 **181**
£110 DM305 ¥28138

LANGONET, CHARLES [B04/69] Fine French Violin: in perfect condition 4760/5950 **3570**
£2183 DM6000 ¥568451

LANTNER, BOHUSLAV [S06/102] Violin w/case: Prague, 1903 855/1368 **1881**
£1100 DM3176 ¥289520

LAURENT, EMILE [C11/171] French Violin: Paris, 1928 3940/5910 **6501**
£3300 DM9577 ¥826980

LAVEST, J. [B04/143] French Violin in very good condition: Montlugon, c. 1935 2380/2975 **1666**
£1019 DM2800 ¥265277

LAZARE, ROBERT [P03/361] Violin w/case, violin: London, 1986 411/658 **615**
£374 DM1037 ¥95669

LE CYR, JAMES FERDINAND [P07/108] Good Violin w/case, rib to back slightly unglued: Los Angeles, 1916 (Nicholas Mushkin, Las Vegas, June, 1986) 910/1274 **1301**
£715 DM2101 ¥194551

LE CYR, JAMES FERDINAND [S03/54] American Violin w/case: Los Angeles, 1916 (Nicholas Mushkin, Las Vegas, June 16, 1986) 1368/1710 **NS**

LECHI, ANTONIO [P02/52] Violin 680/1020 **1496**
£880 DM2473 ¥216040

LECHI, ANTONIO [P03/250] Violin: 1923 658/986 **723**
£440 DM1220 ¥112552

LECHI, ANTONIO [P06/104] Violin w/case, bow: Cremona, 1922 864/1037 **950**
£550 DM1592 ¥146520

BARAK NORMAN
Fine and Important Viol: London, 1692
Sotheby's, London, June 14, 1990, Lot 287

LECHI, ANTONIO [P06/154] Violin w/case, bow: Cremona, 1923 691/864 **836**
£484 DM1401 ¥128938

LECHI, ANTONIO [S11/215] Violin: Cremona, 1923 1965/2948 **NS**

LECHI, ANTONIO [S06/82] Italian Violin w/case: Cremona, 1921 1197/1539 **1129**
£660 DM1906 ¥173712

LEE, H. W. [P09/121] Good Violin w/case, good condition: London, 1924 935/1309 **NS**

LEE, H. W. [C06/277] English Violin w/case 1032/1376 **NS**

LEGNANI, LUIGI (ascribed to) [S06/67] Violin w/case: Naples, c. 1770 5130/5985 **6019**
£3520 DM10164 ¥926464

LEIDOLFF, JOHANN CHRISTOPH [P03/227] Violin: Vienna, 1748 986/1315 **1085**
£660 DM1830 ¥168828

LOCKE, GEORGE HERBERT [P03/173] Violin: Shrewsbury, 1906 822/986 **904**
£550 DM1525 ¥140690

LONGMAN & BRODERIP [P09/142] Violin painted purfling: London, c. 1780 748/935 **1193**
£638 DM1888 ¥164030

LONGMAN & BRODERIP [C11/123] English Violin w/case: London 1379/1773 **975**
£495 DM1436 ¥124047

LONGMAN & LUKEY [P11/81] English Violin: London, c. 1790 491/688 **NS**

LONGSON, F. H. [P10/87] Good Violin: Stockport, 1880 1176/1372 **NS**

LONGSON, J. L. [P03/216] Violin w/case, bow: Stockport, 1880 658/822 **1628**
£990 DM2745 ¥253242

LOTT, JOHN [S06/210] Fine English Violin: London, mid 19th C. (W. E. Hill & Sons, London, February 8, 1899) 42750/59850 **41382**
£24200 DM69878 ¥6369440

LOUVET, F. [B04/248] French Violin restored condition: Paris, 1729 893/1488 **833**
£509 DM1400 ¥132639

LOVERI, CARLO [P06/113] Italian Violin w/case, bow, good condition: Naples, 1917 1296/1727 **1995**
£1155 DM3344 ¥307692

LOWENDALL, LOUIS [Sk11/177] German Violin w/case: Berlin, 1906 600/800 **1100**
£561 DM1639 ¥141900

LOWENDALL, LOUIS [P02/170] Violin w/violin: Berlin, 1894 595/765 **972**
£572 DM1607 ¥140426

LOWENDALL, LOUIS [P02/190] Violin w/case: Dresden, 1884 255/425 **299**
£176 DM495 ¥43208

LOWENDALL, LOUIS [P03/238] Violin w/case, good condition: Berlin, c. 1890 329/493 **326**
£198 DM549 ¥50648

LOWENDALL, LOUIS [P06/141] Good Violin w/case, 2 bows: Berlin, 1896 691/1037 **1235**
£715 DM2070 ¥190476

LOWENDALL, LOUIS [P06/192] Good Violin w/case, 2 bows: Berlin, c. 1900 518/691 **874**
£506 DM1465 ¥134798

LOWENDALL, LOUIS [P10/56] Violin w/case: Dresden, c. 1900 235/353 **280**
£143 DM423 ¥35092

LOWENDALL, LOUIS [P11/390] Good Violin w/case, bow, good condition: Dresden, c. 1890 295/491 **346**
£176 DM508 ¥44546

LUCCI, GIUSEPPE [C06/150] Italian Violin: Rome, 1974 (Maker's) 3096/4300 **4919**
£2860 DM8265 ¥753810

LUCCI, GIUSEPPE [C03/316] Italian Violin w/case: Rome, 1982 (Maker's, June 8, 1982) 4884/6512 **10745**
£6600 DM18381 ¥1696860

LUFF, WILLIAM H. [P03/179] Fine Violin w/case: London, 1978 4932/6576 **5787**
£3520 DM9761 ¥900416

LUFF, WILLIAM H. [P09/69] Violin w/case, cover, mint condition: London, 1959 (Maker's, 1969) 4675/6545 **5348**
£2860 DM8466 ¥735306

LUFF, WILLIAM H. [C06/322] Good English Violin w/case: London, 1974 5160/6880 **5676**
£3300 DM9537 ¥869781

LUPOT, NICOLAS [S03/63] Fine French Violin w/case: Paris, c. 1811 (Roland Baumgartner, Basel, April 8, 1986) 51300/68400 **75240**
£44000 DM121880 ¥11149600

LUPOT, NICOLAS [S06/14] Fine Violin w/case: Paris, c. 1800 (Max Zoller & Son, Amsterdam, October 7, 1970) 41040/51300 **52668**
£30800 DM88935 ¥8106560

LUTSCHG, GUSTAV [C03/299] Swiss Violin: Bern, 1912 2768/3256 **4656**
£2860 DM7965 ¥735306

MACPHERSON, H. [C06/80] Violin w/case: 1905 516/688 **568**
£330 DM954 ¥86978

MAGNIERE, GABRIEL [P10/69] Good Violin w/case, fine condition: Mirecourt, 1899 1176/1764 **2695**
£1375 DM4066 ¥337425

MALAKOFF, BRUGERE [S03/324] French Violin: Marseille, 1892 3420/5130 **6019**
£3520 DM9750 ¥891968

MANGENOT, P. [B04/22] French Violin in very good condition: Mirecourt, c. 1910 893/1488 **952**
£582 DM1600 ¥151587

MANGENOT, PAUL [S06/66] French Violin w/case: Mirecourt 2394/2736 **2257**
£1320 DM3811 ¥347424

MANSUY [B04/250] French Violin in good condition: c. 1870 595/1190 **536**
£328 DM900 ¥85268

MARAVIGLIA, GUIDO (attributed to) [P10/82] Good Violin w/case, good condition 980/1372 **2182**
£1113 DM3292 ¥273179

MARCHI, GIOVANNI (ascribed to) [C06/137] Interesting Violin w/case, 2 bows 4300/6020 **4730**
£2750 DM7947 ¥724818

MARIANI, ANTONIO [Sk11/116] Italian Violin w/case: Pesaro, mid 17th C. 2000/3000 **2090**
£1066 DM3114 ¥269610

MARIANI, ANTONIO [S06/91] Italian Violin w/case, 2 bows: Pesaro, c. 1660 20520/27360 **24453**
£14300 DM41291 ¥3763760

MARSHALL, JOHN [P10/77] Good Violin overall good condition: Aberdeen, c. 1880 1372/1764 **NS**

MARSHALL, JOHN [S03/316] Violin: London, 1754 1710/2565 **3386**
£1980 DM5485 ¥501732

MARTIN, E. [Sk11/229] Saxon Violin w/case, bow 200/300 **358**
£182 DM533 ¥46118

MARTIN, J. [B04/35] English Violin in good condition: Paris, 1808 1190/1785 **1012**
£619 DM1700 ¥161061

MARTIN FAMILY, (MEMBER OF) [S03/306] Violin: Markneukirchen 855/1197 **2633**
£1540 DM4266 ¥390236

MARTINO, GIUSEPPE [Sk11/157] Violin w/case, bow: Boston, 1922 800/900 **2200**
£1122 DM3278 ¥283800

MARTIRENGHI, MARCELLO [C03/344] Italian Violin: Venice, 1948 3256/4884 **6805**
£4180 DM11641 ¥1074678

MASAFIJA, DIMITRI [C11/147] Italian Violin: Cremona, 1981 985/1576 **1560**
£792 DM2298 ¥198475

MAST, J. [B04/74] Exceptionally Fine Violin: Toulouse, 1820 (B. Millant, Paris, 1986) 7140/8330 **7735**
£4731 DM13000 ¥1231643

MAST, JOSEPH LAURENT [S11/389] Violin w/2 violins: Toulouse, c. 1810 1965/2948 **1945**
£990 DM2893 ¥247995

MATHIEU, NICOLAS [C03/142] French Violin w/case, 2 bows 977/1628 **537**
£330 DM919 ¥84843

MAUCOTEL, CHARLES [S03/194] Violin: London, 1859 2565/4275 **5267**
£3080 DM8532 ¥780472

MAYSON, WALTER [P03/190] Violin w/case, 2 bows, minor repairs required: Windermere, 1884 411/740 **1230**
£748 DM2074 ¥191338

MAYSON, WALTER [P03/241] Violin w/case: 1880 411/575 **687**
£418 DM1159 ¥106924

MAYSON, WALTER [S11/211] Violin w/case: Manchester, 1877 1965/2948 **NS**

MAYSON, WALTER [S03/31] Violin w/case, bow: Manchester, 1890 1197/1710 **NS**

MAYSON, WALTER [S03/311] English Violin: Manchester, 1895 (Stansfield Mayson, Manchester, June 2, 1908) 1368/2052 **NS**

MAYSON, WALTER [S03/323] Violin: Manchester, 1890 1368/2052 **2445**
£1430 DM3961 ¥362362

MAYSON, WALTER [S03/358] English Violin w/case, bow: Manchester, 1894 (Maker's, October, 1894) 1368/2052 **1411**
£825 DM2285 ¥209055

MAYSON, WALTER [S03/51] Violin: Manchester, 1892 1026/1368 **NS**

MAYSON, WALTER [C11/309] English Violin: 1892 985/1576 **1040**
£528 DM1532 ¥132317

MAYSON, WALTER [C03/122] English Violin: Manchester, 1892 814/1140 **985**
£605 DM1685 ¥155545

MAYSON, WALTER H. [P09/65] Violin good condition: Manchester, 1892 842/1216 **823**
£440 DM1302 ¥113124

MAYSON, WALTER H. [P09/88] Good Violin w/case, bow, good condition: London, 1899 1496/2244 **1481**
£792 DM2344 ¥203623

MAYSON, WALTER H. [P11/87] Good Violin w/case, 2 bows, good condition: Manchester, 1898 1572/2358 **1513**
£770 DM2221 ¥194887

MEAD, L. J. [P02/21] Violin Cosham, 1957: w/case, bow 425/595 **524**
£308 DM865 ¥75614

MEEK, JAMES [Sk11/142] English Violin w/case, bow: Carlisle, 1904 (Robert Alton, Liverpool, March, 1931) 800/1000 **1430**
£729 DM2131 ¥184470

MEINEL, EUGEN [P03/105] Good Violin excellent condition (minus endpin and tailpiece): Markneukirchen, c. 1900 3288/4932 **4702**
£2860 DM7931 ¥731588

MEINEL, OSKAR [Sk11/209] German Violin w/case: Markneukirchen, 1963 200/300 **495**
£252 DM738 ¥63855

MELEGARI, MICHELE & PIETRO [S11/206] Violin w/case, 2 bows: Turin, 1872 3930/7860 **8214**
£4180 DM12214 ¥1047090

MENNESSON, EMILE [C03/167] French Violin: 1890 1302/1628 **2507**
£1540 DM4289 ¥395934

MERLING, PAULI [S11/192] Violin w/case, bow: Copenhagen, 1927 2948/3930 **4755**
£2420 DM7071 ¥606210

MERLING, PAULI [C03/326] Danish Violin: Copenhagen, 1911 1140/1628 **1254**
£770 DM2144 ¥197967

MEUROT, L. (attributed to) [P03/106] Good Violin w/case, cover 1644/2466 **2170**
£1320 DM3660 ¥337656

MEUROT, L. (attributed to) [P11/180] Good French Violin good condition 1179/1572 **1081**
£550 DM1587 ¥139205

MILLANT, R. & M. [B04/144] French Violin in very good condition: Paris, c. 1930 2083/2975 **1964**
£1201 DM3300 ¥312648

MILTON, LOUIS [C11/293] English Violin w/case: Bedford, 1928 1576/2364 **3251**
£1650 DM4788 ¥413490

MIREMONT [S03/366] Violin w/violin: Paris, c. 1850 342/513 **NS**

MOCKEL, OSWALD [B04/30] Fine German Violin outstanding state of preservation: Berlin, 1873 1190/1785 **2023**
£1237 DM3400 ¥322122

MOCKEL, OTTO [P02/75] Violin: Berlin, 1889 1020/1360 **1964**
£1155 DM3246 ¥283553

MOITESSIER, LOUIS [P09/50] Violin: Mirecourt, c. 1800 1496/1683 **NS**

MOITESSIER, LOUIS [P11/196] Violin: Mirecourt, c. 1800 1376/1572 **NS**

MONK, JOHN KING [P06/441] Violin triple bass bar arrangement: Merton, March, 1894 259/432 **266**
£154 DM446 ¥41026

MONNIG, FRITZ [P02/29] Violin w/case, slightly crackled 1020/1190 **2044**
£1202 DM3378 ¥295165

MONNIG, FRITZ [P03/195] Violin w/case: Vienna, 1938 1644/2466 **2170**
£1320 DM3660 ¥337656

MONTAGNANA, DOMENICO [S11/370] Italian Violin: Venice, c. 1728 (Rudolph Wurlitzer, New York, July 14, 1938) 157200/196500 **172920**
£88000 DM257136 ¥22044000

MONTANI, COSTANTE [S03/333] Violin w/case: Milan, 1930 (Dario D'Attili, Dumont, August 13, 1981) 4275/6840 **4703**
£2750 DM7617 ¥696850

MOODY, G. T. [P06/146] Violin w/case, top right table corner fragment missing: Southampton, 1916 432/605 **988**
£572 DM1656 ¥152381

MORIZOT, RENE [P07/82] Violin: Mirecourt, 1956 728/910 **1101**
£605 DM1777 ¥164620

MOUGENOT, L. [B04/68] Fine French Violin in perfect condition: Mirecourt, 1924 5355/6545 **5355**
£3275 DM9000 ¥852676

MOUGENOT, LEON [C06/295] French Violin: 1948 1376/2064 **3027**
£1760 DM5086 ¥463883

MOUGENOT, LEON (attributed to) [C06/127] French Violin 1376/2064 **2081**
£1210 DM3497 ¥318920

MOUGENOT, LEON (workshop of) [S11/97] Violin: Mirecourt, early 20th C. 1965/2358 **1729**
£880 DM2571 ¥220440

MOYA, HIDALGO [P09/79] Good Violin w/case, bow, old repair lower right table: 1918 (Colchester Violin Shop, December, 1988) 2244/3366 **3291**
£1760 DM5210 ¥452496

MOYA, HIDALGO [C06/308] Violin w/case: 1914 1376/2064 **1419**
£825 DM2384 ¥217445

MOZZANI, LUIGI [P03/228] Violin good condition: Bologna, 1931 986/1315 **1447**
£880 DM2440 ¥225104

MOZZANI, LUIGI [C11/134] Italian Violin: 1917 1970/2955 **2492**
£1265 DM3671 ¥317009

MULLER, JOSEPH [P02/165] Violin: Schoenbach, 1888 340/510 **374**
£220 DM618 ¥54010

NAFISSI, CARLO [P09/179] Good Violin w/case: Gubbio, 1879 5610/9350 **NS**

NAFISSI, CARLO [P11/88] Good Violin w/case: Gubbio, 1879 2948/4913 **NS**

NEFF, JOSEPH [Sk11/203] American Violin w/case: Philadelphia, mid 19th C. 400/500 **468**
£238 DM697 ¥60308

NEFF, JOSEPH [Sk11/215] American Violin w/case: Philadelphia, 1853 600/800 **330**
£168 DM492 ¥42570

NEUNER, LUDWIG [S06/21] Violin: Mittenwald, c. 1890 1197/1710 **2257**
£1320 DM3811 ¥347424

NEUNER, MATHIAS [P06/157] Violin repaired crack on lower right flank table: Mittenwald, c. 1860 345/518 **494**
£286 DM828 ¥76190

NEUNER, N. [B04/224] German Child's Violin in good condition: Mittenwald, first half, 19th C. 417/536 **446**
£273 DM750 ¥71056

NEUNER & HORNSTEINER [P02/64] Violin: 1912 255/425 **598**
£352 DM989 ¥86416

NEUNER & HORNSTEINER [P09/317] Small-Size Violin w/violin: c. 1880 561/748 **658**
£352 DM1042 ¥90499

NEUNER & HORNSTEINER [P10/35] Good Violin: Mittenwald, c. 1870 490/686 **517**
£264 DM781 ¥64786

NEUNER & HORNSTEINER [S11/183] German Violin w/case, bow: Mittenwald, 1894 1965/2948 **NS**

NEUNER & HORNSTEINER [S06/399] German Violin: Mittenwald, 1879 1197/1710 **1881**
£1100 DM3176 ¥289520

NEUNER & HORNSTEINER (attributed to) [P07/88] Violin w/case 455/637 **921**
£506 DM1487 ¥137683

NICOLAS, DIDIER (L'AINE) [Sk11/220] French Violin w/case, bow: Mirecourt 700/800 **605**
£309 DM901 ¥78045

NICOLAS, DIDIER (L'AINE) [P06/78] French Violin: Mirecourt, c. 1820 691/1037 **NS**

NICOLAS, DIDIER (L'AINE) [P09/135] Violin: c. 1820 655/935 **994**
£531 DM1573 ¥136597

NICOLAS, DIDIER (L'AINE) [P10/32] Good Violin open crack, lower table, requires restoration: c. 1840 1372/1764 **2587**
£1320 DM3903 ¥323928

NICOLAS, DIDIER (L'AINE) [P10/79] French Violin w/case, regluing required, old restoration scroll: c. 1800 1372/1764 **NS**

NICOLAS, DIDIER (L'AINE) [P11/174] Violin w/case: c. 1830 1376/1768 **NS**

NICOLAS, DIDIER (L'AINE) [P11/193] French Violin w/case, bow: c. 1810 982/1376 **NS**

NICOLAS, DIDIER (L'AINE) [S11/13] French Violin w/case, bow: Mirecourt 1179/1572 **2270**
£1155 DM3375 ¥289328

NICOLAS, DIDIER (L'AINE) [S11/31] Violin w/case, 2 bows 1572/2358 **1945**
£990 DM2893 ¥247995

NICOLAS, DIDIER (L'AINE) [S11/369] French Violin: Mirecourt 3930/5895 **NS**

NICOLAS, DIDIER (L'AINE) [B04/153] Attractive French Violin in perfect condition 4165/5355 **4046**
£2475 DM6800 ¥644244

NICOLAS, DIDIER (L'AINE) [B04/352] French Violin in good condition: Mirecourt, c. 1830 1785/2380 **1666**
£1019 DM2800 ¥265277

NICOLAS, DIDIER (L'AINE) [S03/330] Violin: Mirecourt, c. 1830 1026/1368 **941**
£550 DM1523 ¥139370

NICOLAS, DIDIER (L'AINE) [S03/349] Violin: Mirecourt, mid 19th C. 855/1197 **846**
£495 DM1371 ¥125433

NICOLAS, DIDIER (L'AINE) [S06/99] French Violin w/case: Mirecourt 1197/1710 **1693**
£990 DM2859 ¥260568

NICOLAS, DIDIER (L'AINE) [C11/329] French Violin 3152/3940 **5634**
£2860 DM8300 ¥716716

NOLLI, MARCO [P03/249] Violin good condition: Cremona, 1985 1151/1480 **1808**
£1100 DM3050 ¥281380

NORMAN, BARAK [S11/387] Violin: London, 1710 1572/2358 **NS**

NORMAN, BARAK [S03/227] Violin: London, c. 1720 1710/3420 **NS**

ODDONE, CARLO GIUSEPPE [S11/402] Violin: Turin, 1928 11790/17685 **21615**
£11000 DM32142 ¥2755500

ODDONE, CARLO GIUSEPPE [S06/5] Italian Violin w/case: Turin, 1931 20520/25650 **18810**
£11000 DM31762 ¥2895200

ODDONE, CARLO GIUSEPPE [C03/189] Italian Violin: Turin, 1929 19536/24420 **23280**
£14300 DM39825 ¥3676530

OLDFIELD, W. [P07/79] Violin w/case: Westmorland, 1904 455/637 **NS**

OLDFIELD, W. [P10/21] Good Violin in good condition: Westmoreland, 1904 588/784 **604**
£308 DM911 ¥75583

OLIVIER, CHRISTIAN [P07/83] Good Violin: 1925 637/910 **1481**
£814 DM2392 ¥221489

ORLANDINI, A. [B04/156] Italian Violin: Parma, 1968 3570/4760 **2975**
£1819 DM5000 ¥473709

ORNATI, GIUSEPPE [S11/12] Violin: Milan, 1939 7860/11790 **NS**

ORTEGA, ASENCIO (attributed to) [C03/356] Interesting Violin 8140/9768 **NS**

OTTO, RUDI [Sk11/109] German Violin w/case: Bremen, 1952 1800/2200 **1980**
£1010 DM2950 ¥255420

OWEN, JOHN W. [P09/125] Good Violin w/case, bow, good condition: Leeds, 1898 2244/3366 **2468**
£1320 DM3907 ¥339372

PALZINI, GIANBATTISTA [Sk11/146] Modern Italian Violin w/case: Verona, 1945 1500/2000 **1980**
£1010 DM2950 ¥255420

PANORMO, EDWARD FERDINAND (attributed to) [P03/141] English Violin: c. 1840 1315/1973 **NS**

PANORMO, EDWARD FERDINAND (attributed to) [P07/49] Violin 546/910 **NS**

PANORMO, GEORGE [S11/109] English Violin w/case: London, c. 1800 (W. E. Hill & Sons, London, November 25, 1919) 11790/15720 **12969**
£6600 DM19285 ¥1653300

PANORMO, GEORGE [S03/356] English Violin w/case: London, c. 1800 (W. E. Hill & Sons, London, November 25, 1919) 11970/17100 **NS**

PANORMO, VINCENZO [S11/400] Fine English Violin w/case: London, c. 1790 (W. E. Hill & Sons, London, April 18, 1961) 58950/68775 **64845**
£33000 DM96426 ¥8266500

PANORMO, VINCENZO [B04/195] Violin in excellent condition: Paris, 1790 47600/5950 **44625**
£27292 DM75000 ¥7105635

PANORMO, VINCENZO [S06/76] Fine Violin w/case: London, c. 1790 17100/25650 **20691**
£12100 DM34939 ¥3184720

PANORMO, VINCENZO [C06/335] Fine Violin w/case 34400/51600 **52976**
£30800 DM89012 ¥8117956

PANORMO, VINCENZO (attributed to) [S03/221] Violin: (Bein & Fushi, Chicago, August 17, 1984) 4275/5985 **10534**
£6160 DM17063 ¥1560944

PAPAGEORGIOU, GEORGES D. [S11/195] Turkish Violin: Constantinople, 1929 2358/2948 **3026**
£1540 DM4500 ¥385770

PARKER, DANIEL (attributed to) [C11/177] Fine English Violin w/case 9850/15760 **10402**
£5280 DM15323 ¥1323168

PARTL, CHRISTIAN FRANZ [C11/164] Austrian Violin: Vienna, 1750 2955/3940 **2925**
£1485 DM4309 ¥372141

PARTL, CHRISTIAN FRANZ [C03/343] Austrian Violin: Vienna, 1750 4070/4884 **NS**

GIOVANNI FRANCESCO PRESSENDA
Fine Italian Violin: Turin, 1837
Christie's, London, June 13, 1990, Lot 336

PATTERSON, W. D. [P03/180] Good Violin w/case, cover: Cremona, 1975 822/1151 **1121**
£682 DM1891 ¥174456

PEARCE, GEORGE [S03/193] Violin: London, c. 1840 3078/4275 **4138**
£2420 DM6703 ¥613228

PEDRAZZINI, GIUSEPPE [P03/114] Fine Violin w/case, cover, bow: Milan, 1924 13152/19728 **22605**
£13750 DM38129 ¥3517250

PEDRAZZINI, GIUSEPPE [S06/412] Violin: Milan, 1919 (Giuseppe Ornati, Milan, September 22, 1962) 8550/11970 **NS**

PEDRAZZINI, GIUSEPPE [S06/7] Violin: Milan, 1919 (Giuseppe Ornati, Milan, October 24, 1960) 8550/11970 **NS**

PELIZON, ANTONIO [C06/116] Violin 6880/8600 **NS**

PENZL, IGNAZ [P02/27] Violin w/case, 2 bows 340/510 **823**
£484 DM1360 ¥118822

PENZL, IGNAZ [P02/33] Violin w/case, bow: Fleissen 510/765 **1047**
£616 DM1731 ¥151228

PERRIN, E. J. (FILS) [S11/121] Violin: Mirecourt, c. 1850 1965/2948 **NS**

PERRY, L. A. [P02/98] Good Violin w/case: Deganwy, 1984 850/1190 **NS**

PERRY, L. A. [P07/37A] Good Violin w/case: Deganwy 910/1274 **601**
£330 DM970 ¥89793

PERRY, STEPHEN [Sk11/193] American Violin w/case: Lowell, 1938 200/300 **385**
£196 DM574 ¥49665

PERRY, THOMAS [Sk11/221] Violin w/2 cases, 2 bows, violin: Dublin, late 18th C. 700/900 **1650**
£841 DM2459 ¥212850

PERRY, THOMAS [S03/205] Violin: Dublin, c. 1810 1368/2052 **1505**
£880 DM2438 ¥222992

PFRETZSCHNER, CARL FRIEDRICH (attributed to) [P03/231] Interesting Violin w/case, cover, bow, repair on lower right table 1315/1973 **1447**
£880 DM2440 ¥225104

PFRETZSCHNER, G. A. [Sk11/188] German Violin w/case: Markneukirchen, early 20th C. 800/1000 **935**
£477 DM1393 ¥120615

PHILLIPSON, EDWARD [P02/82] Violin w/case: Cumberland, 1907 340/510 **473**
£278 DM782 ¥68323

PHILLIPSON, EDWARD [P06/161] Violin: Cumberland, 1920 432/605 **494**
£286 DM828 ¥76190

PICCIONE, EMILIO [C03/148] Italian Violin: 1776 3256/4884 **8059**
£4950 DM13786 ¥1272645

PIERRAY, CLAUDE [P03/153] French Violin w/case, cover: Paris, c. 1720 1480/2466 **1266**
£770 DM2135 ¥196966

PIERRAY, CLAUDE [S11/409] French Violin w/case, bow: Paris, c. 1730 (W. E. Hill & Sons, London, February 3, 1954) 4913/7860 **6052**
£3080 DM9000 ¥771540

PIERRAY, CLAUDE (attributed to) [P03/142] Violin w/case, bow, restored: Paris, c. 1730 2466/4110 **NS**

PIERRAY, CLAUDE (attributed to) [P06/124] Violin w/case, bow, restorations 1382/2073 **1045**
£605 DM1751 ¥161172

PIERRAY, CLAUDE (attributed to) [C11/176] French Violin w/case, bow 5910/7880 **5851**
£2970 DM8619 ¥744282

PILAT, PAUL [C06/114] Violin: 1947 5160/6880 **7190**
£4180 DM12080 ¥1101723

PILLEMENT, FRANCOIS [P07/106] Small-size French Violin w/case, minor wing restoration, right soundhole: c. 1800 364/546 **320**
£176 DM517 ¥47890

PILLEMENT, FRANCOIS [P07/56] French Violin w/case: c. 1800 546/728 **641**
£352 DM1034 ¥95779

PIPER, W. [C11/324] English Violin w/case: Birmingham, 1984 (Maker's) 1182/1576 **1300**
£660 DM1915 ¥165396

PIQUE, FRANCOIS LOUIS [S11/117] French Violin w/case, cover, bow: Paris, 1811 (W. E. Hill & Sons, London, June 6, 1904) 29475/39300 **36746**
£18700 DM54641 ¥4684350

PIQUE, FRANCOIS LOUIS [S06/94] French Violin w/case, cover: Paris, 1811 (W. E. Hill & Sons, London, June 6, 1904) 34200/51300 **NS**

PIRETTI, ENRICO [C11/301] Italian Violin: 1955 (Maker's, December 4, 1987) 2364/3546 **4334**
£2200 DM6384 ¥551320

PIROT, CLAUDE [S11/15] French Violin w/2 cases, 3 bows, violin: Paris, 1806 7860/11790 **14266**
£7260 DM21214 ¥1818630

PLACHT, JOHANN FRANZ [S06/214] Violin w/case: Schoenbach, late 18th C. 1368/2052 **1505**
£880 DM2541 ¥231616

PLUMEREL, JEAN [P06/190] Violin: Mirecourt, c. 1760 432/691 **760**
£440 DM1274 ¥117216

POLITI, ENRICO & RAUL [C03/334] Italian Violin: Rome, 1959 9768/13024 **NS**

POLLASTRI, AUGUSTO [S11/106] Violin w/case: Bologna, 1920 11790/15720 **NS**

POLLASTRI, AUGUSTO [S11/187] Violin w/case: Bologna, 1926 11790/15720 **NS**

POLLASTRI, AUGUSTO (attributed to) [S06/409] Italian Violin: (Carlo Carfagna, Rome, February 5, 1990) 6840/10260 **NS**

POLLASTRI, GAETANO [B04/269] Fine Italian Violin in perfect condition: Bologna, 1947 16660/19040 **14875**
£9097 DM25000 ¥2368545

POLLER, PAUL [B04/217] German Violin in good condition: Munich, 1920 119/298 **357**
£218 DM600 ¥56845

POSTACCHINI, ANDREA [S03/200] Violin w/case: Fermo, 1818 (J. & A. Beare, London, July 12, 1961) 20520/27360 **20691**
£12100 DM33517 ¥3066140

POSTIGLIONE, VINCENZO [B04/270] Fine Italian Violin: Naples, 1908 10710/14875 **16660**
£10189 DM28000 ¥2652770

POSTIGLIONE, VINCENZO [C03/185] Italian Violin: Naples, 1889 6512/8140 **13431**
£8250 DM22976 ¥2121075

PRAGA, EUGENIO (ascribed to) [C06/328] Violin w/case: (Dario D'Attili, May 11, 1979) 8600/10320 **NS**

PRESSENDA, GIOVANNI FRANCESCO [P06/174] Violin w/case: Turin, 1835 51825/69100 **62708**
£36300 DM105088 ¥9670320

PRESSENDA, GIOVANNI FRANCESCO [S03/371] Fine Violin w/case: Turin, 1841 (Max Moller, Amsterdam, February 1, 1954) 102600/119700 **NS**

PRESSENDA, GIOVANNI FRANCESCO [S03/56] Fine Violin w/case, cover, bow: Turin, 1833 68400/102600 **NS**

PRESSENDA, GIOVANNI FRANCESCO [C06/336] Fine Italian Violin: Turin, 1837 (Max Moller, July 28, 1949) 94600/120400 **104060**
£60500 DM174845 ¥15945985

PRESTON, JOHN [P07/32] Violin w/case: London, c. 1770 182/273 **320**
£176 DM517 ¥47890

PULLAR, E. F. [P07/103] English Violin w/case: London, 1922 455/637 **501**
£275 DM808 ¥74827

PYNE, GEORGE [S03/346] English Violin: London, 1908 3420/5130 **3574**
£2090 DM5789 ¥529606

PYNE, GEORGE [S06/95] English Violin w/case: London, 1910 2565/3420 **2633**
£1540 DM4447 ¥405328

PYNE, GEORGE [C06/306] English Violin: 1899 2064/2580 **2081**
£1210 DM3497 ¥318920

RAFFE, E. H. [S03/216] Violin 1197/1710 **1505**
£880 DM2438 ¥222992

RAFFE, E. H. [S03/35] German Violin w/case, 2 bows: Nuremburg, 1794 6840/10260 **7524**
£4400 DM12188 ¥1114960

RANCE, J. F. [S03/22] Violin w/case, cover, bow: Watford, 1940 1026/1368 **2069**
£1210 DM3352 ¥306614

RAPOPORT, HAIM [S11/209] Violin w/case, cover: Tel Aviv, 1964 (Maker's, January 3, 1966) 4913/6877 **NS**

RAPOPORT, HAIM [S03/20] Violin w/case, cover: Tel Aviv, 1964 (Maker's, January 3, 1966) 10260/11970 **NS**

RASURA, VINCENZO (ascribed to) [S03/27] Violin w/case, bow: Lugo, 1783 5130/8550 **4703**
£2750 DM7617 ¥696850

RAUCH, SEBASTIAN [B04/151] German Violin in good condition: Wratislavia, 1776 2678/3273 **1785**
£1092 DM3000 ¥284225

RAUCH, THOMAS [S06/20] Bohemian Violin w/case: Breslau, second quarter, 18th C. 1710/2565 **1693**
£990 DM2859 ¥260568

RAYMOND, ROBERT JOHN [P09/154] Violin w/case: Bulmer, 1965 561/748 **453**
£242 DM716 ¥62218

REICHEL, JOHANN FRIEDRICH [C11/328] German Violin 1576/2364 **NS**

REITER, JOHANN [B04/41] Fine Violin in perfect condition: Mittenwald, 1939 1190/1785 **1190**
£728 DM2000 ¥189484

REMY [C11/136] French Violin w/case, 2 bows 1379/1970 **1409**
£715 DM2075 ¥179179

REMY [C06/105] French Violin w/case 1204/1720 **1324**
£770 DM2225 ¥202949

RENISTO, ANDREAS [S11/92] Italian Violin w/case: 1928 2358/3537 **3026**
£1540 DM4500 ¥385770

RICHARDSON, ARTHUR [Sk11/124] Good English Violin w/case: Devon, 1925 2500/3500 **4070**
£2076 DM6064 ¥525030

RICHARDSON, ARTHUR [P06/204] Good Violin w/case: Crediton Devon, 1929 3455/5182 **3801**
£2200 DM6369 ¥586080

RICHARDSON, ARTHUR [S03/317] Violin: Crediton, 1926 1197/1710 **NS**

RICHTER, ECKART [P11/59] Good Violin good condition: Markneukirchen, 1980 786/1179 **NS**

RICHTER, G. [B04/38] German Violin in perfect condition: Markneukirchen, 1988 1190/2380 **1607**
£983 DM2700 ¥255803

RIDGE [S03/39] English or Scottish Violin: 1849 1368/2052 **NS**

RINALDI, MARENGO ROMANUS [B04/180] Fine Italian Violin in perfect condition: Turin, 1896 17850/20825 **17255**
£10553 DM29000 ¥2747512

ROBINSON, WILLIAM [P06/91] Good Violin w/case, excellent condition: London, 1929 (Maker's) 1037/1727 **4371**
£2530 DM7324 ¥673992

ROBINSON, WILLIAM [P07/114] Violin: London, 1930 546/728 **829**
£455 DM1338 ¥123914

ROBINSON, WILLIAM [C11/122] English Violin w/case: London, 1922 1182/1576 **1842**
£935 DM2713 ¥234311

ROCCA, ENRICO [B04/185] Excellent Italian Violin in excellent condition: Genoa, 1900 17850/23800 **16065**
£9825 DM27000 ¥2558029

ROCCA, GIUSEPPE [C06/337] Fine Italian Violin: Turin, 19th C. (W. E. Hill & Sons, March 10, 1921) 86000/111800 **113520**
£66000 DM190740 ¥17395620

JOSE ROMANILLOS
Concert Guitar: Semley, 1972
Sotheby's, London, November 22, 1990, Lot 166

ROCCA, JOSEPH [S03/378] Fine Violin w/case, cover: Turin, 1850 (W. E. Hill & Sons, London, June 4, 1935) 102600/119700 **161766**
£94600 DM262042 ¥23971640

ROGERI, GIOVANNI BATTISTA [S11/33] Fine Violin: Brecia, 1699 (W. E. Hill & Sons, Great Missenden, February 7, 1983) 98250/137550 **121044**
£61600 DM179995 ¥15430800

ROGERI, PIETRO GIACOMO [S11/396] Fine and Important Italian Violin w/case: Brescia, 1721 (Rudolph Wurlitzer, New York, November 3, 1926) 196500/235800 **NS**

ROST, FRANZ GEORGE [P06/127] Good Violin w/case: London, 1913 1123/1641 **2280**
£1320 DM3821 ¥351648

ROTH, ERNST HEINRICH [Sk11/178] German Violin w/case: Bubenreuth, 1961 800/1000 **880**
£449 DM1311 ¥113520

ROTH, ERNST HEINRICH [P06/119] Violin w/case, bow: Markneukirchen, c. 1940 518/691 **912**
£528 DM1529 ¥140659

ROTH, ERNST HEINRICH [P06/70] Violin w/case, bow, post restoration on table: Markneukirchen 518/864 **1558**
£902 DM2611 ¥240293

ROTH, ERNST HEINRICH [P09/112] Good Violin good condition: Markneukirchen, 1930 748/935 **1337**
£715 DM2116 ¥183826

ROUMEN, JOHANNES ARNOLDUS [S06/11] Dutch Violin w/case, fitted to Baroque specification: Amsterdam, c. 1860 8550/11970 **NS**

ROVESCALLI, T. [B04/53] Fine Italian Violin in perfect condition: Cremona, 1932 5355/7140 **4760**
£2911 DM8000 ¥757934

RUGGIERI, FRANCESCO [S11/120] Fine Violin: Cremona, 1696 (Cyril Woodcock, London, February 23, 1955) 137550/176850 **NS**

RUGGIERI, FRANCESCO [C03/362] Fine Italian Violin w/case, cover, scroll by Andrea Guarneri: (W. E. Hill & Sons, November 6, 1928) 81400/97680 **80586**
£49500 DM137857 ¥12726450

RUGGIERI, VINCENZO [S06/15] Fine Italian Violin: Cremona, 1694 (Albert Caressa, Paris, February 15, 1926) 119700/153900 **NS**

RUGGIERI, VINCENZO (attributed to) [S06/220] Violin w/case: (Hamma & Co., Stuttgart, December 27, 1939) 51300/68400 **NS**

RUSHWORTH & DREAPER [S11/105] Violin w/violin, constructed to left hand spec.: Liverpool, c. 1920 1179/1572 **NS**

RUSHWORTH & DREAPER [S06/69] English Violin w/case, bow: Liverpool 1026/1368 **3574**
£2090 DM6035 ¥550088

SALSEDO, LUIGI [S11/4] Violin: 1926 1965/2358 **3675**
£1870 DM5464 ¥468435

SALSEDO, LUIGI (attributed to) [S03/232] Italian Violin: first quarter, 20th C. 3420/5130 **4891**
£2860 DM7922 ¥724724

SALZARD, FRANCOIS [P10/31] Violin: c. 1850 588/784 **510**
£260 DM770 ¥63804

SANDER, CARL [P06/203] Violin w/case: Mittenwald, c. 1960 518/691 **950**
£550 DM1592 ¥146520

SANDNER, EDI [P11/404] Modern Full-Size Violin w/violin, 2 cases, good condition: Mittenwald 688/1081 **778**
£396 DM1142 ¥100228

SANNINO, VINCENZO [S11/193] Violin: Rome, 1918 (G. B. Morassi, Cremona) 7860/9825 **NS**

SANNINO, VINCENZO (attributed to) [C06/286] Interesting Violin: Naples, 1912 (Dario D'Attili, November 26, 1989) 5160/6880 **10406**
£6050 DM17484 ¥1594599

SARFATI, G. [B04/145] French Violin in perfect condition: 1938 1785/2678 **1666**
£1019 DM2800 ¥265277

SCARAMPELLA, STEFANO [B04/183] Italian Violin in perfect condition: Mantua, 1905 20825/23800 **22610**
£13828 DM38000 ¥3600188

SCHALLER, REINHOLD [B04/229] German Violin in good condition: Dresden, 1879 119/298 **446**
£273 DM750 ¥71056

SCHAU, CARL [C03/154] Austrian Violin: Schwechat, 1907 977/1302 **NS**

SCHEERER, JOHN [S03/34] English Violin: London, 1906 684/1026 **1317**
£770 DM2133 ¥195118

SCHEINLEIN, M. F. [B04/261] German Violin in good condition, scroll repaired: Langenfeldt, 1702 1785/2380 **1666**
£1019 DM2800 ¥265277

SCHMIDT, E. R. & CO. [P06/439] German Violin w/case, cover: c. 1900 345/518 **323**
£187 DM541 ¥49817

SCHMIDT, E. R. & CO. [P10/34] Good Violin in good condition: Saxony, c. 1880 490/686 **690**
£352 DM1041 ¥86381

SCHMIDT, E. R. & CO. [C03/313] German Violin w/case 651/977 **1522**
£935 DM2604 ¥240388

SCHMIDT, JOHANN MARTIN [S11/110] Violin: Pressburg, 1809 1376/1965 **NS**

SCHMIDT, REINHOLD [Sk11/179] Saxon Violin w/case, 2 bows 800/1000 **770**
£393 DM1147 ¥99330

SCHMITT, LUCIEN [C06/86] French Violin: Grenoble, 1924 2064/2580 **3406**
£1980 DM5722 ¥521869

SCHOENFELDER, JOHANN GEORG [B04/64] Fine German Violin w/case, cover, in very good condition: Markneukirchen, c. 1780 (Hamma & Co., Stuttgart, 1980) 5355/6545 **5058**
£3093 DM8500 ¥805305

SCHROEDER, JOHN G. [Sk11/239] American Violin w/case: New York 800/1200 **715**
£365 DM1065 ¥92235

SCHUSTER, C. J. & SON [P06/81] Violin: Markneukirchen, c. 1910 207/311 **323**
£187 DM541 ¥49817

SCHWARZ, GIOVANNI [S03/355] Violin: Venice, 1929 5985/8550 **9781**
£5720 DM15844 ¥1449448

SCHWARZ, HEINRICH [P11/197] Violin w/case, 2 bows: Leipzig, 1894 786/982 **757**
£385 DM1111 ¥97444

SCHWEITZER, JOHANN BAPTISTE (attributed to) [P02/73] Good Violin overall good condition: Budapest, c. 1840 1530/2040 **2899**
£1705 DM4791 ¥418578

SCOLARI, GIORGIO [C11/157] Italian Violin: Cremona, 1982 4925/6895 **4984**
£2530 DM7342 ¥634018

SCOLARI, GIORGIO [C03/164] Italian Violin w/case: Cremona, 1978 3256/4884 **7521**
£4620 DM12867 ¥1187802

SDERCI, LUCIANO [S06/219] Italian Violin: Florence, 1965 5985/7695 **NS**

SDERCI, LUCIANO (attributed to) [C11/338] Italian Violin 7880/11820 **8668**
£4400 DM12769 ¥1102640

SEIDEL, CHRISTIAN WILHELM [P02/88] Violin w/case, 2 bows, good condition: Markneukirchen, c. 1890 595/935 **1159**
£682 DM1916 ¥167431

SEIDEL, JOHANN MICHAEL [P06/458] Violin w/violin: Markneukirchen, c. 1800 294/432 **418**
£242 DM701 ¥64469

SERAPHIN, SANCTUS (attributed to) [S11/406] Good Violin: (Alfred Schmid, Munich, January 25, 1917) 29475/49125 **NS**

SERAPHIN, SANCTUS (attributed to) [S06/402] Violin: (Alfred Schmid, Munich, January 25, 1917) 59850/76950 **NS**

SGARABOTTO, PIETRO [C03/128] Italian Violin w/case: Parma, 1958 4884/8140 **8954**
£5500 DM15317 ¥1414050

SGARBI, ANTONIO [S03/328] Violin: Rome, 1900 5130/8550 **NS**

SIEGA, ETTORE & SON (ascribed to) [S11/212] Violin w/case: Venice, 1930 2948/3930 **4107**
£2090 DM6107 ¥523545

SILVESTRE, PIERRE [S11/1] Violin w/case, 3 bows, violin: Lyon, 1859 11790/15720 **15563**
£7920 DM23142 ¥1983960

SILVESTRE & MAUCOTEL [S11/126] Fine Violin w/case, bow: Paris, 1911 (Makers', September 23, 1911) 15720/23580 **15130**
£7700 DM22499 ¥1928850

SIMON, FRANZ [P06/171] Violin w/case, bow: Salzburg, c. 1780 3455/4319 **NS**

SIMON, FRANZ [P09/111] Violin w/case, bow: Salzburg, c. 1780 1496/2992 **1851**
£990 DM2930 ¥254529

SIMOUTRE, NICHOLAS EUGENE [P06/156] Violin: c. 1870 (Beare & Son, London, 1909) 345/518 **4371**
£2530 DM7324 ¥673992

SIMPSON, JAMES & JOHN [S03/321] Violin: London, c. 1790 1710/2565 **3950**
£2310 DM6399 ¥585354

SIMPSON, THOMAS [S06/385] English Violin w/case, 2 bows: Birmingham, 1916 1197/1539 **1129**
£660 DM1906 ¥173712

SMILLIE, ALEXANDER [S03/231] Scottish Violin w/case: Glasgow, 1915 1368/2052 **1505**
£880 DM2438 ¥222992

SMILLIE, ALEXANDER [C11/334] Scottish Violin w/case, bow: Glasgow, 1905 1970/2955 **4117**
£2090 DM6065 ¥523754

SOFFRITTI, ETTORE [P06/155] Fine Violin excellent condition: (Lennart Lee, Goteborg, 1987) 8637/13820 **NS**

SORSANO, SPIRITO [S06/213] Italian Violin w/case, bow: Cunei, 1733 (Silvestre & Maucotel, Paris, October 15, 1905) 47880/59850 **58311**
£34100 DM98464 ¥8975120

SOUBEYRAN, MARC [S11/23] Baroque Violin w/case, bow: 1982 2948/3930 **NS**

STADLMANN, JOHANN JOSEPH [S03/52] Violin: Vienna, 1766 3420/5130 **NS**

STADLMANN, JOHANN JOSEPH [S03/53] Violin w/case: Vienna, 1765 2565/3420 **2633**
£1540 DM4266 ¥390236

STAINER, JACOB [Sk11/115] Fine Violin w/case: Absam, 1655 (Dario D'Attili, Dumont, June 15, 1989) 40000/50000 **50600**
£25806 DM75394 ¥6527400

STAINER, MARCUS (attributed to) [Sk11/125] Tyrolian Violin w/case: (Rudolf Wurlitzer, New York, August 26, 1943) 3000/4000 **2860**
£1459 DM4261 ¥368940

STANLEY, ROBERT A. [P11/198] Violin w/case, bow, violin: Manchester, 1917 1179/1572 **1621**
£825 DM2380 ¥208808

STIRRAT, DAVID [S03/305] Violin: Edinburgh, 1814 1026/1710 **NS**

STIRRAT, DAVID [S06/403] Violin w/case, bow: Edinburgh, 1912 3420/4275 **4463**
£2610 DM7536 ¥686952

STORIONI, CARLO [P11/78] Good Violin w/case, 2 bows, good condition: 1890 688/1081 **1837**
£935 DM2697 ¥236649

STORIONI, LORENZO [C03/192] Good Italian Violin w/case, bow: Cremona, 1770 48840/65120 **68050**
£41800 DM116413 ¥10746780

STRADIVARI, ANTONIO [S11/127] Important Violin "The Dancla": Cremona, 1703 (Carl Machler, Zurich, January 15, 1959) **NS**

STRADIVARI, ANTONIO [S06/406] Important Violin The "Ex-Armand von Vecsey": Cremona, 1709 (Dario D'Attili, Dumont, February 7, 1984) 684000/855000 **NS**

STRADIVARI, ANTONIO [C11/360] Important Violin "The Mendelssohn": Cremona, 1720 (Rembert Wurlitzer, September 12, 1956) 1083500/1280500 **1776940**
£902000 DM2617604 ¥226041200

STRADIVARI, OMOBONO [S06/105] Important Italian Violin w/case: Cremona, 1732 (Hamma & Co., Stuttgart, July 6, 1961) 256500/427500 **NS**

STRAUB, SIMON [B04/264] German Violin w/case, in very good condition: Rothenbach, 1785 4165/4760 **4463**
£2729 DM7500 ¥710564

SUZUKI, M. [P02/203] Good Full-Size Violin w/violin: 1911 204/306 **430**
£253 DM711 ¥62112

TARASCONI, G. [B04/71] Fine Italian Violin in very good condition: Milan, 1897 8925/11900 **8330**
£5095 DM14000 ¥1326385

TARR, SHELLEY [C11/298] English Violin w/case, 2 bows: Manchester, 1892 1379/1773 **NS**

TASSINI, MARCO [S11/371] Italian Violin w/case, 2 bows: 1925 1965/2948 **2053**
£1045 DM3053 ¥261773

TAVEGIA, CARLO ANTONIO [S11/87] Interesting Italian Violin unpurfled, original condition: Milan, 1731 3930/5895 **4323**
£2200 DM6428 ¥551100

TAVEGIA, CARLO ANTONIO [S03/197] Interesting Italian Violin original condition: Milan, 1731 6840/10260 **NS**

TECCHLER, DAVID [C03/360] Fine Violin: Rome, 18th C. (W. E. Hill & Sons, December 7, 1900) 26048/32560 **26862**
£16500 DM45952 ¥4242150

TECCHLER, DAVID (attributed to) [P03/196] Interesting Violin: (K. M. Lawrence & Co., Liverpool, April, 1980) 4110/5754 **4702**
£2860 DM7931 ¥731588

TENUCCI, EUGEN [B04/170] Fine Violin in excellent condition: Zurich, 1919 6545/7735 **5950**
£3639 DM10000 ¥947418

TERMANINI, PIETRO [S03/206] Italian Violin w/case: Modena, second half, 18th C. 8550/11970 **12227**
£7150 DM19805 ¥1811810

TESTORE, CARLO [C11/180] Good Italian Violin w/case: Milan, 1746 29550/39400 **41173**
£20900 DM60652 ¥5237540

TESTORE, CARLO (attributed to) [S11/382] Violin w/case, bow: (Laurence Naisby, Liverpool, December 5, 1956) 15720/23580 **29180**
£14850 DM43392 ¥3719925

TESTORE, CARLO ANTONIO [C11/359] Fine Italian Violin: Milan, 1745 35460/49250 **47674**
£24200 DM70228 ¥6064520

TESTORE, CARLO GIUSEPPE [S11/365] Violin w/case: Milan, c. 1710 (San Domenico, Cardiff, July 5, 1989) 15720/19650 **NS**

TESTORE, CARLO GIUSEPPE [S06/401] Violin w/case: Milan, c. 1710 (San Domenico Str. Inst., Cardiff, July 5, 1989) 3420/5130 **NS**

TESTORE FAMILY (MEMBER OF) [S03/226] Violin: Milan, early 18th C. 3420/5130 **3386**
£1980 DM5485 ¥501732

TESTORE FAMILY (MEMBER OF) [S03/313] Italian Violin: Milan, first half, 18th C. 10260/15390 **16553**
£9680 DM26814 ¥2452912

THIBOUT, JACQUES PIERRE [S03/32] French Violin w/case: Paris, c. 1820 4788/5985 **4703**
£2750 DM7617 ¥696850

THIBOUVILLE-LAMY [P03/242] Violin w/case, bow: Mirecourt, c. 1910 411/575 **940**
£572 DM1586 ¥146318

THIBOUVILLE-LAMY [P03/92] Violin w/case, bow, minor wing repair required: c. 1910 411/575 **940**
£572 DM1586 ¥146318

THIBOUVILLE-LAMY [P03/95] French Violin: c. 1900 493/658 **760**
£462 DM1281 ¥118180

THIBOUVILLE-LAMY [P06/121] Attractive Violin w/case, bow: Mirecourt 1382/1727 **1995**
£1155 DM3344

THIBOUVILLE-LAMY [P06/134] Violin w/case, bow: Mirecourt, c. 1900 518/691 **722**
£418 DM1210 ¥111355

THIBOUVILLE-LAMY [P06/168] Good French Violin w/case, bow, good condition: Mirecourt, c. 1890 518/691 **918**
£531 DM1538 ¥141538

THIBOUVILLE-LAMY [P06/405] Violin: Mirecourt, c. 1920 259/432 **494**
£286 DM828 ¥76190

THIBOUVILLE-LAMY [P06/444] Violin w/case, bow: Mirecourt, c. 1900 207/345 **190**
£110 DM318 ¥29304

THIBOUVILLE-LAMY [P06/472] French Violin: Mirecourt, c. 1880 345/518 **591**
£342 DM990 ¥91135

THIBOUVILLE-LAMY [P06/82] Violin: Mirecourt, c. 1920 173/259 **NS**

THIBOUVILLE-LAMY [P06/87] French Violin w/case, good condition: c. 1900 518/691 **532**
£308 DM892 ¥82051

THIBOUVILLE-LAMY [P06/88] French Violin w/case, good condition: c. 1900 518/691 **494**
£286 DM828 ¥76190

THIBOUVILLE-LAMY [P07/112] Small-size French Violin w/case, bow: c. 1910 255/400 **761**
£418 DM1228 ¥113738

THIBOUVILLE-LAMY [P07/173] Three-Quarter Size Violin w/violin, minus pegs, tailpiece: Mirecourt, c. 1940 273/455 **601**
£330 DM970 ¥89793

THIBOUVILLE-LAMY [P09/287] Small-Size French Violin: Mirecourt, c. 1900 281/467 **576**
£308 DM912 ¥79187

THIBOUVILLE-LAMY [P09/73] Violin minus top nut and tailpiece: Mirecourt, c. 1880 842/1029 **NS**

THIBOUVILLE-LAMY [P10/160] Good Violin: Mirecourt, c. 1920 98/196 **323**
£165 DM488 ¥40491

THIBOUVILLE-LAMY [P10/211] Violin w/violin, 2 cases: Mirecourt 196/294 **474**
£242 DM716 ¥59387

THIBOUVILLE-LAMY [P11/310] Full Size Violin w/case, 2 bows, good condition: Mirecourt, c. 1920 157/236 **497**
£253 DM730 ¥64034

THIBOUVILLE-LAMY [P11/96] Violin minus top nut and tailpiece: Mirecourt, c. 1880 590/786 **605**
£308 DM889 ¥77955

THIBOUVILLE-LAMY, J. [P02/69] Violin minus tailpiece: Mirecourt, c. 1930 340/510 **673**
£396 DM1113 ¥97218

THIBOUVILLE-LAMY, J. [P06/440] French Violin: Mirecourt, c. 1900 345/518 **1102**
£638 DM1847 ¥169963

THIBOUVILLE-LAMY, J. [P07/107] French Violin w/case, bow: c. 1910 273/455 **440**
£242 DM711 ¥65848

THIBOUVILLE-LAMY, J. [P10/15] French Violin in good condition: c. 1900 588/784 **893**
£455 DM1347 ¥111755

THIBOUVILLE-LAMY, J. [P11/315] Violin w/case, bow: Mirecourt, c. 1910 295/491 **281**
£143 DM413 ¥36193

THIBOUVILLE-LAMY, J. [P11/332] Small-Size Violin: Mirecourt, c. 1900 197/393 **648**
£330 DM952 ¥83523

THIBOUVILLE-LAMY, J. (workshop of) [Sk11/138] French Violin w/case, 2 bows 1000/1500 **4950**
£2524 DM7376 ¥638550

THIBOUVILLE-LAMY, JEROME [P02/77] Good Violin minus tailpiece: Mirecourt, c. 1880 425/595 **1029**
£605 DM1700 ¥148528

THIBOUVILLE-LAMY, JEROME [P03/91] Violin w/case, bow: Mirecourt, c. 1920 411/575 **760**
£462 DM1281 ¥118180

THIBOUVILLE-LAMY, JEROME [P10/174] Good Small-Size Violin w/2 cases, violin: Mirecourt, c. 1900 353/549 **776**
£396 DM1171 ¥97178

THIBOUVILLE-LAMY, JEROME [P10/241] Violin w/violin: Mirecourt, c. 1920 235/431 **595**
£304 DM898 ¥74503

THIBOUVILLE-LAMY, JEROME [S11/107] Violin w/violin: Mirecourt, c. 1900 1179/1572 **1210**
£616 DM1800 ¥154308

THIBOUVILLE-LAMY, JEROME [S11/112] Violin w/case, 2 bows: Mirecourt, c. 1920 1376/1572 **2162**
£1100 DM3214 ¥275550

THIBOUVILLE-LAMY, JEROME [S11/22] French Violin w/case, bow: Mirecourt, early 20th C. 1376/1965 **2162**
£1100 DM3214 ¥275550

THIBOUVILLE-LAMY, JEROME [S03/361] French Violin w/violin: Mirecourt, 20th C. 1710/2565 **NS**

THIBOUVILLE-LAMY, JEROME [S03/368] French Violin: Mirecourt, c. 1870 1026/1539 **752**
£440 DM1219 ¥111496

THIBOUVILLE-LAMY, JEROME [S06/203] Violin w/2 cases, violin: Paris, c. 1900 1710/2565 **1693**
£990 DM2859 ¥260568

THIBOUVILLE-LAMY, JEROME [S06/88] French Violin w/case, bow: Mirecourt, first quarter, 20th C. 1710/2565 **NS**

THIER, JOSEPH (attributed to) [P02/57] Violin w/case, 2 bows: Innsbruck, c. 1930 510/850 **1085**
£638 DM1793 ¥156629

THIR, MATHIAS [Sk11/140] Viennese Violin w/case, bow: late 18th C. 2500/3500 **NS**

THIR, MATHIAS [C11/333] Austrian Violin: Vienna 1970/2955 **1950**
£990 DM2873 ¥248094

THIR, MATHIAS [C03/179] Austrian Violin: Vienna, 18th C. 2930/4070 **NS**

THIR, MATHIAS (attributed to) [P11/189] Violin w/case, good overall condition 1376/1965 **4971**
£2530 DM7299 ¥640343

THOMPSON, CHARLES & SAMUEL [P03/128] Violin minor restoration required: London, c. 1770 822/1151 **868**
£528 DM1464 ¥135062

THOMPSON, CHARLES & SAMUEL [P03/191] Good Violin w/case, bow: London, 1783 1480/2466 **1628**
£990 DM2745 ¥253242

THOMPSON, CHARLES & SAMUEL [P06/249] English Violin: London, c. 1790 1037/1382 **NS**

THOMPSON, CHARLES & SAMUEL [S03/217] Violin w/2 violins: London, c. 1780 2052/3078 **2445**
£1430 DM3961 ¥362362

THOMPSON & SON [S11/25] Violin w/2 cases, 2 bows, 3 violins: late 18th C. 1965/2948 **4971**
£2530 DM7393 ¥633765

THOMSON [P06/89] Violin: Aberdeen, 1858 345/518 **304**
£176 DM510 ¥46886

THORBURN, S. W. [P06/437] Violin: Symington Mill 345/518 **361**
£209 DM605 ¥55678

THOUVENEL, CHARLES [P09/149] Violin w/case, 2 bows: Luneville, c. 1790 2244/3366 **2366**
£1265 DM3744 ¥325231

THOW, J. [P07/78] Violin w/case: c. 1870 455/637 **561**
£308 DM905 ¥83807

TILLER, G. W. [P11/296] Violin good condition: Boscombe, 1915 491/688 **735**
£374 DM1079 ¥94659

TIM-GEIGEN [P07/86] Good Violin w/case: c. 1910 910/1274 **1401**
£770 DM2262 ¥209517

TOBIN, RICHARD [P06/95] Violin w/case, some old restored worm: London, c. 1800 1382/2073 **NS**

TOBIN, RICHARD [P10/54] Violin w/case, some old restored worm: London, c. 1800 980/1372 **NS**

TOBIN, RICHARD [S03/209] English Violin w/case: London, early 19th C. 2565/4275 **NS**

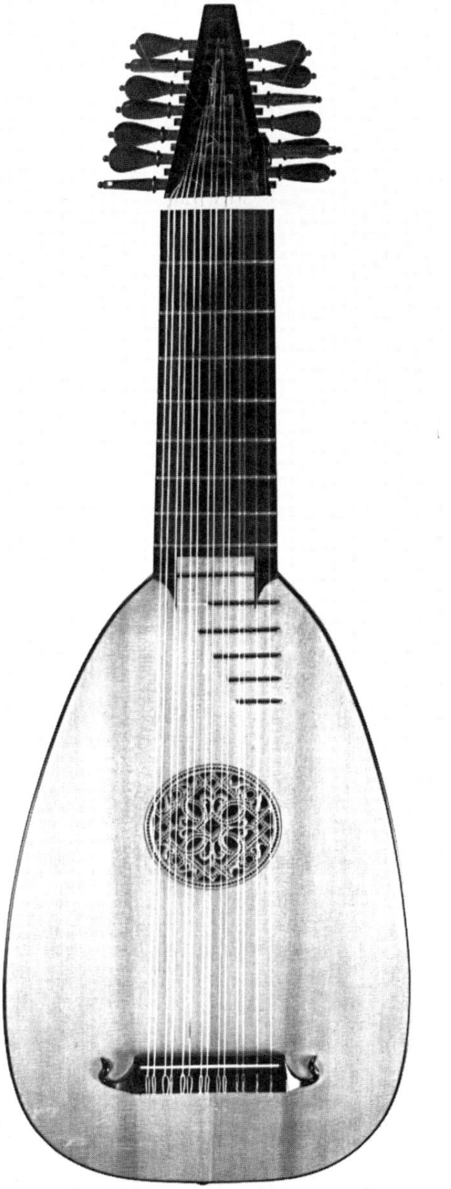

DAVID RUBIO
Lute: Semley, 1967
Sotheby's, London, November 22, 1990, Lot 167

TOBIN, RICHARD [S03/43] Violin: London, c. 1810
1026/1368 NS

TOBIN, RICHARD (attributed to) [P03/187] Good Violin repaired
986/1480 **904**
£550 DM1525 ¥140690

TOMASSINI, DOMENICO (ascribed to) [S03/33] Violin w/case: Viterbo, 1820
2565/3420 **4138**
£2420 DM6703 ¥613228

TONONI, CARLO [S11/410] Italian Violin w/case, 2 bows: Venice, mid 18th C. (J. & A. Beare, London, July 26, 1935)
39300/49125 **38907**
£19800 DM57856 ¥4959900

TWEEDALE, CHARLES L. [P09/182] Violin w/case, bow: Weston, 1924
748/1122 **741**
£396 DM1172 ¥101812

VALENZANO, JOANNES MARIA [S06/397] Violin: Piedmont, 1794 (W. E. Hill & Sons, London, April 28, 1949)
25650/34200 **28215**
£16500 DM47644 ¥4342800

VALENZANO, JOANNES MARIA [S06/8] Fine Italian Violin w/case: Rome, 1826 (Hamma & Co., Stuttgart, April 21, 1959)
51300/59850 **60192**
£35200 DM101640 ¥9264640

VALENZANO, JOANNES MARIA (ascribed to) [S11/85] Italian Violin w/case: (Chardon & Fils, Paris, November 30, 1945)
29475/39300 NS

VAUTELINT, N. PIERRE [S06/208] Violin w/case: Paris, 1904
1197/1710 **5267**
£3080 DM8894 ¥810656

VENTAPANE, LORENZO [P06/266] Violin w/case, faint restoration near post on back: Naples, 1824 (J. & A. Beare, London, April, 1947)
8637/17275 **25653**
£14850 DM42991 ¥3956040

VENTAPANE, LORENZO [S11/373] Violin: Naples, 1837 (Dario D'Attili, December 19, 1989)
4913/6877 **9511**
£4840 DM14142 ¥1212420

VENTAPANE, LORENZO [S06/189] Italian Violin w/case: Naples, 1810 (Otto Stam, Utrecht, March 3, 1979)
25650/34200 **35739**
£20900 DM60349 ¥5500880

VENTAPANE, LORENZO (attributed to) [S11/392] Fine Italian Violin w/case: (Dykes & Sons, London, September 1, 1923)
35370/43230 NS

VERINI, ANDREA [P09/147] Violin w/case: 1884
935/1496 **2880**
£1540 DM4558 ¥395934

VICKERS, J. E. [P07/46] Modern Violin w/case, bow
728/1092 **1059**
£582 DM1710 ¥158335

VICKERS, J. E. [P11/191] Violin w/case, bow, good condition
786/1179 **1541**
£784 DM2263 ¥198506

VINACCIA FAMILY (MEMBER OF) [S11/376] Italian Violin w/case: Naples, c. 1775 (Dario D'Attili, Dumont, February 19, 1986)
15720/23580 NS

VINCENT, ALFRED [P06/126] Good Violin w/case, good condition: 1923
3455/5182 **4561**
£2640 DM7643 ¥703296

VINCENT, ALFRED [P06/205] Fine Violin w/case, bow: London, c. 1910
4319/6046 **6461**
£3740 DM10827 ¥996336

VINCENT, ALFRED [P06/96] Violin w/case, bow: London, 1924
2073/3109 **4751**
£2750 DM7961 ¥732600

VINCENT, ALFRED (attributed to) [P09/183] Violin w/case, bow, slight heat affected varnish, lower back, table
3740/4675 **4114**
£2200 DM6512 ¥565620

VISCONTI, DOMENICO (attributed to) [C06/317] Italian Violin
2064/3096 **1892**
£1100 DM3179 ¥289927

VLUMMENS, DOMINIC [S06/103] Violin w/case: London, 1925
3420/5130 **3950**
£2310 DM6670 ¥607992

VOIGT, ARNOLD [C03/321] German Violin w/case, bow
651/814 **985**
£605 DM1685 ¥155545

VOIGT, JOHANN GEORG [P06/396] Violin w/case, old restorations: 1789
432/605 NS

VOIGT, PAUL [P02/102] Violin: Manchester, 1907
1020/1360 **1159**
£682 DM1916 ¥167431

VOLLER BROTHERS [C06/331] Fine Violin
20640/25800 **24596**
£14300 DM41327 ¥3769051

VON DOLLING, (YOUNGER) [P10/170] Good Violin minor repair at button, otherwise good condition: c. 1900
392/588 NS

VUILLAUME, JEAN BAPTISTE [P11/200] Fine Violin w/case, fine condition: Paris, c. 1840 (Rembert Wurlitzer, New York, 1963)
49125/68775 **64845**
£33000 DM95205 ¥8352300

VUILLAUME, JEAN BAPTISTE [S11/179] Violin: Paris, 1849
15720/23580 NS

VUILLAUME, JEAN BAPTISTE [S11/207] Fine Violin w/case: Paris, mid 19th C.
49125/58950 **54037**
£27500 DM80355 ¥6888750

VUILLAUME, JEAN BAPTISTE [S11/411] Violin w/case: Paris, c. 1850
11790/15720 **24857**
£12650 DM36963 ¥3168825

VUILLAUME, JEAN BAPTISTE [B04/181] French Violin in very good condition: Paris, 1853 (B. Millant, Paris, 1988)
17850/20825 **16660**
£10189 DM28000 ¥2652770

VUILLAUME, JEAN BAPTISTE [B04/193] Fine French Violin in very good condition: Paris, 1844
44625/53550 **41650**
£25473 DM70000 ¥6631926

VUILLAUME, JEAN BAPTISTE [B04/83] Important French Violin in mint condition: Paris (E. Vatelot, Paris, 1973)
23800/29750 **22610**
£13828 DM38000 ¥3600188

VUILLAUME, JEAN BAPTISTE [C03/183] French Violin: Paris, 1844
13024/19536 NS

VUILLAUME, JEAN BAPTISTE [C03/357] Good French Violin: Paris, 1847
16280/24420 **17013**
£10450 DM29103 ¥2686695

VUILLAUME, JEAN BAPTISTE (ascribed to) [C06/329] French Violin w/case: (Robert Wurlitzer, January 20, 1965) 13760/20640 **17974**
£10450 DM30200 ¥2754307

VUILLAUME, JEAN BAPTISTE (workshop of) [C11/354] French Violin w/case, bow: 1864
15760/23640 **39006**
£19800 DM57460 ¥4961880

VUILLAUME, NICHOLAS [S11/119] Child's Violin w/case,: Brussels, c. 1860 5895/7860 **5404**
£2750 DM8035 ¥688875

VUILLAUME, NICHOLAS [C06/149] Fine French Violin w/case: (Dario D'Attili, February 10, 1977)
17200/25800 **14758**
£8580 DM24796 ¥2261431

VUILLAUME, SEBASTIAN [P06/176] Fine Violin w/case, cover, bow, excellent condition: Paris, 1857
3455/5182 **4371**
£2530 DM7324 ¥673992

VUILLAUME, SEBASTIAN [S11/26] Violin w/case, cover: Paris, c. 1865 (Helmuth A. Keller, Philadelphia, April 7, 1969)
11790/15720 **NS**

VUILLAUME, SEBASTIAN [S03/236] Violin w/case, cover: Paris, c. 1865 (Helmuth A. Keller, Philadelphia, April 7, 1969) 17100/25650 **NS**

VUILLAUME, SEBASTIAN [S03/359] Fine French Violin: Paris, c. 1870 (William Moennig & Son, Philadelphia, May 24, 1968) 25650/30780 **NS**

WAGNER, BENEDICT (attributed to) [Sk11/158] South German Violin w/case, bow 1500/2000 **1540**
£785 DM2295 ¥198660

WALKER, WILLIAM [P06/122] Violin w/case, bow, good condition: Beith, 1885 691/1209 **NS**

WALKER, WILLIAM [P11/192] Good Violin w/case, minor wing repair required: Mid Calder, 1905
1376/1768 **2860**
£1455 DM4199 ¥368336

WALTON, WILLIAM [C06/298] English Violin w/case: 1915 774/1118 **851**
£495 DM1431 ¥130467

WAMSLEY, PETER [P11/84] Violin w/case, Baroque condition: London, 1738 1179/1572 **1729**
£880 DM2539 ¥222728

WAMSLEY, PETER [S11/367] Violin: London, second quarter, 18th C. (W. E. Hill & Sons, London, February 11, 1942) 3537/3930 **5188**
£2640 DM7714 ¥661320

WAMSLEY, PETER [B04/31] English Violin needs repair: London, 1748 1785/2975 **893**
£546 DM1500 ¥142113

WAMSLEY, PETER [S03/336] Fine English Violin: London, 1748 (W. E. Hill & Sons, London, January 3, 1933) 5985/8550 **8465**
£4950 DM13711 ¥1254330

WAMSLEY, PETER [S03/5] Violin: second quarter, 18th C. 3078/3420 **NS**

WAMSLEY, PETER [S06/207] Violin w/case, cover: London, 1730 3420/5130 **3762**
£2200 DM6352 ¥579040

WANNER, MICHAEL [P06/114] Violin: Mittenwald, 1885 605/777 **912**
£528 DM1529 ¥140659

WARD, GEORGE [C06/92] Irish Violin w/case: Dublin, 1751 1376/2064 **1419**
£825 DM2384 ¥217445

WASSERMANN, JOSEPH [S03/189] Violin w/case, cover, 2 bows: Moravia, 1805 (J. J. Van De Geest, October 1, 1948) 3420/5130 **5643**
£3300 DM9141 ¥836220

WEIGERT, JOHANN BLASIUS [Sk11/110] Tyrolian Violin w/case: Linz 1800/2200 **2090**
£1066 DM3114 ¥269610

WHEDBEE, WILLIAM [Sk11/156] Contemporary American Violin w/case: Chicago, 1986
1000/1500 **1540**
£785 DM2295 ¥198660

WHITBREAD, W. W. [P02/194] Violin w/case, cover: Port Morsly, 1921 255/425 **324**
£190 DM535 ¥46719

WHITE, ASA WARREN [Sk11/148] American Violin w/case: Boston, 1872 1000/2000 **715**
£365 DM1065 ¥92235

WHITE, H. N. & CO. [Sk11/225] American Violin w/case, bow: Nashua, 1919 400/500 **330**
£168 DM492 ¥42570

WHITMARSH, EDWIN [C11/325] English Violin w/case, bow: London, 1921 788/1182 **1517**
£770 DM2235 ¥192962

WHITMARSH, EMANUEL [P09/97] Violin w/case, 2 bows: London, 1901 935/1309 **1131**
£605 DM1791 ¥155545

WIDHALM, LEOPOLD [Sk11/107] German Violin w/case: Nurnberg, 18th C. 1500/2500 **4070**
£2076 DM6064 ¥525030

WIDHALM, LEOPOLD [P09/52] Violin w/case, bow: Nurnberg, 18th C. 748/935 **1122**
£600 DM1776 ¥154260

WIDHALM, LEOPOLD [B04/178] Very Fine Violin in perfect condition: Nurnberg, c. 1760 (Hamma & Co., Stuttgart, 1981) 17850/20825 **17255**
£10553 DM29000 ¥2747512

WIDHALM, LEOPOLD [S03/214] Bavarian Violin w/case: Nuremburg, 1734 3420/5130 **4138**
£2420 DM6703 ¥613228

WILKANOWSKI, W. [Sk11/167] American Violin w/case, 2 bows: Brooklyn, c. 1925 200/300 **605**
£309 DM901 ¥78045

WILKANOWSKI, W. [Sk11/175] American Violin: Brooklyn, 1951 300/400 **990**
£505 DM1475 ¥127710

WILKINSON, JOHN [S11/405] Violin w/case: London, 1930 3930/5895 **NS**

WILKINSON, WILLIAM & PERRY, THOMAS [P09/85] Violin w/case, bow: Dublin, 1804 1496/2244 **1481**
£792 DM2344 ¥203623

WILSON, TOM [P02/38] Violin: Grimsby, 1948
255/510 **355**
£209 DM587 ¥51310

JACOB STAINER
Fine Violin: Absam, 1655
Skinner, Boston, November 11, 1990, Lot 115

WINTERLING, G. [B04/165] Excellent German Violin in perfect condition: Hamburg, c. 1925 (H. Schicker, Freiburg, 1986) 8925/10710 **9223**
£5640 DM15500 ¥1468498

WINTERLING, G. [B04/271] German Violin in very good condition: Krailling, 1920 5950/8330 **5355**
£3275 DM9000 ¥852676

WITHERS, EDWARD [S11/194] English Violin: London, c. 1880 1965/2948 **3026**
£1540 DM4500 ¥385770

WOLFF BROS. [P02/196] Violin open crack on table at tailpiece: Kreuznach, 1909 340/510 **374**
£220 DM618 ¥54010

WOLFF BROS. [P02/45] Violin good condition: Kreuznach, 1887 340/510 **449**
£264 DM742 ¥64812

WOLFF BROS. [P03/369] Violin w/case: Kreuznach, c. 1860 132/197 **271**
£165 DM458 ¥42207

WOLFF BROS. [P06/425] Violin w/case, 2 bows, minor top left table restoration: 1904 345/518 **456**
£264 DM764 ¥70330

WOLFF BROS. [P06/443] Violin w/case, bow: Kreuznach, 1906 259/432 **418**
£242 DM701 ¥64469

WOLFF BROS. [P10/229] Small-Size Violin w/case, bow, good condition: 1906 294/392 **819**
£418 DM1236 ¥102577

WOLFF BROS. [P11/292] Good Full-Size Violin w/violin, 2 cases, minor wing crack: Kreuznach, 1890 393/590 **432**
£220 DM635 ¥55682

WOULDHAVE, JOHN [P09/181] Violin w/case, bow: North Shields, 1858 748/1122 **NS**

ZACH, THOMAS (attributed to) [P03/165] Good Violin w/case, cover, bow 2466/4110 **2532**
£1540 DM4270 ¥393932

ZANIER, FERRUCCIO [B04/54] Italian Violin in very good condition: Trieste, c. 1935 4165/5355 **3868**
£2365 DM6500 ¥615822

ZEMITIS, M. [B04/28] Russian Violin in very good condition: Riga, c. 1950 1190/1785 **1131**
£691 DM1900 ¥180009

ZETTWITZ, WILLIAM [S03/192] Violin w/case, 2 bows: Auckland, 1920 1197/1710 **NS**

ZIMMERMAN, FRIEDERICH [P06/226] Violin w/case, bow: Dresden, c. 1900 432/691 **646**
£374 DM1083 ¥99634

VIOLIN BOW

ADAM, GRAND [C11/283] Very Fine Silver Violin Bow: (Jean-Jacques Millant, December 6, 1988) 7880/13790 **16253**
£8250 DM23941 ¥2067450

ALVEY, BRIAN [C03/78] Silver Violin Bow 407/570 **NS**

ALVEY, BRIAN [C03/93] Gold and Tortoiseshell Violin Bow 1628/1954 **1970**
£1210 DM3370 ¥311091

APPARUT, GEORGES [B04/90] Silver French Violin Bow in very good condition 833/1190 **952**
£582 DM1600 ¥151587

BAUSCH, L. [P09/153] Silver Violin Bow 224/337 **309**
£165 DM488 ¥42421

BAUSCH, L. [P11/162] Silver Violin Bow 295/491 **324**
£165 DM476 ¥41762

BAZIN [P11/140] Silver Violin Bow 393/590 **1470**
£748 DM2158 ¥189319

BAZIN, C. [P07/158] Silver Violin Bow minus one eye 364/546 **507**
£278 DM818 ¥75725

BAZIN, C. [P10/111] Silver Violin Bow minus hair 235/353 **345**
£176 DM520 ¥43190

BAZIN, CHARLES [P06/289] Silver Violin Bow 605/777 **1995**
£1155 DM3344 ¥307692

BAZIN, CHARLES [P07/136] Silver Violin Bow 273/455 **440**
£242 DM711 ¥65848

BAZIN, CHARLES [P09/242] Nickel Violin Bow w/bow 561/935 **741**
£396 DM1172 ¥101812

BAZIN, CHARLES [P09/243] Nickel Violin Bow w/bow 467/655 **329**
£176 DM521 ¥45250

BAZIN, CHARLES [P10/100] Silver Violin Bow 392/588 **1537**
£784 DM2319 ¥192467

BAZIN, CHARLES [S03/283] French Silver and Ivory Violin Bow: Paris 855/1197 **941**
£550 DM1523 ¥139370

BAZIN, CHARLES [S06/55] Silver Violin Bow: Mirecourt 855/1197 **1223**
£715 DM2065 ¥188188

BAZIN, CHARLES [C11/251] Silver Violin Bow 1576/2364 **2059**
£1045 DM3033 ¥261877

BAZIN, CHARLES [C06/244] Silver Violin Bow 1204/1720 **946**
£550 DM1589 ¥144964

BAZIN, LOUIS [Sk11/67] Nickel Violin Bow 400/500 **330**
£168 DM492 ¥42570

BAZIN, LOUIS [P11/166] Silver Violin Bow minus hair 393/590 **865**
£440 DM1269 ¥111364

BAZIN, LOUIS [B04/308] Silver French Violin Bow in very good condition: Mirecourt, c. 1940 1190/1785 **1131**
£691 DM1900 ¥180009

BAZIN, LOUIS [C06/225] Silver Violin Bow 688/1032 **795**
£462 DM1335 ¥121769

BAZIN, LOUIS [C06/237] Silver Violin Bow 1204/1720 **2649**
£1540 DM4451 ¥405898

BAZIN FAMILY (MEMBER OF) [S06/227] Fine Gold and Tortoiseshell Violin Bow: Paris, c. 1930
2052/3078 **NS**

BEARE, JOHN & ARTHUR [C11/261] Gold Violin Bow 1576/1970 **2384**
£1210 DM3511 ¥303226

BERNARDEL, GUSTAVE [P09/226] Silver Violin Bow
467/748 **946**
£506 DM1498 ¥130093

BERNARDEL, GUSTAVE [B04/104] Silver French Violin Bow in very good condition 1785/2380 **1726**
£1055 DM2900 ¥274751

BERNARDEL, GUSTAVE [S03/276] Silver Violin Bow: Paris 1197/1539 **2445**
£1430 DM3961 ¥362362

BERNARDEL, GUSTAVE [S06/340] Silver Violin Bow: Paris 1026/1368 **NS**

BERNARDEL, LEON [P11/119] Silver Violin Bow
786/1179 **951**
£484 DM1396 ¥122500

BERNARDEL, LEON [S03/264] Silver Violin Bow: Paris 1197/1539 **1693**
£990 DM2742 ¥250866

BERNARDEL, RENE [S03/82] Silver Violin Bow stick repaired: Paris 855/1197 **2069**
£1210 DM3352 ¥306614

BISCH, PAUL [Sk11/66] Silver French Violin Bow: Paris 800/1000 **770**
£393 DM1147 ¥99330

BRAND, KARL [P02/109] Silver Violin Bow w/violin bow 136/255 **243**
£143 DM402 ¥35107

BRIGGS, JAMES WILLIAM [S03/101] Silver Violin Bow: Glasgow 684/1026 **564**
£330 DM914 ¥83622

BRISTOW, STEPHEN [P02/107] Violin Bow
595/850 **711**
£418 DM1175 ¥102619

BULTITUDE, A. R. [P11/144] Chased Gold Violin Bow 1179/1768 **2162**
£1100 DM3174 ¥278410

BULTITUDE, ARTHUR [S11/56] Gold and Tortoiseshell Violin Bow: Hawkhurst
3930/5895 **3458**
£1760 DM5143 ¥440880

BULTITUDE, ARTHUR [C11/207] Silver Violin Bow
985/1379 **1300**
£660 DM1915 ¥165396

BUTHOD, CHARLES [P09/240] Gold Violin Bow frog restored 935/1122 **NS**

BUTHOD, CHARLES [P11/218] Gold Violin Bow frog with restoration 590/786 **NS**

BUTHOD, CHARLES [P11/241] Silver Violin Bow w/2 bows 295/491 **281**
£143 DM413 ¥36193

BUTHOD, CHARLES [S11/346] Chased Silver Violin Bow: Paris 786/1179 **NS**

CALLIER, FRANK [Sk11/60] Silver Violin Bow
400/500 **605**
£309 DM901 ¥78045

CALLIER, FRANK [Sk11/63] Gold Violin Bow
1000/1500 **1320**
£673 DM1967 ¥170280

CARESSA, ALBERT [S11/247] Silver Violin Bow: Paris 1376/1768 **1729**
£880 DM2571 ¥220440

CARESSA & FRANCAIS [S03/273] Silver Violin Bow: Paris 1539/2052 **2916**
£1705 DM4723 ¥432047

CARESSA & FRANCAIS [S06/383] Silver Violin Bow: Paris 1368/1710 **NS**

CARRODUS [P10/107] Silver Violin Bow
490/686 **893**
£455 DM1347 ¥111755

CHADWICK [B04/101] Silver English Violin Bow in very good condition: London 1190/1785 **893**
£546 DM1500 ¥142113

CHANOT, JOSEPH ANTHONY [S11/349] Silver Violin Bow: London 1179/1572 **2594**
£1320 DM3857 ¥330660

CHARDON, CHANOT [B04/288] Silver French Violin Bow repaired under wrapping 357/476 **387**
£237 DM650 ¥61582

COLLIN-MEZIN [S11/62] Silver Violin Bow: Paris
982/1572 **1297**
£660 DM1929 ¥165330

COLLIN-MEZIN [S03/253] Silver Violin Bow: Paris
1368/1710 **NS**

CUNIOT-HURY [P06/252] Silver Violin Bow
518/691 **1235**
£715 DM2070 ¥190476

CUNIOT-HURY [P11/171] Nickel Violin Bow
295/491 **298**
£152 DM438 ¥38421

CUNIOT-HURY, EUGENE [S03/281] Silver Violin Bow: Mirecourt, c. 1900 855/1197 **1411**
£825 DM2285 ¥209055

DARCHE, HILAIRE [P11/139] Silver Violin Bow
590/884 **908**
£462 DM1333 ¥116932

DELIVET, AUGUSTE [S11/253] Silver Violin Bow: Paris 1572/1965 **NS**

DODD [P11/165] Violin Bow minus hair and lapping: c. 1830 491/688 **473**
£241 DM695 ¥60972

DODD [S11/267] Violin Bow head and handle repaired: London 1376/1965 **NS**

DODD [S11/66] Ivory English Violin Bow: c. 1800
2358/2948 **2594**
£1320 DM3857 ¥330660

DODD [B04/110] Silver English Violin Bow in very good condition: London, early 19th C.
3570/4165 **3451**
£2111 DM5800 ¥549502

DODD [C11/206] Silver Violin Bow 1182/1576 **1300**
£660 DM1915 ¥165396

DODD, EDWARD [S06/365] Ivory Violin Bow: London, c. 1780 1710/2565 **2822**
£1650 DM4764 ¥434280

DODD, JAMES [S11/262] Silver and Ivory Violin Bow: London, c. 1840 2358/3537 **NS**

DODD, JAMES [S06/228] Gold and Tortoiseshell Violin Bow: London, c. 1850 (H. J. Eldridge, November 22, 1907) 3420/6840 **3762**
£2200 DM6352 ¥579040

DODD, JAMES [C11/271] Ivory Violin Bow 1576/2364 **1842**
£935 DM2713 ¥234311

DODD, JOHN [S11/223] Violin Bow: Kew 2358/2948 **NS**

DODD, JOHN [S11/48] Silver and Ivory Violin Bow head repaired: Kew, c. 1820 1179/1572 **2810**
£1430 DM4178 ¥358215

DODD, JOHN [S06/28] English Violin Bow: London, early 19th C. 5130/6840 **NS**

DODD, JOHN [S06/342] Silver and Ivory Violin Bow head repaired: Kew, c. 1820 1710/3420 **NS**

DODD, JOHN [S06/343] Ivory Violin Bow: Kew, c. 1780 1368/2052 **1223**
£715 DM2065 ¥188188

DODD, JOHN [S06/345] Silver and Ivory Violin Bow: Kew, c. 1800 1368/2052 **1223**
£715 DM2065 ¥188188

DODD, JOHN (ascribed to) [S06/353] Ivory Violin Bow 1197/1539 **NS**

DODD, JOHN (attributed to) [P11/85] Violin Bow 393/590 **476**
£242 DM698 ¥61250

DODD, JOHN (attributed to) [C03/69] Silver Violin Bow 1302/1954 **1254**
£770 DM2144 ¥197967

DODD FAMILY (MEMBER OF) [S03/79] Gold Violin Bow repairs on handle and on stick near lapping: London 684/1026 **NS**

DODD FAMILY (MEMBER OF) [C03/271] Silver English Violin Bow 1302/1954 **2328**
£1430 DM3983 ¥367653

DOLLING, KURT [C03/64] Silver Violin Bow 326/488 **394**
£242 DM674 ¥62218

DORFLER, D. [P07/148] Gold Violin Bow 109/182 **254**
£140 DM410 ¥38012

DOTSCHKAIL, R. [B04/305] Gold German Violin Bow in very good condition: c. 1970 1190/1785 **1071**
£655 DM1800 ¥170535

DUGAD, ANDRE [S06/379] Silver Violin Bow: Paris 513/855 **339**
£198 DM572 ¥52114

DUPUY, GEORGE [S06/378] Silver Violin Bow: Paris 855/1197 **NS**

DURRSCHMIDT, O. [B04/291] Silver German Violin Bow: c. 1970 417/536 **357**
£218 DM600 ¥56845

DURRSCHMIDT, OTTO [Sk11/79] Silver Violin Bow 350/450 **550**
£280 DM820 ¥70950

DURRSCHMIDT, OTTO [P06/305] Gilt Violin Bow 345/432 **798**
£462 DM1337 ¥123077

DURRSCHMIDT, OTTO [P06/322] Silver Violin Bow 259/432 **247**
£143 DM414 ¥38095

DURRSCHMIDT, OTTO [P07/45] Good Silver Violin Bow 364/546 **360**
£198 DM582 ¥53876

DURRSCHMIDT, OTTO [P09/224] Silver Violin Bow 374/561 **329**
£176 DM521 ¥45250

DURRSCHMIDT, OTTO [P11/240] Silver Violin Bow 295/491 **324**
£165 DM476 ¥41762

EULRY, CLEMENT [S06/121] Gold Violin Bow: Mirecourt, c. 1850 3420/5130 **3386**
£1980 DM5717 ¥521136

EURY, NICOLAS [S03/72] Silver Violin Bow: Paris (Jean-Jacques Millant, Paris, October 18, 1989) 10260/13680 **NS**

EURY, NICOLAS [S06/26] Silver Violin Bow handle repaired: Paris, c. 1820 4275/5985 **8276**
£4840 DM13975 ¥1273888

FETIQUE, JULES [Sk11/82] Silver Violin Bow 1000/1500 **2200**
£1122 DM3278 ¥283800

FETIQUE, VICTOR [P11/225] Silver Violin Bow stick spliced on upper half 295/491 **NS**

FETIQUE, VICTOR [S11/224] Silver Violin Bow: Paris 3930/4913 **6268**
£3190 DM9321 ¥799095

FETIQUE, VICTOR [S11/70] Silver French Violin Bow: Paris 1179/1572 **3242**
£1650 DM4821 ¥413325

FETIQUE, VICTOR [S03/75] Silver Violin Bow: Paris 1710/2565 **2069**
£1210 DM3352 ¥306614

FETIQUE, VICTOR [S06/142] Gold and Tortoiseshell Violin Bow: Paris 3420/5130 **5267**
£3080 DM8894 ¥810656

FETIQUE, VICTOR [S06/250] Silver Violin Bow head repaired: Paris 1368/1710 **1317**
£770 DM2223 ¥202664

FETIQUE, VICTOR [S06/41] Gold Violin Bow: Paris 2052/2565 **2257**
£1320 DM3811 ¥347424

FINKEL, SIEGFRIED [Sk11/86] Silver Violin Bow 600/800 **770**
£393 DM1147 ¥99330

FRANCAIS, EMILE [S06/57] Silver Violin Bow: Paris 1026/1368 **1505**
£880 DM2541 ¥231616

FRANCAIS, EMILE [S06/58] Silver Violin Bow: Paris 1026/1368 **1693**
£990 DM2859 ¥260568

FRANCAIS, EMILE [S06/59] Silver Violin Bow: Paris 1026/1368 **NS**

GAND & BERNARDEL [S03/255] Silver Violin Bow: Paris 1539/2052 **2633**
£1540 DM4266 ¥390236

GEIPEL, RICHARD [P06/314] Silver Violin Bow 259/432 **NS**

GEIPEL, RICHARD [P10/96] Silver Violin Bow 157/294 **302**
£154 DM455 ¥37792

GEROME, ROGER [B04/307] Silver French Violin Bow in very good condition: Mirecourt, c. 1960 1071/1309 **774**
£473 DM1300 ¥123164

GEROME, ROGER [S06/56] Gold Violin Bow 1368/2052 **NS**

GILLET, R. [B04/106] Silver French Violin Bow in very good condition: Paris, c. 1940 (B. Millant, Paris) 2380/2975 **2083**
£1274 DM3500 ¥331596

GLASEL [B04/306] Silver Violin Bow in very good condition: Paris 1190/1785 **1071**
£655 DM1800 ¥170535

GOTZ [P03/265] Silver Violin Bow 329/493 **NS**

GOTZ, CONRAD [P03/272] Silver Violin Bow handle worn: c. 1880 164/329 **651**
£396 DM1098 ¥101297

GOTZ, CONRAD [S03/90] German Silver and Tortoiseshell Violin Bow: (Leslie Sheppard, Holt, December 10, 1977) 855/1197 **941**
£550 DM1523 ¥139370

GUETTER, OTTO [P07/155] Silver Violin Bow w/bow 218/400 **645**
£354 DM1041 ¥96378

HAGEMANN, F. R. [P02/119] Silver Violin Bow 204/306 **NS**

HAGEMANN, F. R. [P06/294] Silver Violin Bow 138/207 **190**
£110 DM318 ¥29304

HAMMIG, W. H. [P06/303] Silver Violin Bow 345/432 **NS**

HAMMIG, W. H. [P10/92] Silver Violin Bow 235/353 **323**
£165 DM488 ¥40491

HART & SON [S11/236] Silver Violin Bow: London 1179/1572 **NS**

HART & SON [S03/271] Silver Violin Bow: London 855/1197 **NS**

HEL, PIERRE [S03/282] Silver Violin Bow: Lille, c. 1925 684/1026 **1129**
£660 DM1828 ¥167244

HENRY, JOSEPH [S11/351] Gold and Tortoiseshell Violin Bow: Paris, mid 19th C. (Kenneth Warren & Son, Chicago, February 10, 1975) 19650/23580 **NS**

HERMANN, LOTHAR [C06/233] Silver Violin Bow 516/688 **473**
£275 DM795 ¥72482

HERRMANN, A. [P03/270] Silver Violin Bow 247/329 **579**
£352 DM976 ¥90042

HERRMANN, A. [P07/151] Silver Violin Bow (Two) 273/455 **368**
£202 DM595 ¥55073

HERRMANN, EDWARD [Sk11/102] Silver Violin Bow 300/400 **468**
£238 DM697 ¥60308

HERRMANN, W. [P03/257] Silver Violin Bow 329/493 **624**
£380 DM1052 ¥97076

HILL, W. E. & SONS [Sk11/62] Gold Violin Bow w/case 3000/4000 **3300**
£1683 DM4917 ¥425700

HILL, W. E. & SONS [Sk11/84A] Silver and Ivory Violin Bow 1000/1500 **1320**
£673 DM1967 ¥170280

HILL, W. E. & SONS [P02/104] Silver Violin Bow 595/680 **1272**
£748 DM2102 ¥183634

HILL, W. E. & SONS [P02/105] Silver Violin Bow 595/680 **823**
£484 DM1360 ¥118822

HILL, W. E. & SONS [P03/125] Silver Violin Bow 658/904 **1628**
£990 DM2745 ¥253242

HILL, W. E. & SONS [P03/158] Silver Violin Bow 1315/1644 **1411**
£858 DM2379 ¥219476

HILL, W. E. & SONS [P03/161] Silver Violin Bow 411/575 **1121**
£682 DM1891 ¥174456

HILL, W. E. & SONS [P03/163] Silver Violin Bow 740/904 **1899**
£1155 DM3203 ¥295449

HILL, W. E. & SONS [P03/256] Silver Violin Bow 986/1151 **NS**

HILL, W. E. & SONS [P03/269] Silver Violin Bow 329/493 **344**
£209 DM580 ¥53462

HILL, W. E. & SONS [P03/282] Silver Violin Bow minus hair and part lapping 164/329 **398**
£242 DM671 ¥61904

HILL, W. E. & SONS [P06/179] Good Silver Violin Bow 864/1382 **1710**
£990 DM2866 ¥263736

HILL, W. E. & SONS [P06/253] Silver Violin Bow 691/950 **1178**
£682 DM1974 ¥181685

HILL, W. E. & SONS [P06/284] Silver Violin Bow 691/864 **988**
£572 DM1656 ¥152381

HILL, W. E. & SONS [P06/285] Silver Violin Bow minus hair 518/691 **988**
£572 DM1656 ¥152381

LORENZO STORIONI
Good Italian Violin: Cremona, 1770
Christie's, London, March 28, 1990, Lot 192

HILL, W. E. & SONS [P06/290] Silver Violin Bow 1382/1900 **1368**
£792 DM2293 ¥210989

HILL, W. E. & SONS [P07/74] Violin Bow w/violin, case 546/728 **1161**
£638 DM1874 ¥173600

HILL, W. E. & SONS [P07/76] Violin Bow 546/728 **881**
£484 DM1422 ¥131696

HILL, W. E. & SONS [P09/105] Good Silver Violin Bow 842/1029 **1748**
£935 DM2768 ¥240389

HILL, W. E. & SONS [P09/108] Good Violin Bow minus hair, frog damaged 935/1496 **1481**
£792 DM2344 ¥203623

HILL, W. E. & SONS [P09/151] Fine Presentation Gold Violin Bow 3740/5610 **4525**
£2420 DM7163 ¥622182

HILL, W. E. & SONS [P09/192] Good Silver Violin Bow w/case 1309/2057 **2777**
£1485 DM4396 ¥381793

HILL, W. E. & SONS [P09/195] Silver Violin Bow 748/935 **1399**
£748 DM2214 ¥192311

HILL, W. E. & SONS [P09/70] Good Silver Violin Bow 935/1309 **1440**
£770 DM2279 ¥197967

HILL, W. E. & SONS [P10/108] Three-Quarter Size Silver Violin Bow 490/686 **1186**
£605 DM1789 ¥148467

HILL, W. E. & SONS [P11/136] Silver Violin Bow 982/1179 **1254**
£638 DM1841 ¥161478

HILL, W. E. & SONS [P11/137] Silver Violin Bow 786/1081 **1081**
£550 DM1587 ¥139205

HILL, W. E. & SONS [P11/141] Silver Violin Bow minus hair 786/982 **1513**
£770 DM2221 ¥194887

HILL, W. E. & SONS [P11/157] Silver Violin Bow 982/1376 **2363**
£1202 DM3469 ¥304302

HILL, W. E. & SONS [P11/205] Silver Violin Bow 688/884 **865**
£440 DM1269 ¥111364

HILL, W. E. & SONS [S11/220] Silver Violin Bow: London, 1947 2948/3930 **2810**
£1430 DM4178 ¥358215

HILL, W. E. & SONS [S11/230] Silver Violin Bow: London 1376/1965 **1513**
£770 DM2250 ¥192885

HILL, W. E. & SONS [S11/238] Silver Violin Bow: London 982/1376 **1081**
£550 DM1607 ¥137775

HILL, W. E. & SONS [S11/250] Gold Violin Bow: London 3930/4913 **NS**

HILL, W. E. & SONS [S11/263] Silver and Ivory Violin Bow head repaired: London 1572/1965 **1405**
£715 DM2089 ¥179108

HILL, W. E. & SONS [S11/264] Silver Violin Bow: London 1965/2948 **3026**
£1540 DM4500 ¥385770

HILL, W. E. & SONS [S11/350] Fine Silver Violin Bow: London, 1977 3537/4913 **5188**
£2640 DM7714 ¥661320

HILL, W. E. & SONS [S11/63] Silver and Tortoiseshell Violin Bow: London 2948/4913 **4755**
£2420 DM7071 ¥606210

HILL, W. E. & SONS [S11/72] Gold Violin Bow head pinned: London, 1935 1179/1572 **1081**
£550 DM1607 ¥137775

HILL, W. E. & SONS [S11/81] Silver Violin Bow: London, 1933 2751/3144 **3675**
£1870 DM5464 ¥468435

HILL, W. E. & SONS [B04/113] Gold and Tortoiseshell English Violin Bow in fine condition: London, c. 1934 4760/5355 **5355**
£3275 DM9000 ¥852676

HILL, W. E. & SONS [B04/310] Silver English Violin Bow in good condition: London, 1965 1190/1785 **1190**
£728 DM2000 ¥189484

HILL, W. E. & SONS [S03/106] Silver Violin Bow: London 855/1197 **1223**
£715 DM1981 ¥181181

HILL, W. E. & SONS [S03/107] Silver Violin Bow: London, 1931 855/1197 **1317**
£770 DM2133 ¥195118

HILL, W. E. & SONS [S03/108] Silver and Tortoiseshell Violin Bow: London, 1933 2565/3420 **4514**
£2640 DM7313 ¥668976

HILL, W. E. & SONS [S03/110] Silver and Tortoiseshell Violin Bow: London 2565/342 **2445**
£1430 DM3961 ¥362362

HILL, W. E. & SONS [S03/257] Silver Violin Bow: London 2052/2565 **2633**
£1540 DM4266 ¥390236

HILL, W. E. & SONS [S03/266] Silver Violin Bow: London 2052/2565 **2633**
£1540 DM4266 ¥390236

HILL, W. E. & SONS [S03/297] Engraved Gold Violin Bow: London, c. 1928 1710/2565 **3762**
£2200 DM6094 ¥557480

HILL, W. E. & SONS [S03/74] Silver and Tortoiseshell Violin Bow w/violin bow: London 2052/3078 **2445**
£1430 DM3961 ¥362362

HILL, W. E. & SONS [S03/80] Silver Violin Bow: London, 1929 1710/2565 **1881**
£1100 DM3047 ¥278740

HILL, W. E. & SONS [S03/83] Silver Violin Bow: London 1197/1368 **1693**
£990 DM2742 ¥250866

HILL, W. E. & SONS [S03/87] Silver Violin Bow: London 1368/2052 **1317**
£770 DM2133 ¥195118

HILL, W. E. & SONS [S03/89] Silver Violin Bow: London 1710/2565 **NS**

HILL, W. E. & SONS [S03/92] Silver Violin Bow: London 2394/3078 **2445**
£1430 DM3961 ¥362362

HILL, W. E. & SONS [S03/94] Silver Violin Bow: London, 1928 2394/2736 **2822**
£1650 DM4570 ¥418110

HILL, W. E. & SONS [S03/97] Silver Violin Bow: London 1197/1710 **1317**
£770 DM2133 ¥195118

HILL, W. E. & SONS [S06/122] Silver Violin Bow: London 2565/3420 **3198**
£1870 DM5400 ¥492184

HILL, W. E. & SONS [S06/224] Gold Violin Bow: London, 1910 3420/5130 **3386**
£1980 DM5717 ¥521136

HILL, W. E. & SONS [S06/226] Gold and Tortoiseshell Violin Bow: London, 1937 3420/5130 **4891**
£2860 DM8258 ¥752752

HILL, W. E. & SONS [S06/24] Silver Violin Bow: London, 1929 1026/1368 **846**
£495 DM1429 ¥130284

HILL, W. E. & SONS [S06/245] Silver and Ivory Violin Bow: London 2565/3420 **NS**

HILL, W. E. & SONS [S06/247] Child's Silver Violin Bow: London 513/855 **NS**

HILL, W. E. & SONS [S06/248] Violin Bow: London 1026/1368 **NS**

HILL, W. E. & SONS [S06/255] Silver Violin Bow: London 1710/2565 **2069**
£1210 DM3494 ¥318472

HILL, W. E. & SONS [S06/30] Silver Violin Bow: London, 1927 1026/1368 **NS**

HILL, W. E. & SONS [S06/337] Silver Violin Bow: London 2052/2736 **NS**

HILL, W. E. & SONS [S06/352] Silver Violin Bow: London, 1929 1710/2052 **NS**

HILL, W. E. & SONS [S06/372] Silver Violin Bow: London 1368/2052 **1505**
£880 DM2541 ¥231616

HILL, W. E. & SONS [S06/375] Silver Violin Bow: London 855/1026 **846**
£495 DM1429 ¥130284

HILL, W. E. & SONS [S06/381] Silver and Tortoiseshell Violin Bow: London 1368/2052 **1411**
£825 DM2382 ¥217140

HILL, W. E. & SONS [C11/201] Silver Violin Bow 1576/2364 **2167**
£1100 DM3192 ¥275660

HILL, W. E. & SONS [C11/209] Silver Violin Bow 1576/2364 **2167**
£1100 DM3192 ¥275660

HILL, W. E. & SONS [C11/216] Gold Violin Bow 1970/2955 **2600**
£1320 DM3831 ¥330792

HILL, W. E. & SONS [C11/235] Silver Violin Bow 788/1182 **910**
£462 DM1341 ¥115777

HILL, W. E. & SONS [C11/238] Silver Violin Bow 1576/1970 **3684**
£1870 DM5427 ¥468622

HILL, W. E. & SONS [C11/243] Silver Violin Bow 788/1182 **NS**

HILL, W. E. & SONS [C11/246] Silver Violin Bow 1576/2364 **NS**

HILL, W. E. & SONS [C11/247] Silver and Tortoiseshell Violin Bow 2758/3546 **NS**

HILL, W. E. & SONS [C11/250] Silver Violin Bow 591/985 **823**
£418 DM1213 ¥104751

HILL, W. E. & SONS [C11/253] Silver Violin Bow 2364/2955 **2600**
£1320 DM3831 ¥330792

HILL, W. E. & SONS [C11/263] Ivory Violin Bow 2758/3546 **NS**

HILL, W. E. & SONS [C06/212] Silver Violin Bow 860/1204 **1135**
£660 DM1907 ¥173956

HILL, W. E. & SONS [C06/220] Silver Violin Bow without lapping 1032/1720 **1892**
£1100 DM3179 ¥289927

HILL, W. E. & SONS [C06/243] Silver and Tortoiseshell Violin Bow 2580/3096 **2838**
£1650 DM4768 ¥434891

HILL, W. E. & SONS [C03/264] Silver Violin Bow 488/651 **985**
£605 DM1685 ¥155545

HILL, W. E. & SONS [C03/291] Gold and Tortoiseshell Violin Bow 2442/3256 **4656**
£2860 DM7965 ¥735306

HILL, W. E. & SONS [C03/296] Engraved Gold and Tortoiseshell Violin Bow 3256/4070 **4656**
£2860 DM7965 ¥735306

HILL, W. E. & SONS [C03/76] Engraved Gold and Tortoiseshell Violin Bow 3256/4070 **5731**
£3520 DM9803 ¥904992

HOYER, C. A. [P11/163] Good Silver Violin Bow w/bow, minus hair 393/688 **865**
£440 DM1269 ¥111364

HOYER, G. [B04/287] Silver German Violin Bow in very good condition: Markneukirchen, c. 1950 357/476 **387**
£237 DM650 ¥61582

HOYER, OTTO A. [Sk11/55] Silver Violin Bow 400/500 **935**
£477 DM1393 ¥120615

HOYER, OTTO A. [Sk11/88] Silver Violin Bow: Paris, 1922 600/800 **1045**
£533 DM1557 ¥134805

HOYER, OTTO A. [C11/240] Silver Violin Bow 985/1576 **1734**
£880 DM2554 ¥220528

HUMS, ALBIN [P06/307] Gilt Violin Bow 345/518 **836**
£484 DM1401 ¥128938

HUMS, ALBIN [C11/204] Silver Violin Bow 591/788 **NS**

DAVID TECCHLER
Fine Violin: Rome, 18th C.
Christie's, London, March 28, 1990, Lot 360

HUMS, ALBIN [C06/238] Silver Violin Bow
688/1032 **NS**

HUMS, ALBIN [C03/287] Silver Violin Bow
814/1140 **1701**
£1045 DM2910 ¥268669

HUMS, W. [P11/164] Silver Violin Bow
295/491 **238**
£121 DM349 ¥30625

HUSSON, CHARLES CLAUDE (attributed to) [C03/260]
Gold Violin Bow 1628/2442 **NS**

KESSLER [P10/110] Silver Violin Bow whalebone lapping: Berlin 196/294 **431**
£220 DM651 ¥53988

KITTEL FAMILY (MEMBER OF) (ascribed to) [C03/106]
Gold Violin Bow 4884/6512 **4656**
£2860 DM7965 ¥735306

KNOPF, HENRY RICHARD [Sk11/59] Silver Violin Bow without hair: New York 200/300 **550**
£280 DM820 ¥70950

LABERTE [B04/303] Silver French Violin Bow in very good condition: Mirecourt, c. 1930
595/1190 **536**
£328 DM900 ¥85268

LABERTE, MARC [B04/87] Nickel French Violin Bow in good condition: c. 1940 893/1190 **774**
£473 DM1300 ¥123164

LABERTE, MARC (ascribed to) [S06/377] Silver Violin Bow 513/684 **339**
£198 DM572 ¥52114

LAFLEUR (ascribed to) [C03/270] Silver Violin Bow
1954/2930 **NS**

LAFLEUR, JOSEPH RENE [S11/252] Silver Violin Bow: Paris, c. 1860 3930/4913 **NS**

LAFLEUR, JOSEPH RENE (ascribed to) [C11/260]
Ivory Violin Bow 2955/3940 **1625**
£825 DM2394 ¥206745

LAMY, A. [P09/209] Silver Violin Bow: Paris, c. 1880 748/935 **NS**

LAMY, A. [B04/114] Silver French Violin Bow in excellent condition: Paris, second half, 19th C.
4165/5355 **4463**
£2729 DM7500 ¥710564

LAMY, ALFRED [S11/219] Silver Violin Bow: Paris
3930/5895 **4323**
£2200 DM6428 ¥551100

LAMY, ALFRED [S11/222] Silver Violin Bow: Paris, c. 1900 (Etienne Vatelot, Paris, March 17, 1976)
3537/4913 **5836**
£2970 DM8678 ¥743985

LAMY, ALFRED [S11/344] Silver Violin Bow head repaired: Paris 1179/1572 **1297**
£660 DM1929 ¥165330

LAMY, ALFRED [S03/300] Silver Violin Bow: Paris
1710/2565 **3010**
£1760 DM4875 ¥445984

LAMY, ALFRED [S06/42] Silver Violin Bow: Paris
1368/1710 **NS**

LAMY, ALFRED [C11/217] Silver Violin Bow
1970/2955 **2384**
£1210 DM3511 ¥303226

LAMY, ALFRED [C11/270] Silver Violin Bow
5910/7880 **NS**

LAMY, ALFRED [C11/275] Silver Violin Bow: (Jean-Jacques Millant, December 6, 1988)
4925/6895 **6934**
£3520 DM10215 ¥882112

LAMY, ALFRED [C06/241] Silver Violin Bow
1204/1720 **NS**

LAMY, ALFRED [C06/251] Silver Violin Bow
2064/2580 **NS**

LAMY, ALFRED [C06/259] Silver Violin Bow
2580/3096 **NS**

LAMY, ALFRED [C06/261] Silver Violin Bow
3440/5160 **6054**
£3520 DM10173 ¥927766

LAMY, ALFRED [C03/75] Silver Violin Bow
4884/6512 **6805**
£4180 DM11641 ¥1074678

LAMY, ALFRED JOSEPH [S06/354] Silver Violin Bow handle repaired: Paris 2565/3420 **4138**
£2420 DM6988 ¥636944

LEBLANC, P. R. [B04/297] Silver Violin Bow in very good condition 476/595 **476**
£291 DM800 ¥75793

LEBLANC, P. R. [B04/298] Silver Violin Bow in very good condition 536/655 **476**
£291 DM800 ¥75793

LEBLANC, P. R. [B04/299] Silver Violin Bow in very good condition 536/655 **536**
£328 DM900 ¥85268

LEBLANC, P. R. [B04/300] Silver Violin Bow in very good condition 476/595 **417**
£255 DM700 ¥66319

LERMETZ [P09/244] Silver Violin Bow w/bow: c. 1920 187/374 **185**
£99 DM293 ¥25453

LOTTE, FRANCOIS [S11/60] Silver Violin Bow: Paris (Jean-Francois Raffin, Paris, April 26, 1990)
982/1572 **1038**
£528 DM1543 ¥132264

LOTTE, FRANCOIS [S03/280] Nickel Violin Bow: Mirecourt, c. 1916 684/1026 **941**
£550 DM1523 ¥139370

LOTTE, FRANCOIS [C03/278] Silver Violin Bow
651/977 **716**
£440 DM1225 ¥113124

LOWENDALL, LOUIS [P10/90] Nickel and Ivory Violin Bow 157/235 **NS**

LUPOT, FRANCOIS [S03/73] Gold Violin Bow: Paris (Jean-Jacques Millant, Paris, October 23, 1989)
10260/13680 **13167**
£7700 DM21329 ¥1951180

LUPOT, FRANCOIS (attributed to) [C03/71] Silver Violin Bow 1954/2442 **5372**
£3300 DM9190 ¥848430

Lupot, Nicolas [C06/256] Silver Violin Bow
5160/6020 **NS**

Maire, Nicolas [S11/79] Silver Violin Bow w/box: Paris, third quarter, 19th C. 3930/5895 **8646**
£4400 DM12857 ¥1102200

Maire, Nicolas [B04/120] Silver French Violin Bow: Paris, second half, 19th C. 8925/10710 **8628**
£5277 DM14500 ¥1373756

Maire, Nicolas [S06/29] Silver Violin Bow w/bow box: Paris, third quarter, 19th C. 5130/6840 **NS**

Martin [P09/71] Silver Violin Bow: Leipzig
374/561 **370**
£198 DM586 ¥50906

Maure, Pierre [P06/288] Good Silver Violin Bow
777/1037 **874**
£506 DM1465 ¥134798

Meauchand [C11/230] Rare Violin Bow
3940/5910 **6068**
£3080 DM8938 ¥771848

Meauchand (attributed to) [C11/229] Rare Violin Bow 3940/5910 **6068**
£3080 DM8938 ¥771848

Meinel, Eugen [Sk11/100] Silver Violin Bow
200/300 **110**
£56 DM164 ¥14190

Meinel, Eugen [P07/159] Silver Violin Bow minus lapping and hair 364/546 **414**
£228 DM669 ¥61957

Millant, B. [B04/91] Silver French Violin Bow in very good condition: Paris, 1959 1190/1785 **1488**
£910 DM2500 ¥236855

Miquel, E. [S03/102] Silver Violin Bow
684/1026 **527**
£308 DM853 ¥78047

Moller, Max [S06/237] Silver Violin Bow: Amsterdam 1197/1539 **1317**
£770 DM2223 ¥202664

Morizot [Sk11/97] Ivory and Silver Violin Bow
800/1000 **1210**
£617 DM1803 ¥156090

Morizot [S06/60] Silver Violin Bow: Mirecourt
1026/1368 **1129**
£660 DM1906 ¥173712

Morizot, Louis [P03/268] Violin Bow
411/740 **760**
£462 DM1281 ¥118180

Morizot, Louis [P11/170] Nickel Violin Bow w/bow 295/491 **298**
£152 DM438 ¥38421

Morizot, Louis [S03/76] Nickel Violin Bow: Mirecourt, 1930 513/684 **1035**
£605 DM1676 ¥153307

Morizot, Louis [S06/106] Silver Violin Bow: Mirecourt 1026/1368 **1223**
£715 DM2065 ¥188188

Morizot, Louis [S06/107] Silver Violin Bow: Mirecourt 1026/1368 **1223**
£715 DM2065 ¥188188

Morizot, Louis [C03/90] Nickel Violin Bow
244/326 **627**
£385 DM1072 ¥98983

Mougenot, Georges [S06/112] Silver Violin Bow: Brussels 855/1197 **941**
£550 DM1588 ¥144760

Muhl [P06/306] Gilt Violin Bow 259/345 **798**
£462 DM1337 ¥123077

Nurnberger, Albert [Sk11/89] Silver Violin Bow
600/800 **1100**
£561 DM1639 ¥141900

Nurnberger, Albert [Sk11/95] Silver Violin Bow
300/400 **660**
£337 DM983 ¥85140

Nurnberger, Albert [P11/122] Good Silver Violin Bow 786/1179 **1729**
£880 DM2539 ¥222728

Nurnberger, Albert [P11/138] Silver Violin Bow
393/590 **605**
£308 DM889 ¥77955

Nurnberger, Albert [P11/158] Silver Violin Bow
236/354 **249**
£127 DM365 ¥32017

Nurnberger, Albert [S11/257] Silver Violin Bow: Markneukirchen 1376/1768 **2162**
£1100 DM3214 ¥275550

Nurnberger, Albert [S11/45] Silver Violin Bow: Markneukirchen 786/1179 **1124**
£572 DM1671 ¥143286

Nurnberger, Albert [B04/103] Silver German Violin Bow in very good condition: Markneukirchen, c. 1920 1785/2380 **1666**
£1019 DM2800 ¥265277

Nurnberger, Albert [B04/111] Gold and Tortoiseshell German Violin Bow in splendid condition: Markneukirchen, c. 1930
3570/4165 **4046**
£2475 DM6800 ¥644244

Nurnberger, Albert [S03/272] Silver Violin Bow: Markneukirchen 855/1197 **1693**
£990 DM2742 ¥250866

Nurnberger, Albert [S03/291] Gold Violin Bow: Markneukirchen 1368/1710 **1411**
£825 DM2285 ¥209055

Nurnberger, Albert [S06/133] Silver Violin Bow: Markneukirchen 855/1197 **1035**
£605 DM1747 ¥159236

Nurnberger, Albert [S06/134] Silver Violin Bow: Markneukirchen 855/1197 **1035**
£605 DM1747 ¥159236

Nurnberger, Albert [S06/135] Nickel Violin Bow: Markneukirchen 684/1026 **941**
£550 DM1588 ¥144760

Nurnberger, Albert [S06/136] Silver Violin Bow: Markneukirchen 855/1197 **941**
£550 DM1588 ¥144760

Nurnberger, Albert [S06/40] Silver Violin Bow: Markneukirchen 855/1197 **941**
£550 DM1588 ¥144760

NURNBERGER, ALBERT [C11/222] Silver Violin Bow 788/1182 **1409**
£715 DM2075 ¥179179

NURNBERGER, ALBERT [C11/236] Silver Violin Bow 985/1182 **1084**
£550 DM1596 ¥137830

NURNBERGER, ALBERT [C03/62] Silver Violin Bow 651/977 **NS**

NURNBERGER, ALBERT [C03/73] Gold and Tortoiseshell Violin Bow 1465/1954 **2149**
£1320 DM3676 ¥339372

NURNBERGER, ALBERT [C03/79] Silver Violin Bow 326/488 **716**
£440 DM1225 ¥113124

OUCHARD, E. [B04/88] Nickel French Violin Bow in very good condition: c. 1930 595/833 **1131**
£691 DM1900 ¥180009

OUCHARD, E. [B04/92] Silver French Violin Bow in very good condition: Mirecourt, c. 1930 1190/1785 **1071**
£655 DM1800 ¥170535

OUCHARD, EMILE [P02/117] Nickel Violin Bow 340/510 **1159**
£682 DM1916 ¥167431

OUCHARD, EMILE [P03/160] Silver Violin Bow 411/575 **1664**
£1012 DM2806 ¥258870

OUCHARD, EMILE [S11/228] Nickel Violin Bow 786/1179 **NS**

PAESOLD, RODERICH [P06/221] Gold Violin Bow 432/777 **418**
£242 DM701 ¥64469

PAESOLD, RODERICH [P06/222] Gold Violin Bow 432/777 **570**
£330 DM955 ¥87912

PAESOLD, RODERICH [P06/300] Gilt Violin Bow 518/691 **532**
£308 DM892 ¥82051

PAJEOT [S11/243] Gold Violin Bow: Mirecourt 3930/5895 **NS**

PAJEOT [C06/254] Silver Violin Bow 2580/3440 **NS**

PAJEOT (attributed to) [C11/259] Silver Violin Bow without hair 1970/2955 **6934**
£3520 DM10215 ¥882112

PAJEOT, (FILS) [S11/249] Silver Violin Bow: Mirecourt, c. 1840 5895/7860 **5620**
£2860 DM8357 ¥716430

PAJEOT, (FILS) [S11/57] Silver Violin Bow: Mirecourt, c. 1815 5895/7860 **9078**
£4620 DM13500 ¥1157310

PAJEOT, (PERE) [B04/119] Silver French Violin Bow in very good condition: 19th C. 8925/10710 **8330**
£5095 DM14000 ¥1326385

PAQUOTTE BROS. [S11/64] Silver Violin Bow: Paris 1965/2358 **1945**
£990 DM2893 ¥247995

PAQUOTTE BROS. [S03/254] Silver Violin Bow: Paris 2052/3078 **NS**

PAULUS, JOHANNES O. [B04/285] Silver German Violin Bow in very good condition: c. 1970 357/476 **387**
£237 DM650 ¥61582

PECCATTE, DOMINIQUE [S11/55] Silver Violin Bow: Paris, c. 1840 (W. D. Watson, Denham, June 20th, 1964) 15720/23580 **16211**
£8250 DM24106 ¥2066625

PECCATTE, DOMINIQUE [C11/284] Fine Gold Violin Bow: (Jean-Jacques Millant, December 6, 1988) 23640/31520 **39006**
£19800 DM57460 ¥4961880

PECCATTE, DOMINIQUE (attributed to) [S11/50] Silver Violin Bow 4913/6877 **6052**
£3080 DM9000 ¥771540

PECCATTE, FRANCOIS [S03/91] Silver Violin Bow: Paris, c. 1850 5130/6840 **11286**
£6600 DM18282 ¥1672440

PENZEL [P07/153] Silver Violin Bow w/3 bows 364/546 **1059**
£582 DM1710 ¥158335

PENZEL, K. [B04/276] Nickel German Violin Bow in good condition: c. 1960 179/238 **149**
£91 DM250 ¥23685

PERSOIS (attributed to) [C11/273] Gold and Tortoiseshell Violin Bow 9850/13790 **9752**
£4950 DM14365 ¥1240470

PFRETZSCHNER, F. C. [B04/86] Silver German Violin Bow in very good condition: Markneukirchen, c. 1935 595/1190 **833**
£509 DM1400 ¥132639

PFRETZSCHNER, H. R. [Sk11/57] Nickel Violin Bow 300/400 **440**
£224 DM656 ¥56760

PFRETZSCHNER, H. R. [P06/316] Silver Violin Bow 432/605 **665**
£385 DM1115 ¥102564

PFRETZSCHNER, H. R. [B04/277] Silver German Violin Bow head repaired: Markneukirchen, c. 1920 119/238 **149**
£91 DM250 ¥23685

PFRETZSCHNER, H. R. [B04/279] Silver German Violin Bow in good condition: Markneukirchen, c. 1920 357/476 **417**
£255 DM700 ¥66319

PFRETZSCHNER, H. R. [S06/117] Silver Violin Bow: Markneukirchen 684/1026 **752**
£440 DM1270 ¥115808

PFRETZSCHNER, H. R. [S06/118] Gold Violin Bow: Markneukirchen 1026/1368 **1166**
£682 DM1969 ¥179502

PFRETZSCHNER, H. R. [S06/119] Silver Violin Bow: Markneukirchen 855/1197 **1035**
£605 DM1747 ¥159236

PFRETZSCHNER, H. R. [S06/120] Silver Violin Bow: Markneukirchen 855/1197 **NS**

PFRETZSCHNER, H. R. [S06/127] Silver Violin Bow: Markneukirchen 855/1197 **NS**

PFRETZSCHNER, H. R. [S06/128] Silver Violin Bow: Markneukirchen 855/1197 **NS**

PFRETZSCHNER, H. R. [S06/129] Silver Violin Bow: Markneukirchen 855/1197 **941**
£550 DM1588 ¥144760

PFRETZSCHNER, H. R. [S06/140] Silver Violin Bow: Markneukirchen 855/1197 **NS**

PFRETZSCHNER, H. R. [S06/229] Silver Violin Bow: Markneukirchen 855/1197 **NS**

PFRETZSCHNER, H. R. [S06/346] Silver Violin Bow: Markneukirchen 1026/1368 **NS**

PFRETZSCHNER, H. R. [C06/232] Silver Violin Bow 688/860 **1892**
£1100 DM3179 ¥289927

PFRETZSCHNER, H. R. [C03/102] Silver Violin Bow 488/651 **573**
£352 DM980 ¥265277

PFRETZSCHNER, H. R. [C03/82] Silver Violin Bow 407/570 **752**
£462 DM1287 ¥118780

PFRETZSCHNER, T. H. [P10/99] Silver Violin Bow 294/490 **446**
£228 DM673 ¥55878

PFRETZSCHNER, W. A. [P06/308] Gilt Violin Bow 259/432 **798**
£462 DM1337 ¥123077

PFRETZSCHNER, W. A. [P09/221] Silver Violin Bow 374/561 **453**
£242 DM716 ¥62218

PFRETZSCHNER, W. A. [S06/373] Silver Violin Bow: Markneukirchen 1026/1368 **NS**

PILLOT [S11/342] Nickel and Ivory Violin Bow: Paris, early 19th C. (Rembert Wurlitzer, New York, February 13, 1954) 2948/3930 **NS**

PILLOT [S03/301] Nickel and Ivory Violin Bow: Paris, early 19th C. (Rembert Wurlitzer, New York, February 13, 1954) 2565/3420 **NS**

POIRSON [B04/102] Silver French Violin Bow in very good condition: c. 1910 1785/2380 **1666**
£1019 DM2800 ¥30

PRAGER, AUGUST EDWIN [P10/103] Nickel Violin Bow w/2 bows **744**
£380 DM1122 ¥93129

PRAGER, AUGUST EDWIN [P10/109] Silver Violin Bow wear at handle 235/314 **604**
£308 DM911 ¥75583

PRAGER, GUSTAV [C06/221] Silver Violin Bow 516/860 **568**
£330 DM954 ¥86978

PRAGER, GUSTAV [C06/229] Silver Violin Bow 516/860 **568**
£330 DM954 ¥86978

PRAGER, GUSTAV [C03/283] Silver Violin Bow 488/651 **573**
£352 DM980 ¥90499

PRAGER, GUSTAV [C03/80] Silver Violin Bow 326/488 **681**
£418 DM1164 ¥107468

RAU, AUGUST [P03/115] Silver Violin Bow 411/575 **326**
£198 DM549 ¥50648

RAU, AUGUST [B04/293] Silver German Violin Bow in good condition: Markneukirchen, c.1935 595/1190 **833**
£509 DM1400 ¥132639

RAU, AUGUST [B04/85] Silver German Violin Bow in perfect condition: Markneukirchen, c. 1940 893/1190 **952**
£582 DM1600 ¥151587

RAU, AUGUST [C03/274] Silver Violin Bow 651/977 **1074**
£660 DM1838 ¥169686

RETFORD, WILLIAM C. [S11/58] Silver Violin Bow: London 4913/6877 **8214**
£4180 DM12214 ¥1047090

RICHAUME, ANDRE [C11/244] Silver Violin Bow 985/1576 **3684**
£1870 DM5427 ¥468622

RUSHWORTH & DREAPER [P07/101] Silver Violin Bow w/case, viola 182/364 **601**
£330 DM970 ¥89793

SALCHOW, WILLIAM [S11/73] Silver Violin Bow: New York 1965/2948 **2810**
£1430 DM4178 ¥358215

SANDNER, A. E. [Sk11/58] Silver Violin Bow 350/450 **440**
£224 DM656 ¥56760

SARTORY, EUGENE [Sk11/84] Silver Violin Bow 3000/4000 **4620**
£2356 DM6884 ¥595980

SARTORY, EUGENE [P03/112] Silver Violin Bow 3288/4110 **6872**
£4180 DM11591 ¥1069244

SARTORY, EUGENE [P03/113] Silver Violin Bow 3288/4932 **7053**
£4290 DM11896 ¥1097382

SARTORY, EUGENE [P03/116] Silver Violin Bow minus lapping 3288/4932 **7595**
£4620 DM12811 ¥1181796

SARTORY, EUGENE [P03/122] Silver Violin Bow fine condition: Paris (W. E. Hill & Sons, London, 1959) 3288/4932 **9042**
£5500 DM15252 ¥1406900

SARTORY, EUGENE [P03/123] Silver Violin Bow 1315/1973 **1989**
£1210 DM3355 ¥309518

SARTORY, EUGENE [P03/162] Gold Violin Bow repairs to head 2466/2959 **6031**
£3669 DM10173 ¥938402

SARTORY, EUGENE [P03/207] Silver Violin Bow 3288/4932 **NS**

SARTORY, EUGENE [P06/175] Good Silver Violin Bow minor repair at ivory face 5182/6910 **7601**
£4400 DM12738 ¥1172160

SARTORY, EUGENE [P06/265] Silver Violin Bow restoration at ivory face and upper stick 1382/2073 **NS**

SARTORY, EUGENE [S11/340] Silver Violin Bow: Paris 4913/5895 **9511**
£4840 DM14142 ¥1212420

JEAN-BAPTISTE VUILLAUME
Fine Violin: Paris, mid 19th C.
Sotheby's, London, November 22, 1990, Lot 207

SARTORY, EUGENE [S11/80] Silver Violin Bow: Paris 3340/4520 **NS**

SARTORY, EUGENE [B04/105] Silver French Violin Bow 2083/2678 **1785**
£1092 DM3000 ¥284225

SARTORY, EUGENE [B04/118] Silver French Violin Bow in excellent condition: Paris, c. 1935 5950/7140 **5950**
£3639 DM10000 ¥947418

SARTORY, EUGENE [S03/112] Silver Violin Bow: Paris 4275/5985 **7148**
£4180 DM11579 ¥1059212

SARTORY, EUGENE [S03/294] Gold Violin Bow: Paris 3078/3762 **4891**
£2860 DM7922 ¥724724

SARTORY, EUGENE [S03/298] Silver Violin Bow: Paris 4275/5985 **6772**
£3960 DM10969 ¥1003464

SARTORY, EUGENE [S03/299] Silver Violin Bow: Paris 2565/4275 **3762**
£2200 DM6094 ¥557480

SARTORY, EUGENE [S03/85] Silver Violin Bow: Paris 2565/4275 **4514**
£2640 DM7313 ¥668976

SARTORY, EUGENE [S06/48] Silver Violin Bow: Paris 3420/4275 **6395**
£3740 DM10799 ¥984368

SARTORY, EUGENE [S06/49] Silver Violin Bow: Paris 3420/4275 **5643**
£3300 DM9529 ¥868560

SARTORY, EUGENE [C11/266] Silver Violin Bow 3940/4925 **NS**

SARTORY, EUGENE [C11/267] Silver Violin Bow 4334/4925 **3684**
£1870 DM5427 ¥468622

SARTORY, EUGENE [C06/260] Silver Violin Bow 3096/4300 **5676**
£3300 DM9537 ¥869781

SARTORY, EUGENE [C03/289] Silver Violin Bow 2442/4070 **4298**
£2640 DM7352 ¥678744

SARTORY, EUGENE [C03/94] Violin Bow without hair 1302/1954 **6805**
£4180 DM11641 ¥1074678

SAUNDERS, S. [C06/267] Silver Violin Bow 4816/6020 **8514**
£4950 DM14305 ¥1304672

SCHREIBER & LUGERT [B04/301] Silver Violin Bow in good condition: Hamburg, c. 1940 595/1190 **774**
£473 DM1300 ¥123164

SCHUBERT PAUL [Sk11/77] Silver Violin Bow 600/800 **NS**

SCHULLER, OTTO [C03/59] Silver Violin Bow 244/326 **340**
£209 DM582 ¥53734

SCHUSTER, ADOLF [C11/233] Silver Violin Bow 493/690 **NS**

SCHUSTER, ADOLF [C06/214] Silver Violin Bow 344/516 **303**
£176 DM509 ¥46388

SCHUSTER, ADOLF [C03/273] Silver Violin Bow 326/488 **466**
£286 DM797 ¥73531

SCHUSTER, ADOLF [C03/282] Silver Violin Bow 326/488 **501**
£308 DM858 ¥79187

SCHUSTER, ADOLF [C03/88] Silver Violin Bow 326/407 **501**
£308 DM858 ¥79187

SCHUSTER, ADOLF C. [P06/304] Silver Violin Bow 190/311 **NS**

SCHUSTER, ADOLF C. [P10/101] Silver Violin Bow 294/490 **1141**
£582 DM1721 ¥142798

SCHWARZ, B. [P09/194] Silver Violin Bow minus hair 467/655 **NS**

SCHWARZ, B. [P11/167] Silver Violin Bow minus hair 295/491 **497**
£253 DM730 ¥64034

SERDET, PAUL [S11/254] Silver Violin Bow: Paris 2358/2948 **3891**
£1980 DM5786 ¥495990

SHANTI-DEVA [P02/115] Silver Violin Bow 850/1190 **129**
£76 DM213 ¥18633

SILVESTRE & MAUCOTEL [S11/261] Silver Violin Bow: Paris, c. 1910 1376/1965 **3675**
£1870 DM5464 ¥468435

SIMON (attributed to) [C03/288] Silver Violin Bow 1954/2442 **2149**
£1320 DM3676 ¥339372

SIMON, PAUL [S11/341] Silver Violin Bow: Paris (Cyril Jacklin, Hailsham, June 29, 1985) 4913/6877 **NS**

SIMON, PAUL (ascribed to) [S03/111] Interesting Silver Violin Bow: Paris 7695/9405 **NS**

SIMONIN [B04/309] Silver French Violin Bow in good condition: c. 1930 1190/1785 **1131**
£691 DM1900 ¥180009

STOESS, A. [B04/281] Silver German Violin Bow in very good condition: c. 1920 298/476 **327**
£200 DM550 ¥52108

SUSS, CHRISTIAN [P09/222] Silver Violin Bow 281/467 **535**
£286 DM847 ¥73531

TAYLOR, MALCOLM [S03/77] Silver Violin Bow 684/1026 **NS**

TAYLOR, MALCOLM [S03/84] Gold Violin Bow 855/1197 **752**
£440 DM1219 ¥111496

TAYLOR, MALCOLM [S06/249] Gold Violin Bow 1026/1368 **1223**
£715 DM2065 ¥188188

THIBOUVILLE-LAMY [P09/193] Silver Violin Bow minus hair 374/561 **453**
£242 DM716 ¥62218

THIBOUVILLE-LAMY [P09/227] Silver Violin Bow
467/655 **329**
£176 DM521 ¥45250

THIBOUVILLE-LAMY [P09/231] Silver French Violin Bow: c. 1930 748/935 **NS**

THIBOUVILLE-LAMY [P11/257] Silver French Violin Bow: c. 1930 590/786 **692**
£352 DM1016 ¥89091

THIBOUVILLE-LAMY [C11/231] Silver Violin Bow w/bow 1576/1970 **NS**

THOMA, MATHIAS [S03/269] Silver Violin Bow
513/855 **NS**

THOMASSIN, CLAUDE [Sk11/84B] Silver Violin Bow
800/1200 **2090**
£1066 DM3114 ¥269610

THOMASSIN, CLAUDE [S03/109] Silver Violin Bow: Paris 1710/2565 **2257**
£1320 DM3656 ¥334488

THOMASSIN, CLAUDE [S03/279] Nickel Violin Bow: Paris 855/1026 **NS**

THOMASSIN, CLAUDE [S03/88] Silver Violin Bow: Paris 1026/1368 **1599**
£935 DM2590 ¥236929

THOMASSIN, CLAUDE [C11/223] Nickel Violin Bow
1182/1576 **2384**
£1210 DM3511 ¥303226

THOMASSIN, CLAUDE (attributed to) [C03/263] Silver Violin Bow 814/1140 **1254**
£770 DM2144 ¥197967

TOURTE, FRANCOIS [Sk11/91] Gold and Tortoiseshell Violin Bow grafted head on the stick
3000/5000 **4950**
£2524 DM7376 ¥638550

TOURTE, FRANCOIS [S06/124] Silver Violin Bow: Paris, c. 1800 (W. E. Hill & Sons, London, February 25, 1937) 11970/15390 **NS**

TOURTE, FRANCOIS [S06/143] Silver Violin Bow: Paris, c. 1780 13680/20520 **16929**
£9900 DM28586 ¥2605680

TOURTE, FRANCOIS [C11/285] Fine Silver Violin Bow: (Jean-Jacques Millant, December 6, 1988)
39400/59100 **43340**
£22000 DM63844 ¥5513200

TOURTE, LOUIS [C11/224] Silver Violin Bow
2955/3940 **3901**
£1980 DM5746 ¥496188

TOURTE, LOUIS (attributed to) [C11/228] Ivory Violin Bow 2955/3940 **4117**
£2090 DM6065 ¥523754

TUBBS, EDWARD [S06/25] Silver Violin Bow: London
4788/5985 **6584**
£3850 DM11117 ¥1013320

TUBBS, EDWARD [C03/63] Silver Violin Bow
651/977 **1074**
£660 DM1838 ¥169686

TUBBS, JAMES [Sk11/94] Silver Violin Bow
1000/1200 **2310**
£1178 DM3442 ¥297990

TUBBS, JAMES [P03/119] Silver Violin Bow slight finger wear on shaft 986/1315 **2532**
£1540 DM4270 ¥393932

TUBBS, JAMES [P03/258] Violin Bow: c. 1880
2466/3288 **NS**

TUBBS, JAMES [P06/200] Silver Violin Bow: c. 1880 864/1382 **4181**
£2420 DM7006 ¥644688

TUBBS, JAMES [P06/269] Silver Violin Bow: c. 1780 1037/1555 **4371**
£2530 DM7324 ¥673992

TUBBS, JAMES [P11/212] Silver Violin Bow
590/786 **646**
£329 DM949 ¥83245

TUBBS, JAMES [S11/61] Silver Violin Bow w/box: London, c. 1880 (Rushworth & Dreaper, Liverpool, September 3, 1956) 3930/5895 **4755**
£2420 DM7071 ¥606210

TUBBS, JAMES [S11/83] Silver Violin Bow: London
2948/3930 **3891**
£1980 DM5786 ¥495990

TUBBS, JAMES [B04/109] Silver English Violin Bow in very good condition: London, second half, 19th C.
3570/4165 **3273**
£2001 DM5500 ¥521080

TUBBS, JAMES [B04/112] Silver English Violin Bow in very good condition: London, late 19th C.
4165/4760 **2975**
£1819 DM5000 ¥473709

TUBBS, JAMES [S03/93] Silver Violin Bow: London
3420/5130 **3762**
£2200 DM6094 ¥557480

TUBBS, JAMES [S06/123] Silver Violin Bow: London
4788/5985 **5079**
£2970 DM8576 ¥781704

TUBBS, JAMES [S06/141] Silver Violin Bow: London
2565/3420 **2822**
£1650 DM4764 ¥434280

TUBBS, JAMES [S06/254] Silver Violin Bow: London
2565/3420 **3010**
£1760 DM5082 ¥463232

TUBBS, JAMES [S06/333] Silver Violin Bow w/case, cover, violin: London (H. Milne, London, March 9, 1915) 2565/3420 **4326**
£2530 DM7305 ¥665896

TUBBS, JAMES [S06/341] Silver Violin Bow head damaged: London, c. 1870 855/1368 **941**
£550 DM1588 ¥144760

TUBBS, JAMES [S06/344] Silver Violin Bow head damaged: London 2052/2736 **1881**
£1100 DM3176 ¥289520

TUBBS, JAMES [C11/213] Silver Violin Bow
788/1182 **NS**

TUBBS, JAMES [C11/248] Silver Violin Bow
1970/2955 **2167**
£1100 DM3192 ¥275660

TUBBS, JAMES [C11/264] Silver Violin Bow
4728/5516 **2817**
£1430 DM4150 ¥358358

TUBBS, JAMES [C11/265] Silver Violin Bow: (Joseph Roda, October 18, 1967) 4728/5516 **NS**

TUBBS, JAMES [C06/234] Silver Violin Bow 860/1376 **NS**

TUBBS, JAMES [C06/258] Silver Violin Bow 2580/4300 **3216**
£1870 DM5404 ¥492876

TUBBS, WILLIAM [P10/104] Silver Violin Bow some restoration and wear at handle: c. 1850 980/1372 **1289**
£658 DM1945 ¥161424

TUBBS, WILLIAM [S03/95] Silver Violin Bow w/case, cover, violin, bow: London 2565/4275 **3010**
£1760 DM4875 ¥445984

TUBBS, WILLIAM (attributed to) [P10/115] English Violin Bow stick attributed to Tubbs, w/bow 392/588 **647**
£330 DM976 ¥80982

TUBBS FAMILY, (MEMBER OF) [S11/239] Silver Violin Bow: London, c. 1840 1965/2948 **NS**

TUBBS FAMILY, (MEMBER OF) [S03/262] Silver Violin Bow: London, c. 1840 1710/2565 **NS**

VAN DER MEER, KAREL [P07/133] Silver Violin Bow 546/728 **NS**

VAN DER MEER, KAREL [P11/186] Silver Violin Bow 393/590 **696**
£354 DM1022 ¥89648

VAN DER MEER, KAREL [S11/345] Gold and Tortoiseshell Violin Bow: Amsterdam 1965/2948 **2270**
£1155 DM3375 ¥289328

VAN DER MEER, KAREL [S03/290] Silver Violin Bow: Amsterdam 855/1197 **1035**
£605 DM1676 ¥153307

VIDOUDEZ, FRANCOIS [S03/278] Silver Violin Bow w/violin bow: Geneva 855/1368 **1129**
£660 DM1828 ¥167244

VIGNERON, ANDRE [Sk11/84C] Silver Violin Bow 1600/1800 **2420**
£1234 DM3606 ¥312180

VIGNERON, ANDRE [S11/235] Silver Violin Bow: Paris 1179/1572 **2378**
£1210 DM3536 ¥303105

VIGNERON, ANDRE [S06/36] Silver Violin Bow: Paris 1197/1539 **1317**
£770 DM2223 ¥202664

VIGNERON, ANDRE [S06/37] Silver Violin Bow: Paris 1368/1710 **1881**
£1100 DM3176 ¥289520

VILLAUME, G. [B04/302] Silver French Violin Bow in very good condition: Nancy, c. 1930 595/1190 **357**
£218 DM600 ¥56845

VOIGT, ARNOLD [P09/228] Silver Violin Bow 374/561 **741**
£396 DM1172 ¥101812

VOIRIN, FRANCOIS NICOLAS [P06/262] Silver Violin Bow: (Rushworth & Dreaper, Liverpool, 1947) 1209/1555 **3610**
£2090 DM6051 ¥556776

VOIRIN, FRANCOIS NICOLAS [P11/143] Silver Violin Bow 1179/1572 **2162**
£1100 DM3174 ¥278410

VOIRIN, FRANCOIS NICOLAS [S11/221] Silver Violin Bow: Paris, c. 1860 5895/6877 **5836**
£2970 DM8678 ¥743985

VOIRIN, FRANCOIS NICOLAS [S11/251] Silver Violin Bow: Paris 4913/6877 **7133**
£3630 DM10607 ¥909315

VOIRIN, FRANCOIS NICOLAS [S11/59] Gold and Tortoiseshell Violin Bow: Paris 7860/11790 **9943**
£5060 DM14785 ¥1267530

VOIRIN, FRANCOIS NICOLAS [B04/117] Silver French Violin Bow in very good condition: Paris, c. 1860 5950/7140 **NS**

VOIRIN, FRANCOIS NICOLAS [S03/252] Silver Violin Bow: Paris 4275/5130 **4703**
£2750 DM7617 ¥56845

VOIRIN, FRANCOIS NICOLAS [S03/274] Silver Violin Bow: Paris 4275/5130 **4703**
£2750 DM7617 ¥696850

VOIRIN, FRANCOIS NICOLAS [S03/81] Silver Violin Bow: Paris 4275/5985 **6772**
£3960 DM10969 ¥1003464

VOIRIN, FRANCOIS NICOLAS [S06/47] Silver Violin Bow: Paris 2565/3420 **3950**
£2310 DM6670 ¥607992

VOIRIN, FRANCOIS NICOLAS [C11/272] Fine Gold Violin Bow 9850/13790 **16253**
£8250 DM23941 ¥2067450

VOIRIN, FRANCOIS NICOLAS [C11/274] Gold Violin Bow 6895/8865 **NS**

VOIRIN, FRANCOIS NICOLAS [C11/277] Silver Violin Bow 4925/6895 **5634**
£2860 DM8300 ¥716716

VOIRIN, FRANCOIS NICOLAS [C06/253] Silver Violin Bow 3440/5160 **5676**
£3300 DM9537 ¥869781

VOIRIN, FRANCOIS NICOLAS [C03/294] Silver Violin Bow 4070/4884 **5372**
£3300 DM9190 ¥848430

VOIRIN, J. [B04/89] Nickel French Violin Bow in good condition 595/893 **714**
£437 DM1200 ¥113690

VOIRIN, JOSEPH [P03/159] Silver Violin Bow 658/822 **832**
£506 DM1403 ¥129435

VUILLAUME, JEAN BAPTISTE [Sk11/85] Silver Violin Bow: Paris 800/1200 **2090**
£1066 DM3114 ¥269610

VUILLAUME, JEAN BAPTISTE [Sk11/96] Silver Violin Bow 2000/3000 **2420**
£1234 DM3606 ¥312180

VUILLAUME, JEAN BAPTISTE [S06/371] Silver Violin Bow: Paris, c. 1870 2565/3420 **NS**

VUILLAUME, JEAN BAPTISTE (ascribed to) [S03/292] Silver Violin Bow 1368/1710 **2069**
£1210 DM3352 ¥306614

VUILLAUME, JEAN BAPTISTE (workshop of) [C11/258] Silver Violin Bow: (Dario D'Attili, April 25, 1984) 3546/4925 **7585**
£3850 DM11173 ¥964810

WALTON, WILLIAM [S06/225] Gold Violin Bow: Paris, c. 1830 (Hart & Son, London, December 6, 1935) 5985/8550 **NS**

WEICHOLD, A. R. [P03/259] Silver Violin Bow 329/493 **470**
£286 DM793 ¥73159

WEICHOLD, R. [P03/267] Silver Violin Bow 132/247 **579**
£352 DM976 ¥90042

WEICHOLD, R. [P06/309] Good Silver Violin Bow: Dresden 432/605 **646**
£374 DM1083 ¥99634

WEICHOLD, R. [P06/320] Silver Violin Bow 432/605 **760**
£440 DM1274 ¥117216

WEICHOLD, R. [P09/223] Silver Violin Bow 327/467 **617**
£330 DM977 ¥84843

WEICHOLD, R. [P09/237] Silver Violin Bow 374/561 **535**
£286 DM847 ¥73531

WEICHOLD, RICHARD [Sk11/56] Silver Violin Bow: Dresden 250/350 **495**
£252 DM738 ¥63855

WEICHOLD, RICHARD [P10/112] Silver Violin Bow minus hair, ferule replaced: Dresden 196/294 **280**
£143 DM423 ¥35092

WEICHOLD, RICHARD [S06/335] Silver Violin Bow: Dresden 513/684 **NS**

WEICHOLD, RICHARD [C11/245] Silver Violin Bow w/bow 1576/1970 **NS**

WEICHOLD, RICHARD [C03/96] Silver Violin Bow 488/651 **1164**
£715 DM1991 ¥183826

WEICHOLD, RICHARD [C03/99] Silver Violin Bow 814/1140 **1433**
£880 DM2451 ¥226248

WEIDHAAS, PAUL [B04/295] Silver German Violin Bow in very good condition: Markneukirchen, c. 1930 595/1190 **714**
£437 DM1200 ¥113690

WEIDHAAS, PAUL [B04/304] Gold and Tortoiseshell German Violin Bow in very good condition: Markneukirchen, c. 1930 1071/1488 **3094**
£1892 DM5200 ¥492657

WEIDHAAS, PAUL [C11/241A] Silver Violin Bow 985/1379 **1084**
£550 DM1596 ¥137830

WEIDHAAS, PAUL [C03/265] Silver Violin Bow 326/488 **394**
£242 DM674 ¥62218

WEIDHAAS, PAUL [C03/285] Silver Violin Bow 488/651 **537**
£330 DM919 ¥84843

WERRO, JEAN [P10/106] Silver Violin Bow 490/686 **645**
£329 DM973 ¥80712

WILSON, GARNER [P02/108] Silver Violin Bow 510/680 **785**
£462 DM1298 ¥113421

WILSON, GARNER [P03/120] Good Silver Violin Bow 822/986 **NS**

WILSON, GARNER [P06/301] Good Silver Violin Bow 605/777 **NS**

WILSON, GARNER [P06/310] Silver Violin Bow 345/518 **418**
£242 DM701 ¥64469

WILSON, GARNER [S11/343] Gold and Tortoiseshell Violin Bow: Bury St. Edmunds 1572/1965 **1405**
£715 DM2089 ¥179108

WILSON, GARNER [S11/44] Gold Violin Bow: Bury St. Edmunds 1179/1768 **NS**

WILSON, GARNER [S06/239] Silver Violin Bow 1197/1539 **NS**

WILSON, GARNER [S06/27] Gold and Tortoiseshell Violin Bow: Bury St. Edmunds 1710/2565 **NS**

WILSON, JAMES J. T. [P09/189] Silver Violin Bow 281/467 **1337**
£715 DM2116 ¥183826

WILSON, JAMES J. T. [P10/95] Silver Violin Bow 490/686 **733**
£374 DM1106 ¥91780

WINKLER, FRANZ [P07/154] Silver Violin Bow w/bow 455/637 **645**
£354 DM1041 ¥96378

WINKLER, FRANZ [S11/347] Gold and Tortoiseshell German Violin Bow 1179/1572 **NS**

WINTERLING, GEORGE [B04/284] Silver German Violin Bow in very good condition: Hamburg, c. 1920 417/714 **387**
£237 DM650 ¥61582

WOODFIELD, J. D. [P10/117] Silver Violin Bow 392/588 **NS**

WUNDERLICH, F. R. [C06/257] Gold Violin Bow 1204/1720 **1419**
£825 DM2384 ¥217445

ZIMMER, E. W. [B04/294] Silver German Violin Bow in good condition: c. 1960 417/536 **357**
£218 DM600 ¥56845

VIOLONCELLO

AIRETON, EDMUND (attributed to) [P02/142] English Violoncello w/cover, bow, fair condition 1020/1360 **2992**
£1760 DM4946 ¥432080

BAILLY, PAUL (ascribed to) [S06/308] French Violoncello: Paris 3420/5130 **NS**

BANKS, JAMES & HENRY (attributed to) [P07/165] Violoncello 5460/9100 **NS**

BANKS, JAMES & HENRY (attributed to) [P09/254] Violoncello minus lower right corner on the back: c. 1780 5610/7480 **5348**
£2860 DM8466 ¥735306

BARRETT, JOHN [S11/305] English Violoncello: London, 1741 11790/15720 **NS**

BETTS, JOHN [S11/324] English Violoncello: London, c. 1800 23580/29475 **33503**
£17050 DM49820 ¥4271025

BOULANGEOT, EMILE [S11/310] French Violoncello w/case: Lyon, 1925 (Etienne Vatelot, Paris, March 5, 1985) 9825/9825 **9727**
£4950 DM14464 ¥1239975

BOULANGEOT, EMILE [S03/156] French Violoncello w/case: Lyon, 1925 (Etienne Vatelot, Paris, March 5, 1985) 10260/13680 **NS**

CAPPA, GOFFREDO [S11/312] Violoncello w/case: Saluzzo, late 17th C. (W. H. Tibbalds, Brighton, July 9, 1938) 23580/31440 **37826**
£19250 DM56248 ¥4822125

CONIA, STEFANO [S03/180] Italian Violoncello w/case: Cremona, 1973 (Maker's, June 17, 1973) 13680/17100 **14108**
£8250 DM22852 ¥2090550

CONTINO, ALFREDO (attributed to) [P11/282] Italian Violoncello w/cover: (Lennart Lee, Gotheborg, September, 1988) 5895/7860 **6052**
£3080 DM8886 ¥779548

CORSBY, GEORGE (attributed to) [C11/90] English Violoncello 3940/5910 **3467**
£1760 DM5108 ¥441056

CRASKE, GEORGE [C03/228] English Violoncello: 1830 1628/3256 **6805**
£4180 DM11641 ¥1074678

CROSS, NATHANIEL [S06/330] Fine English Violoncello w/case: London, 1733 (W. E. Hill & Sons, London, October 19, 1938) 11970/15390 **16929**
£9900 DM28586 ¥2605680

DE COMBLE, AMBROSE [S11/332] Violoncello w/cover: Tournai, mid 18th C. 3930/5895 **4107**
£2090 DM6107 ¥523545

DEGANI, EUGENIO [P06/348] Violoncello minus small part of top right corner back, lower rib repair: Venice, 1894 25912/34550 **25653**
£14850 DM42991 ¥3956040

DERAZEY, HONORE (workshop of) [C11/96] French Violoncello 3940/5910 **9101**
£4620 DM13407 ¥1157772

DERAZEY, JUSTIN [P09/272] French Violoncello minus the front, neck with graft and fingerboard: c. 1875 748/1122 **1481**
£792 DM2344 ¥203623

DIEHL, JOHANN [S03/181] Violoncello w/case, bow: Mainz, 1831 5130/8550 **28967**
£16940 DM46924 ¥4292596

DODD, THOMAS [C03/247] English Violoncello: Covent Garden (L. P. Balmforth, June 30, 1955) 9768/13024 **15466**
£9500 DM26457 ¥2442450

DUKE, RICHARD [S03/171] Violoncello: London, c. 1760 5130/8550 **3010**
£1760 DM4875 ¥445984

FORSTER, WILLIAM [S11/336] Violoncello w/case, "The Royal George": London, c. 1790 58950/78600 **NS**

FURBER, HENRY [S06/329] Violoncello w/case: London, 1886 4275/5985 **8653**
£5060 DM14611 ¥1331792

FURBER, JOHN [P02/149] Violoncello: St. Luke, 1820 136/306 **860**
£506 DM1422 ¥124223

FURBER, JOHN (attributed to) [P07/164] Good Violoncello 6370/9100 **7407**
£4070 DM11958 ¥1107447

GADDA, GAETANO [B04/182] Violoncello in perfect condition: Mantua, 1953 16660/19040 **15470**
£9461 DM26000 ¥2463287

GAFFINO, JOSEPH [S11/325] Violoncello: Paris, 1778 23580/29475 **NS**

GAGLIANO, GIOVANNI [S03/169] Italian Violoncello w/case, bow: Naples, c. 1805 30780/37620 **28215**
£16500 DM45705 ¥4181100

GOULDING & CO. [P06/366] English Violoncello w/cover: London, c. 1800 605/1123 **2185**
£1265 DM3662 ¥336996

GRANCINO, GIOVANNI [S11/330] Violoncello w/case, 2 bows, simulated purfling: Milan, c. 1700 78600/117900 **82137**
£41800 DM122140 ¥10470900

GUERSAN, LOUIS [S11/311] Violoncello w/case: Paris, 1738 13755/17685 **NS**

GUERSAN, LOUIS (ascribed to) [C11/108] French Violoncello: (Charles Enel, January 19, 1950) 15760/23640 **NS**

HARRIS, CHARLES [S11/307] English Violoncello w/case, 2 bows: London, c. 1800 7860/9825 **7781**
£3960 DM11571 ¥991980

HARRIS, CHARLES [S03/173] English Violoncello w/case, 2 bows: London, c. 1800 8550/11970 **NS**

HART & SON [S03/168] Violoncello w/case, bow: London, 1889 3078/4275 **3762**
£2200 DM6094 ¥557480

HILL, JOSEPH [S03/182] English Violoncello w/case: London, c. 1760 (W. E. Hill & Sons, London, December 10, 1908) 25650/34200 **22572**
£13200 DM36564 ¥3344880

HILL, LOCKEY (attributed to) [S11/334] Violoncello: (Ralph P. Powell, Smethwick, May 24, 1957) 3930/4913 **NS**

HJORTH, EMIL & SON [S03/172] Danish Violoncello w/cover: Copenhagen, 1944 6840/10260 **8465**
£4950 DM13711 ¥1254330

HOFMANS, MATHIAS [S11/322] Violoncello w/cover, 2 bows: Antwerp, c. 1700 5895/9825 **12969**
£6600 DM19285 ¥1653300

HOYER, JOHANN FRIEDERICH [S11/315] German Violoncello w/cover, bow: Klingenthal, 1766 5895/7860 **NS**

HOYER, JOHANN FRIEDERICH [S06/307] German Violoncello w/cover, bow: Klingenthal, 1766
6840/10260 **NS**

HUBICKA, JULIUS A. [C06/201] Good Violoncello w/case: Prague, 1926 10320/13760 **17028**
£9900 DM28611 ¥2609343

JAIS, ANDREAS [S06/298] Child's Violoncello w/case: Tolz, 1713 1710/3420 **2633**
£1540 DM4447 ¥405328

JOHNSON, JOHN (attributed to) [P09/262] Violoncello w/cover, minus two table corners, painted purfling 7480/11220 **NS**

JORIO, VINCENZO [S03/165] Fine Violoncello w/case, 2 bows: Naples, c. 1840
17100/25650 **16929**
£9900 DM27423 ¥2508660

KENNEDY, THOMAS [S06/326] Violoncello w/case, 2 bows: London, mid 19th C. 8550/11970 **14108**
£8250 DM23822 ¥2171400

KENNEDY, THOMAS (ascribed to) [S11/327] Small Violoncello w/case: London 5895/9825 **5404**
£2750 DM8035 ¥688875

KREUZINGER, FRIEDRICH [Sk11/45] Modern German Violoncello w/case 1200/1500 **1320**
£673 DM1967 ¥170280

KRINER, JOSEPH [S03/175] Violoncello: Wurzburg, 1851 5130/6840 **4703**
£2750 DM7617 ¥696850

LABERTE-HUMBERT BROS. [P11/286] Violoncello w/cover, 2 bows: Mirecourt, 1927 982/1572 **4539**
£2310 DM6664 ¥584661

LEEB, ANDREAS CARL [S06/296] Austrian Violoncello w/cover, bow: Vienna, 1807
5130/8550 **7900**
£4620 DM13340 ¥1215984

LONGMAN & BRODERIP [S11/314] Composite English Violoncello inked simulated purfling: late 18th C. 2948/3930 **NS**

LONGMAN & BRODERIP [S03/176] Composite English Violoncello: late 18th C. 2565/3420 **NS**

LONGMAN & BRODERIP [C11/95] English Violoncello: London 7880/9850 **NS**

LONGMAN & LUKEY [C03/233] English Violoncello: London 1628/3256 **8596**
£5280 DM14705 ¥1357488

LONGMAN & LUKEY [C03/252] English Violoncello: London 13024/16280 **13431**
£8250 DM22976 ¥2121075

LOWENDALL, LOUIS [S06/300] Violoncello w/cover: Berlin, 1899 2052/3078 **4138**
£2420 DM6988 ¥636944

MARCHI, GIOVANNI ANTONIO [S06/299] Violoncello w/case: Bologna, 1764 10260/13680 **27275**
£15950 DM46056 ¥4198040

NAMY, JEAN THEODORE [S06/294] French Violoncello w/cover, Baroque specification: Paris, late 18th C. 17100/20520 **NS**

NEUNER & HORNSTEINER [S11/323] Violoncello w/cover: Mittenwald, 1889 4913/6877 **7133**
£3630 DM10607 ¥909315

NEUNER & HORNSTEINER [S03/167] Bavarian Violoncello w/case: Mittenwald, 1862
5985/7695 **NS**

NICOLAS [C06/203] Good French Violoncello w/case: Paris, 1806 17200/25800 **17028**
£9900 DM28611 ¥2609343

OTTO, MAX [Sk11/48] German Violoncello w/case: Markneukirchen, early 20th C. 1800/2200 **NS**

OWEN, JOHN W. [P09/257] Good Violoncello: Leeds, 1926 6545/9350 **8639**
£4620 DM13675 ¥1187802

PILLEMENT, FRANCOIS [P03/305] Violoncello w/cover: Paris, c. 1800 1973/2630 **NS**

PILLEMENT, FRANCOIS [S11/331] Violoncello w/cover: Mirecourt, c. 1800 5895/9825 **NS**

PRECUB, FLOREA [B04/82] Romanian Violoncello in very good condition: 1971 4165/5355 **3868**
£2365 DM6500 ¥615822

PRESCOTT, GRAHAM [S06/295] Violoncello w/case: Concord, late 19th C. 1026/1368 **846**
£495 DM1429 ¥130284

PRESTON, JAMES [P02/144] English Violoncello w/cover, lower center back joint open: London, c. 1760 1020/1360 **2899**
£1705 DM4791 ¥418578

PURDAY, T. E. [C03/227] English Violoncello: London 4884/6512 **11640**
£7150 DM19913 ¥1838265

PYNE, GEORGE [S06/297] Violoncello: London, c. 1910 5130/8550 **7900**
£4620 DM13340 ¥1215984

QUARGNAL, RUDOLFO [B04/60] Italian Violoncello in good condition: Gradisca d'Isonzo, 1978
4760/5950 **4165**
£2547 DM7000 ¥663193

RAMBAUX, CLAUDE VICTOR [S03/153] Violoncello w/case: Paris, c. 1840 17100/25650 **NS**

RAUTMANN, CARL [S06/325] Violoncello: Brunswick, 1853 3420/5130 **6395**
£3740 DM10799 ¥984368

RICHARDSON, ARTHUR [C11/105] English Violoncello w/case: Crediton Devon, 1921
9850/11820 **9752**
£4950 DM14365 ¥1240470

RICHARDSON, ARTHUR [C03/229] English Violoncello w/case: Devon, 1921 9768/13024 **NS**

ROCCA, ENRICO [S11/328] Fine Violoncello w/case: Genoa, 1906 (Peter Paul Prier, Salt Lake City, April 28, 1978) 98250/137550 **NS**

ROCCA, ENRICO (attributed to) [S03/147] Violoncello w/case: Genoa, 1901 (Friederich Bohm, Berlin, April 4, 1970) 42750/59850 **NS**

RODIANI, GIOVITA (attributed to) [Sk11/44] Interesting Violoncello w/case: (Rudolf Wurlitzer, New York, September 10, 1947) 6000/8000 **6600**
£3366 DM9834 ¥851400

ROGERI, GIOVANNI BATTISTA (ascribed to) [S06/293] Italian Violoncello w/case 59850/85500 **NS**

ROTH, ERNST HEINRICH [P11/274] Fine Violoncello: Bubenreuth Erlangen, 1970 3930/5895 **7565**
£3850 DM11107 ¥974435

ROTTENBURGH, JEAN HYACINTHE [S06/304] Violoncello w/case: Brussels, 1753 (Hug & Co., Zurich, March 30, 1962) 13680/20520 **15424**
£9020 DM26045 ¥2374064

RUGGIERI & GUARNERI, FRANCESCO & P. [S11/329] Italian Violoncello w/case: (Raymond Casey, Worcester, August 29, 1956) 35370/43230 **45392**
£23100 DM67498 ¥5786550

RUSHWORTH & DREAPER [C11/102] English Violoncello: 1922 6895/8865 **NS**

SCHUTZ [S11/316] Violoncello 2948/3930 **3026**
£1540 DM4500 ¥385770

SGARBI, GIUSEPPE [B04/190] Important Italian Violoncello in very good condition: Modena, 1893 29750/35700 **27370**
£16739 DM46000 ¥4358123

SMITH, THOMAS [P06/360] Violoncello w/cover, bow: London, 1760 2591/4319 **3420**
£1980 DM5732 ¥527472

SMITH, THOMAS (attributed to) [P03/304] Violoncello 3288/4932 **5407**
£3289 DM9120 ¥841326

SORSANO, SPIRITO (attributed to) [S11/333] Fine Violoncello: (Emile Francais, Paris, December 12, 1951) 29475/39300 **30261**
£15400 DM44999 ¥3857700

STEWART, N. [S03/178] Violoncello w/case, bow: mid 19th C. 8550/11970 **13030**
£7620 DM21107 ¥1930908

SYMINGTON, GEORGE [P06/347] Scottish Violoncello w/bow, restoration on table: Kilmarnock, August, 1883 518/691 **1330**
£770 DM2229 ¥205128

TESTORE FAMILY (MEMBER OF) (attributed to) [S03/160] Italian Violoncello: c. 1700 (Chardon & fils, Paris, January 8, 1958) 17100/25650 **19751**
£11550 DM31993 ¥2926770

THIBOUVILLE-LAMY [P09/265] Violoncello w/cover: Mirecourt, c. 1900 2805/4675 **3086**
£1650 DM4884 ¥424215

THIBOUVILLE-LAMY, J. [P06/334] Good French Violoncello minor open crack lower left table: Paris, c. 1900 2073/3109 **5701**
£3300 DM9553 ¥879120

TIRIOT [B04/319] French Violoncello: Paris, c. 1800 1190/1785 **833**
£509 DM1400 ¥132639

TOBIN, RICHARD [S03/151] Fine Violoncello w/case, 2 bows: London, early 19th C. (W. E. Hill & Sons, London, February 17, 1948) 17100/25650 **23513**
£13750 DM38087 ¥3484250

TOBIN, RICHARD (ascribed to) [S11/338] English Violoncello w/case: London, early 19th C. 9825/11790 **NS**

VENTAPANE, LORENZO [S06/313] Small Italian Violoncello w/case, 2 bows: Naples, first quarter, 19th C. 17100/25650 **NS**

VUILLAUME, JEAN BAPTISTE [S03/161] Fine French Violoncello: Paris, 1855 59850/85500 **NS**

VUILLAUME, JEAN BAPTISTE (workshop of) [C03/251] French Violoncello: Paris, 1842 24420/32560 **26862**
£16500 DM45952 ¥4242150

WAMSLEY, PETER [P06/361] Violoncello w/case, bow, minor restoration and overall cleaning required: London, c. 1730 13820/20730 **NS**

WAMSLEY, PETER [P11/277] Violoncello w/case, bow: London, c. 1730 15720/18668 **NS**

WAMSLEY, PETER [S03/157] English Violoncello w/cover: London, mid 18th C. 5130/6840 **NS**

WERNER, ERICH [P02/135] Violoncello good condition: Bubenreuth, 1988 1360/1700 **1683**
£990 DM2782 ¥243045

WIDHALM, LEOPOLD [S11/339] Violoncello w/case: Nuremburg, c. 1770 13755/19650 **NS**

WOLFF BROS. [S03/155] Violoncello: Kreuznach, 1896 2565/4275 **5267**
£3080 DM8532 ¥780472

VIOLONCELLO BOW

ADAM, J. [B04/115] Silver French Violoncello Bow in excellent condition: Mirecourt, late 18th C. 3570/4760 **3570**
£2183 DM6000 ¥568451

ALVEY, BRIAN [S03/113] Silver Violoncello Bow: Sunbury-on-Thames 1197/1710 **NS**

BAUSCH [P09/199] Nickel Violoncello Bow 281/374 **329**
£176 DM521 ¥45250

BAUSCH [P11/187] Violoncello Bow w/4 bows 393/590 **298**
£152 DM438 ¥38421

BAUSCH, L. [P09/205] Silver Violoncello Bow 281/467 **411**
£220 DM651 ¥56562

BAUSCH, L. (attributed to) [P09/204] Silver Violoncello Bow 318/467 **329**
£176 DM521 ¥45250

BAZIN [C03/257] Silver Violoncello Bow 488/814 **1164**
£715 DM1991 ¥183826

BAZIN, CHARLES [C03/92] Silver Violoncello Bow 977/1302 **1164**
£715 DM1991 ¥183826

BAZIN, CHARLES NICHOLAS [S11/352] Silver French Violoncello Bow: Mirecourt (Pierre Guillaume, Brussels, June 8, 1989) 1376/1965 **2162**
£1100 DM3214 ¥275550

BAZIN, CHARLES NICHOLAS [S06/367] Gold Violoncello Bow: Mirecourt, c. 1900 1710/2565 **1787**
£1045 DM3017 ¥275044

BAZIN, LOUIS [S11/233] Silver Violoncello Bow: Mirecourt, c. 1930 1572/2358 **1513**
£770 DM2250 ¥192885

BROWN, JAMES (attributed to) [P09/219] Silver Violoncello Bow minus lapping: c. 1830 561/748 **NS**

BROWN, JAMES (attributed to) [P11/220] Silver Violoncello Bow minus lapping 393/590 **476**
£242 DM698 ¥61250

BRYANT, PERCIVAL WILFRED [S06/355] Silver Violoncello Bow: Brighton 855/1197 **NS**

BRYANT, PERCIVAL WILFRED [S06/357] Silver Violoncello Bow w/2 bows: Brighton 855/1197 **1223**
£715 DM2065 ¥188188

BULTITUDE, A. R. [P11/236] Silver Violoncello Bow 1179/1572 **1989**
£1012 DM2920 ¥256137

CUNIOT-HURY [S11/47] Silver Violoncello Bow: Mirecourt 982/1376 **NS**

DODD, JOHN [S11/245] Composite Silver Violoncello Bow stick by John Dodd, head pinned: Kew, c. 1830 (Rembert Wurlitzer, New York, July 8, 1957) 590/982 **540**
£275 DM804 ¥68888

DODD, JOHN [S06/349] Silver and Ivory Violoncello Bow: Kew, c. 1830 3420/5130 **3386**
£1980 DM5717 ¥521136

DODD FAMILY (MEMBER OF) [S11/231] Silver Violoncello Bow: London, first half, 19th C. 1965/2948 **2053**
£1045 DM3053 ¥261773

DOLLING, HEINZ [P11/247] Silver Violoncello Bow 491/688 **646**
£329 DM949 ¥83245

DOLLING, HEINZ [S11/260] Chased Gold Violoncello Bow: Wurnitzgrun 1965/2948 **NS**

DORFLER, D. [P07/149] 5 Violoncello Bows 364/546 **1658**
£911 DM2676 ¥247829

DORFLER, EGIDIUS [S06/33] Gold Violoncello Bow w/3 bows 1539/2394 **2069**
£1210 DM3494 ¥318472

DUPUY, GEORGE [S03/247] Silver Violoncello Bow: Paris 2052/3078 **1599**
£935 DM2590 ¥236929

DURRSCHMIDT, O. [B04/292] Silver German Violoncello Bow in very good condition: c. 1970 417/595 **357**
£218 DM600 ¥56845

EULRY, CLEMENT [C06/265] Silver Violoncello Bow 2580/3096 **NS**

FETIQUE, VICTOR [S06/44] Silver Violoncello Bow: Paris 4275/5130 **NS**

FETIQUE, VICTOR [S06/46] Silver Violoncello Bow: Paris 5130/6840 **NS**

FETIQUE, VICTOR [C06/236] Silver Violoncello Bow 1720/2580 **2649**
£1540 DM4451 ¥405898

FETIQUE, VICTOR (ascribed to) [S03/248] Gold Violoncello Bow stick repaired at handle: Paris 1710/2565 **NS**

FINKEL, SIEGFRIED [Sk11/72] Gold Violoncello Bow 800/1200 **1430**
£729 DM2131 ¥184470

FORSTER [C06/266] Silver Violoncello Bow 3440/4300 **3406**
£1980 DM5722 ¥521869

FRITSCH, JEAN [P06/349] Silver Violoncello Bow 432/864 **798**
£462 DM1337 ¥123077

GEROME, ROGER [P10/137] Good Silver and Tortoiseshell Violoncello Bow: Mirecourt 1176/1764 **NS**

GLESEL, C. [S11/76] Silver Violoncello Bow: Paris 982/1572 **NS**

GLESEL, C. [S06/241] Silver Violoncello Bow: Paris 855/1368 **NS**

HART [P10/139] Silver Violoncello Bow 784/1176 **992**
£506 DM1496 ¥124172

HART & SON [P09/201] Fine Silver Violoncello Bow 1309/1683 **1748**
£935 DM2768 ¥240389

HERMANN, LOTHAR [C11/202] Silver Violoncello Bow 788/1182 **NS**

HERMANN, LOTHAR [C03/60] Silver Violoncello Bow 814/977 **NS**

HILL, W. E. & SONS [Sk11/73] Silver Violoncello Bow 800/1000 **1100**
£561 DM1639 ¥141900

HILL, W. E. & SONS [Sk11/74A] Gold Violoncello Bow 2000/3000 **2530**
£1290 DM3770 ¥326370

HILL, W. E. & SONS [P02/120] Silver Violoncello Bow 680/1020 **1159**
£682 DM1916 ¥167431

HILL, W. E. & SONS [P06/357] Silver Violoncello Bow head pinned 691/1037 **874**
£506 DM1465 ¥134798

HILL, W. E. & SONS [P06/362] Good Silver Violoncello Bow 1382/1900 **2090**
£1210 DM3503 ¥322344

HILL, W. E. & SONS [P09/192A] Good Silver Violoncello Bow 1122/1496 **1604**
£858 DM2540 ¥220592

HILL, W. E. & SONS [P09/196] Silver Violoncello Bow 935/1309 **1892**
£1012 DM2996 ¥260185

HILL, W. E. & SONS [P09/197] Silver Violoncello Bow 935/1309 **1892**
£1012 DM2996 ¥260185

HILL, W. E. & SONS [P09/213] Good Silver Violoncello Bow 1870/2805 **2263**
£1210 DM3582 ¥311091

HILL, W. E. & SONS [P09/261] Silver Violoncello Bow 748/1122 **NS**

HILL, W. E. & SONS [P11/145] Silver Violoncello Bow 786/1179 **2378**
£1210 DM3491 ¥306251

HILL, W. E. & SONS [P11/237] Silver Violoncello Bow repair three inches from the head 491/688 **324**
£165 DM476 ¥41762

HILL, W. E. & SONS [S11/237] Silver Violoncello Bow: London 2948/3930 **3458**
£1760 DM5143 ¥440880

HILL, W. E. & SONS [S11/246] Silver Violoncello Bow: London 1376/1965 **NS**

HILL, W. E. & SONS [S11/68] Gold and Tortoiseshell Violoncello Bow head pinned: London 1965/2358 **3026**
£1540 DM4500 ¥385770

HILL, W. E. & SONS [S11/69] Silver Violoncello Bow head repaired: London 1179/1572 **NS**

HILL, W. E. & SONS [S11/74] Silver Violoncello Bow w/box: London 1965/2948 **1945**
£990 DM2893 ¥247995

HILL, W. E. & SONS [B04/311] Silver English Violoncello Bow in very good condition: London 2975/3570 **2083**
£1274 DM3500 ¥331596

HILL, W. E. & SONS [S03/263] Silver Violoncello Bow: London, 1928 1026/1368 **1166**
£682 DM1889 ¥172819

HILL, W. E. & SONS [S03/268] Silver Violoncello Bow: London 2052/2565 **NS**

HILL, W. E. & SONS [S03/285] Silver Violoncello Bow: London, 1932 1710/2565 **1693**
£990 DM2742 ¥250866

HILL, W. E. & SONS [S03/287] Silver Violoncello Bow: London 1710/2565 **1693**
£990 DM2742 ¥250866

HILL, W. E. & SONS [S06/240] Violoncello Bow: London 2565/3420 **NS**

HILL, W. E. & SONS [S06/348] Silver Violoncello Bow: London, 1953 1710/2565 **1505**
£880 DM2541 ¥231616

HILL, W. E. & SONS [S06/363] Silver Violoncello Bow: London 1368/2052 **NS**

HILL, W. E. & SONS [S06/366] Fine Gold and Tortoiseshell Violoncello Bow: London, 1931 3420/5130 **4514**
£2640 DM7623 ¥694848

HILL, W. E. & SONS [S06/380] Silver Violoncello Bow: London 2052/2565 **1599**
£935 DM2700 ¥246092

HILL, W. E. & SONS [C11/215] Silver Violoncello Bow 1182/1773 **1842**
£935 DM2713 ¥234311

HILL, W. E. & SONS [C06/217] Silver Violoncello Bow w/bow, replacement adjuster 860/1204 **1324**
£770 DM2225 ¥202949

HILL, W. E. & SONS [C06/226] Silver Violoncello Bow 860/1204 **1135**
£660 DM1907 ¥173956

HILL, W. E. & SONS [C06/262] Silver and Tortoiseshell Violoncello Bow 2580/3096 **3027**
£1760 DM5086 ¥463883

HILL, W. E. & SONS [C03/253] Silver Violoncello Bow 1140/1628 **1970**
£1210 DM3370 ¥311091

HILL, W. E. & SONS [C03/262] Silver Violoncello Bow 1628/2442 **1970**
£1210 DM3370 ¥311091

HILL, W. E. & SONS [C03/68] Silver Violoncello Bow 1140/1628 **1612**
£990 DM2757 ¥254529

HILL, W. E. & SONS [C03/83] Silver Violoncello Bow 814/1140 **1522**
£935 DM2604 ¥240388

HOYER, HERMANN ALBERT [P02/139] Silver Violoncello Bow small restoration required 340/510 **430**
£253 DM711 ¥62112

HOYER, OTTO A. [P03/255] Gold Violoncello Bow: 1925 2466/4110 **NS**

HUSSON, CHARLES CLAUDE [Sk11/74] Silver Violoncello Bow: Paris (Bernard Millant, Paris, December 2, 1985) 2500/3500 **3080**
£1571 DM4589 ¥397320

HUSSON, CHARLES CLAUDE [S03/117] Silver Violoncello Bow: Paris 3420/5130 **NS**

KNOPF [B04/283] Silver German Violoncello Bow in good condition: Dresden, 19th C. 476/595 **417**
£255 DM700 ¥66319

KNOPF, W. [Sk11/71] Silver Violoncello Bow: Dresden 800/1000 **880**
£449 DM1311 ¥113520

KUN, JOSEPH [C06/231] Silver Violoncello Bow 344/516 **416**
£242 DM699 ¥63784

LAMY, ALFRED [S11/266] Silver Violoncello Bow: Paris 4913/6877 **NS**

LAMY, ALFRED [S11/364] Silver Violoncello Bow: Paris 5895/7860 **NS**

LAMY, ALFRED [S03/104] Silver Violoncello Bow: Paris 1368/2052 **1317**
£770 DM2133 ¥195118

LAMY, ALFRED [C11/254] Silver Violoncello Bow 2955/4925 **NS**

LAMY, ALFRED [C03/72] Silver Violoncello Bow 4070/5698 **4477**
£2750 DM7659 ¥707025

LAPIERRE, MARCEL [P09/215] Silver Violoncello Bow 748/935 **1029**
£550 DM1628 ¥141405

LEBLANC, P. R. [B04/95] Silver Violoncello Bow in very good condition: c. 1960 714/952 **833**
£509 DM1400 ¥132639

LEBLANC, P. R. [B04/96] Silver Violoncello Bow in very good condition: c. 1960 714/952 **655**
£400 DM1100 ¥104216

LEBLANC, P. R. [B04/97] Silver Violoncello Bow in very good condition: c. 1960 714/952 **655**
£400 DM1100 ¥104216

LEBLANC, P. R. [B04/98] Gold Violoncello Bow in very good condition: c. 1960 1488/2083 **1428**
£873 DM2400 ¥227380

LEFIN [Sk11/70] Silver Violoncello Bow 400/500 **523**
£266 DM779 ¥67403

LOTTE, FRANCOIS [P02/121] Silver Violoncello Bow 510/680 **785**
£462 DM1298 ¥113421

LUPOT, NICOLAS [S06/45] Silver Violoncello Bow: Paris 3762/4788 **NS**

MALINES, GUILLAUME [S11/353] Silver French Violoncello Bow: Paris, c. 1830 (William Salchow, New York, December 28, 1989) 3930/5895 **4539**
£2310 DM6750 ¥578655

MORIZOT, LOUIS [P11/235] Silver Violoncello Bow w/case 491/688 **646**
£329 DM949 ¥83245

MORIZOT, LOUIS [P11/248] Nickel Violoncello Bow 393/590 **NS**

MORIZOT, LOUIS [P11/249] Nickel Violoncello Bow repaired crack on handle 236/354 **NS**

NEUDORFER [P11/239] Nickel Violoncello Bow 295/491 **NS**

NEUVEVILLE, G. C. [P09/203] Silver Violoncello Bow 374/561 **535**
£286 DM847 ¥73531

NEUVEVILLE, G. C. [P10/124] Silver Violoncello Bow 588/882 **1078**
£550 DM1626 ¥134970

NURNBERGER, ALBERT [Sk11/75] Silver Violoncello Bow 300/500 **495**
£252 DM738 ¥63855

NURNBERGER, ALBERT [S11/75] Silver Violoncello Bow: Markneukirchen 1376/1965 **1405**
£715 DM2089 ¥179108

NURNBERGER, ALBERT [S06/370] Silver Violoncello Bow: Markneukirchen 1026/1368 **1881**
£1100 DM3176 ¥289520

NURNBERGER, ALBERT [C11/205] Silver Violoncello Bow 788/1182 **823**
£418 DM1213 ¥104751

NURNBERGER, ALBERT [C03/286] Silver Violoncello Bow 651/814 **788**
£484 DM1348 ¥124436

PAULUS, JOHANNES O. [C03/258] Silver Violoncello Bow 326/488 **501**
£308 DM858 ¥79187

PECCATTE, D. [B04/121] Important Silver French Violoncello Bow in perfect condition: Paris, 19th C. 10710/14875 **11305**
£6914 DM19000 ¥1800094

PFRETZSCHNER, H. R. [Sk11/65] Silver Violoncello Bow 1200/1500 **1045**
£533 DM1557 ¥134805

PFRETZSCHNER, H. R. [P02/147] Silver Violoncello Bow frog restored 425/595 **598**
£352 DM989 ¥86416

PFRETZSCHNER, H. R. [S11/241] Silver Violoncello Bow: Markneukirchen 982/1376 **865**
£440 DM1286 ¥110220

PFRETZSCHNER, H. R. [S11/242] Silver Violoncello Bow w/2 bows: Markneukirchen 786/1179 **1124**
£572 DM1671 ¥143286

PFRETZSCHNER, H. R. [S03/250] Silver Violoncello Bow: Markneukirchen 1197/1539 **1035**
£605 DM1676 ¥153307

PFRETZSCHNER, H. R. [S06/116] Silver Violoncello Bow: Markneukirchen 1026/1368 **NS**

PFRETZSCHNER, H. R. [S06/356] Silver Violoncello Bow: Markneukirchen 1026/1368 **NS**

PFRETZSCHNER, H. R. [S06/358] Silver Violoncello Bow w/2 bows: Markneukirchen 855/1197 **NS**

PFRETZSCHNER, H. R. [C06/222] Silver Violoncello Bow 688/860 **851**
£495 DM1431 ¥130467

PFRETZSCHNER, W. A. [P03/273] Nickel Violoncello Bow 132/164 **470**
£286 DM793 ¥73159

PFRETZSCHNER, W. A. [C03/290] Silver Violoncello Bow 651/814 **573**
£352 DM980 ¥90499

REYNOLDS, J. [P06/351] Silver Violoncello Bow 518/691 **NS**

RIEDL, ALFONS [P11/233] Silver Violoncello Bow w/case 688/884 **NS**

RIEDL, ALFONS [P07/150] 2 Violoncello Bows w/4 bows 281/468 **774**
£414 DM1225 ¥106439

SANDNER, B. [B04/278] Silver German Violoncello Bow in very good condition: c. 1960 179/298 **149**
£91 DM250 ¥23685

SARTORY, EUGENE [P06/341] Silver Violoncello Bow 1727/3109 **NS**

SARTORY, EUGENE [P06/350] Silver Violoncello Bow 5182/6046 **5891**
£3410 DM9872 ¥908424

SARTORY, EUGENE [P10/126] Silver Violoncello Bow restoration to handle and frog 1176/1568 **NS**

SARTORY, EUGENE [S11/361] Silver Violoncello Bow: Paris 7860/9825 **NS**

SARTORY, EUGENE [S11/363] Silver Violoncello Bow: Paris 5895/7860 **NS**

SARTORY, EUGENE [S03/116] Silver Violoncello Bow: Paris 3762/4788 **4138**
£2420 DM6703 ¥613228

SARTORY, EUGENE [S06/369] Silver Violoncello Bow w/box: Paris 3078/4275 **4703**
£2750 DM7941 ¥723800

SARTORY, EUGENE [S06/43] Silver Violoncello Bow: Paris 6840/10260 **NS**

SARTORY, EUGENE [C11/262] Silver Violoncello Bow without lapping 3940/5910 **8668**
£4400 DM12769 ¥1102640

SARTORY, EUGENE [C11/279] Silver Violoncello Bow 5516/6304 **6068**
£3080 DM8938 ¥771848

SARTORY, EUGENE [C03/108] Silver Violoncello Bow 3256/4070 **5014**
£3080 DM8578 ¥791868

SARTORY, EUGENE [C03/295] Silver Violoncello Bow 3256/4070 **5731**
£3520 DM9803 ¥904992

SCHMIDT, C. HANS CARL [C03/281] Silver Violoncello Bow 651/977 **752**
£462 DM1287 ¥118780

SEIFERT, LOTHAR [C03/98] Silver Violoncello Bow 488/651 **501**
£308 DM858 ¥79187

SILVESTRE & MAUCOTEL [P10/138] Silver Violoncello Bow: c. 1900 980/1372 **NS**

THIBOUVILLE-LAMY, J. [P02/122] Silver Violoncello Bow 510/680 **972**
£572 DM1607 ¥140426

THOMASSIN, C. [B04/116] Silver French Violoncello Bow in flawless condition: Paris, c. 1915 5355/5950 **5058**
£3093 DM8500 ¥805305

THOMASSIN, C. [S03/105] Silver Violoncello Bow: Paris, first half, 20th C. 1197/1710 **3386**
£1980 DM5485 ¥501732

THOMASSIN, CLAUDE [S03/289] Nickel Violoncello Bow: Paris 1368/2052 **2257**
£1320 DM3656 ¥334488

TOURTE, LOUIS (attributed to) [C11/269] Ivory Violoncello Bow 10835/11820 **NS**

TUBBS, JAMES [S11/360] Silver Violoncello Bow: London, c. 1880 5895/9825 **5620**
£2860 DM8357 ¥716430

TUBBS, JAMES [C03/280] Silver Violoncello Bow 2930/3582 **5731**
£3520 DM9803 ¥904992

TUBBS, THOMAS (ascribed to) [S06/242] Silver Violoncello Bow repair on handle 1368/2052 **NS**

VAN DER MEER, KAREL [S06/246] Silver Violoncello Bow: Amsterdam 1368/1710 **NS**

VIGNERON, ANDRE [S11/265] Silver Violoncello Bow: Paris 2948/3930 **4323**
£2200 DM6428 ¥551100

VIGNERON, ANDRE [C06/252] Silver Violoncello Bow 1720/2064 **1703**
£990 DM2861 ¥260934

VOIRIN, FRANCOIS NICOLAS [P11/215] Silver Violoncello Bow spliced head: c. 1880 491/688 **473**
£241 DM695 ¥60972

VOIRIN, FRANCOIS NICOLAS [S11/362] Silver Violoncello Bow: Paris, c. 1860 3537/4913 **NS**

VOIRIN, FRANCOIS NICOLAS [S03/114] Silver Violoncello Bow: Paris (Bernard Millant, Paris, November 28, 1989) 5130/6840 **NS**

VOIRIN, FRANCOIS NICOLAS [S03/284] Silver Violoncello Bow: Paris 4275/5985 **4703**
£2750 DM7617 ¥696850

VOIRIN, FRANCOIS NICOLAS [S06/368] Silver Violoncello Bow: Paris 3420/5130 **5267**
£3080 DM8894 ¥810656

VOIRIN, FRANCOIS NICOLAS [C06/263] Silver Violoncello Bow 4300/6020 **3406**
£1980 DM5722 ¥521869

VUILLAUME, JEAN BAPTISTE [S06/347] Silver Violoncello Bow: Paris, c. 1840 (David W. Taylor, Southall) 3420/5130 **4138**
£2420 DM6988 ¥636944

VUILLAUME, JEAN BAPTISTE [C11/256] Silver Violoncello Bow 1970/2955 **NS**

VUILLAUME, JEAN BAPTISTE [C06/264] Silver Violoncello Bow 4300/6020 **NS**

WEICHOLD, R. [P09/198] Silver Violoncello Bow 655/935 **1275**
£682 DM2019 ¥175342

WEICHOLD, RICHARD [C03/95] Silver Violoncello Bow 651/814 **1074**
£660 DM1838 ¥169686

WILSON, GARNER [S11/240] Gold and Tortoiseshell Violoncello Bow: Bury St. Edmunds 1376/1965 **1189**
£605 DM1768 ¥151553

WILSON, GARNER [S06/350] Gold and Tortoiseshell Violoncello Bow: Bury St. Edmunds 1368/2052 **NS**

WILSON, GARNER [S06/374] Silver Violoncello Bow: Bury St. Edmunds 1197/1539 **NS**

WILSON, GARNER [S06/376] Gold Violoncello Bow: Bury St. Edmunds 1197/1710 **1317**
£770 DM2223 ¥202664

WITHERS, GEORGE & SONS [P03/283] Silver Violoncello Bow 247/411 **506**
£308 DM854 ¥78786

WOODFIELD, J. D. [P07/139] Silver Violoncello Bow 546/728 **501**
£275 DM808 ¥74827

WUNDERLICH, F. R. [C03/87] Silver Violoncello Bow 651/814 **573**
£352 DM980 ¥90499

WUNDERLICH, FRITZ [Sk11/87] Silver Violoncello Bow 600/800 **495**
£252 DM738 ¥63855

VIOLONCELLO PICCOLO

BOLINK, JAAP [S06/305] Violoncello Piccolo w/cover: Hilversum 4275/5130 **NS**

WOLFF BROS. [S06/306] German Violoncello Piccolo: Kreuznach, 1894 3420/5130 **3762**
£2200 DM6352 ¥579040

XYLOPHONE

CULLIFORD ROLFE & BARROW [C03/7] Xylophone w/box 163/244 **143**
£88 DM245 ¥22625

Item/Maker	Items Offered	Items Sold	Lowest $	Highest $	Average $
ACCORDION					
Horne, Edgar	1	1	307	307	307
AEOLA					
Wheatstone & Co., C.	1	1	1124	1124	1124
BAGPIPES					
MacDougall, D.	1	0			
BANJO					
Bacon Banjo Co.	1	1	990	990	990
Fairbanks Co., A. C.	1	1	715	715	715
Fiesta	1	1	171	171	171
Libby Bros.	1	1	303	303	303
BANJO MANDOLIN					
Gibson Co.	1	1	165	165	165
BASS RECORDER					
Goble, Robert	1	0			
BASS VIOL DA GAMBA					
Steber, Ernst	1	0			
BASSOON					
Bilton, Richard	1	1	1317	1317	1317
Bocchia, Bono	1	1	495	495	495
Buffet	1	1	330	330	330
Buffet-Crampon & Co.	1	1	361	361	361
Goulding, Wood & Co.	1	0			
Grenser, Johann Heinrich	1	1	12227	12227	12227
Heckel	2	1	10375	10375	10375
Heckel, Wilhelm	1	0			
Milhouse, William	1	0			
Zimmermann, Julius Heinrich	1	1	358	358	358
BUGLE					
Astor & Co., Gerock	1	1	608	608	608
Pace, Charles	1	1	1672	1672	1672
CITHERN					
Preston	1	1	562	562	562
CLARINET					
Bilton, Richard	2	2	1317	1693	1505
Conn, C. G.	1	1	171	171	171
Cramer	1	1	681	681	681
Darche	1	1	543	543	543
Florio, Pietro Grassi	1	1	1129	1129	1129
Goulding & Co.	1	1	361	361	361
Klemm	1	1	758	758	758
Lot, Isadore	1	1	389	389	389
Martin Bros.	1	1	434	434	434
Metzler	1	1	440	440	440
CLARINET					
Otten, John	1	1	280	280	280
Selmer	1	1	209	209	209
Wolf & Co., Robert	1	1	344	344	344
Wood & Ivy	1	1	398	398	398

Item/Maker	*Items Offered*	*Items Sold*	*Lowest $*	*Highest $*	*Average $*
CLAVICHORD					
Goff, Thomas	1	0			
Lindholm, Pehr	1	0			
CONCERTINA					
Crabb, Henry	1	0			
Crabb & Son, H.	1	1	778	778	778
Jeffries, Charles	1	1	367	367	367
Jeffries Bros.	1	1	303	303	303
Lachenal & Co.	3	2	782	1279	1030
Wheatstone & Co., C.	6	5	494	1302	855
CONTRA GUITAR					
Hauser, Hermann	1	0			
CORNOPEAN					
Kohler, John	1	1	3950	3950	3950
CORONET					
Conn, C. G.	1	1	303	303	303
Pepper, J. W.	1	1	385	385	385
DOUBLE BASS					
Cole, James	1	1	11286	11286	11286
Derazey, Justin	1	1	5643	5643	5643
Jacquot Family (member of)	1	1	1760	1760	1760
Panormo, Vincenzo (ascribed to)	1	1	9029	9029	9029
DOUBLE BASS BOW					
Alvey, Brian	1	0			
Bailey, G. E.	1	1	995	995	995
Dotschkail, R.	1	1	696	696	696
Mettal, O.	1	1	547	547	547
Mettal, Walter	1	1	1044	1044	1044
Morizot, Louis	2	1	374	374	374
Paulus, Johannes O.	2	2	945	994	969
Riedl, Alfons	3	3	424	795	655
Vickers, J. E.	3	3	206	344	262
Winkler, Franz	1	1	723	723	723
ENGLISH HORN					
Fornari	1	0			
Loree, Francois	1	1	3595	3595	3595
FLAGEOLET					
Bainbridge	1	1	227	227	227
Hastrick	1	1	398	398	398
Peloubet, C.	1	1	550	550	550
FLUTE					
Boehm & Mendler	1	0			
Cahusac	1	1	607	607	607
Cahusac, Thomas	2	1	617	617	617
Carte, Rudall & Co.	4	3	119	2080	815
Clementi & Co.	1	1	380	380	380
Clinton & Co.	1	1	988	988	988
Crosby, W.	1	1	523	523	523
Florio, Pietro Grassi	2	1	6019	6019	6019
Goulding & Co.	1	1	187	187	187
Goulding & D'Almaine	2	1	361	361	361
Graves, Samuel	1	1	385	385	385
Grenser, Auguste	1	1	18373	18373	18373
Hale, John	1	1	260	260	260

Item/Maker	*Items Offered*	*Items Sold*	*Lowest $*	*Highest $*	*Average $*
Hammig, Philipp	1	1	860	860	860
Haynes Co., William S.	1	1	935	935	935
Holtzapffler	1	0			
Lafleur	1	1	171	171	171
Laurent, Claude	2	1	11919	11919	11919
Lot, Louis	3	2	941	1505	1223
Maker's Guild No. 168	1	0			
Metzler, Valentin	2	1	172	172	172
Milligan	1	0			
Miyazawa & Co.	1	1	1235	1235	1235
Monzani	1	1	3242	3242	3242
Potter, William Henry	2	1	494	494	494
Prowse, Thomas	1	1	995	995	995
Rede, H. W.	1	1	358	358	358
Rudall, George	1	1	1505	1505	1505
FRENCH HORN					
Hawkes & Son	1	1	570	570	570
GUITAR					
Bouchet, Robert	2	2	19454	26334	22894
Contreras, Manuel	1	0			
Gibson Co.	3	3	1210	2640	2053
Guitar Epiphone Co.	1	1	660	660	660
Gutierrez, Manuel	1	0			
Hauser, Hermann	1	1	4323	4323	4323
Kohno, Masaru	2	1	2257	2257	2257
Lacote, Rene	1	1	4323	4323	4323
Martin Co., C. F.	1	1	1760	1760	1760
Mauchant Bros.	1	1	2822	2822	2822
Panormo, Louis	2	2	1483	2633	2058
Ramirez, Jose (III)	1	1	1945	1945	1945
Rinaldi, Marengo Romanus	1	0			
Romanillos, Jose	2	2	6268	15989	11128
HAND HORN					
Raoux, Marcel-Auguste	1	0			
HARP					
Briggs	1	1	1131	1131	1131
Delveau, J.	1	1	1791	1791	1791
Erard, Sebastian	3	2	1505	4514	3010
Erard, Sebastian & Pierre	1	1	995	995	995
Errard	1	1	995	995	995
Light, Edward	1	1	2270	2270	2270
Nadermann, Henry	1	0			
HARPSICHORD					
de Blaise, William	1	1	2081	2081	2081
Dulken, Johan Daniel	1	1	127908	127908	127908
Kirkman, Jacob & Abraham	1	1	99429	99429	99429
HORN					
White, H. N. & Co.	1	1	110	110	110
HURDY GURDY					
Colson	1	1	1729	1729	1729
LUTE					
Romanillos, Jose	1	0			
Rubio, David	2	1	6395	6395	6395
LUTE-GUITAR					
Barry	1	1	389	389	389

Item/Maker	*Items Offered*	*Items Sold*	*Lowest $*	*Highest $*	*Average $*
LYRA GUITAR					
Mozzani, Luigi	1	1	973	973	973
LYRE GUITAR					
Barry	1	1	2600	2600	2600
Mozzani, Luigi	1	0			
MANDOLA					
Maratea, Michele	1	1	185	185	185
MANDOLIN					
Ceccherini, Umberto	1	0			
Embergher, Luigi	1	1	1772	1772	1772
Vinaccia, Gennaro & Alle	1	1	908	908	908
Gibson Co.	1	1	2090	2090	2090
Salsedo, Luigi	1	1	687	687	687
Vinaccia Family (member of) (attributed to)	1	1	2810	2810	2810
OBOE					
Boosey & Hawkes	1	1	224	224	224
Cabart	1	1	103	103	103
Doelling	1	1	1279	1279	1279
Hanken, Gerhard	1	1	1433	1433	1433
Loree, Francois	2	1	4352	4352	4352
Louis	1	1	3027	3027	3027
Milhouse, William	2	2	1693	2633	2163
Nonon, Jacques	1	0			
OBOE D'AMORE					
Loree, Francois	1	1	3027	3027	3027
Louis	1	1	7190	7190	7190
OPHICLEIDE					
Smith, Henry	1	1	912	912	912
PEDAL HARP					
Erard, Sebastian & Pierre	4	4	1837	3026	2405
PIANO					
Atunes, Manuel	1	1	134013	134013	134013
Ball, Jacob	1	1	2053	2053	2053
Bates & Co.	1	1	1035	1035	1035
Bell, S.	1	0			
Beyer, Adam	1	1	1787	1787	1787
Broadwood, John	1	1	1772	1772	1772
Broadwood, John & Sons	5	4	1167	14698	5167
Buntlebart, Gabriel	1	1	2865	2865	2865
Clementi, Muzio	1	1	2865	2865	2865
Froschle, George	1	1	4703	4703	4703
Kirkman, Jacob & Abraham	1	1	8088	8088	8088
Mott, J. H. R.	1	1	985	985	985
Rolfe & Co., William	1	1	3044	3044	3044
PICCOLO					
Bonneville	1	1	1368	1368	1368
Lot, Louis	1	1	2445	2445	2445
PIPES					
Burleigh, David	1	1	530	530	530
POCHETTE					
Jay, Henry (attributed to)	1	1	2880	2880	2880
Tobin, Richard	1	1	3908	3908	3908

Item/Maker	*Items Offered*	*Items Sold*	*Lowest $*	*Highest $*	*Average $*
QUINTON					
Salomon, Jean Baptiste Deshayes	1	1	2069	2069	2069
Wamsley, Peter	1	1	2069	2069	2069
RECORDER					
Dolmetsch, Arnold	1	1	489	489	489
Eichentopf, Johann Heinrich	1	1	2081	2081	2081
SAXOPHONE					
Guinot, Rene	1	0			
SERPENT					
Metzler	1	1	2257	2257	2257
SMALL PIPES					
Reid, Robert & James	1	0			
SPINET					
Barton, Thomas	1	1	21615	21615	21615
Harris, Baker	1	0			
Slade, Benjamin	2	1	11240	11240	11240
TAROGATO					
Stowasser, Janos	1	1	2916	2916	2916
TENOR VIOL					
Heale, Michael	1	0			
Hintz, Frederick	1	1	10346	10346	10346
TROMBONE					
Courtois, Antoine	1	1	303	303	303
Pepper, J. W.	1	1	33	33	33
TRUMPET					
Gisborne	1	1	2565	2565	2565
VIHUELA					
Romanillos, Jose	1	1	2633	2633	2633
VIOL					
Norman, Barak	1	1	52668	52668	52668
VIOLA					
Albanelli, Franco	1	0			
Atkinson, William	2	1	3255	3255	3255
Barbieri, Bruno	1	1	4541	4541	4541
Bisiach, Leandro (jr.)	1	0			
Booth, William	1	1	2532	2532	2532
Bourguignon, Maurice	1	1	3891	3891	3891
Buchner, Rudolf	1	1	1693	1693	1693
Capela, Antonio	2	1	3689	3689	3689
Carletti, Genuzio	1	0			
Chanot, George Adolph	1	0			
Chanot, George Anthony	1	1	6485	6485	6485
Chappuy, Nicolas Augustin	1	1	3908	3908	3908
Chardon & Fils	1	1	6052	6052	6052
Chevrier, Andre	1	0			
Claudot, Pierre	1	1	2499	2499	2499
Cocker, Lawrence	2	2	1693	3574	2633
Colin, Jean Baptiste	2	2	3040	3198	3119
Conia, Stefano	1	1	3595	3595	3595

Item/Maker	*Items Offered*	*Items Sold*	*Lowest $*	*Highest $*	*Average $*
Craske, George	1	1	5404	5404	5404
Cuypers, Johannes Theodorus	1	1	28215	28215	28215
Degani, Eugenio	1	0			
Desideri, Pietro Paolo	1	0			
Dieudonne, Amedee	1	1	3451	3451	3451
Duke, Richard	2	2	4138	5425	4782
Enders, F. & R.	1	1	741	741	741
Epeneel, R. V.	1	0			
Esposti, Piergiuseppe	1	1	3255	3255	3255
Fendt, Bernard	1	1	15989	15989	15989
Forster, William	2	1	6622	6622	6622
Forster, William (II)	2	1	6190	6190	6190
Gabrielli, Giovanni Battista	1	1	34025	34025	34025
Gadda, Gaetano	1	1	5079	5079	5079
Gadda, Mario	1	1	5267	5267	5267
Gand & Bernardel	1	1	23837	23837	23837
Garonnaire, Christian	1	1	6149	6149	6149
Gibson	1	1	760	760	760
Gilbert, Jeffery J.	1	1	3940	3940	3940
Giraud, Franco	1	0			
Glaesel & Herwig	1	1	1682	1682	1682
Gozalan, Mesut	1	1	874	874	874
Guadagnini, Gaetano (attributed to)	1	1	18373	18373	18373
Guersan, Louis	1	1	28171	28171	28171
Gutter, G. W.	1	1	833	833	833
Haenel, Frederick Ewald	1	1	2970	2970	2970
Hammond, John	1	1	1625	1625	1625
Hill, Lockey (attributed to)	1	1	6582	6582	6582
Hill, W. E. & Sons	1	0			
Hudson, George Wulme	1	1	8465	8465	8465
Hyde, Andrew	1	1	715	715	715
Jais, Johannes (ascribed to)	1	1	11286	11286	11286
Keen, W.	1	1	1234	1234	1234
Kennedy, Thomas	1	1	4541	4541	4541
Kilburn, Wilfred	1	0			
Kloz Family (member of)	2	1	4138	4138	4138
Koberling	1	1	841	841	841
Lazare, Robert	2	1	237	237	237
Le Govic, Alain	2	2	721	1281	1001
Lee, Percy	1	1	6068	6068	6068
Littlewood, Gerald	1	1	1189	1189	1189
Lucci, Giuseppe	2	2	6510	6872	6691
Luff, William H.	2	1	6461	6461	6461
Martin, Johann Gottlieb	1	0			
Mezzadri, Alessandro (ascribed to)	1	1	24596	24596	24596
Mockel, Oswald	1	0			
Moinel-Cherpitel	1	0			
Morassi, Giovanni Battista	1	1	6584	6584	6584
Morris, Martin	1	0			
Naisby, Thomas Henry	1	1	3458	3458	3458
Neuner & Hornsteiner	1	1	1292	1292	1292
Obbo, Marcus	1	0			
Pacherel, Pierre	1	1	7568	7568	7568
Panormo, Vincenzo	2	1	54037	54037	54037
Pareschi, Gaetano	2	1	1872	1872	1872
Pedrazzini, Giuseppe	1	0			
Perry, James	1	1	7524	7524	7524
Perry, L. A.	1	1	868	868	868
Perry, Thomas	1	1	9943	9943	9943
Resuche, Charles	2	2	3203	6484	4844
Richardson, Arthur	2	1	3251	3251	3251
Rinaldi, Marengo Romanus	1	1	4138	4138	4138
Rocchi, S.	1	1	5058	5058	5058
Rost, Franz George	1	1	6019	6019	6019
Roth, Ernst Heinrich	3	3	985	1440	1182

Item/Maker	*Items Offered*	*Items Sold*	*Lowest $*	*Highest $*	*Average $*
Sacchi, Giorgio	1	0			
Saunders, Wilfred G.	1	1	1787	1787	1787
Scheinlein, M. F.	1	1	2118	2118	2118
Schmidt, E. R. & Co.	1	1	1324	1324	1324
Schwarz, Giovanni	2	1	8214	8214	8214
Sgarabotto, Gaetano	3	2	7148	10115	8631
Silvestre, Pierre	1	0			
Simonazzi, Amadeo	1	0			
Solomon, Gimpel	2	1	9969	9969	9969
Storioni, Lorenzo (ascribed to)	1	1	63954	63954	63954
Tenucci, Eugen	1	1	2445	2445	2445
Thibouville-Lamy	1	1	1621	1621	1621
Thibouville-Lamy, J.	1	0			
Topham, Carass	1	1	836	836	836
Vettori, Carlo	1	1	2162	2162	2162
Vickers, J. E.	1	1	562	562	562
Voigt, Arnold	1	1	2280	2280	2280
Voigt, E. & P.	1	0			
Vuillaume, Jean Baptiste	1	0			
Vuillaume, Nicholas	1	0			
Walton, R.	1	1	1230	1230	1230
Whitmarsh Family, (member of)	1	1	1530	1530	1530
Withers, George	1	1	1837	1837	1837
Youngson, Alexander	1	0			

VIOLA BOW

Bernardel, Leon	1	1	1513	1513	1513
Bristow, Stephen	2	2	912	1693	1303
Bryant, Percival Wilfred	1	1	2378	2378	2378
Collin-Mezin	1	1	1881	1881	1881
Dodd	2	2	658	2838	1748
Dodd, John	2	2	2633	2810	2722
Dotschkail, R.	1	1	783	783	783
Dupuy, Philippe	1	1	2351	2351	2351
Finkel, Johann S.	1	1	1129	1129	1129
Finkel, Johannes	1	1	1041	1041	1041
Geipel, Richard	2	1	417	417	417
Gerome, Roger	1	1	1904	1904	1904
Gohde, Gregory	1	0			
Hill, W. E. & Sons	6	5	2468	3978	3162
Hoyer, Otto A.	1	0			
Hums, Albin	1	0			
Lamy, Alfred	1	1	6395	6395	6395
Moinel, Amedee	1	1	1736	1736	1736
Muller, E. K.	1	1	451	451	451
Ouchard, Emile	1	0			
Pajeot	1	1	2162	2162	2162
Pajeot, Etienne	1	0			
Penzel	1	1	456	456	456
Penzel, K. Gerhard	1	0			
Pfretzschner, H. R.	2	2	627	1223	925
Pfretzschner, L.	1	1	946	946	946
Rameau, J. S.	1	1	1044	1044	1044
Sartory, Eugene	1	1	6068	6068	6068
Schmidt, C. Hans Carl	1	1	2090	2090	2090
Schuller, Otto	1	1	527	527	527
Thibouville-Lamy	1	0			
Thibouville-Lamy, Jerome	2	2	912	1045	979
Thomassin, Claude	1	1	1787	1787	1787
Tubbs, Edward	1	1	10346	10346	10346
Tubbs, James	2	2	4755	7133	5944
Tunnicliffe, Brian	1	1	1440	1440	1440
van der Meer, Karel	2	2	1100	1945	1523
Wilson, Garner	1	1	1693	1693	1693
Withers, George & Sons	1	1	1470	1470	1470

Item/Maker	Items Offered	Items Sold	Lowest $	Highest $	Average $
ZOPHEL, ERNST WILLY	1	1	645	645	645

VIOLA D'AMORE

Item/Maker	Items Offered	Items Sold	Lowest $	Highest $	Average $
GUIDANTUS, JOANNES FLORENUS (attributed to)	1	0			

VIOLETTA

Item/Maker	Items Offered	Items Sold	Lowest $	Highest $	Average $
GRANCINO, GIOVANNI (III)	1	1	4755	4755	4755

VIOLIN

Item/Maker	Items Offered	Items Sold	Lowest $	Highest $	Average $
ACHNER, PHILIP	1	1	2257	2257	2257
ACOULON, ALFRED (attributed to)	2	1	2594	2594	2594
ACOULON, ALFRED (FILS) (ascribed to)	1	1	1411	1411	1411
ADAMS, HENRY THOMAS	1	1	3339	3339	3339
ADAMSEN, P. P.	1	1	3582	3582	3582
AIRETON, EDMUND	1	0			
AIRETON, EDMUND (ascribed to)	1	1	7349	7349	7349
AITCHISON, FRANK	1	1	494	494	494
ALBANELLI, FRANCO (attributed to)	1	0			
ALBANI, JOSEPH (attributed to)	1	1	5643	5643	5643
ALBERT, CHARLES F.	1	1	1650	1650	1650
ALDRIC, JEAN FRANCOIS	3	2	8925	16117	12521
AMATI, ANTONIO	1	0			
AMATI, ANTONIO & GIROLAMO	1	1	49715	49715	49715
AMATI, ANTONIO & GIROLAMO (ascribed to)	1	0			
AMATI, DOM NICOLO	1	0			
AMATI, NICOLO	1	0			
AMATI, NICOLO (attributed to)	1	1	47025	47025	47025
AMATI FAMILY (MEMBER OF)	1	0			
ANTONIAZZI, ROMEO	1	0			
ANTONIAZZI, ROMEO (ascribed to)	1	1	5676	5676	5676
APPARUT, GEORGES	1	1	2856	2856	2856
ARDERN, JOB	5	4	1124	1900	1450
ASCHAUER, LEO	1	1	1517	1517	1517
ATKINSON, WILLIAM	2	1	4751	4751	4751
AUBRY, JOSEPH	3	3	3094	3784	3443
AUDINOT, NESTOR	1	1	8330	8330	8330
AYLOR, ALBERT	1	1	330	330	330
AZZOLA, LUIGI (ascribed to)	1	1	6019	6019	6019
BAADER & CO.	2	1	1300	1300	1300
BAILLY, PAUL	5	4	5188	9752	7474
BAILLY, PAUL (ascribed to)	1	1	4107	4107	4107
BAILLY, PAUL (attributed to)	1	1	8514	8514	8514
BAILLY, R.	1	1	1547	1547	1547
BAJONI, LUIGI (ascribed to)	1	1	7524	7524	7524
BALESTRIERI, TOMASO	3	2	43263	152218	97741
BANKS, BENJAMIN	1	1	3010	3010	3010
BANKS, JAMES & HENRY (attributed to)	2	1	1401	1401	1401
BARBE, F.	1	1	1250	1250	1250
BARBE, FRANCOIS	1	1	1562	1562	1562
BARBIERI, ENZO	1	1	3198	3198	3198
BARBIERI, PAOLO (ascribed to)	1	1	2633	2633	2633
BARZONI, FRANCOIS	1	1	344	344	344
BASTA, JAN	1	0			
BAUR, MARTIN	1	1	2850	2850	2850
BAZIN, C.	1	0			
BELLOSIO, ANSELMO (attributed to)	1	1	12227	12227	12227
BERGONZI, LORENZO	1	1	2167	2167	2167
BERNARDEL, AUGUST SEBASTIAN	2	2	8235	11000	9617
BERNARDEL, AUGUST SEBASTIEN PHILIPPE	3	3	17850	24990	22431
BERNARDEL, GUSTAVE	2	1	15136	15136	15136
BERNARDEL, LEON	1	1	3940	3940	3940
BERTELLI ENZO	1	1	2916	2916	2916
BETTS	1	1	796	796	796
BETTS, EDWARD (attributed to)	2	2	3703	6510	5106
BETTS, JOHN	2	2	2328	6811	4570
BETTS, JOHN (ascribed to)	1	1	16117	16117	16117

Item/Maker	*Items Offered*	*Items Sold*	*Lowest $*	*Highest $*	*Average $*
BETTS, JOHN (attributed to)	1	1	1297	1297	1297
BIGNAMI, OTELLO (ascribed to)	1	0			
BIRD, CHARLES A. EDWARD	1	1	3040	3040	3040
BISIACH, LEANDRO	3	3	18420	25938	21723
BISIACH, LEANDRO (JR.)	1	0			
BLACKBURN, G. B.	1	1	303	303	303
BLANCHARD, PAUL	1	1	8628	8628	8628
BLANCHART (ascribed to)	1	0			
BLANCHI, ALBERT	2	2	7140	7521	7331
BLONDELET, EMILE	1	1	2069	2069	2069
BLONDELET, H. E.	2	2	1599	1945	1772
BLYTH, WILLIAMSON	1	1	541	541	541
BOLLINGER, JOSEPH	1	1	486	486	486
BONNEL, JOSEPH (attributed to)	1	1	995	995	995
BOOSEY & HAWKES	1	1	823	823	823
BOQUAY, JACQUES (attributed to)	1	0			
BORELLI, ANDREA	1	1	29750	29750	29750
BORLAND, HUGH	1	1	957	957	957
BOSSI, GIUSEPPE	1	0			
BOULANGEOT, EMILE	1	1	9727	9727	9727
BOULANGEOT, EMILE (workshop of)	1	1	1703	1703	1703
BOULLANGIER, CHARLES (attributed to)	1	1	5064	5064	5064
BOURBEAU, E. A.	1	1	648	648	648
BOVIS, FRANCOIS	1	1	13401	13401	13401
BRANDINI, JACOPO	1	0			
BRANDINI, JACOPO (attributed to)	1	1	15136	15136	15136
BRAUND, FREDERICK T.	1	1	836	836	836
BRETON	1	1	1081	1081	1081
BRETON, FRANCOIS	4	3	520	1729	942
BRIERLEY, JOSEPH	1	1	1235	1235	1235
BRIGGS, JAMES WILLIAM	2	2	3675	5267	4471
BRIGGS, JAMES WILLIAM (attributed to)	1	0			
BROUGHTON, LEONARD W.	2	1	446	446	446
BROWN, JAMES (attributed to)	1	1	494	494	494
BROWNE, JOHN	1	0			
BRUCKNER, E.	1	1	1250	1250	1250
BRUGERE, CH.	2	2	4760	6248	5504
BRUGERE, CHARLES GEORGES	2	2	1035	7163	4099
BRUNI, MATEO	1	1	8330	8330	8330
BRYANT, OLE H.	1	1	2860	2860	2860
BUTHOD	1	1	741	741	741
BUTHOD, CHARLES	1	1	1892	1892	1892
BUTHOD, CHARLES LOUIS	2	2	1505	1693	1599
BUTTON & WHITAKER	3	2	752	846	799
BYROM, JOHN	1	1	4551	4551	4551
CABASSE	1	1	646	646	646
CAHUSAC	1	1	1140	1140	1140
CALACE, CAVALIERE RAFFAELE	1	1	3410	3410	3410
CALCAGNI, BERNARDO	3	2	46561	49715	48138
CALLSEN, B.	1	1	1071	1071	1071
CALLSEN, B. (ascribed to)	1	1	39006	39006	39006
CAMILLI, CAMILLUS	1	1	75680	75680	75680
CANDI, ORESTE	1	1	6811	6811	6811
CAPELLINI, VIRGILIO	1	1	3010	3010	3010
CAPICCHIONI, MARINO	1	1	14698	14698	14698
CAPPA, GOFFREDO (ascribed to)	1	0			
CARCASSI, LORENZO (ascribed to)	1	1	8668	8668	8668
CARCASSI, LORENZO & TOMASSO	1	0			
CARESSA, ALBERT	1	1	6917	6917	6917
CARESSA & FRANCAIS (attributed to)	1	1	4340	4340	4340
CARLISLE, JAMES REYNOLD	1	1	248	248	248
CARNY, V.	1	1	2380	2380	2380
CASTAGNERI, ANDREA (attributed to)	1	0			
CASTELLO, PAOLO (ascribed to)	1	1	10745	10745	10745
CAVACEPPI, MARIO	1	1	3080	3080	3080
CAVALLI, ARISTIDE	3	3	1561	2257	1876
CAVALLI, ARISTIDE (workshop of)	1	1	1234	1234	1234

Item/Maker	*Items Offered*	*Items Sold*	*Lowest $*	*Highest $*	*Average $*
CAVANI, GIOVANNI	1	1	5950	5950	5950
CERPI, G.	3	2	1035	1161	1098
CERUTI, GIOVANNI MARIA	1	1	3458	3458	3458
CHAMPION, RENE (ascribed to)	1	1	2090	2090	2090
CHANOT, FRANCIS	1	1	1787	1787	1787
CHANOT, FREDERICK WILLIAM	3	2	2983	8646	5814
CHANOT, G. A.	1	0			
CHANOT, GEORGE	1	1	1791	1791	1791
CHANOT, GEORGE ADOLPH	4	3	2441	8214	5934
CHANOT, GEORGES	2	1	16211	16211	16211
CHANOT, JOSEPH ANTHONY	1	1	1541	1541	1541
CHAPPUY, A.	2	2	833	5355	3094
CHAPPUY, N.	1	1	1428	1428	1428
CHAPPUY, NICOLAS AUGUSTIN	2	2	2069	3040	2555
CHAPPUY, NICOLAS AUGUSTIN (ascribed to)	1	1	1129	1129	1129
CHARTREUX, EUGENE	2	1	648	648	648
CHIPOT, JEAN BAPTISTE	1	0			
CHIPOT-VUILLAUME	4	3	1900	3040	2558
CLARK, SAMUEL	1	1	550	550	550
CLAUDOT, AUGUSTIN	1	1	1190	1190	1190
CLAUDOT, CHARLES	2	1	1131	1131	1131
CLAUDOT, CHARLES (ascribed to)	1	0			
CLAUDOT, NICOLAS	1	1	699	699	699
CLOTELLE, H.	2	1	950	950	950
COLE, JAMES	1	1	2622	2622	2622
COLIN, CLAUDE	2	1	1330	1330	1330
COLIN, JEAN BAPTISTE	5	4	901	2404	1584
COLLENOT, LOUIS	1	1	1428	1428	1428
COLLIN-MEZIN	4	4	1223	3026	2191
COLLIN-MEZIN, CH. J. B.	21	20	672	10710	3400
COLLIN-MEZIN, CH. J. B. (FILS)	2	2	2903	3991	3447
COLTON, WALTER E.	1	1	1980	1980	1980
COMUNI, ANTONIO	1	1	21420	21420	21420
CONIA, STEFANO	2	2	5455	5787	5621
CONTI ALDO	1	1	4984	4984	4984
CONTINO, ALFREDO	1	1	11550	11550	11550
COOPER, HUGH W.	1	1	1509	1509	1509
COPELLI, MAURIZIO	1	1	2660	2660	2660
COUTURIEUX	2	1	647	647	647
CRASKE, GEORGE	14	13	1693	7900	3795
CRASKE, GEORGE (ascribed to)	1	0			
CRASKE, GEORGE (attributed to)	2	2	823	1865	1344
DAL CANTO, GIUSTINO	1	1	1870	1870	1870
DALLA COSTA, ANTONIO	1	1	62683	62683	62683
DARCHE, HILAIRE	1	1	11268	11268	11268
DARTE, AUGUST (attributed to)	1	1	3034	3034	3034
DE RUB, AUGUSTO (ascribed to)	1	0			
DEARLOVE, MARK WILLIAM	1	1	735	735	735
DEBLAYE, ALBERT	1	1	598	598	598
DECHANT, G.	1	1	2090	2090	2090
DEGANI, (WORKSHOP OF)	1	1	19699	19699	19699
DEGANI, EUGENIO	4	4	10850	26004	17622
DEGANI, GIULIO	5	4	5188	15048	10193
DELANOY, ALEXANDRE	2	2	2678	3964	3321
DELIVET, AUGUSTE	1	1	2618	2618	2618
DELLA CORTE, ALFONSO (ascribed to)	1	1	14108	14108	14108
DEMAY	1	1	2023	2023	2023
DERAZEY, HONORE	8	7	1664	10850	4976
DERAZEY, HONORE (attributed to)	1	0			
DERAZEY, JUSTIN	3	2	2865	2975	2920
DEVEAU, JOHN G.	1	1	1141	1141	1141
DIDIER, MARIUS	2	2	1666	2822	2244
DIEHL, A.	1	1	2678	2678	2678
DIEHL, M.	2	2	833	4165	2499
DIEUDONNE, AMEDEE	6	6	2310	3868	2881
DIXON, ALFRED THOMAS	1	1	796	796	796
DOLLENZ, GIOVANNI (ascribed to)	1	0			

Item/Maker	*Items Offered*	*Items Sold*	*Lowest $*	*Highest $*	*Average $*
Dolling, Louis (jun)	2	2	995	1520	1257
Dolling, Robert A.	1	1	825	825	825
Drouin, Charles	1	0			
Duerer, Wilhelm	1	1	329	329	329
Dugade, Aubry	1	1	1975	1975	1975
Dugarde, Aubry	1	1	1438	1438	1438
Duke, Richard	4	3	2470	5787	4644
Dupary, Adolphe	1	1	2270	2270	2270
Eberle, Tomaso	1	1	34672	34672	34672
Eckland, Donald	1	1	3410	3410	3410
Elliot, William	1	1	2470	2470	2470
Enders, F. & R.	1	1	3034	3034	3034
Eyles, Charles	1	0			
Fabricatore, Gennaro	1	1	25585	25585	25585
Fabricatore, Giovanni Battista	1	1	6484	6484	6484
Fabricatore, Giovanni Battista (ascribed to)	1	1	11662	11662	11662
Fabris, Luigi (ascribed to)	1	0			
Fagnola, Hannibal	1	1	20825	20825	20825
Falisse, A.	2	2	2380	3574	2977
Felici, Enrico	1	1	2850	2850	2850
Fendt, Bernard (attributed to)	2	1	3251	3251	3251
Fent, Francois	1	0			
Ferrari, Giuseppe	1	1	2069	2069	2069
Fichtl, M.	1	1	6843	6843	6843
Fichtl, Martin Mathias	1	0			
Ficker, C. S.	1	1	1071	1071	1071
Ficker, Johann Christian	3	3	2378	3325	2838
Ficker Family (member of)	1	0			
Fillion, G.	1	0			
Fiorini, Raffaele (attributed to)	1	1	4767	4767	4767
Fischer, H. A.	1	1	3891	3891	3891
Flambeau, Charles	1	0			
Fleury, Benoit	1	1	1035	1035	1035
Forbes-Whitmore, Anthony	1	1	3420	3420	3420
Forcellini, F.	1	1	4760	4760	4760
Ford, Jacob (attributed to)	1	1	4941	4941	4941
Forrester, Alexander	1	1	785	785	785
Forster, William	1	1	1760	1760	1760
Forster, William (ii)	3	3	2445	9405	4891
Fuchs, W. K.	1	1	990	990	990
Furber, John (attributed to)	1	1	3074	3074	3074
Furber, Matthew (attributed to)	1	1	1041	1041	1041
Furber Family (member of) (attributed to)	1	1	4371	4371	4371
Gabrielli, Giovanni Battista	1	1	67716	67716	67716
Gadda, Gaetano	2	2	11352	12495	11924
Gadda, Mario	2	1	6054	6054	6054
Gagliano, Ferdinand	1	1	88622	88622	88622
Gagliano, Ferdinand (attributed to)	1	1	28380	28380	28380
Gagliano, Gennaro	1	1	56760	56760	56760
Gagliano, Joseph	3	2	27275	43263	35269
Gagliano, Joseph & Antonio	1	1	13200	13200	13200
Gagliano, Nicolo	3	3	23513	89250	59533
Gagliano, Raffaele & Antonio	1	1	30404	30404	30404
Gagliano Family (attributed to)	1	1	21490	21490	21490
Gaida, Giovanni	2	2	11212	15048	13130
Galea, Alfredo G.	1	1	1808	1808	1808
Galla, Anton (attributed to)	1	0			
Gand, Charles Francois (ascribed to)	1	1	26334	26334	26334
Garimberti, F.	1	1	10710	10710	10710
Gavatelli, Alcide	1	1	2182	2182	2182
Gavinies, Francois	1	1	5267	5267	5267
Geissenhof, Franz	1	1	10745	10745	10745
Geissenhof, Franz (attributed to)	1	1	8668	8668	8668
Gemunder, George	1	1	4510	4510	4510
Gerard, Grand	1	1	833	833	833
Germain, Emile	1	1	6501	6501	6501
Gigli, Giulio Cesare	1	1	3010	3010	3010

Item/Maker	*Items Offered*	*Items Sold*	*Lowest $*	*Highest $*	*Average $*
GILBERT, JEFFERY J.	1	1	1317	1317	1317
GILBERT, JEFFERY JAMES	1	1	1599	1599	1599
GILKS, WILLIAM	1	0			
GLASEL, ERNST	1	1	785	785	785
GLASEL, LOUIS	1	1	550	550	550
GLASEL & MOSSNER (attributed to)	1	1	562	562	562
GLASS, JOHANN	1	1	1491	1491	1491
GLENISTER, WILLIAM	2	1	3458	3458	3458
GOBETTI, FRANCESCO	1	1	13543	13543	13543
GOFFRILLER, FRANCESCO	1	1	41382	41382	41382
GOFTON, ROBERT	1	1	1175	1175	1175
GORDON	1	1	690	690	690
GOULDING	1	1	374	374	374
GOULDING (attributed to)	1	1	1520	1520	1520
GOULDING & CO.	1	0			
GRAGNANI, ANTONIO	1	1	34672	34672	34672
GRANCINO, FRANCESCO & GIOVANNI	1	1	8250	8250	8250
GRANCINO, GIOVANNI	1	1	71478	71478	71478
GRANCINO, GEBR.	1	1	20825	20825	20825
GRAND-GERARD, JEAN BAPTISTE	3	2	604	6019	3311
GRANDJON, JULES	1	1	2445	2445	2445
GRATER, THOMAS	1	1	1646	1646	1646
GRIBBEN, P. J.	1	1	289	289	289
GRUNER	1	1	565	565	565
GUADAGNINI, ANTONIO (attributed to)	1	1	21420	21420	21420
GUADAGNINI, FRANCESCO	1	1	12536	12536	12536
GUADAGNIN, G. B. & PIETRO	1	0			
GUADAGNINI, GIOVANNI BATTISTA	4	4	44770	345840	179476
GUARNERI, ANDREA	2	2	32422	53724	43073
GUARNERI, GIUSEPPE (FILIUS ANDREA)	1	1	354486	354486	354486
GUARNERI, GIUSEPPE (FILIUS ANDREA) (attributed to)	1	1	60192	60192	60192
GUARNERI, JOSEPH (DEL GESU) (attributed to)	1	1	31977	31977	31977
GUARNERI, PIETRO (OF MANTUA)	1	0			
GUASTALLA, DANTE	1	1	6395	6395	6395
GUASTALLA, DANTE & ALFREDO	2	2	6019	9900	7960
GUERRA, E.	1	1	18445	18445	18445
GUERRA, EVASIO EMILE	1	1	13167	13167	13167
GUERSAN, LOUIS	2	1	3188	3188	3188
GUERSAN, LOUIS (attributed to)	2	1	908	908	908
GUIDANTUS, JOANNES FLORENUS	2	1	26334	26334	26334
GUIDANTUS, JOANNES FLORENUS (ascribed to)	2	1	12227	12227	12227
HAMMA & CO.	1	1	1547	1547	1547
HAMMETT, THOMAS	1	1	1254	1254	1254
HAMMIG, M.	1	1	4284	4284	4284
HAMMIG, WILHELM HERMAN	1	1	4891	4891	4891
HARDIE, JAMES & SONS	2	2	561	774	668
HARDIE, MATTHEW	1	0			
HARDIE, THOMAS	1	0			
HART & SON	2	2	3403	6052	4728
HAWKES & SON	1	1	1467	1467	1467
HEBERLEIN, HEINRICH TH.	1	1	495	495	495
HEBERLEIN, HEINRICH TH. (JUNIOR)	1	1	1045	1045	1045
HECKEL, RUDOLF	1	1	4656	4656	4656
HEINICKE, MATHIAS	1	1	4463	4463	4463
HEINRICH, THEODORE	1	1	1045	1045	1045
HEL, JOSEPH	2	2	14108	16660	15384
HELD, JOHANN JOSEPH	1	1	3394	3394	3394
HERTL, ANTON	1	1	647	647	647
HESKETH, J. EARL	1	1	2053	2053	2053
HESKETH, THOMAS EARLE	2	2	4702	4703	4702
HILL, HENRY LOCKEY	1	0			
HILL, W. E. & SONS	4	4	5131	10406	6646
HILL, W. E. & SONS (workshop of)	1	0			
HOFFMANN, EDUARD	1	1	43263	43263	43263
HOFMANN, JOHANN MARTIN	1	1	2445	2445	2445
HOFMANS, MATHIAS (ascribed to)	1	0			
HOING, CLIFFORD A.	1	1	1064	1064	1064

Item/Maker	*Items Offered*	*Items Sold*	*Lowest $*	*Highest $*	*Average $*
Hopf	3	3	204	1131	544
Hopf, David	1	1	453	453	453
Hornsteiner, Mathias	2	1	5236	5236	5236
Hudson, George Wulme	3	2	4971	5965	5468
Hutton, Adam	1	1	162	162	162
Iarovoi, Denis	1	0			
Jacobs, Hendrik	1	1	14822	14822	14822
Jacquot, Albert	1	1	12791	12791	12791
Jacquot, Charles	1	1	13090	13090	13090
Jacquot, Charles (ascribed to)	1	0			
Jais, Anton	1	1	711	711	711
Jaura, Wilhelm Thomas	1	0			
Jaura, Wilhelm Thomas (ascribed to)	2	1	5404	5404	5404
Jay, Henry	2	1	1729	1729	1729
Jay, Henry (attributed to)	1	1	1193	1193	1193
Jeune, Laurent	1	1	1250	1250	1250
Johnson, Peter Andreas	1	1	385	385	385
Johnston, Thomas	1	1	266	266	266
Juzek, John	2	2	1964	4181	3072
Kaul, Paul	2	2	3198	7438	5318
Keffer, Joannes	1	1	2023	2023	2023
Kennedy, Thomas	1	1	6395	6395	6395
Kloz, Aegidius	4	4	3223	13090	7595
Kloz, George	1	1	4463	4463	4463
Kloz, Joan Carol	1	1	2660	2660	2660
Kloz, Joseph	1	1	6019	6019	6019
Kloz, Sebastian	1	0			
Kloz, Sebastian (attributed to)	1	1	3223	3223	3223
Kloz, Sebastian (i)	1	1	6081	6081	6081
Kloz Family (member of)	5	4	825	10346	4371
Kloz Family (member of) (attributed to)	1	1	1892	1892	1892
Knorr, P.	1	1	3927	3927	3927
Knupfer, Albert	1	1	988	988	988
Kraft, Peter	1	0			
Kreutzinger, Anton	1	1	1035	1035	1035
Krug, J. Adolph	1	1	770	770	770
Kruse Wilhelm	1	1	707	707	707
Kudanowski, Jan	1	1	2270	2270	2270
Kunze, Wilhelm PAUL	1	0			
L'Anson, Edward (attributed to)	1	0			
Laberte-Humbert Bros.	1	1	1881	1881	1881
Lancaster	1	1	453	453	453
Lancinger, Antonin	1	1	2384	2384	2384
Landolfi, Pietro Antonio	1	1	95106	95106	95106
Lang, J. S.	1	1	181	181	181
Langonet, Charles	1	1	3570	3570	3570
Lantner, Bohuslav	1	1	1881	1881	1881
Laurent, Emile	1	1	6501	6501	6501
Lavest, J.	1	1	1666	1666	1666
Lazare, Robert	1	1	615	615	615
Le Cyr, James Ferdinand	2	1	1301	1301	1301
Lechi, Antonio	6	5	723	1496	1027
Lee, H. W.	1	0			
Legnani, Luigi (ascribed to)	1	1	6019	6019	6019
Leidolff, Johann Christoph	1	1	1085	1085	1085
Locke, George Herbert	1	1	904	904	904
Longman & Broderip	2	2	975	1193	1084
Longman & Lukey	1	0			
Longson, F. H.	1	0			
Longson, J. L.	1	1	1628	1628	1628
Lott, John	1	1	41382	41382	41382
Louvet, F.	1	1	833	833	833
Loveri, Carlo	1	1	1995	1995	1995
Lowendall, Louis	8	8	280	1235	679
Lucci, Giuseppe	2	2	4919	10745	7832
Luff, William H.	3	3	5348	5787	5604
Lupot, Nicolas	2	2	52668	75240	63954

Item/Maker	*Items Offered*	*Items Sold*	*Lowest $*	*Highest $*	*Average $*
Lutschg, Gustav	1	1	4656	4656	4656
Macpherson, H.	1	1	568	568	568
Magniere, Gabriel	1	1	2695	2695	2695
Malakoff, Brugere	1	1	6019	6019	6019
Mangenot, P.	1	1	952	952	952
Mangenot, Paul	1	1	2257	2257	2257
Mansuy	1	1	536	536	536
Maraviglia, Guido (attributed to)	1	1	2182	2182	2182
Marchi, Giovanni (ascribed to)	1	1	4730	4730	4730
Mariani, Antonio	2	2	2090	24453	13272
Marshall, John	2	1	3386	3386	3386
Martin, E.	1	1	358	358	358
Martin, J.	1	1	1012	1012	1012
Martin Family, (member of)	1	1	2633	2633	2633
Martino, Giuseppe	1	1	2200	2200	2200
Martirenghi, Marcello	1	1	6805	6805	6805
Masafija, Dimitri	1	1	1560	1560	1560
Mast, J.	1	1	7735	7735	7735
Mast, Joseph Laurent	1	1	1945	1945	1945
Mathieu, Nicolas	1	1	537	537	537
Maucotel, Charles	1	1	5267	5267	5267
Mayson, Walter	7	6	687	2445	1300
Mayson, Walter H.	3	3	823	1513	1272
Mead, L. J.	1	1	524	524	524
Meek, James	1	1	1430	1430	1430
Meinel, Eugen	1	1	4702	4702	4702
Meinel, Oskar	1	1	495	495	495
Melegari, Michele & Pietro	1	1	8214	8214	8214
Mennesson, Emile	1	1	2507	2507	2507
Merling, Pauli	2	2	1254	4755	3004
Meurot, L. (attributed to)	2	2	1081	2170	1625
Millant, R. & M.	1	1	1964	1964	1964
Milton, Louis	1	1	3251	3251	3251
Miremont	1	0			
Mockel, Oswald	1	1	2023	2023	2023
Mockel, Otto	1	1	1964	1964	1964
Moitessier, Louis	1	0			
Monk, John King	1	1	266	266	266
Monnig, Fritz	2	2	2044	2170	2107
Montagnana, Domenico	1	1	172920	172920	172920
Montani, Costante	1	1	4703	4703	4703
Moody, G. T.	1	1	988	988	988
Morizot, Rene	1	1	1101	1101	1101
Mougenot, L.	1	1	5355	5355	5355
Mougenot, Leon	1	1	3027	3027	3027
Mougenot, Leon (attributed to)	1	1	2081	2081	2081
Mougenot, Leon (workshop of)	1	1	1729	1729	1729
Moya, Hidalgo	2	2	1419	3291	2355
Mozzani, Luigi	2	2	1447	2492	1969
Muller, Joseph	1	1	374	374	374
Nafissi, Carlo	1	0			
Neff, Joseph	2	2	330	468	399
Neuner, Ludwig	1	1	2257	2257	2257
Neuner, Mathias	1	1	494	494	494
Neuner, N.	1	1	446	446	446
Neuner & Hornsteiner	5	4	517	1881	914
Neuner & Hornsteiner (attributed to)	1	1	921	921	921
Nicolas, Didier (l'aine)	12	11	605	5634	2112
Nolli, Marco	1	1	1808	1808	1808
Norman, Barak	1	0			
Oddone, Carlo Giuseppe	3	3	18810	23280	21235
Oldfield, W.	2	1	604	604	604
Olivier, Christian	1	1	1481	1481	1481
Orlandini, A.	1	1	2975	2975	2975
Ornati, Giuseppe	1	0			
Ortega, Asencio (attributed to)	1	0			
Otto,Rudi	1	1	1980	1980	1980

Item/Maker	*Items Offered*	*Items Sold*	*Lowest $*	*Highest $*	*Average $*
Owen, John W.	1	1	2468	2468	2468
Palzini, Gianbattista	1	1	1980	1980	1980
Panormo, Edward Ferdinand (attributed to)	1	0			
Panormo, George	2	1	12969	12969	12969
Panormo, Vincenzo	4	4	20691	64845	45784
Panormo, Vincenzo (attributed to)	1	1	10534	10534	10534
Papageorgiou, Georges D.	1	1	3026	3026	3026
Parker, Daniel (attributed to)	1	1	10402	10402	10402
Partl, Christian Franz	2	1	2925	2925	2925
Patterson, W. D.	1	1	1121	1121	1121
Pearce, George	1	1	4138	4138	4138
Pedrazzini, Giuseppe	2	1	22605	22605	22605
Pelizon, Antonio	1	0			
Penzl, Ignaz	2	2	823	1047	935
Perrin, E. J. (fils)	1	0			
Perry, L. A.	2	1	601	601	601
Perry, Stephen	1	1	385	385	385
Perry, Thomas	2	2	1505	1650	1577
Pfretzschner, Carl Friedrich (attributed to)	1	1	1447	1447	1447
Pfretzschner, G. A.	1	1	935	935	935
Phillipson, Edward	2	2	473	494	484
Piccione, Emilio	1	1	8059	8059	8059
Pierray, Claude	2	2	1266	6052	3659
Pierray, Claude (attributed to)	3	2	1045	5851	3448
Pilat, Paul	1	1	7190	7190	7190
Pillement, Francois	2	2	320	641	480
Piper, W.	1	1	1300	1300	1300
Pique, Francois Louis	2	1	36746	36746	36746
Piretti, Enrico	1	1	4334	4334	4334
Pirot, Claude	1	1	14266	14266	14266
Placht, Johann Franz	1	1	1505	1505	1505
Plumerel, Jean	1	1	760	760	760
Politi, Enrico & Raul	1	0			
Pollastri, Augusto	1	0			
Pollastri, Augusto (attributed to)	1	0			
Pollastri, Gaetano	1	1	14875	14875	14875
Poller, Paul	1	1	357	357	357
Postacchini, Andrea	1	1	20691	20691	20691
Postiglione, Vincenzo	2	2	13431	16660	15046
Praga, Eugenio (ascribed to)	1	0			
Pressenda, Giovanni Francesco	3	2	62708	104060	83384
Preston, John	1	1	320	320	320
Pullar, E. F.	1	1	501	501	501
Pyne, George	3	3	2081	3574	2763
Raffe, E. H.	2	2	1505	7524	4514
Rance, J. F.	1	1	2069	2069	2069
Rapoport, Haim	1	0			
Rasura, Vincenzo (ascribed to)	1	1	4703	4703	4703
Rauch, Sebastian	1	1	1785	1785	1785
Rauch, Thomas	1	1	1693	1693	1693
Raymond, Robert John	1	1	453	453	453
Reichel, Johann Friedrich	1	0			
Reiter, Johann	1	1	1190	1190	1190
Remy	2	2	1324	1409	1366
Renisto, Andreas	1	1	3026	3026	3026
Richardson, Arthur	3	2	3801	4070	3935
Richter, Eckart	1	0			
Richter, G.	1	1	1607	1607	1607
Ridge	1	0			
Rinaldi, Marengo Romanus	1	1	17255	17255	17255
Robinson, William	3	3	829	4371	2347
Rocca, Enrico	1	1	16065	16065	16065
Rocca, Giuseppe	1	1	113520	113520	113520
Rocca, Joseph	1	1	161766	161766	161766
Rogeri, Giovanni Battista	1	1	121044	121044	121044
Rogeri, Pietro Giacomo	1	0			
Rost, Franz George	1	1	2280	2280	2280

Item/Maker	*Items Offered*	*Items Sold*	*Lowest $*	*Highest $*	*Average $*
Roth, Ernst Heinrich	4	4	880	1558	1172
Roumen, Johannes Arnoldus	1	0			
Rovescalli, T.	1	1	4760	4760	4760
Ruggieri, Francesco	2	1	80586	80586	80586
Ruggieri, Vincenzo	1	0			
Ruggieri, Vincenzo (attributed to)	1	0			
Rushworth & Dreaper	2	1	3574	3574	3574
Salsedo, Luigi	1	1	3675	3675	3675
Salsedo, Luigi (attributed to)	1	1	4891	4891	4891
Salzard, Francois	1	1	561	561	561
Sander, Carl	1	1	950	950	950
Sandner, Edi	1	1	778	778	778
Sannino, Vincenzo	1	0			
Sannino, Vincenzo (attributed to)	1	1	10406	10406	10406
Sarfati, G.	1	1	1666	1666	1666
Scarampella, Stefano	1	1	22610	22610	22610
Schaller, Reinhold	1	1	446	446	446
Schau, Carl	1	0			
Scheerer, John	1	1	1317	1317	1317
Scheinlein, M. F.	1	1	1666	1666	1666
Schmidt, E. R. & Co.	3	3	323	1522	845
Schmidt, Johann Martin	1	0			
Schmidt, Reinhold	1	1	770	770	770
Schmitt, Lucien	1	1	3406	3406	3406
Schoenfelder, Johann Georg	1	1	5058	5058	5058
Schroeder, John G.	1	1	715	715	715
Schuster, C. J. & Son	1	1	323	323	323
Schwarz, Giovanni	1	1	9781	9781	9781
Schwarz, Heinrich	1	1	757	757	757
Schweitzer, Johann Baptiste (attributed to)	1	1	2899	2899	2899
Scolari, Giorgio	2	2	4984	7521	6253
Sderci, Luciano	1	0			
Sderci, Luciano (attributed to)	1	1	8668	8668	8668
Seidel, Christian Wilhelm	1	1	1159	1159	1159
Seidel, Johann Michael	1	1	418	418	418
Seraphin, Sanctus (attributed to)	1	0			
Sgarabotto, Pietro	1	1	8954	8954	8954
Sgarbi, Antonio	1	0			
Siega, Ettore & Son (ascribed to)	1	1	4107	4107	4107
Silvestre, Pierre	1	1	15563	15563	15563
Silvestre & Maucotel	1	1	15130	15130	15130
Simon, Franz	2	1	1851	1851	1851
Simoutre, Nicholas Eugene	1	1	4371	4371	4371
Simpson, James & John	1	1	3950	3950	3950
Simpson, Thomas	1	1	1129	1129	1129
Smillie, Alexander	2	2	1505	4117	2811
Soffritti, Ettore	1	0			
Sorsano, Spirito	1	1	58311	58311	58311
Soubeyran, Marc	1	0			
Stadlmann, Johann Joseph	2	1	2633	2633	2633
Stainer, Jacob	1	1	50600	50600	50600
Stainer, Marcus (attributed to)	1	1	2860	2860	2860
Stanley, Robert A.	1	1	1621	1621	1621
Stirrat, David	2	1	4463	4463	4463
Storioni, Carlo	1	1	1837	1837	1837
Storioni, Lorenzo	1	1	68050	68050	68050
Stradivari, Antonio	2	1	1776940	1776940	1776940
Stradivari, Omobono	1	0			
Straub, Simon	1	1	4463	4463	4463
Suzuki, M.	1	1	430	430	430
Tarasconi, G.	1	1	8330	8330	8330
Tarr, Shelley	1	0			
Tassini, Marco	1	1	2053	2053	2053
Tavegia, Carlo Antonio	2	1	4323	4323	4323
Tecchler, David	1	1	26862	26862	26862
Tecchler, David (attributed to)	1	1	4702	4702	4702
Tenucci, Eugen	1	1	5950	5950	5950

Item/Maker	Items Offered	Items Sold	Lowest $	Highest $	Average $
Termanini, Pietro	1	1	12227	12227	12227
Testore, Carlo	1	1	41173	41173	41173
Testore, Carlo (attributed to)	1	1	29180	29180	29180
Testore, Carlo Antonio	1	1	47674	47674	47674
Testore, Carlo Giuseppe	1	0			
Testore Family (member of)	2	2	3386	16553	9969
Thibout, Jacques Pierre	1	1	4703	4703	4703
Thibouville-Lamy	17	16	190	1995	686
Thibouville-Lamy, J.	6	6	281	1102	673
Thibouville-Lamy, J. (workshop of)	1	1	4950	4950	4950
Thibouville-Lamy, Jerome	9	8	595	2162	1122
Thier, Joseph (attributed to)	1	1	1085	1085	1085
Thir, Mathias	2	1	1950	1950	1950
Thir, Mathias (attributed to)	1	1	4971	4971	4971
Thompson, Charles & Samuel	4	3	868	2445	1647
Thompson & Son	1	1	4971	4971	4971
Thomson	1	1	304	304	304
Thorburn, S. W.	1	1	361	361	361
Thouvenel, Charles	1	1	2366	2366	2366
Thow, J.	1	1	561	561	561
Tiller, G. W.	1	1	735	735	735
Tim-Geigen	1	1	1401	1401	1401
Tobin, Richard	1	0			
Tobin, Richard (attributed to)	1	1	904	904	904
Tomassini, Domenico (ascribed to)	1	1	4138	4138	4138
Tononi, Carlo	1	1	38907	38907	38907
Tweedale, Charles L.	1	1	741	741	741
Valenzano, Joannes Maria	2	2	28215	60192	44204
Valenzano, Joannes Maria (ascribed to)	1	0			
Vautelint, N. Pierre	1	1	5267	5267	5267
Ventapane, Lorenzo	3	3	9511	35739	23634
Ventapane, Lorenzo (attributed to)	1	0			
Verini, Andrea	1	1	2880	2880	2880
Vickers, J. E.	2	2	1059	1541	1300
Vinaccia Family (member of)	1	0			
Vincent, Alfred	3	3	4561	6461	5257
Vincent, Alfred (attributed to)	1	1	4114	4114	4114
Visconti, Domenico (attributed to)	1	1	1892	1892	1892
Vlummens, Dominic	1	1	3950	3950	3950
Voigt, Arnold	1	1	985	985	985
Voigt, Johann Georg	1	0			
Voigt, Paul	1	1	1159	1159	1159
Voller Brothers	1	1	24596	24596	24596
Von Dolling, (younger)	1	0			
Vuillaume, Jean Baptiste	8	7	16660	64845	34525
Vuillaume, Jean Baptiste (ascribed to)	1	1	17974	17974	17974
Vuillaume, Jean Baptiste (workshop of)	1	1	39006	39006	39006
Vuillaume, Nicholas	2	2	5404	14758	10081
Vuillaume, Sebastian	2	1	4371	4371	4371
Wagner, Benedict (attributed to)	1	1	1540	1540	1540
Walker, William	2	1	2860	2860	2860
Walton, William	1	1	851	851	851
Wamsley, Peter	6	5	893	8465	4007
Wanner, Michael	1	1	912	912	912
Ward, George	1	1	1419	1419	1419
Wassermann, Joseph	1	1	5643	5643	5643
Weigert, Johann Blasius	1	1	2090	2090	2090
Whedbee, William	1	1	1540	1540	1540
Whitbread, W. W.	1	1	324	324	324
White, Asa Warren	1	1	715	715	715
White, H. N. & Co.	1	1	330	330	330
Whitmarsh, Edwin	1	1	1517	1517	1517
Whitmarsh, Emanuel	1	1	1131	1131	1131
Widhalm, Leopold	4	4	1234	17255	6674
Wilkanowski, W.	2	2	605	990	798
Wilkinson, John	1	0			
Wilkinson, William & Perry, Thomas	1	1	1481	1481	1481

Item/Maker	*Items Offered*	*Items Sold*	*Lowest $*	*Highest $*	*Average $*
Wilson, Tom	1	1	355	355	355
Winterling, G.	2	2	5355	9223	7289
Withers, Edward	1	1	3026	3026	3026
Wolff Bros.	7	7	271	819	460
Wouldhave, John	1	0			
Zach, Thomas (attributed to)	1	1	2532	2532	2532
Zanier, Ferruccio	1	1	3868	3868	3868
Zemitis, M.	1	1	1131	1131	1131
Zettwitz, William	1	0			
Zimmerman, Friederich	1	1	646	646	646

VIOLIN BOW

Alvey, Brian	2	1	1970	1970	1970
Apparut, Georges	1	1	952	952	952
Bausch, L.	2	2	309	324	316
Bazin	1	1	1470	1470	1470
Bazin, C.	2	2	345	507	426
Bazin, Charles	9	9	329	2059	1134
Bazin, Louis	5	5	330	2649	1154
Bazin Family (member of)	1	0			
Beare, John & Arthur	1	1	2384	2384	2384
Bernardel, Gustave	4	3	946	2445	1706
Bernardel, Leon	2	2	951	1693	1322
Bernardel, Rene	1	1	2069	2069	2069
Bisch, Paul	1	1	770	770	770
Brand, Karl	1	1	243	243	243
Briggs, James William	1	1	564	564	564
Bristow, Stephen	1	1	711	711	711
Bultitude, A. R.	1	1	2162	2162	2162
Bultitude, Arthur	2	2	1300	3458	2379
Buthod, Charles	2	1	281	281	281
Callier, Frank	2	2	605	1320	963
Caressa, Albert	1	1	1729	1729	1729
Caressa & Francais	2	1	2916	2916	2916
Carrodus	1	1	893	893	893
Chadwick	1	1	893	893	893
Chanot, Joseph Anthony	1	1	2594	2594	2594
Chardon, Chanot	1	1	387	387	387
Collin-Mezin	2	1	1297	1297	1297
Cuniot-Hury	2	2	298	1235	767
Cuniot-Hury, Eugene	1	1	1411	1411	1411
Darche, Hilaire	1	1	908	908	908
Delivet, Auguste	1	0			
Dodd	5	4	473	3451	1955
Dodd, Edward	1	1	2822	2822	2822
Dodd, James	3	2	1842	3762	2802
Dodd, John	3	2	1223	2810	2016
Dodd, John (ascribed to)	1	0			
Dodd, John (attributed to)	2	2	476	1254	865
Dodd Family (member of)	2	1	2328	2328	2328
Dolling, Kurt	1	1	394	394	394
Dorfler, D.	1	1	254	254	254
Dotschkail, R.	1	1	1071	1071	1071
Dugad, Andre	1	1	339	339	339
Dupuy, George	1	0			
Durrschmidt, O.	1	1	357	357	357
Durrschmidt, Otto	6	6	247	798	435
Eulry, Clement	1	1	3386	3386	3386
Eury, Nicolas	2	1	8276	8276	8276
Fetique, Jules	1	1	2200	2200	2200
Fetique, Victor	7	6	1317	6268	3403
Finkel, Siegfried	1	1	770	770	770
Francais, Emile	3	2	1505	1693	1599
Gand & Bernardel	1	1	2633	2633	2633
Geipel, Richard	2	1	302	302	302
Gerome, Roger	2	1	774	774	774
Gillet, R.	1	1	2083	2083	2083

Item/Maker	Items Offered	Items Sold	Lowest $	Highest $	Average $
GLASEL	1	1	1071	1071	1071
GOTZ	1	0			
GOTZ, CONRAD	2	2	651	941	796
GRAND ADAM	1	1	16253	16253	16253
GUETTER, OTTO	1	1	645	645	645
HAGEMANN, F. R.	2	1	190	190	190
HAMMIG, W. H.	2	1	323	323	323
HART & SON	1	0			
HEL, PIERRE	1	1	1129	1129	1129
HENRY, JOSEPH	1	0			
HERMANN, LOTHAR	1	1	473	473	473
HERRMANN, A.	3	3	368	746	564
HERRMANN, EDWARD	1	1	468	468	468
HERRMANN, W.	1	1	624	624	624
HILL, W. E. & SONS	65	64	344	5731	2162
HOYER, C. A.	1	1	865	865	865
HOYER, G.	1	1	387	387	387
HOYER, OTTO A.	3	3	935	1734	1238
HUMS, ALBIN	3	2	836	1701	1269
HUMS, W.	1	1	238	238	238
HUSSON, CHARLES CLAUDE (attributed to)	1	0			
KESSLER	1	1	431	431	431
KITTEL FAMILY (MEMBER OF) (ascribed to)	1	1	4656	4656	4656
KNOPF, HENRY RICHARD	1	1	550	550	550
LABERTE	1	1	536	536	536
LABERTE, MARC	1	1	774	774	774
LABERTE, MARC (ascribed to)	1	1	339	339	339
LAFLEUR (ascribed to)	1	0			
LAFLEUR, JOSEPH RENE	1	0			
LAFLEUR, JOSEPH RENE (ascribed to)	1	1	1625	1625	1625
LAMY, A.	2	1	4463	4463	4463
LAMY, ALFRED	10	9	281	6934	4103
LAMY, ALFRED JOSEPH	1	1	4138	4138	4138
LEBLANC, P. R.	3	3	417	536	476
LERMETZ	1	1	185	185	185
LOTTE, FRANCOIS	3	3	716	1038	898
LOWENDALL, LOUIS	1	0			
LUPOT, FRANCOIS	1	1	13167	13167	13167
LUPOT, FRANCOIS (attributed to)	1	1	5372	5372	5372
LUPOT, NICOLAS	1	0			
MAIRE, NICOLAS	3	2	8628	8646	8637
MARTIN	1	1	370	370	370
MAURE, PIERRE	1	1	874	874	874
MEAUCHAND	1	1	6068	6068	6068
MEAUCHAND (attributed to)	1	1	6068	6068	6068
MEINEL, EUGEN	2	2	110	414	262
MILLANT, B.	1	1	1488	1488	1488
MIQUEL, E.	1	1	527	527	527
MOLLER, MAX	1	1	1317	1317	1317
MORIZOT	2	2	1129	1210	1169
MORIZOT, LOUIS	5	5	298	1223	788
MOUGENOT, GEORGES	1	1	941	941	941
MUHL	1	1	798	798	798
NURNBERGER, ALBERT	18	17	249	4046	1399
OUCHARD, E.	2	2	1071	1131	1101
OUCHARD, EMILE	3	2	1159	1664	1412
PAESOLD, RODERICH	3	3	418	570	507
PAJEOT	1	0			
PAJEOT (attributed to)	1	1	6934	6934	6934
PAJEOT, (FILS)	2	2	5620	9078	7349
PAJEOT, (PERE)	1	1	8330	8330	8330
PAQUOTTE BROS.	2	1	1945	1945	1945
PAULUS, JOHANNES O.	1	1	387	387	387
PECCATTE, DOMINIQUE	2	2	16211	39006	27609
PECCATTE, DOMINIQUE (attributed to)	1	1	6052	6052	6052
PECCATTE, FRANCOIS	1	1	11286	11286	11286
PENZEL	1	1	1059	1059	1059

Item/Maker	*Items Offered*	*Items Sold*	*Lowest $*	*Highest $*	*Average $*
PENZEL, K.	1	1	149	149	149
PERSOIS (attributed to)	1	1	9752	9752	9752
PFRETZSCHNER, F. C.	1	1	833	833	833
PFRETZSCHNER, H. R.	12	11	149	1892	798
PFRETZSCHNER, T. H.	1	1	446	446	446
PFRETZSCHNER, W. A.	3	2	453	798	625
PILLOT	1	0			
POIRSON	1	1	1666	1666	1666
PRAGER, AUGUST EDWIN	2	2	604	744	674
PRAGER, GUSTAV	3	3	568	681	607
RAU, AUGUST	4	4	326	1074	796
RETFORD, WILLIAM C.	1	1	8214	8214	8214
RICHAUME, ANDRE	1	1	3684	3684	3684
RUSHWORTH & DREAPER	1	1	601	601	601
SALCHOW, WILLIAM	1	1	2810	2810	2810
SANDNER, A. E.	1	1	440	440	440
SARTORY, EUGENE	23	22	1785	9511	5802
SAUNDERS, S.	1	1	8514	8514	8514
SCHREIBER & LUGERT	1	1	774	774	774
SCHUBERT PAUL	1	0			
SCHULLER, OTTO	1	1	340	340	340
SCHUSTER, ADOLF	4	3	303	501	423
SCHUSTER, ADOLF C.	2	2	361	1141	751
SCHWARZ, B.	2	1	497	497	497
SERDET, PAUL	1	1	3891	3891	3891
SHANTI-DEVA	1	1	129	129	129
SILVESTRE & MAUCOTEL	1	1	3675	3675	3675
SIMON (attributed to)	1	1	2149	2149	2149
SIMON, PAUL	1	0			
SIMON, PAUL (ascribed to)	1	0			
SIMONIN	1	1	1131	1131	1131
STOESS, A.	1	1	327	327	327
SUSS, CHRISTIAN	1	1	535	535	535
TAYLOR, MALCOLM	3	2	752	1223	988
THIBOUVILLE-LAMY	4	3	329	692	491
THOMA, MATHIAS	1	0			
THOMASSIN, CLAUDE	5	4	1599	2384	2082
THOMASSIN, CLAUDE (attributed to)	1	1	1254	1254	1254
TOURTE, FRANCOIS	4	3	4950	43340	21740
TOURTE, LOUIS	1	1	3901	3901	3901
TOURTE, LOUIS (attributed to)	1	1	4117	4117	4117
TUBBS, EDWARD	2	2	1074	6584	3829
TUBBS, JAMES	20	19	646	5079	3103
TUBBS, WILLIAM	2	2	1289	3010	2149
TUBBS, WILLIAM (attributed to)	1	1	647	647	647
TUBBS FAMILY, (MEMBER OF)	1	0			
VAN DER MEER, KAREL	4	3	696	2270	1333
VIDOUDEZ, FRANCOIS	1	1	1129	1129	1129
VIGNERON, ANDRE	4	4	1317	2420	1999
VILLAUME, G.	1	1	357	357	357
VOIGT, ARNOLD	1	1	741	741	741
VOIRIN, FRANCOIS NICOLAS	13	12	2162	16253	6420
VOIRIN, J.	1	1	714	714	714
VOIRIN, JOSEPH	1	1	832	832	832
VUILLAUME, JEAN BAPTISTE	3	2	2090	2420	2255
VUILLAUME, JEAN BAPTISTE (ascribed to)	1	1	2069	2069	2069
VUILLAUME, JEAN BAPTISTE (workshop of)	1	1	7585	7585	7585
WALTON, WILLIAM	1	0			
WEICHOLD, A. R.	1	1	470	470	470
WEICHOLD, R.	5	5	535	760	627
WEICHOLD, RICHARD	5	4	280	1433	843
WEIDHAAS, PAUL	5	5	394	3094	1165
WERRO, JEAN	1	1	645	645	645
WILSON, GARNER	4	3	418	1405	869
WILSON, JAMES J. T.	2	2	733	1337	1035
WINKLER, FRANZ	2	1	645	645	645
WINTERLING, GEORGE	1	1	387	387	387

Item/Maker	Items Offered	Items Sold	Lowest $	Highest $	Average $
WOODFIELD, J. D.	1	0			
WUNDERLICH, F. R.	1	1	1419	1419	1419
ZIMMER, E. W.	1	1	357	357	357
VIOLONCELLO					
AIRETON, EDMUND (attributed to)	1	1	2992	2992	2992
BAILLY, PAUL (ascribed to)	1	0			
BANKS, JAMES & HENRY (attributed to)	2	1	5348	5348	5348
BARRETT, JOHN	1	0			
BETTS, JOHN	1	1	33503	33503	33503
BOULANGEOT, EMILE	2	1	9727	9727	9727
CAPPA, GOFFREDO	1	1	37826	37826	37826
CONIA, STEFANO	1	1	14108	14108	14108
CONTINO, ALFREDO (attributed to)	1	1	6052	6052	6052
CORSBY, GEORGE (attributed to)	1	1	3467	3467	3467
CRASKE, GEORGE	1	1	6805	6805	6805
CROSS, NATHANIEL	1	1	16929	16929	16929
DE COMBLE, AMBROSE	1	1	4107	4107	4107
DEGANI, EUGENIO	1	1	25653	25653	25653
DERAZEY, HONORE (workshop of)	1	1	9101	9101	9101
DERAZEY, JUSTIN	1	1	1481	1481	1481
DIEHL, JOHANN	1	1	28967	28967	28967
DODD, THOMAS	1	1	15466	15466	15466
DUKE, RICHARD	1	1	3010	3010	3010
FORSTER, WILLIAM	1	0			
FURBER, HENRY	1	1	8653	8653	8653
FURBER, JOHN	1	1	860	860	860
FURBER, JOHN (attributed to)	1	1	7407	7407	7407
GADDA, GAETANO	1	1	15470	15470	15470
GAFFINO, JOSEPH	1	0			
GAGLIANO, GIOVANNI	1	1	28215	28215	28215
GOULDING & CO.	1	1	2185	2185	2185
GRANCINO, GIOVANNI	1	1	82137	82137	82137
GUERSAN, LOUIS	1	0			
GUERSAN, LOUIS (ascribed to)	1	0			
HARRIS, CHARLES	2	1	7781	7781	7781
HART & SON	1	1	3762	3762	3762
HERMANN, LOTHAR	1	0			
HILL, JOSEPH	1	1	22572	22572	22572
HILL, LOCKEY (attributed to)	1	0			
HJORTH, EMIL & SON	1	1	8465	8465	8465
HOFMANS, MATHIAS	1	1	12969	12969	12969
HOYER, JOHANN FRIEDERICH	1	0			
HUBICKA, JULIUS A.	1	1	17028	17028	17028
JAIS, ANDREAS	1	1	2633	2633	2633
JOHNSON, JOHN (attributed to)	1	0			
JORIO, VINCENZO	1	1	16929	16929	16929
KENNEDY, THOMAS	1	1	14108	14108	14108
KENNEDY, THOMAS (ascribed to)	1	1	5404	5404	5404
KREUZINGER, FRIEDRICH	1	1	1320	1320	1320
KRINER, JOSEPH	1	1	4703	4703	4703
LABERTE-HUMBERT BROS.	1	1	4539	4539	4539
LEEB, ANDREAS CARL	1	1	7900	7900	7900
LONGMAN & BRODERIP	1	0			
LONGMAN & LUKEY	2	2	8596	13431	11013
LOWENDALL, LOUIS	1	1	4138	4138	4138
MARCHI, GIOVANNI ANTONIO	1	1	27275	27275	27275
NAMY, JEAN THEODORE	1	0			
NEUNER & HORNSTEINER	2	1	7133	7133	7133
NICOLAS	1	1	17028	17028	17028
OTTO, MAX	1	0			
OWEN, JOHN W.	1	1	8639	8639	8639
PILLEMENT, FRANCOIS	1	0			
PRECUB, FLOREA	1	1	3868	3868	3868
PRESCOTT, GRAHAM	1	1	846	846	846
PRESTON, JAMES	1	1	2899	2899	2899
PURDAY, T. E.	1	1	11640	11640	11640

Item/Maker	*Items Offered*	*Items Sold*	*Lowest $*	*Highest $*	*Average $*
Pyne, George	1	1	7900	7900	7900
Quargnal, Rudolfo	1	1	4165	4165	4165
Rambaux, Claude Victor	1	0			
Rautmann, Carl	1	1	6395	6395	6395
Richardson, Arthur	2	1	9752	9752	9752
Rocca, Enrico	1	0			
Rocca, Enrico (attributed to)	1	0			
Rodiani, Giovita (attributed to)	1	1	6600	6600	6600
Rogeri, Giovanni Battista (ascribed to)	1	0			
Roth, Ernst Heinrich	1	1	7565	7565	7565
Rottenburgh, Jean Hyacinthe	1	1	15424	15424	15424
Ruggieri & Guarneri, Francesco & P.	1	1	45392	45392	45392
Rushworth & Dreaper	1	0			
Schutz	1	1	3026	3026	3026
Sgarbi, Giuseppe	1	1	27370	27370	27370
Smith, Thomas	1	1	3420	3420	3420
Smith, Thomas (attributed to)	1	1	5407	5407	5407
Sorsano, Spirito (attributed to)	1	1	30261	30261	30261
Stewart, N.	1	1	13030	13030	13030
Symington, George	1	1	1330	1330	1330
Testore Family (member of) (attributed to)	1	1	19751	19751	19751
Thibouville-Lamy	1	1	3086	3086	3086
Thibouville-Lamy, J.	1	1	5701	5701	5701
Tiriot	1	1	833	833	833
Tobin, Richard	1	1	23513	23513	23513
Tobin, Richard (ascribed to)	1	0			
Ventapane, Lorenzo	1	0			
Vuillaume, Jean Baptiste	1	0			
Vuillaume, Jean Baptiste (workshop of)	1	1	26862	26862	26862
Wamsley, Peter	1	0			
Werner, Erich	1	1	1683	1683	1683
Widhalm, Leopold	1	0			
Wolff Bros.	1	1	5267	5267	5267

VIOLONCELLO BOW

Adam, J.	1	1	3570	3570	3570
Alvey, Brian	1	0			
Bausch	2	2	298	329	314
Bausch, L.	1	1	411	411	411
Bausch, L. (attributed to)	1	1	329	329	329
Bazin	1	1	1164	1164	1164
Bazin, Charles	1	1	1164	1164	1164
Bazin, Charles Nicholas	2	2	1787	2162	1974
Bazin, Louis	1	1	1513	1513	1513
Brown, James (attributed to)	2	1	476	476	476
Bryant, Percival Wilfred	2	1	1223	1223	1223
Bultitude, A. R.	1	1	1989	1989	1989
Cuniot-Hury	1	0			
Dodd, John	2	2	540	3386	1963
Dodd Family (member of)	1	1	2053	2053	2053
Dolling, Heinz	2	1	646	646	646
Dorfler, D.	1	1	1658	1658	1658
Dorfler, Egidius	1	1	2069	2069	2069
Dupuy, George	1	1	1599	1599	1599
Durrschmidt, O.	1	1	357	357	357
Eulry, Clement	1	0			
Fetique, Victor	2	1	2649	2649	2649
Fetique, Victor (ascribed to)	1	0			
Finkel, Siegfried	1	1	1430	1430	1430
Forster	1	1	3406	3406	3406
Fritsch, Jean	1	1	798	798	798
Gerome, Roger	1	0			
Glesel, C.	1	0			
Hart	1	1	992	992	992
Hart & Son	1	1	1748	1748	1748
Hermann, Lothar	1	0			
Hill, W. E. & Sons	27	26	324	4514	1909

Item/Maker	*Items Offered*	*Items Sold*	*Lowest $*	*Highest $*	*Average $*
HOYER, HERMANN ALBERT	1	1	430	430	430
HOYER, OTTO A.	1	0			
HUSSON, CHARLES CLAUDE	2	1	3080	3080	3080
KNOPF	1	1	417	417	417
KNOPF, W.	1	1	880	880	880
KUN, JOSEPH	1	1	416	416	416
LAMY, ALFRED	3	2	1317	4477	2897
LAPIERRE, MARCEL	1	1	1029	1029	1029
LEBLANC, P. R.	3	3	655	1428	972
LEFIN	1	1	523	523	523
LOTTE, FRANCOIS	1	1	785	785	785
LUPOT, NICOLAS	1	0			
MALINES, GUILLAUME	1	1	4539	4539	4539
MORIZOT, LOUIS	2	1	646	646	646
NEUDORFER	1	0			
NEUVEVILLE, G. C.	2	2	535	1078	806
NURNBERGER, ALBERT	5	5	495	1881	1078
PAULUS, JOHANNES O.	1	1	501	501	501
PECCATTE, D.	1	1	11305	11305	11305
PFRETZSCHNER, H. R.	7	6	598	1124	920
PFRETZSCHNER, W. A.	2	2	470	573	522
REYNOLDS, J.	1	0			
RIEDL, ALFONS	2	1	829	829	829
SANDNER, B.	1	1	149	149	149
SARTORY, EUGENE	8	7	4138	8668	5745
SCHMIDT, C. HANS CARL	1	1	752	752	752
SEIFERT, LOTHAR	1	1	501	501	501
SILVESTRE & MAUCOTEL	1	0			
THIBOUVILLE-LAMY, J.	1	1	972	972	972
THOMASSIN, C.	2	2	3386	5058	4222
THOMASSIN, CLAUDE	1	1	2257	2257	2257
TOURTE, LOUIS (attributed to)	1	0			
TUBBS, JAMES	2	2	5620	5731	5675
TUBBS, THOMAS (ascribed to)	1	0			
VAN DER MEER, KAREL	1	0			
VIGNERON, ANDRE	2	2	1703	4323	3013
VOIRIN, FRANCOIS NICOLAS	5	4	473	5267	3462
VUILLAUME, JEAN BAPTISTE	2	1	4138	4138	4138
WEICHOLD, R.	1	1	1275	1275	1275
WEICHOLD, RICHARD	1	1	1074	1074	1074
WILSON, GARNER	3	2	1189	1317	1253
WITHERS, GEORGE & SONS	1	1	506	506	506
WOODFIELD, J. D.	1	1	501	501	501
WUNDERLICH, F. R.	1	1	573	573	573
WUNDERLICH, FRITZ	1	1	495	495	495

VIOLONCELLO PICCOLO

BOLINK, JAAP	1	0			
WOLFF BROS.	1	1	3762	3762	3762

XYLOPHONE

CULLIFORD ROLFE & BARROW	1	1	143	143	143

Item/Maker	*Items Offered*	*Items Sold*	*Lowest DM*	*Highest DM*	*Average DM*
ACCORDION					
Horne, Edgar	1	1	519	519	519
AEOLA					
Wheatstone & Co., C.	1	1	1671	1671	1671
BAGPIPES					
MacDougall, D.	1	0			
BANJO					
Bacon Banjo Co.	1	1	1475	1475	1475
Fairbanks Co., A. C.	1	1	1065	1065	1065
Fiesta	1	1	287	287	287
Libby Bros.	1	1	451	451	451
BANJO MANDOLIN					
Gibson Co.	1	1	246	246	246
BASS RECORDER					
Goble, Robert	1	0			
BASS VIOL DA GAMBA					
Steber, Ernst	1	0			
BASSOON					
Bilton, Richard	1	1	2223	2223	2223
Bocchia, Bono	1	1	738	738	738
Buffet	1	1	492	492	492
Buffet-Crampon & Co.	1	1	605	605	605
Goulding, Wood & Co.	1	0			
Grenser, Johann Heinrich	1	1	20646	20646	20646
Heckel	2	1	15428	15428	15428
Heckel, Wilhelm	1	0			
Milhouse, William	1	0			
Zimmermann, Julius Heinrich	1	1	533	533	533
BUGLE					
Astor & Co., Gerock	1	1	1019	1019	1019
Pace, Charles	1	1	2802	2802	2802
CITHERN					
Preston	1	1	825	825	825
CLARINET					
Bilton, Richard	2	2	2223	2859	2541
Conn, C. G.	1	1	287	287	287
Cramer	1	1	1164	1164	1164
Darche	1	1	915	915	915
Florio, Pietro Grassi	1	1	1906	1906	1906
Goulding & Co.	1	1	605	605	605
Klemm	1	1	1117	1117	1117
Lot, Isadore	1	1	571	571	571
Martin Bros.	1	1	732	732	732
Metzler	1	1	656	656	656
Otten, John	1	1	452	452	452
Selmer	1	1	350	350	350
Wolf & Co., Robert	1	1	580	580	580
Wood & Ivy	1	1	671	671	671
CLAVICHORD					
Goff, Thomas	1	0			
Lindholm, Pehr	1	0			

Item/Maker	*Items Offered*	*Items Sold*	*Lowest DM*	*Highest DM*	*Average DM*
CONCERTINA					
Crabb, Henry	1	0			
Crabb & Son, H.	1	1	1142	1142	1142
Jeffries, Charles	1	1	546	546	546
Jeffries Bros.	1	1	444	444	444
Lachenal & Co.	3	2	1237	2160	1699
Wheatstone & Co., C.	6	5	781	2196	1392
CONTRA GUITAR					
Hauser, Hermann	1	0			
CORNOPEAN					
Kohler, John	1	1	6670	6670	6670
CORONET					
Conn, C. G.	1	1	451	451	451
Pepper, J. W.	1	1	574	574	574
DOUBLE BASS					
Cole, James	1	1	19058	19058	19058
Derazey, Justin	1	1	9141	9141	9141
Jacquot Family (member of)	1	1	2622	2622	2622
Panormo, Vincenzo (ascribed to)	1	1	14626	14626	14626
DOUBLE BASS BOW					
Alvey, Brian	1	0			
Bailey, G. E.	1	1	1678	1678	1678
Dotschkail, R.	1	1	1022	1022	1022
Mettal, O.	1	1	803	803	803
Mettal, Walter	1	1	1533	1533	1533
Morizot, Louis	2	1	549	549	549
Paulus, Johannes O.	2	2	1387	1460	1423
Riedl, Alfons	3	3	622	1168	962
Vickers, J. E.	3	3	326	580	418
Winkler, Franz	1	1	1220	1220	1220
ENGLISH HORN					
Fornari	1	0			
Loree, Francois	1	1	6040	6040	6040
FLAGEOLET					
Bainbridge	1	1	381	381	381
Hastrick	1	1	671	671	671
Peloubet, C.	1	1	820	820	820
FLUTE					
Boehm & Mendler	1	0			
Cahusac	1	1	894	894	894
Cahusac, Thomas	2	1	977	977	977
Carte, Rudall & Co.	4	3	179	3508	1367
Clementi & Co.	1	1	637	637	637
Clinton & Co.	1	1	1656	1656	1656
Crosby, W.	1	1	779	779	779
Florio, Pietro Grassi	2	1	10164	10164	10164
Goulding & Co.	1	1	309	309	309
Goulding & D'Almaine	2	1	605	605	605
Graves, Samuel	1	1	574	574	574
Grenser, Auguste	1	1	27321	27321	27321
Hale, John	1	1	420	420	420
Hammig, Philipp	1	1	1470	1470	1470
Haynes Co., William S.	1	1	1393	1393	1393
Holtzapffler	1	0			
Lafleur	1	1	287	287	287
Laurent, Claude	2	1	17557	17557	17557

Item/Maker	Items Offered	Items Sold	Lowest DM	Highest DM	Average DM
Lot, Louis	3	2	1588	2541	2065
Maker's Guild No. 168	1	0			
Metzler, Valentin	2	1	260	260	260
Milligan	1	0			
Miyazawa & Co.	1	1	2070	2070	2070
Monzani	1	1	4821	4821	4821
Potter, William Henry	2	1	781	781	781
Prowse, Thomas	1	1	1678	1678	1678
Rede, H. W.	1	1	533	533	533
Rudall, George	1	1	2541	2541	2541
FRENCH HORN					
Hawkes & Son	1	1	955	955	955
GUITAR					
Bouchet, Robert	2	2	28928	44467	36698
Contreras, Manuel	1	0			
Gibson Co.	3	3	1803	3934	3059
Guitar Epiphone Co.	1	1	983	983	983
Gutierrez, manuel	1	0			
Hauser, Hermann	1	1	6428	6428	6428
Kohno, Masaru	2	1	3811	3811	3811
Lacote, Rene	1	1	6428	6428	6428
Martin Co., C. F.	1	1	2622	2622	2622
Mauchant Bros.	1	1	4764	4764	4764
Panormo, Louis	2	2	2501	4447	3474
Ramirez, Jose (III)	1	1	2893	2893	2893
Rinaldi, Marengo Romanus	1	0			
Romanillos, Jose	2	2	9321	26998	18160
HAND HORN					
Raoux, Marcel-Auguste	1	0			
HARP					
Briggs	1	1	1791	1791	1791
Delveau, J.	1	1	3063	3063	3063
Erard, Sebastian	3	2	2541	7623	5082
Erard, Sebastian & Pierre	1	1	1678	1678	1678
Errard	1	1	1678	1678	1678
Light, Edward	1	1	3332	3332	3332
Nadermann, Henry	1	0			
HARPSICHORD					
de Blaise, William	1	1	3497	3497	3497
Dulken, Johan Daniel	1	1	207196	207196	207196
Kirkman, Jacob & Abraham	1	1	147853	147853	147853
HORN					
White, H. N. & Co.	1	1	164	164	164
HURDY GURDY					
Colson	1	1	2539	2539	2539
LUTE					
Romanillos, Jose	1	0			
Rubio, David	2	1	10799	10799	10799
LUTE-GUITAR					
Barry	1	1	571	571	571
LYRA GUITAR					
Barry	1	1	3831	3831	3831
Mozzani, Luigi	2	1	1428	1428	1428

Item/Maker	Items Offered	Items Sold	Lowest DM	Highest DM	Average DM
MANDOLA					
Maratea, Michele	1	1	293	293	293
MANDOLIN					
Ceccherini, Umberto	1	0			
Embergher, Luigi	1	1	2602	2602	2602
Vinaccia, Gennaro & Alle	1	1	1333	1333	1333
Gibson Co.	1	1	3114	3114	3114
Salsedo, Luigi	1	1	1159	1159	1159
Vinaccia Family (member of) (attributed to)	1	1	4126	4126	4126
OBOE					
Boosey & Hawkes	1	1	371	371	371
Cabart	1	1	170	170	170
Doelling	1	1	2160	2160	2160
Hanken, Gerhard	1	1	2451	2451	2451
Loree, Francois	2	1	7312	7312	7312
Louis	1	1	5086	5086	5086
Milhouse, William	2	2	2859	4447	3653
Nonon, Jacques	1	0			
OBOE D'AMORE					
Loree, Francois	1	1	5086	5086	5086
Louis	1	1	12080	12080	12080
OPHICLEIDE					
Smith, Henry	1	1	1529	1529	1529
PEDAL HARP					
Erard, Sebastian & Pierre	4	4	2732	4500	3576
PIANO					
Atunes, Manuel	1	1	199280	199280	199280
Ball, Jacob	1	1	3053	3053	3053
Bates & Co.	1	1	1676	1676	1676
Bell, S.	1	0			
Beyer, Adam	1	1	3017	3017	3017
Broadwood, John	1	1	2636	2636	2636
Broadwood, John & Sons	5	4	1736	21857	7862
Buntlebart, Gabriel	1	1	4902	4902	4902
Clementi, Muzio	1	1	4902	4902	4902
Froschle, George	1	1	7617	7617	7617
Kirkman, Jacob & Abraham	1	1	13102	13102	13102
Mott, J. H. R.	1	1	1685	1685	1685
Rolfe & Co., William	1	1	5208	5208	5208
PICCOLO					
Bonneville	1	1	2293	2293	2293
Lot, Louis	1	1	4129	4129	4129
PIPES					
Burleigh, David	1	1	890	890	890
POCHETTE					
Jay, Henry (attributed to)	1	1	4558	4558	4558
Tobin, Richard	1	1	6186	6186	6186
QUINTON					
Salomon, Jean Baptiste Deshayes	1	1	3494	3494	3494
Wamsley, Peter	1	1	3494	3494	3494
RECORDER					
Dolmetsch, Arnold	1	1	826	826	826
Eichentopf, Johann Heinrich	1	1	3497	3497	3497

Item/Maker	*Items Offered*	*Items Sold*	*Lowest DM*	*Highest DM*	*Average DM*
SAXOPHONE					
Guinot, Rene	1	0			
SERPENT					
Metzler	1	1	3811	3811	3811
SMALL PIPES					
Reid, Robert & James	1	0			
SPINET					
Barton, Thomas	1	1	32142	32142	32142
Harris, Baker	1	0			
Slade, Benjamin	2	1	16714	16714	16714
TAROGATO					
Stowasser, Janos	1	1	4923	4923	4923
TENOR VIOL					
Heale, Michael	1	0			
Hintz, Frederick	1	1	17469	17469	17469
TROMBONE					
Courtois, Antoine	1	1	451	451	451
Pepper, J. W.	1	1	49	49	49
TRUMPET					
Gisborne	1	1	4299	4299	4299
VIHUELA					
Romanillos, Jose	1	1	4447	4447	4447
VIOL					
Norman, Barak	1	1	88935	88935	88935
VIOLA					
Albanelli, Franco	1	0			
Atkinson, William	2	1	5491	5491	5491
Barbieri, Bruno	1	1	7630	7630	7630
Bisiach, Leandro (jr.)	1	0			
Booth, William	1	1	4270	4270	4270
Bourguignon, Maurice	1	1	5786	5786	5786
Buchner, Rudolf	1	1	2742	2742	2742
Capela, Antonio	2	1	6200	6200	6200
Carletti, Genuzio	1	0			
Chanot, George Adolph	1	0			
Chanot, George Anthony	1	1	9521	9521	9521
Chappuy, Nicolas Augustin	1	1	6186	6186	6186
Chardon & Fils	1	1	9000	9000	9000
Chevrier, Andre	1	0			
Claudot, Pierre	1	1	4200	4200	4200
Cocker, Lawrence	2	2	2859	5789	4324
Colin, Jean Baptiste	2	2	5095	5400	5247
Conia, Stefano	1	1	6040	6040	6040
Craske, George	1	1	8035	8035	8035
Cuypers, Johannes Theodorus	1	1	45705	45705	45705
Degani, Eugenio	1	0			
Desideri, Pietro Paolo	1	0			
Dieudonne, Amedee	1	1	5800	5800	5800
Duke, Richard	2	2	6988	9151	8069
Enders, F. & R.	1	1	1172	1172	1172
Epeneel, R. V.	1	0			
Esposti, Piergiuseppe	1	1	5491	5491	5491
Fendt, Bernard	1	1	26998	26998	26998
Forster, William	2	1	11126	11126	11126

Item/Maker	*Items Offered*	*Items Sold*	*Lowest DM*	*Highest DM*	*Average DM*
Forster, William (ii)	2	1	10027	10027	10027
Gabrielli, Giovanni Battista	1	1	58206	58206	58206
Gadda, Gaetano	1	1	8227	8227	8227
Gadda, Mario	1	1	8532	8532	8532
Gand & Bernardel	1	1	35114	35114	35114
Garonnaire, Christian	1	1	10371	10371	10371
Gibson	1	1	1274	1274	1274
Gilbert, Jeffery J.	1	1	6740	6740	6740
Giraud, Franco	1	0			
Glaesel & Herwig	1	1	2537	2537	2537
Gozalan, Mesut	1	1	1465	1465	1465
Guadagnini, Gaetano (attributed to)	1	1	27321	27321	27321
Guersan, Louis	1	1	41499	41499	41499
Gutter, G. W.	1	1	1400	1400	1400
Haenel, Frederick Ewald	1	1	4425	4425	4425
Hammond, John	1	1	2394	2394	2394
Hill, Lockey (attributed to)	1	1	10419	10419	10419
Hill, W. E. & Sons	1	0			
Hudson, George Wulme	1	1	14293	14293	14293
Hyde, Andrew	1	1	1065	1065	1065
Jais, Johannes (ascribed to)	1	1	18282	18282	18282
Keen, W.	1	1	1954	1954	1954
Kennedy, Thomas	1	1	7630	7630	7630
Kilburn, Wilfred	1	0			
Kloz Family (member of)	2	1	6988	6988	6988
Koberling	1	1	1357	1357	1357
Lazare, Robert	2	1	358	358	358
Le Govic, Alain	2	2	1163	2068	1616
Lee, Percy	1	1	8938	8938	8938
Littlewood, Gerald	1	1	1768	1768	1768
Lucci, Giuseppe	2	2	10981	11591	11286
Luff, William H.	2	1	10827	10827	10827
Martin, Johann Gottlieb	1	0			
Mezzadri, Alessandro (ascribed to)	1	1	41327	41327	41327
Mockel, Oswald	1	0			
Moinel-Cherpitel	1	0			
Morassi, Giovanni Battista	1	1	10664	10664	10664
Morris, Martin	1	0			
Naisby, Thomas Henry	1	1	5143	5143	5143
Neuner & Hornsteiner	1	1	2165	2165	2165
Obbo, Marcus	1	0			
Pacherel, Pierre	1	1	12716	12716	12716
Panormo, Vincenzo	2	1	80355	80355	80355
Pareschi, Gaetano	2	1	3157	3157	3157
Pedrazzini, Giuseppe	1	0			
Perry, James	1	1	12705	12705	12705
Perry, L. A.	1	1	1464	1464	1464
Perry, Thomas	1	1	14598	14598	14598
Resuche, Charles	2	2	5171	9643	7407
Richardson, Arthur	2	1	4788	4788	4788
Rinaldi, Marengo Romanus	1	1	6703	6703	6703
Rocchi, S.	1	1	8500	8500	8500
Rost, Franz George	1	1	10164	10164	10164
Roth, Ernst Heinrich	3	3	1685	2279	1940
Sacchi, Giorgio	1	0			
Saunders, Wilfred G.	1	1	3017	3017	3017
Scheinlein, M. F.	1	1	3110	3110	3110
Schmidt, E. R. & Co.	1	1	2225	2225	2225
Schwarz, Giovanni	2	1	12214	12214	12214
Sgarabotto, Gaetano	3	2	12070	17000	14535
Silvestre, Pierre	1	0			
Simonazzi, Amadeo	1	0			
Solomon, Gimpel	2	1	16834	16834	16834
Storioni, Lorenzo (ascribed to)	1	1	107992	107992	107992
Tenucci, Eugen	1	1	3961	3961	3961
Thibouville-Lamy	1	1	2380	2380	2380
Thibouville-Lamy, J.	1	0			

Item/Maker	*Items Offered*	*Items Sold*	*Lowest DM*	*Highest DM*	*Average DM*
Topham, Carass	1	1	1401	1401	1401
Vettori, Carlo	1	1	3214	3214	3214
Vickers, J. E.	1	1	825	825	825
Voigt, Arnold	1	1	3821	3821	3821
Voigt, E. & P.	1	0			
Vuillaume, Jean Baptiste	1	0			
Vuillaume, Nicholas	1	0			
Walton, R.	1	1	2066	2066	2066
Whitmarsh Family, (member of)	1	1	2564	2564	2564
Withers, George	1	1	2732	2732	2732
Youngson, Alexander	1	0			

VIOLA BOW

Bernardel, Leon	1	1	2250	2250	2250
Bristow, Stephen	2	2	1529	2742	2135
Bryant, Percival Wilfred	1	1	3536	3536	3536
Collin-Mezin	1	1	3176	3176	3176
Dodd	2	2	1042	4768	2905
Dodd, John	2	2	4126	4266	4196
Dotschkail, R.	1	1	1264	1264	1264
Dupuy, Philippe	1	1	3965	3965	3965
Finkel, Johann S.	1	1	1828	1828	1828
Finkel, Johannes	1	1	1748	1748	1748
Geipel, Richard	2	1	700	700	700
Gerome, Roger	1	1	3200	3200	3200
Gohde, Gregory	1	0			
Hill, W. E. & Sons	6	5	3907	6711	5218
Hoyer, Otto A.	1	0			
Hums, Albin	1	0			
Lamy, Alfred	1	1	10799	10799	10799
Moinel, Amedee	1	1	2618	2618	2618
Muller, E. K.	1	1	731	731	731
Ouchard, Emile	1	0			
Pajeot	1	1	3214	3214	3214
Pajeot, Etienne	1	0			
Penzel	1	1	764	764	764
Penzel, K. Gerhard	1	0			
Pfretzschner, H. R.	2	2	1072	2065	1568
Pfretzschner, L.	1	1	1498	1498	1498
Rameau, J. S.	1	1	1533	1533	1533
Sartory, Eugene	1	1	8938	8938	8938
Schmidt, C. Hans Carl	1	1	3503	3503	3503
Schuller, Otto	1	1	853	853	853
Thibouville-Lamy	1	0			
Thibouville-Lamy, Jerome	2	2	1529	1751	1640
Thomassin, Claude	1	1	3017	3017	3017
Tubbs, Edward	1	1	16758	16758	16758
Tubbs, James	2	2	6982	10607	8794
Tunnicliffe, Brian	1	1	2279	2279	2279
van der Meer, Karel	2	2	1639	2893	2266
Wilson, Garner	1	1	2859	2859	2859
Withers, George & Sons	1	1	2186	2186	2186
Zophel, Ernst Willy	1	1	1041	1041	1041

VIOLA D'AMORE

Guidantus, Joannes Florenus (attributed to)	1	0			

VIOLETTA

Grancino, Giovanni (III)	1	1	7071	7071	7071

VIOLIN

Achner, Philip	1	1	3656	3656	3656
Acoulon, Alfred (attributed to)	2	1	3808	3808	3808
Acoulon, Alfred (fils) (ascribed to)	1	1	2285	2285	2285
Adams, Henry Thomas	1	1	5391	5391	5391

Item/Maker	*Items Offered*	*Items Sold*	*Lowest DM*	*Highest DM*	*Average DM*
Adamsen, P. P.	1	1	6127	6127	6127
Aireton, Edmund	1	0			
Aireton, Edmund (ascribed to)	1	1	10928	10928	10928
Aitchison, Frank	1	1	828	828	828
Albanelli, Franco (attributed to)	1	0			
Albani, Joseph (attributed to)	1	1	9529	9529	9529
Albert, Charles F.	1	1	2459	2459	2459
Aldric, Jean Francois	3	2	15000	27571	21286
Amati, Antonio	1	0			
Amati, Antonio & Girolamo	1	1	72991	72991	72991
Amati, Antonio & Girolamo (ascribed to)	1	0			
Amati, Dom Nicolo	1	0			
Amati, Nicolo	1	0			
Amati, Nicolo (attributed to)	1	1	76175	76175	76175
Amati Family (member of)	1	0			
Antoniazzi, Romeo	1	0			
Antoniazzi, Romeo (ascribed to)	1	1	9537	9537	9537
Apparut, Georges	1	1	4800	4800	4800
Ardern, Job	5	4	1650	3184	2375
Aschauer, Leo	1	1	2235	2235	2235
Atkinson, William	2	1	7961	7961	7961
Aubry, Joseph	3	3	5200	6358	5786
Audinot, Nestor	1	1	14000	14000	14000
Aylor, Albert	1	1	492	492	492
Azzola, Luigi (ascribed to)	1	1	9750	9750	9750
Baader & Co.	2	1	1915	1915	1915
Bailly, Paul	5	4	7714	14365	11861
Bailly, Paul (ascribed to)	1	1	6107	6107	6107
Bailly, Paul (attributed to)	1	1	14305	14305	14305
Bailly, R.	1	1	2600	2600	2600
Bajoni, Luigi (ascribed to)	1	1	12705	12705	12705
Balestrieri, Tomaso	3	2	73054	260397	166726
Banks, Benjamin	1	1	4875	4875	4875
Banks, James & Henry (attributed to)	2	1	2114	2114	2114
Barbe, F.	1	1	2100	2100	2100
Barbe, Francois	1	1	2521	2521	2521
Barbieri, Enzo	1	1	5400	5400	5400
Barbieri, Paolo (ascribed to)	1	1	4266	4266	4266
Barzoni, Francois	1	1	580	580	580
Basta, Jan	1	0			
Baur, Martin	1	1	4777	4777	4777
Bazin, C.	1	0			
Bellosio, Anselmo (attributed to)	1	1	19805	19805	19805
Bergonzi, Lorenzo	1	1	3192	3192	3192
Bernardel, August Sebastian	2	2	12130	16390	14260
Bernardel, August Sebastien Philippe	3	3	30000	42000	37764
Bernardel, Gustave	2	1	25432	25432	25432
Bernardel, Leon	1	1	6740	6740	6740
Bertelli Enzo	1	1	4723	4723	4723
Betts	1	1	1342	1342	1342
Betts, Edward (attributed to)	2	2	5861	10981	8421
Betts, John	2	2	3983	11444	7713
Betts, John (ascribed to)	1	1	27571	27571	27571
Betts, John (attributed to)	1	1	1904	1904	1904
Bignami, Otello (ascribed to)	1	0			
Bird, Charles A. Edward	1	1	5095	5095	5095
Bisiach, Leandro	3	3	27134	38570	33558
Bisiach, Leandro (jr.)	1	0			
Blackburn, G. B.	1	1	444	444	444
Blanchard, Paul	1	1	14500	14500	14500
Blanchart (ascribed to)	1	0			
Blanchi, Albert	2	2	12000	12867	12433
Blondelet, Emile	1	1	3352	3352	3352
Blondelet, H. E.	2	2	2590	2893	2741
Blyth, Williamson	1	1	912	912	912
Bollinger, Joseph	1	1	804	804	804
Bonnel, Joseph (attributed to)	1	1	1678	1678	1678

Item/Maker	*Items Offered*	*Items Sold*	*Lowest DM*	*Highest DM*	*Average DM*
Boosey & Hawkes	1	1	1302	1302	1302
Boquay, Jacques (attributed to)	1	0			
Borelli, Andrea	1	1	50000	50000	50000
Borland, Hugh	1	1	1614	1614	1614
Bossi, Giuseppe	1	0			
Boulangeot, Emile	1	1	14464	14464	14464
Boulangeot, Emile (workshop of)	1	1	2861	2861	2861
Boullangier, Charles (attributed to)	1	1	8541	8541	8541
Bourbeau, E. A.	1	1	952	952	952
Bovis, Francois	1	1	19676	19676	19676
Brandini, Jacopo	1	0			
Brandini, Jacopo (attributed to)	1	1	25432	25432	25432
Braund, Frederick T.	1	1	1401	1401	1401
Breton	1	1	1607	1607	1607
Breton, Francois	4	3	824	2571	1436
Brierley, Joseph	1	1	2070	2070	2070
Briggs, James William	2	2	5395	8894	7144
Briggs, James William (attributed to)	1	0			
Broughton, Leonard W.	2	1	673	673	673
Brown, James (attributed to)	1	1	828	828	828
Browne, John	1	0			
Bruckner, E.	1	1	2100	2100	2100
Brugere, CH.	2	2	8000	10500	9250
Brugere, Charles Georges	2	2	1676	12254	6965
Bruni, Mateo	1	1	14000	14000	14000
Bryant, Ole H.	1	1	4261	4261	4261
Buthod	1	1	1172	1172	1172
Buthod, Charles	1	1	3179	3179	3179
Buthod, Charles Louis	2	2	2438	2742	2590
Button & Whitaker	3	2	1219	1429	1324
Byrom, John	1	1	6704	6704	6704
Cabasse	1	1	949	949	949
Cahusac	1	1	1911	1911	1911
Calace, Cavaliere Raffaele	1	1	5081	5081	5081
Calcagni, Bernardo	3	2	73927	79651	76789
Callsen, B.	1	1	1800	1800	1800
Callsen, B. (ascribed to)	1	1	57460	57460	57460
Camilli, Camillus	1	1	127160	127160	127160
Candi, Oreste	1	1	11444	11444	11444
Capellini, Virgilio	1	1	4875	4875	4875
Capicchioni, Marino	1	1	21857	21857	21857
Cappa, Goffredo (ascribed to)	1	0			
Carcassi, Lorenzo (ascribed to)	1	1	12769	12769	12769
Carcassi, Lorenzo & Tomasso	1	0			
Caressa, Albert	1	1	10285	10285	10285
Caressa & Francais (attributed to)	1	1	7321	7321	7321
Carlisle, James Reynold	1	1	369	369	369
Carny, V.	1	1	4000	4000	4000
Castagneri, Andrea (attributed to)	1	0			
Castello, Paolo (ascribed to)	1	1	18381	18381	18381
Cavaceppi, Mario	1	1	4589	4589	4589
Cavalli, Aristide	3	3	2632	3811	3103
Cavalli, Aristide (workshop of)	1	1	1954	1954	1954
Cavani, Giovanni	1	1	10000	10000	10000
Cerpi, G.	3	2	1676	1874	1775
Ceruti, Giovanni Maria	1	1	5143	5143	5143
Champion, Rene (ascribed to)	1	1	3114	3114	3114
Chanot, Francis	1	1	2895	2895	2895
Chanot, Frederick William	3	2	4379	12857	8618
Chanot, G. A.	1	0			
Chanot, George	1	1	3063	3063	3063
Chanot, George Adolph	4	3	4118	12214	9303
Chanot, Georges	2	1	23801	23801	23801
Chanot, Joseph Anthony	1	1	2263	2263	2263
Chappuy, A.	2	2	1400	9000	5200
Chappuy, N.	1	1	2400	2400	2400
Chappuy, Nicolas Augustin	2	2	3494	5095	4295

Item/Maker	Items Offered	Items Sold	Lowest DM	Highest DM	Average DM
Chappuy, Nicolas Augustin (ascribed to)	1	1	1906	1906	1906
Chartreux, Eugene	2	1	952	952	952
Chipot, Jean Baptiste	1	0			
Chipot-Vuillaume	4	3	3184	5095	4098
Clark, Samuel	1	1	820	820	820
Claudot, Augustin	1	1	2000	2000	2000
Claudot, Charles	2	1	1900	1900	1900
Claudot, Charles (ascribed to)	1	0			
Claudot, Nicolas	1	1	1107	1107	1107
Clotelle, H.	2	1	1592	1592	1592
Cole, James	1	1	4423	4423	4423
Colin, Claude	2	1	2229	2229	2229
Colin, Jean Baptiste	5	4	1454	4028	2546
Collenot, Louis	1	1	2400	2400	2400
Collin-Mezin	4	4	1981	4570	3477
Collin-Mezin, Ch. J. B.	22	21	990	18000	5516
Collin-Mezin, Ch. J. B. (fils)	2	2	4686	6687	5687
Colton, Walter E.	1	1	2950	2950	2950
Comuni, Antonio	1	1	36000	36000	36000
Conia, Stefano	2	2	9211	9761	9486
Conti Aldo	1	1	7342	7342	7342
Contino, Alfredo	1	1	17210	17210	17210
Cooper, Hugh W.	1	1	2277	2277	2277
Copelli, Maurizio	1	1	4458	4458	4458
Couturieux	2	1	976	976	976
Craske, George	14	13	2742	13340	6152
Craske, George (ascribed to)	1	0			
Craske, George (attributed to)	2	2	1213	2739	1976
Dal Canto, Giustino	1	1	2786	2786	2786
dalla Costa, Antonio	1	1	93212	93212	93212
Darche, Hilaire	1	1	16599	16599	16599
Darte, August (attributed to)	1	1	4469	4469	4469
de Rub, Augusto (ascribed to)	1	0			
Dearlove, Mark William	1	1	1079	1079	1079
Deblaye, Albert	1	1	989	989	989
Dechant, G.	1	1	3114	3114	3114
Degani, (workshop of)	1	1	33698	33698	33698
Degani, Eugenio	4	4	18302	38306	27979
Degani, Giulio	5	4	7616	24376	15998
Delanoy, Alexandre	2	2	4500	6399	5449
Delivet, Auguste	1	1	4400	4400	4400
Della Corte, Alfonso (ascribed to)	1	1	23822	23822	23822
Demay	1	1	3400	3400	3400
Derazey, Honore	8	7	2806	18302	8017
Derazey, Honore (attributed to)	1	0			
Derazey, Justin	3	2	4902	5000	4951
Deveau, John G.	1	1	1721	1721	1721
Didier, Marius	2	2	2800	4764	3782
Diehl, A.	1	1	4500	4500	4500
Diehl, M.	2	2	1400	7000	4200
Dieudonne, Amedee	6	6	3442	6500	4694
Dixon, Alfred Thomas	1	1	1342	1342	1342
Dollenz, Giovanni (ascribed to)	1	0			
Dolling, Louis (jun)	2	2	1678	2548	2113
Dolling, Robert A.	1	1	1229	1229	1229
Drouin, Charles	1	0			
Duerer, Wilhelm	1	1	551	551	551
Dugade, Aubry	1	1	3199	3199	3199
Dugarde, Aubry	1	1	2170	2170	2170
Duke, Richard	4	3	4140	9761	7813
Dupary, Adolphe	1	1	3815	3815	3815
Eberle, Tomaso	1	1	51075	51075	51075
Eckland, Donald	1	1	5081	5081	5081
Elliot, William	1	1	4140	4140	4140
Enders, F. & R.	1	1	4469	4469	4469
Eyles, Charles	1	0			
Fabricatore, Gennaro	1	1	43000	43000	43000

Item/Maker	*Items Offered*	*Items Sold*	*Lowest DM*	*Highest DM*	*Average DM*
FABRICATORE, GIOVANNI BATTISTA	1	1	9643	9643	9643
FABRICATORE, GIOVANNI BATTISTA (ascribed to)	1	1	18891	18891	18891
FABRIS, LUIGI (ascribed to)	1	0			
FAGNOLA, HANNIBAL	1	1	35000	35000	35000
FALISSE, A.	2	2	4000	5789	4895
FELICI, ENRICO	1	1	4777	4777	4777
FENDT, BERNARD (attributed to)	2	1	4788	4788	4788
FENT, FRANCOIS	1	0			
FERRARI, GIUSEPPE	1	1	3352	3352	3352
FICHTL, M.	1	1	11500	11500	11500
FICHTL, MARTIN MATHIAS	1	0			
FICKER, C. S.	1	1	1800	1800	1800
FICKER, JOHANN CHRISTIAN	3	3	3536	5573	4411
FICKER FAMILY (MEMBER OF)	1	0			
FILLION, G.	1	0			
FIORINI, RAFFAELE (attributed to)	1	1	7023	7023	7023
FISCHER, H. A.	1	1	5712	5712	5712
FLAMBEAU, CHARLES	1	0			
FLEURY, BENOIT	1	1	1676	1676	1676
FORBES-WHITMORE, ANTHONY	1	1	5732	5732	5732
FORCELLINI, F.	1	1	8000	8000	8000
FORD, JACOB (attributed to)	1	1	8280	8280	8280
FORRESTER, ALEXANDER	1	1	1298	1298	1298
FORSTER, WILLIAM	1	1	2622	2622	2622
FORSTER, WILLIAM (II)	3	3	4129	15235	7978
FUCHS, W. K.	1	1	1475	1475	1475
FURBER, JOHN (attributed to)	1	1	5186	5186	5186
FURBER, MATTHEW (attributed to)	1	1	1681	1681	1681
FURBER FAMILY (MEMBER OF) (attributed to)	1	1	7324	7324	7324
GABRIELLI, GIOVANNI BATTISTA	1	1	114345	114345	114345
GADDA, GAETANO	2	2	19074	21000	20037
GADDA, MARIO	2	1	10173	10173	10173
GAGLIANO, FERDINAND	1	1	131782	131782	131782
GAGLIANO, FERDINAND (attributed to)	1	1	47685	47685	47685
GAGLIANO, GENNARO	1	1	95370	95370	95370
GAGLIANO, JOSEPH	3	2	44181	70081	57131
GAGLIANO, JOSEPH & ANTONIO	1	1	19668	19668	19668
GAGLIANO, NICOLO	3	3	38087	150000	99752
GAGLIANO, RAFFAELE & ANTONIO	1	1	50952	50952	50952
GAGLIANO FAMILY (attributed to)	1	1	36762	36762	36762
GAIDA, GIOVANNI	2	2	18912	24376	21644
GALEA, ALFREDO G.	1	1	3050	3050	3050
GALLA, ANTON (attributed to)	1	0			
GAND, CHARLES FRANCOIS (ascribed to)	1	1	42658	42658	42658
GARIMBERTI, F.	1	1	18000	18000	18000
GAVATELLI, ALCIDE	1	1	3292	3292	3292
GAVINIES, FRANCOIS	1	1	8532	8532	8532
GEISSENHOF, FRANZ	1	1	18381	18381	18381
GEISSENHOF, FRANZ (attributed to)	1	1	12769	12769	12769
GEMUNDER, GEORGE	1	1	6720	6720	6720
GERARD, GRAND	1	1	1400	1400	1400
GERMAIN, EMILE	1	1	9577	9577	9577
GIGLI, GIULIO CESARE	1	1	5082	5082	5082
GILBERT, JEFFERY J.	1	1	2133	2133	2133
GILBERT, JEFFERY JAMES	1	1	2590	2590	2590
GILKS, WILLIAM	1	0			
GLASEL, ERNST	1	1	1298	1298	1298
GLASEL, LOUIS	1	1	820	820	820
GLASEL & MOSSNER (attributed to)	1	1	825	825	825
GLASS, JOHANN	1	1	2190	2190	2190
GLENISTER, WILLIAM	2	1	5143	5143	5143
GOBETTI, FRANCESCO	1	1	22869	22869	22869
GOFFRILLER, FRANCESCO	1	1	69878	69878	69878
GOFTON, ROBERT	1	1	1983	1983	1983
GORDON	1	1	1041	1041	1041
GOULDING	1	1	618	618	618
GOULDING (attributed to)	1	1	2548	2548	2548

Item/Maker	*Items Offered*	*Items Sold*	*Lowest DM*	*Highest DM*	*Average DM*
Goulding & Co.	1	0			
Gragnani, Antonio	1	1	51075	51075	51075
Grancino, Francesco & Giovanni	1	1	12293	12293	12293
Grancino, Giovanni	1	1	115786	115786	115786
Grancino, Gebr.	1	1	35000	35000	35000
Grand-Gerard, Jean Baptiste	3	2	911	9750	5331
Grandjon, Jules	1	1	3961	3961	3961
Grater, Thomas	1	1	2720	2720	2720
Gribben, P. J.	1	1	488	488	488
Gruner	1	1	950	950	950
Guadagnini, Antonio (attributed to)	1	1	36000	36000	36000
Guadagnini, Francesco	1	1	21444	21444	21444
Guadagnin, G. B. & Pietro	1	0			
Guadagnini, Giovanni Battista	4	4	76587	514272	285882
Guarneri, Andrea	2	2	48213	91905	70059
Guarneri, Giuseppe (filius andrea)	1	1	527129	527129	527129
Guarneri, Giuseppe (filius andrea) (attributed to)	1	1	97504	97504	97504
Guarneri, Joseph (del gesu) (attributed to)	1	1	53996	53996	53996
Guarneri, Pietro (of mantua)	1	0			
Guastalla, Dante	1	1	10360	10360	10360
Guastalla, Dante & Alfredo	2	2	9750	14751	12251
Guerra, E.	1	1	31000	31000	31000
Guerra, Evasio Emile	1	1	22234	22234	22234
Guersan, Louis	2	1	5047	5047	5047
Guersan, Louis (attributed to)	2	1	1333	1333	1333
Guidantus, Joannes Florenus	2	1	44467	44467	44467
Guidantus, Joannes Florenus (ascribed to)	2	1	20646	20646	20646
Hamma & Co.	1	1	2600	2600	2600
Hammett, Thomas	1	1	1841	1841	1841
Hammig, M.	1	1	7200	7200	7200
Hammig, Wilhelm Herman	1	1	7922	7922	7922
Hardie, James & Sons	2	2	927	1280	1103
Hardie, Matthew	1	0			
Hardie, Thomas	1	0			
Hart & Son	2	2	5494	9000	7247
Hawkes & Son	1	1	2322	2322	2322
Heberlein, Heinrich Th.	1	1	738	738	738
Heberlein, Heinrich Th. (Junior)	1	1	1557	1557	1557
Heckel, Rudolf	1	1	7965	7965	7965
Heinicke, Mathias	1	1	7500	7500	7500
Heinrich, Theodore	1	1	1557	1557	1557
Hel, Joseph	2	2	22852	28000	25426
Held, Johann Joseph	1	1	5372	5372	5372
Hertl, Anton	1	1	976	976	976
Hesketh, J. Earl	1	1	3053	3053	3053
Hesketh, Thomas Earle	2	2	7931	7941	7936
Hill, Henry Lockey	1	0			
Hill, W. E. & Sons	4	4	8598	17484	11203
Hill, W. E. & Sons (workshop of)	1	0			
Hoffmann, Eduard	1	1	70081	70081	70081
Hofmann, Johann Martin	1	1	3961	3961	3961
Hofmans, Mathias (ascribed to)	1	0			
Hoing, Clifford A.	1	1	1783	1783	1783
Hopf	3	3	337	1900	912
Hopf, David	1	1	716	716	716
Hornsteiner, Mathias	2	1	8800	8800	8800
Hudson, George Wulme	3	2	7393	9442	8418
Hutton, Adam	1	1	244	244	244
Iarovoi, Denis	1	0			
Jacobs, Hendrik	1	1	24839	24839	24839
Jacquot, Albert	1	1	20720	20720	20720
Jacquot, Charles	1	1	22000	22000	22000
Jacquot, Charles (ascribed to)	1	0			
Jais, Anton	1	1	1175	1175	1175
Jaura, Wilhelm Thomas	1	0			
Jaura, Wilhelm Thomas (ascribed to)	2	1	8035	8035	8035
Jay, Henry	2	1	2571	2571	2571

Item/Maker	Items Offered	Items Sold	Lowest DM	Highest DM	Average DM
Martino, Giuseppe	1	1	3278	3278	3278
Martirenghi, Marcello	1	1	11641	11641	11641
Masafija, Dimitri	1	1	2298	2298	2298
Mast, J.	1	1	13000	13000	13000
Mast, Joseph Laurent	1	1	2893	2893	2893
Mathieu, Nicolas	1	1	919	919	919
Maucotel, Charles	1	1	8532	8532	8532
Mayson, Walter	7	6	1159	3961	2116
Mayson, Walter H.	3	3	1302	2344	1956
Mead, L. J.	1	1	865	865	865
Meek, James	1	1	2131	2131	2131
Meinel, Eugen	1	1	7931	7931	7931
Meinel, Oskar	1	1	738	738	738
Melegari, Michele & Pietro	1	1	12214	12214	12214
Mennesson, Emile	1	1	4289	4289	4289
Merling, Pauli	2	2	2144	7071	4608
Meurot, L. (attributed to)	2	2	1587	3660	2624
Millant, R. & M.	1	1	3300	3300	3300
Milton, Louis	1	1	4788	4788	4788
Miremont	1	0			
Mockel, Oswald	1	1	3400	3400	3400
Mockel, Otto	1	1	3246	3246	3246
Moitessier, Louis	1	0			
Monk, John King	1	1	446	446	446
Monnig, Fritz	2	2	3378	3660	3519
Montagnana, Domenico	1	1	257136	257136	257136
Montani, Costante	1	1	7617	7617	7617
Moody, G. T.	1	1	1656	1656	1656
Morizot, Rene	1	1	1777	1777	1777
Mougenot, L.	1	1	9000	9000	9000
Mougenot, Leon	1	1	5086	5086	5086
Mougenot, Leon (attributed to)	1	1	3497	3497	3497
Mougenot, Leon (workshop of)	1	1	2571	2571	2571
Moya, Hidalgo	2	2	2384	5210	3797
Mozzani, Luigi	2	2	2440	3671	3056
Muller, Joseph	1	1	618	618	618
Nafissi, Carlo	1	0			
Neff, Joseph	2	2	492	697	594
Neuner, Ludwig	1	1	3811	3811	3811
Neuner, Mathias	1	1	828	828	828
Neuner, N.	1	1	750	750	750
Neuner & Hornsteiner	5	4	781	3176	1497
Neuner & Hornsteiner (attributed to)	1	1	1487	1487	1487
Nicolas, Didier (l'aine)	12	11	901	8300	3300
Nolli, Marco	1	1	3050	3050	3050
Norman, Barak	1	0			
Oddone, Carlo Giuseppe	3	3	31762	39825	34577
Oldfield, W.	2	1	911	911	911
Olivier, Christian	1	1	2392	2392	2392
Orlandini, A.	1	1	5000	5000	5000
Ornati, Giuseppe	1	0			
Ortega, Asencio (attributed to)	1	0			
Otto,Rudi	1	1	2950	2950	2950
Owen, John W.	1	1	3907	3907	3907
Palzini, Gianbattista	1	1	2950	2950	2950
Panormo, Edward Ferdinand (attributed to)	1	0			
Panormo, George	2	1	19285	19285	19285
Panormo, Vincenzo	4	4	34939	96426	73844
Panormo, Vincenzo (attributed to)	1	1	17063	17063	17063
Papageorgiou, Georges D.	1	1	4500	4500	4500
Parker, Daniel (attributed to)	1	1	15323	15323	15323
Partl, Christian Franz	2	1	4309	4309	4309
Patterson, W. D.	1	1	1891	1891	1891
Pearce, George	1	1	6703	6703	6703
Pedrazzini, Giuseppe	2	1	38129	38129	38129
Pelizon, Antonio	1	0			
Penzl, Ignaz	2	2	1360	1731	1546

Item/Maker	*Items Offered*	*Items Sold*	*Lowest DM*	*Highest DM*	*Average DM*
JAY, HENRY (attributed to)	1	1	1888	1888	1888
JEUNE, LAURENT	1	1	2100	2100	2100
JOHNSON, PETER ANDREAS	1	1	574	574	574
JOHNSTON, THOMAS	1	1	446	446	446
JUZEK, JOHN	2	2	3246	7006	5126
KAUL, PAUL	2	2	5180	12500	8840
KEFFER, JOANNES	1	1	3400	3400	3400
KENNEDY, THOMAS	1	1	10799	10799	10799
KLOZ, AEGIDIUS	4	4	5514	22000	12345
KLOZ, GEORGE	1	1	7500	7500	7500
KLOZ, JOAN CAROL	1	1	4458	4458	4458
KLOZ, JOSEPH	1	1	9750	9750	9750
KLOZ, SEBASTIAN	1	0			
KLOZ, SEBASTIAN (attributed to)	1	1	5514	5514	5514
KLOZ, SEBASTIAN (I)	1	1	10190	10190	10190
KLOZ FAMILY (MEMBER OF)	5	4	1229	17469	7024
KLOZ FAMILY (MEMBER OF) (attributed to)	1	1	3179	3179	3179
KNORR, P.	1	1	6600	6600	6600
KNUPFER, ALBERT	1	1	1656	1656	1656
KRAFT, PETER	1	0			
KREUTZINGER, ANTON	1	1	1676	1676	1676
KRUG, J. ADOLPH	1	1	1147	1147	1147
KRUSE WILHELM	1	1	1193	1193	1193
KUDANOWSKI, JAN	1	1	3815	3815	3815
KUNZE, WILHELM PAUL	1	0			
L'ANSON, EDWARD (attributed to)	1	0			
LABERTE-HUMBERT BROS.	1	1	3047	3047	3047
LANCASTER	1	1	716	716	716
LANCINGER, ANTONIN	1	1	3511	3511	3511
LANDOLFI, PIETRO ANTONIO	1	1	141425	141425	141425
LANG, J. S.	1	1	305	305	305
LANGONET, CHARLES	1	1	6000	6000	6000
LANTNER, BOHUSLAV	1	1	3176	3176	3176
LAURENT, EMILE	1	1	9577	9577	9577
LAVEST, J.	1	1	2800	2800	2800
LAZARE, ROBERT	1	1	1037	1037	1037
LE CYR, JAMES FERDINAND	2	1	2101	2101	2101
LECHI, ANTONIO	6	5	1220	2473	1718
LEE, H. W.	1	0			
LEGNANI, LUIGI (ascribed to)	1	1	10164	10164	10164
LEIDOLFF, JOHANN CHRISTOPH	1	1	1830	1830	1830
LOCKE, GEORGE HERBERT	1	1	1525	1525	1525
LONGMAN & BRODERIP	2	2	1436	1888	1662
LONGMAN & LUKEY	1	0			
LONGSON, F. H.	1	0			
LONGSON, J. L.	1	1	2745	2745	2745
LOTT, JOHN	1	1	69878	69878	69878
LOUVET, F.	1	1	1400	1400	1400
LOVERI, CARLO	1	1	3344	3344	3344
LOWENDALL, LOUIS	8	8	423	2070	1094
LUCCI, GIUSEPPE	2	2	8265	18381	13323
LUFF, WILLIAM H.	3	3	8466	9761	9255
LUPOT, NICOLAS	2	2	88935	121880	105407
LUTSCHG, GUSTAV	1	1	7965	7965	7965
MACPHERSON, H.	1	1	954	954	954
MAGNIERE, GABRIEL	1	1	4066	4066	4066
MALAKOFF, BRUGERE	1	1	9750	9750	9750
MANGENOT, P.	1	1	1600	1600	1600
MANGENOT, PAUL	1	1	3811	3811	3811
MANSUY	1	1	900	900	900
MARAVIGLIA, GUIDO (attributed to)	1	1	3292	3292	3292
MARCHI, GIOVANNI (ascribed to)	1	1	7947	7947	7947
MARIANI, ANTONIO	2	2	3114	41291	22203
MARSHALL, JOHN	2	1	5485	5485	5485
MARTIN, E.	1	1	533	533	533
MARTIN, J.	1	1	1700	1700	1700
MARTIN FAMILY, (MEMBER OF)	1	1	4266	4266	4266

Item/Maker	*Items Offered*	*Items Sold*	*Lowest DM*	*Highest DM*	*Average DM*
Perrin, E. J. (fils)	1	0			
Perry, L. A.	2	1	970	970	970
Perry, Stephen	1	1	574	574	574
Perry, Thomas	2	2	2438	2459	2448
Pfretzschner, Carl Friedrich (attributed to)	1	1	2440	2440	2440
Pfretzschner, G. A.	1	1	1393	1393	1393
Phillipson, Edward	2	2	782	828	805
Piccione, Emilio	1	1	13786	13786	13786
Pierray, Claude	2	2	2135	9000	5567
Pierray, Claude (attributed to)	3	2	1751	8619	5185
Pilat, Paul	1	1	12080	12080	12080
Pillement, Francois	2	2	517	1034	776
Piper, W.	1	1	1915	1915	1915
Pique, Francois Louis	2	1	54641	54641	54641
Piretti, Enrico	1	1	6384	6384	6384
Pirot, Claude	1	1	21214	21214	21214
Placht, Johann Franz	1	1	2541	2541	2541
Plumerel, Jean	1	1	1274	1274	1274
Politi, Enrico & Raul	1	0			
Pollastri, Augusto	1	0			
Pollastri, Augusto (attributed to)	1	0			
Pollastri, Gaetano	1	1	25000	25000	25000
Poller, Paul	1	1	600	600	600
Postacchini, Andrea	1	1	33517	33517	33517
Postiglione, Vincenzo	2	2	22976	28000	25488
Praga, Eugenio (ascribed to)	1	0			
Pressenda, Giovanni Francesco	3	2	105088	174845	139967
Preston, John	1	1	517	517	517
Pullar, E. F.	1	1	808	808	808
Pyne, George	3	3	3497	5789	4578
Raffe, E. H.	2	2	2438	12188	7313
Rance, J. F.	1	1	3352	3352	3352
Rapoport, Haim	1	0			
Rasura, Vincenzo (ascribed to)	1	1	7617	7617	7617
Rauch, Sebastian	1	1	3000	3000	3000
Rauch, Thomas	1	1	2859	2859	2859
Raymond, Robert John	1	1	716	716	716
Reichel, Johann Friedrich	1	0			
Reiter, Johann	1	1	2000	2000	2000
Remy	2	2	2075	2225	2150
Renisto, Andreas	1	1	4500	4500	4500
Richardson, Arthur	3	2	6064	6369	6217
Richter, Eckart	1	0			
Richter, G.	1	1	2700	2700	2700
Ridge	1	0			
Rinaldi, Marengo Romanus	1	1	29000	29000	29000
Robinson, William	3	3	1338	7324	3792
Rocca, Enrico	1	1	27000	27000	27000
Rocca, Giuseppe	1	1	190740	190740	190740
Rocca, Joseph	1	1	262042	262042	262042
Rogeri, Giovanni Battista	1	1	179995	179995	179995
Rogeri, Pietro Giacomo	1	0			
Rost, Franz George	1	1	3821	3821	3821
Roth, Ernst Heinrich	4	4	1311	2611	1892
Roumen, Johannes Arnoldus	1	0			
Rovescalli, T.	1	1	8000	8000	8000
Ruggieri, Francesco	2	1	137857	137857	137857
Ruggieri, Vincenzo	1	0			
Ruggieri, Vincenzo (attributed to)	1	0			
Rushworth & Dreaper	2	1	6035	6035	6035
Salsedo, Luigi	1	1	5464	5464	5464
Salsedo, Luigi (attributed to)	1	1	7922	7922	7922
Salzard, Francois	1	1	846	846	846
Sander, Carl	1	1	1592	1592	1592
Sandner, Edi	1	1	1142	1142	1142
Sannino, Vincenzo	1	0			
Sannino, Vincenzo (attributed to)	1	1	17484	17484	17484

Item/Maker	*Items Offered*	*Items Sold*	*Lowest DM*	*Highest DM*	*Average DM*
SARFATI, G.	1	1	2800	2800	2800
SCARAMPELLA, STEFANO	1	1	38000	38000	38000
SCHALLER, REINHOLD	1	1	750	750	750
SCHAU, CARL	1	0			
SCHEERER, JOHN	1	1	2133	2133	2133
SCHEINLEIN, M. F.	1	1	2800	2800	2800
SCHMIDT, E. R. & CO.	3	3	541	2604	1395
SCHMIDT, JOHANN MARTIN	1	0			
SCHMIDT, REINHOLD	1	1	1147	1147	1147
SCHMITT, LUCIEN	1	1	5722	5722	5722
SCHOENFELDER, JOHANN GEORG	1	1	8500	8500	8500
SCHROEDER, JOHN G.	1	1	1065	1065	1065
SCHUSTER, C. J. & SON	1	1	541	541	541
SCHWARZ, GIOVANNI	1	1	15844	15844	15844
SCHWARZ, HEINRICH	1	1	1111	1111	1111
SCHWEITZER, JOHANN BAPTISTE (attributed to)	1	1	4791	4791	4791
SCOLARI, GIORGIO	2	2	7342	12867	10104
SDERCI, LUCIANO	1	0			
SDERCI, LUCIANO (attributed to)	1	1	12769	12769	12769
SEIDEL, CHRISTIAN WILHELM	1	1	1916	1916	1916
SEIDEL, JOHANN MICHAEL	1	1	701	701	701
SERAPHIN, SANCTUS (attributed to)	1	0			
SGARABOTTO, PIETRO	1	1	15317	15317	15317
SGARBI, ANTONIO	1	0			
SIEGA, ETTORE & SON (ascribed to)	1	1	6107	6107	6107
SILVESTRE, PIERRE	1	1	23142	23142	23142
SILVESTRE & MAUCOTEL	1	1	22499	22499	22499
SIMON, FRANZ	2	1	2930	2930	2930
SIMOUTRE, NICHOLAS EUGENE	1	1	7324	7324	7324
SIMPSON, JAMES & JOHN	1	1	6399	6399	6399
SIMPSON, THOMAS	1	1	1906	1906	1906
SMILLIE, ALEXANDER	2	2	2438	6065	4251
SOFFRITTI, ETTORE	1	0			
SORSANO, SPIRITO	1	1	98464	98464	98464
SOUBEYRAN, MARC	1	0			
STADLMANN, JOHANN JOSEPH	2	1	4266	4266	4266
STAINER, JACOB	1	1	75394	75394	75394
STAINER, MARCUS (attributed to)	1	1	4261	4261	4261
STANLEY, ROBERT A.	1	1	2380	2380	2380
STIRRAT, DAVID	2	1	7536	7536	7536
STORIONI, CARLO	1	1	2697	2697	2697
STORIONI, LORENZO	1	1	116413	116413	116413
STRADIVARI, ANTONIO	2	1	2617604	2617604	2617604
STRADIVARI, OMOBONO	1	0			
STRAUB, SIMON	1	1	7500	7500	7500
SUZUKI, M.	1	1	711	711	711
TARASCONI, G.	1	1	14000	14000	14000
TARR, SHELLEY	1	0			
TASSINI, MARCO	1	1	3053	3053	3053
TAVEGIA, CARLO ANTONIO	2	1	6428	6428	6428
TECCHLER, DAVID	1	1	45952	45952	45952
TECCHLER, DAVID (attributed to)	1	1	7931	7931	7931
TENUCCI, EUGEN	1	1	10000	10000	10000
TERMANINI, PIETRO	1	1	19805	19805	19805
TESTORE, CARLO	1	1	60652	60652	60652
TESTORE, CARLO (attributed to)	1	1	43392	43392	43392
TESTORE, CARLO ANTONIO	1	1	70228	70228	70228
TESTORE, CARLO GIUSEPPE	1	0			
TESTORE FAMILY (MEMBER OF)	2	2	5485	26814	16149
THIBOUT, JACQUES PIERRE	1	1	7617	7617	7617
THIBOUVILLE-LAMY	17	16	318	3344	1120
THIBOUVILLE-LAMY, J.	6	6	413	1847	1064
THIBOUVILLE-LAMY, J. (workshop of)	1	1	7376	7376	7376
THIBOUVILLE-LAMY, JEROME	9	8	898	3214	1768
THIER, JOSEPH (attributed to)	1	1	1793	1793	1793
THIR, MATHIAS	2	1	2873	2873	2873
THIR, MATHIAS (attributed to)	1	1	7299	7299	7299

Item/Maker	Items Offered	Items Sold	Lowest DM	Highest DM	Average DM
THOMPSON, CHARLES & SAMUEL	4	3	1464	3961	2724
THOMPSON & SON	1	1	7393	7393	7393
THOMSON	1	1	510	510	510
THORBURN, S. W.	1	1	605	605	605
THOUVENEL, CHARLES	1	1	3744	3744	3744
THOW, J.	1	1	905	905	905
TILLER, G. W.	1	1	1079	1079	1079
TIM-GEIGEN	1	1	2262	2262	2262
TOBIN, RICHARD	1	0			
TOBIN, RICHARD (attributed to)	1	1	1525	1525	1525
TOMASSINI, DOMENICO (ascribed to)	1	1	6703	6703	6703
TONONI, CARLO	1	1	57856	57856	57856
TWEEDALE, CHARLES L.	1	1	1172	1172	1172
VALENZANO, JOANNES MARIA	2	2	47644	101640	74642
VALENZANO, JOANNES MARIA (ascribed to)	1	0			
VAUTELINT, N. PIERRE	1	1	8894	8894	8894
VENTAPANE, LORENZO	3	3	14142	60349	39161
VENTAPANE, LORENZO (attributed to)	1	0			
VERINI, ANDREA	1	1	4558	4558	4558
VICKERS, J. E.	2	2	1710	2263	1986
VINACCIA FAMILY (MEMBER OF)	1	0			
VINCENT, ALFRED	3	3	7643	10827	8810
VINCENT, ALFRED (attributed to)	1	1	6512	6512	6512
VISCONTI, DOMENICO (attributed to)	1	1	3179	3179	3179
VLUMMENS, DOMINIC	1	1	6670	6670	6670
VOIGT, ARNOLD	1	1	1685	1685	1685
VOIGT, JOHANN GEORG	1	0			
VOIGT, PAUL	1	1	1916	1916	1916
VOLLER BROTHERS	1	1	41327	41327	41327
VON DOLLING, (YOUNGER)	1	0			
VUILLAUME, JEAN BAPTISTE	8	7	28000	95205	53947
VUILLAUME, JEAN BAPTISTE (ascribed to)	1	1	30200	30200	30200
VUILLAUME, JEAN BAPTISTE (workshop of)	1	1	57460	57460	57460
VUILLAUME, NICHOLAS	2	2	8035	24796	16416
VUILLAUME, SEBASTIAN	2	1	7324	7324	7324
WAGNER, BENEDICT (attributed to)	1	1	2295	2295	2295
WALKER, WILLIAM	2	1	4199	4199	4199
WALTON, WILLIAM	1	1	1431	1431	1431
WAMSLEY, PETER	6	5	1500	13711	6363
WANNER, MICHAEL	1	1	1529	1529	1529
WARD, GEORGE	1	1	2384	2384	2384
WASSERMANN, JOSEPH	1	1	9141	9141	9141
WEIGERT, JOHANN BLASIUS	1	1	3114	3114	3114
WHEDBEE, WILLIAM	1	1	2295	2295	2295
WHITBREAD, W. W.	1	1	535	535	535
WHITE, ASA WARREN	1	1	1065	1065	1065
WHITE, H. N. & CO.	1	1	492	492	492
WHITMARSH, EDWIN	1	1	2235	2235	2235
WHITMARSH, EMANUEL	1	1	1791	1791	1791
WIDHALM, LEOPOLD	4	4	1954	29000	10930
WILKANOWSKI, W.	2	2	901	1475	1188
WILKINSON, JOHN	1	0			
WILKINSON, WILLIAM & PERRY, THOMAS	1	1	2344	2344	2344
WILSON, TOM	1	1	587	587	587
WINTERLING, G.	2	2	9000	15500	12250
WITHERS, EDWARD	1	1	4500	4500	4500
WOLFF BROS.	7	7	458	1236	736
WOULDHAVE, JOHN	1	0			
ZACH, THOMAS (attributed to)	1	1	4270	4270	4270
ZANIER, FERRUCCIO	1	1	6500	6500	6500
ZEMITIS, M.	1	1	1900	1900	1900
ZETTWITZ, WILLIAM	1	0			
ZIMMERMAN, FRIEDERICH	1	1	1083	1083	1083
VIOLIN BOW					
ALVEY, BRIAN	2	1	3370	3370	3370
APPARUT, GEORGES	1	1	1600	1600	1600
BAUSCH, L.	2	2	476	488	482

Item/Maker	*Items Offered*	*Items Sold*	*Lowest DM*	*Highest DM*	*Average DM*
Bazin	1	1	2158	2158	2158
Bazin, C.	2	2	520	818	669
Bazin, Charles	9	9	521	3344	1809
Bazin, Louis	5	5	492	4451	1889
Bazin Family (member of)	1	0			
Beare, John & Arthur	1	1	3511	3511	3511
Bernardel, Gustave	4	3	1498	3961	2786
Bernardel, Leon	2	2	1396	2742	2069
Bernardel, Rene	1	1	3352	3352	3352
Bisch, Paul	1	1	1147	1147	1147
Brand, Karl	1	1	402	402	402
Briggs, James William	1	1	914	914	914
Bristow, Stephen	1	1	1175	1175	1175
Bultitude, A. R.	1	1	3174	3174	3174
Bultitude, Arthur	2	2	1915	5143	3529
Buthod, Charles	2	1	413	413	413
Callier, Frank	2	2	901	1967	1434
VIOLIN BOW					
Caressa, Albert	1	1	2571	2571	2571
Caressa & Francais	2	1	4723	4723	4723
Carrodus	1	1	1347	1347	1347
Chadwick	1	1	1500	1500	1500
Chanot, Joseph Anthony	1	1	3857	3857	3857
Chardon, Chanot	1	1	650	650	650
Collin-Mezin	2	1	1929	1929	1929
Cuniot-Hury	2	2	438	2070	1254
Cuniot-Hury, Eugene	1	1	2285	2285	2285
Darche, Hilaire	1	1	1333	1333	1333
Delivet, Auguste	1	0			
Dodd	5	4	695	5800	3067
Dodd, Edward	1	1	4764	4764	4764
Dodd, James	3	2	2713	6352	4533
Dodd, John	3	2	2065	4178	3122
Dodd, John (ascribed to)	1	0			
Dodd, John (attributed to)	2	2	698	2144	1421
Dodd Family (member of)	2	1	3983	3983	3983
Dolling, Kurt	1	1	674	674	674
Dorfler, D.	1	1	410	410	410
Dotschkail, R.	1	1	1800	1800	1800
Dugad, Andre	1	1	572	572	572
Dupuy, George	1	0			
Durrschmidt, O.	1	1	600	600	600
Durrschmidt, Otto	6	6	414	1337	692
Eulry, Clement	1	1	5717	5717	5717
Eury, Nicolas	2	1	13975	13975	13975
Fetique, Jules	1	1	3278	3278	3278
Fetique, Victor	7	6	2223	9321	5404
Finkel, Siegfried	1	1	1147	1147	1147
Francais, Emile	3	2	2541	2859	2700
Gand & Bernardel	1	1	4266	4266	4266
Geipel, Richard	2	1	455	455	455
Gerome, Roger	2	1	1300	1300	1300
Gillet, R.	1	1	3500	3500	3500
Glasel	1	1	1800	1800	1800
Gotz	1	0			
Gotz, Conrad	2	2	1098	1523	1311
Grand Adam	1	1	23941	23941	23941
Guetter, Otto	1	1	1041	1041	1041
Hagemann, F. R.	2	1	318	318	318
Hammig, W. H.	2	1	488	488	488
Hart & Son	1	0			
Hel, Pierre	1	1	1828	1828	1828
Henry, Joseph	1	0			
Hermann, Lothar	1	1	795	795	795
Herrmann, A.	3	3	595	1095	889
Herrmann, Edward	1	1	697	697	697

Item/Maker	*Items Offered*	*Items Sold*	*Lowest DM*	*Highest DM*	*Average DM*
Herrmann, W.	1	1	1052	1052	1052
Hill, W. E. & Sons	66	65	580	9803	3427
Hoyer, C. A.	1	1	1269	1269	1269
Hoyer, G.	1	1	650	650	650
Hoyer, Otto A.	3	3	1393	2554	1835
Hums, Albin	3	2	1401	2910	2156
Hums, W.	1	1	349	349	349
Husson, Charles Claude (attributed to)	1	0			
Kessler	1	1	651	651	651
Kittel Family (member of) (ascribed to)	1	1	7965	7965	7965
Knopf, Henry Richard	1	1	820	820	820
Laberte	1	1	900	900	900
Laberte, Marc	1	1	1300	1300	1300
Laberte, Marc (ascribed to)	1	1	572	572	572
Lafleur (ascribed to)	1	0			
Lafleur, Joseph Rene	1	0			
Lafleur, Joseph Rene (ascribed to)	1	1	2394	2394	2394
Lamy, A.	2	1	7500	7500	7500
Lamy, Alfred	10	9	413	11641	6429
Lamy, Alfred Joseph	1	1	6988	6988	6988
Leblanc, P. R.	3	3	700	900	800
Lermetz	1	1	293	293	293
Lotte, Francois	3	3	1225	1543	1431
Lowendall, Louis	1	0			
Lupot, Francois	1	1	21329	21329	21329
Lupot, Francois (attributed to)	1	1	9190	9190	9190
Lupot, Nicolas	1	0			
Maire, Nicolas	3	2	12857	14500	13678
Martin	1	1	586	586	586
Maure, Pierre	1	1	1465	1465	1465
Meauchand	1	1	8938	8938	8938
Meauchand (attributed to)	1	1	8938	8938	8938
Meinel, Eugen	2	2	164	669	416
Millant, B.	1	1	2500	2500	2500
Miquel, E.	1	1	853	853	853
Moller, Max	1	1	2223	2223	2223
Morizot	2	2	1803	1906	1854
Morizot, Louis	5	5	438	2065	1306
Mougenot, Georges	1	1	1588	1588	1588
Muhl	1	1	1337	1337	1337
Nurnberger, Albert	18	17	365	6800	2226
Ouchard, E.	2	2	1800	1900	1850
Ouchard, Emile	3	2	1916	2806	2361
Paesold, Roderich	3	3	701	955	849
Pajeot	1	0			
Pajeot (attributed to)	1	1	10215	10215	10215
Pajeot, (fils)	2	2	8357	13500	10928
Pajeot, (pere)	1	1	14000	14000	14000
Paquotte Bros.	2	1	2893	2893	2893
Paulus, Johannes O.	1	1	650	650	650
Peccatte, Dominique	2	2	24106	57460	40783
Peccatte, Dominique (attributed to)	1	1	9000	9000	9000
Peccatte, Francois	1	1	18282	18282	18282
Penzel	1	1	1710	1710	1710
Penzel, K.	1	1	250	250	250
Persois (attributed to)	1	1	14365	14365	14365
Pfretzschner, F. C.	1	1	1400	1400	1400
Pfretzschner, H. R.	12	11	250	3179	1340
Pfretzschner, T. H.	1	1	673	673	673
Pfretzschner, W. A.	3	2	716	1337	1027
Pillot	1	0			
Poirson	1	1	2800	2800	2800
Prager, August Edwin	2	2	911	1122	1016
Prager, Gustav	3	3	954	1164	1033
Rau, August	4	4	549	1838	1347
Retford, William C.	1	1	12214	12214	12214
Richaume, Andre	1	1	5427	5427	5427

Item/Maker	*Items Offered*	*Items Sold*	*Lowest DM*	*Highest DM*	*Average DM*
RUSHWORTH & DREAPER	1	1	970	970	970
SALCHOW, WILLIAM	1	1	4178	4178	4178
SANDNER, A. E.	1	1	656	656	656
SARTORY, EUGENE	23	22	3000	15252	9546
SAUNDERS, S.	1	1	14305	14305	14305
SCHREIBER & LUGERT	1	1	1300	1300	1300
SCHUBERT PAUL	1	0			
SCHULLER, OTTO	1	1	582	582	582
SCHUSTER, ADOLF	4	3	509	858	721
SCHUSTER, ADOLF C.	2	2	605	1721	1163
SCHWARZ, B.	2	1	730	730	730
SERDET, PAUL	1	1	5786	5786	5786
SHANTI-DEVA	1	1	213	213	213
SILVESTRE & MAUCOTEL	1	1	5464	5464	5464
SIMON (attributed to)	1	1	3676	3676	3676
SIMON, PAUL	1	0			
SIMON, PAUL (ascribed to)	1	0			
SIMONIN	1	1	1900	1900	1900
STOESS, A.	1	1	550	550	550
SUSS, CHRISTIAN	1	1	847	847	847
TAYLOR, MALCOLM	3	2	1219	2065	1642
THIBOUVILLE-LAMY	4	3	521	1016	751
THOMA, MATHIAS	1	0			
THOMASSIN, CLAUDE	5	4	2590	3656	3218
THOMASSIN, CLAUDE (attributed to)	1	1	2144	2144	2144
TOURTE, FRANCOIS	4	3	7376	63844	33269
TOURTE, LOUIS	1	1	5746	5746	5746
TOURTE, LOUIS (attributed to)	1	1	6065	6065	6065
TUBBS, EDWARD	2	2	1838	11117	6477
TUBBS, JAMES	20	19	949	8576	5036
TUBBS, WILLIAM	2	2	1945	4875	3410
TUBBS, WILLIAM (attributed to)	1	1	976	976	976
TUBBS FAMILY, (MEMBER OF)	1	0			
VAN DER MEER, KAREL	4	3	1022	3375	2024
VIDOUDEZ, FRANCOIS	1	1	1828	1828	1828
VIGNERON, ANDRE	4	4	2223	3606	3135
VILLAUME, G.	1	1	600	600	600
VOIGT, ARNOLD	1	1	1172	1172	1172
VOIRIN, FRANCOIS NICOLAS	13	12	3174	23941	9960
VOIRIN, J.	1	1	1200	1200	1200
VOIRIN, JOSEPH	1	1	1403	1403	1403
VUILLAUME, JEAN BAPTISTE	3	2	3114	3606	3360
VUILLAUME, JEAN BAPTISTE (ascribed to)	1	1	3352	3352	3352
VUILLAUME, JEAN BAPTISTE (workshop of)	1	1	11173	11173	11173
WALTON, WILLIAM	1	0			
WEICHOLD, A. R.	1	1	793	793	793
WEICHOLD, R.	5	5	847	1274	1031
WEICHOLD, RICHARD	5	4	423	2451	1401
WEIDHAAS, PAUL	5	5	674	5200	1918
WERRO, JEAN	1	1	973	973	973
WILSON, GARNER	4	3	701	2089	1363
WILSON, JAMES J. T.	2	2	1106	2116	1611
WINKLER, FRANZ	2	1	1041	1041	1041
WINTERLING, GEORGE	1	1	650	650	650
WOODFIELD, J. D.	1	0			
WUNDERLICH, F. R.	1	1	2384	2384	2384
ZIMMER, E. W.	1	1	600	600	600

VIOLONCELLO

AIRETON, EDMUND (attributed to)	1	1	4946	4946	4946
BAILLY, PAUL (ascribed to)	1	0			
BANKS, JAMES & HENRY (attributed to)	2	1	8466	8466	8466
BARRETT, JOHN	1	0			
BETTS, JOHN	1	1	49820	49820	49820
BOULANGEOT, EMILE	2	1	14464	14464	14464
CAPPA, GOFFREDO	1	1	56248	56248	56248
CONIA, STEFANO	1	1	22852	22852	22852

Item/Maker	*Items Offered*	*Items Sold*	*Lowest DM*	*Highest DM*	*Average DM*
CONTINO, ALFREDO (attributed to)	1	1	8886	8886	8886
CORSBY, GEORGE (attributed to)	1	1	5108	5108	5108
CRASKE, GEORGE	1	1	11641	11641	11641
CROSS, NATHANIEL	1	1	28586	28586	28586
DE COMBLE, AMBROSE	1	1	6107	6107	6107
DEGANI, EUGENIO	1	1	42991	42991	42991
DERAZEY, HONORE (workshop of)	1	1	13407	13407	13407
DERAZEY, JUSTIN	1	1	2344	2344	2344
DIEHL, JOHANN	1	1	46924	46924	46924
DODD, THOMAS	1	1	26457	26457	26457
DUKE, RICHARD	1	1	4875	4875	4875
FORSTER, WILLIAM	1	0			
FURBER, HENRY	1	1	14611	14611	14611
FURBER, JOHN	1	1	1422	1422	1422
FURBER, JOHN (attributed to)	1	1	11958	11958	11958
GADDA, GAETANO	1	1	26000	26000	26000
GAFFINO, JOSEPH	1	0			
GAGLIANO, GIOVANNI	1	1	45705	45705	45705
GOULDING & CO.	1	1	3662	3662	3662
GRANCINO, GIOVANNI	1	1	122140	122140	122140
GUERSAN, LOUIS	1	0			
GUERSAN, LOUIS (ascribed to)	1	0			
HARRIS, CHARLES	2	1	11571	11571	11571
HART & SON	1	1	6094	6094	6094
HERMANN, LOTHAR	1	0			
HILL, JOSEPH	1	1	36564	36564	36564
HILL, LOCKEY (attributed to)	1	0			
HJORTH, EMIL & SON	1	1	13711	13711	13711
HOFMANS, MATHIAS	1	1	19285	19285	19285
HOYER, JOHANN FRIEDERICH	1	0			
HUBICKA, JULIUS A.	1	1	28611	28611	28611
JAIS, ANDREAS	1	1	4447	4447	4447
JOHNSON, JOHN (attributed to)	1	0			
JORIO, VINCENZO	1	1	27423	27423	27423
KENNEDY, THOMAS	1	1	23822	23822	23822
KENNEDY, THOMAS (ascribed to)	1	1	8035	8035	8035
KREUZINGER, FRIEDRICH	1	1	1967	1967	1967
KRINER, JOSEPH	1	1	7617	7617	7617
LABERTE-HUMBERT BROS.	1	1	6664	6664	6664
LEEB, ANDREAS CARL	1	1	13340	13340	13340
LONGMAN & BRODERIP	1	0			
LONGMAN & LUKEY	2	2	14705	22976	18841
LOWENDALL, LOUIS	1	1	6988	6988	6988
MARCHI, GIOVANNI ANTONIO	1	1	46056	46056	46056
NAMY, JEAN THEODORE	1	0			
NEUNER & HORNSTEINER	2	1	10607	10607	10607
NICOLAS	1	1	28611	28611	28611
OTTO, MAX	1	0			
OWEN, JOHN W.	1	1	13675	13675	13675
PILLEMENT, FRANCOIS	1	0			
PRECUB, FLOREA	1	1	6500	6500	6500
PRESCOTT, GRAHAM	1	1	1429	1429	1429
PRESTON, JAMES	1	1	4791	4791	4791
PURDAY, T. E.	1	1	19913	19913	19913
PYNE, GEORGE	1	1	13340	13340	13340
QUARGNAL, RUDOLFO	1	1	7000	7000	7000
RAMBAUX, CLAUDE VICTOR	1	0			
RAUTMANN, CARL	1	1	10799	10799	10799
RICHARDSON, ARTHUR	2	1	14365	14365	14365
ROCCA, ENRICO	1	0			
ROCCA, ENRICO (attributed to)	1	0			
RODIANI, GIOVITA (attributed to)	1	1	9834	9834	9834
ROGERI, GIOVANNI BATTISTA (ascribed to)	1	0			
ROTH, ERNST HEINRICH	1	1	11107	11107	11107
ROTTENBURGH, JEAN HYACINTHE	1	1	26045	26045	26045
RUGGIERI & GUARNERI, FRANCESCO & P.	1	1	67498	67498	67498
RUSHWORTH & DREAPER	1	0			

Item/Maker	*Items Offered*	*Items Sold*	*Lowest DM*	*Highest DM*	*Average DM*
Schutz	1	1	4500	4500	4500
Sgarbi, Giuseppe	1	1	46000	46000	46000
Smith, Thomas	1	1	5732	5732	5732
Smith, Thomas (attributed to)	1	1	9120	9120	9120
Sorsano, Spirito (attributed to)	1	1	44999	44999	44999
Stewart, N.	1	1	21107	21107	21107
Symington, George	1	1	2229	2229	2229
Testore Family (member of) (attributed to)	1	1	31993	31993	31993
Thibouville-Lamy	1	1	4884	4884	4884
Thibouville-Lamy, J.	1	1	9553	9553	9553
Tiriot	1	1	1400	1400	1400
Tobin, Richard	1	1	38087	38087	38087
Tobin, Richard (ascribed to)	1	0			
Ventapane, Lorenzo	1	0			
Vuillaume, Jean Baptiste	1	0			
Vuillaume, Jean Baptiste (workshop of)	1	1	45952	45952	45952
Wamsley, Peter	1	0			
Werner, Erich	1	1	2782	2782	2782
Widhalm, Leopold	1	0			
Wolff Bros.	1	1	8532	8532	8532

VIOLONCELLO BOW

Item/Maker	*Items Offered*	*Items Sold*	*Lowest DM*	*Highest DM*	*Average DM*
Adam, J.	1	1	6000	6000	6000
Alvey, Brian	1	0			
Bausch	2	2	438	521	479
Bausch, L.	1	1	651	651	651
Bausch, L. (attributed to)	1	1	521	521	521
Bazin	1	1	1991	1991	1991
Bazin, Charles	1	1	1991	1991	1991
Bazin, Charles Nicholas	2	2	3017	3214	3116
Bazin, Louis	1	1	2250	2250	2250
Brown, James (attributed to)	2	1	698	698	698
Bryant, Percival Wilfred	2	1	2065	2065	2065
Bultitude, A. R.	1	1	2920	2920	2920
Cuniot-Hury	1	0			
Dodd, John	2	2	804	5717	3260
Dodd Family (member of)	1	1	3053	3053	3053
Dolling, Heinz	2	1	949	949	949
Dorfler, D.	1	1	2676	2676	2676
Dorfler, Egidius	1	1	3494	3494	3494
Dupuy, George	1	1	2590	2590	2590
Durrschmidt, O.	1	1	600	600	600
Eulry, Clement	1	0			
Fetique, Victor	2	1	4451	4451	4451
Fetique, Victor (ascribed to)	1	0			
Finkel, Siegfried	1	1	2131	2131	2131
Forster	1	1	5722	5722	5722
Fritsch, Jean	1	1	1337	1337	1337
Gerome, Roger	1	0			
Glesel, C.	1	0			
Hart	1	1	1496	1496	1496
Hart & Son	1	1	2768	2768	2768
Hermann, Lothar	1	0			
Hill, W. E. & Sons	27	26	476	7623	3060
Hoyer, Hermann Albert	1	1	711	711	711
Hoyer, Otto A.	1	0			
Husson, Charles Claude	2	1	4589	4589	4589
Knopf	1	1	700	700	700
Knopf, W.	1	1	1311	1311	1311
Kun, Joseph	1	1	699	699	699
Lamy, Alfred	3	2	2133	7659	4896
Lapierre, Marcel	1	1	1628	1628	1628
Leblanc, P. R.	3	3	1100	2400	1633
Lefin	1	1	779	779	779
Lotte, Francois	1	1	1298	1298	1298
Lupot, Nicolas	1	0			
Malines, Guillaume	1	1	6750	6750	6750

Item/Maker	Items Offered	Items Sold	Lowest DM	Highest DM	Average DM
Morizot, Louis	2	1	949	949	949
Neudorfer	1	0			
Neuveville, G. C.	2	2	847	1626	1236
Nurnberger, Albert	5	5	738	3176	1713
Paulus, Johannes O.	1	1	858	858	858
Peccatte, D.	1	1	19000	19000	19000
Pfretzschner, H. R.	7	6	989	1676	1435
Pfretzschner, W. A.	2	2	793	980	887
Reynolds, J.	1	0			
Riedl, Alfons	2	1	1338	1338	1338
Sandner, B.	1	1	250	250	250
Sartory, Eugene	8	7	6703	12769	9229
Schmidt, C. Hans Carl	1	1	1287	1287	1287
Seifert, Lothar	1	1	858	858	858
Silvestre & Maucotel	1	0			
Thibouville-Lamy, J.	1	1	1607	1607	1607
Thomassin, C.	2	2	5485	8500	6992
Thomassin, Claude	1	1	3656	3656	3656
Tourte, Louis (attributed to)	1	0			
Tubbs, James	2	2	8357	9803	9080
Tubbs, Thomas (ascribed to)	1	0			
van der Meer, Karel	1	0			
Vigneron, Andre	2	2	2861	6428	4645
Voirin, Francois Nicolas	5	4	695	8894	5732
Vuillaume, Jean Baptiste	2	1	6988	6988	6988
Weichold, R.	1	1	2019	2019	2019
Weichold, Richard	1	1	1838	1838	1838
Wilson, Garner	3	2	1768	2223	1996
Withers, George & Sons	1	1	854	854	854
Woodfield, J. D.	1	1	808	808	808
Wunderlich, F. R.	1	1	980	980	980
Wunderlich, Fritz	1	1	738	738	738

VIOLONCELLO PICCOLO

Item/Maker	Items Offered	Items Sold	Lowest DM	Highest DM	Average DM
Bolink, Jaap	1	0			
Wolff Bros.	1	1	6352	6352	6352

XYLOPHONE

Item/Maker	Items Offered	Items Sold	Lowest DM	Highest DM	Average DM
Culliford Rolfe & Barrow	1	1	245	245	245

Item/Maker	*Items Offered*	*Items Sold*	*Lowest £*	*Highest £*	*Average £*
ACCORDION					
Horne, Edgar	1	1	187	187	187
AEOLA					
Wheatstone & Co., C.	1	1	572	572	572
BAGPIPES					
MacDougall, D.	1	0			
BANJO					
Bacon Banjo Co.	1	1	505	505	505
Fairbanks Co., A. C.	1	1	365	365	365
Fiesta	1	1	99	99	99
Libby Bros.	1	1	154	154	154
BANJO MANDOLIN					
Gibson Co.	1	1	84	84	84
BASS RECORDER					
Goble, Robert	1	0			
BASS VIOL DA GAMBA					
Steber, Ernst	1	0			
BASSOON					
Bilton, Richard	1	1	770	770	770
Bocchia, Bono	1	1	252	252	252
Buffet	1	1	168	168	168
Buffet-Crampon & Co.	1	1	209	209	209
Goulding, Wood & Co.	1	0			
Grenser, Johann Heinrich	1	1	7150	7150	7150
Heckel	2	1	5280	5280	5280
Heckel, Wilhelm	1	0			
Milhouse, William	1	0			
Zimmermann, Julius Heinrich	1	1	182	182	182
BUGLE					
Astor & Co., Gerock	1	1	352	352	352
Pace, Charles	1	1	968	968	968
CITHERN					
Preston	1	1	286	286	286
CLARINET					
Bilton, Richard	2	2	770	990	880
Conn, C. G.	1	1	99	99	99
Cramer	1	1	418	418	418
Darche	1	1	330	330	330
Florio, Pietro Grassi	1	1	660	660	660
Goulding & Co.	1	1	209	209	209
Klemm	1	1	385	385	385
Lot, Isadore	1	1	198	198	198
Martin Bros.	1	1	264	264	264
Metzler	1	1	224	224	224
Otten, John	1	1	154	154	154
Selmer	1	1	121	121	121
Wolf & Co., Robert	1	1	209	209	209
Wood & Ivy	1	1	242	242	242
CLAVICHORD					
Goff, Thomas	1	0			
Lindholm, Pehr	1	0			

Item/Maker	Items Offered	Items Sold	Lowest £	Highest £	Average £
CONCERTINA					
Crabb, Henry	1	0			
Crabb & Son, H.	1	1	396	396	396
Jeffries, Charles	1	1	187	187	187
Jeffries Bros.	1	1	154	154	154
Lachenal & Co.	3	2	418	748	583
Wheatstone & Co., C.	6	5	264	792	484
CONTRA GUITAR					
Hauser, Hermann	1	0			
CORNOPEAN					
Kohler, John	1	1	2310	2310	2310
CORONET					
Conn, C. G.	1	1	154	154	154
Pepper, J. W.	1	1	196	196	196
DOUBLE BASS					
Cole, James	1	1	6600	6600	6600
Derazey, Justin	1	1	3300	3300	3300
Jacquot Family (member of)	1	1	898	898	898
Panormo, Vincenzo (ascribed to)	1	1	5280	5280	5280
DOUBLE BASS BOW					
Alvey, Brian	1	0			
Bailey, G. E.	1	1	605	605	605
Dotschkail, R.	1	1	354	354	354
Mettal, O.	1	1	278	278	278
Mettal, Walter	1	1	531	531	531
Morizot, Louis	2	1	190	190	190
Paulus, Johannes O.	2	2	481	506	493
Riedl, Alfons	3	3	216	405	333
Vickers, J. E.	3	3	110	209	147
Winkler, Franz	1	1	440	440	440
ENGLISH HORN					
Fornari	1	0			
Loree, Francois	1	1	2090	2090	2090
FLAGEOLET					
Bainbridge	1	1	132	132	132
Hastrick	1	1	242	242	242
Peloubet, C.	1	1	280	280	280
FLUTE					
Boehm & Mendler	1	0			
Cahusac	1	1	308	308	308
Cahusac, Thomas	2	1	330	330	330
Carte, Rudall & Co.	4	3	61	1265	490
Clementi & Co.	1	1	220	220	220
Clinton & Co.	1	1	572	572	572
Crosby, W.	1	1	266	266	266
Florio, Pietro Grassi	2	1	3520	3520	3520
Goulding & Co.	1	1	110	110	110
Goulding & D'Almaine	2	1	209	209	209
Graves, Samuel	1	1	196	196	196
Grenser, Auguste	1	1	9350	9350	9350
Hale, John	1	1	143	143	143
Hammig, Philipp	1	1	528	528	528
Haynes Co., William S.	1	1	477	477	477
Holtzapffler	1	0			
Lafleur	1	1	99	99	99
Laurent, Claude	2	1	6050	6050	6050

Item/Maker	*Items Offered*	*Items Sold*	*Lowest £*	*Highest £*	*Average £*
Lot, Louis	3	2	550	880	715
Maker's Guild No. 168	1	0			
Metzler, Valentin	2	1	88	88	88
Milligan	1	0			
Miyazawa & Co.	1	1	715	715	715
Monzani	1	1	1650	1650	1650
Potter, William Henry	2	1	264	264	264
Prowse, Thomas	1	1	605	605	605
Rede, H. W.	1	1	182	182	182
Rudall, George	1	1	880	880	880
FRENCH HORN					
Hawkes & Son	1	1	330	330	330
GUITAR					
Bouchet, Robert	2	2	9900	15400	12650
Contreras, Manuel	1	0			
Gibson Co.	3	3	617	1346	1047
Guitar Epiphone Co.	1	1	337	337	337
Gutierrez, manuel	1	0			
Hauser, Hermann	1	1	2200	2200	2200
Kohno, Masaru	2	1	1320	1320	1320
Lacote, Rene	1	1	2200	2200	2200
Martin Co., C. F.	1	1	898	898	898
Mauchant Bros.	1	1	1650	1650	1650
Panormo, Louis	2	2	902	1540	1221
Ramirez, Jose (III)	1	1	990	990	990
Rinaldi, Marengo Romanus	1	0			
Romanillos, Jose	2	2	3190	9350	6270
HAND HORN					
Raoux, Marcel-Auguste	1	0			
HARP					
Briggs	1	1	605	605	605
Delveau, J.	1	1	1100	1100	1100
Erard, Sebastian	3	2	880	2640	1760
Erard, Sebastian & Pierre	1	1	605	605	605
Errard	1	1	605	605	605
Light, Edward	1	1	1155	1155	1155
Nadermann, Henry	1	0			
HARPSICHORD					
de Blaise, William	1	1	1210	1210	1210
Dulken, Johan Daniel	1	1	74800	74800	74800
Kirkman, Jacob & Abraham	1	1	50600	50600	50600
HORN					
White, H. N. & Co.	1	1	56	56	56
HURDY GURDY					
Colson	1	1	880	880	880
LUTE					
Romanillos, Jose	1	0			
Rubio, David	2	1	3740	3740	3740
LUTE-GUITAR					
Barry	1	1	198	198	198
LYRA GUITAR					
Barry	1	1	1320	1320	1320
Mozzani, Luigi	2	1	495	495	495

Item/Maker	*Items Offered*	*Items Sold*	*Lowest £*	*Highest £*	*Average £*
MANDOLA					
Maratea, Michele	1	1	99	99	99
MANDOLIN					
Ceccherini, Umberto	1	0			
Embergher, Luigi	1	1	902	902	902
Vinaccia, Gennaro & Alle	1	1	462	462	462
Gibson Co.	1	1	1066	1066	1066
Salsedo, Luigi	1	1	418	418	418
Vinaccia Family (member of) (attributed to)	1	1	1430	1430	1430
OBOE					
Boosey & Hawkes	1	1	132	132	132
Cabart	1	1	61	61	61
Doelling	1	1	748	748	748
Hanken, Gerhard	1	1	880	880	880
Loree, Francois	2	1	2530	2530	2530
Louis	1	1	1760	1760	1760
Milhouse, William	2	2	990	1540	1265
Nonon, Jacques	1	0			
OBOE D'AMORE					
Loree, Francois	1	1	1760	1760	1760
Louis	1	1	4180	4180	4180
OPHICLEIDE					
Smith, Henry	1	1	528	528	528
PEDAL HARP					
Erard, Sebastian & Pierre	4	4	935	1540	1224
PIANO					
Atunes, Manuel	1	1	68200	68200	68200
Ball, Jacob	1	1	1045	1045	1045
Bates & Co.	1	1	605	605	605
Bell, S.	1	0			
Beyer, Adam	1	1	1045	1045	1045
Broadwood, John	1	1	902	902	902
Broadwood, John & Sons	5	4	594	7480	2720
Buntlebart, Gabriel	1	1	1760	1760	1760
Clementi, Muzio	1	1	1760	1760	1760
Froschle, George	1	1	2750	2750	2750
Kirkman, Jacob & Abraham	1	1	4730	4730	4730
Mott, J. H. R.	1	1	605	605	605
Rolfe & Co., William	1	1	1870	1870	1870
PICCOLO					
Bonneville	1	1	792	792	792
Lot, Louis	1	1	1430	1430	1430
PIPES					
Burleigh, David	1	1	308	308	308
POCHETTE					
Jay, Henry (attributed to)	1	1	1540	1540	1540
Tobin, Richard	1	1	2090	2090	2090
QUINTON					
Salomon, Jean Baptiste Deshayes	1	1	1210	1210	1210
Wamsley, Peter	1	1	1210	1210	1210
RECORDER					
Dolmetsch, Arnold	1	1	286	286	286
Eichentopf, Johann Heinrich	1	1	1210	1210	1210

Item/Maker	*Items Offered*	*Items Sold*	*Lowest £*	*Highest £*	*Average £*
SAXOPHONE					
Guinot, Rene	1	0			
SERPENT					
Metzler	1	1	1320	1320	1320
SMALL PIPES					
Reid, Robert & James	1	0			
SPINET					
Barton, Thomas	1	1	11000	11000	11000
Harris, Baker	1	0			
Slade, Benjamin	2	1	5720	5720	5720
TAROGATO					
Stowasser, Janos	1	1	1705	1705	1705
TENOR VIOL					
Heale, Michael	1	0			
Hintz, Frederick	1	1	6050	6050	6050
TROMBONE					
Courtois, Antoine	1	1	154	154	154
Pepper, J. W.	1	1	17	17	17
TRUMPET					
Gisborne	1	1	1485	1485	1485
VIHUELA					
Romanillos, Jose	1	1	1540	1540	1540
VIOL					
Norman, Barak	1	1	30800	30800	30800
VIOLA					
Albanelli, Franco	1	0			
Atkinson, William	2	1	1980	1980	1980
Barbieri, Bruno	1	1	2640	2640	2640
Bisiach, Leandro (jr.)	1	0			
Booth, William	1	1	1540	1540	1540
Bourguignon, Maurice	1	1	1980	1980	1980
Buchner, Rudolf	1	1	990	990	990
Capela, Antonio	2	1	2256	2256	2256
Carletti, Genuzio	1	0			
Chanot, George Adolph	1	0			
Chanot, George Anthony	1	1	3300	3300	3300
Chappuy, Nicolas Augustin	1	1	2090	2090	2090
Chardon & Fils	1	1	3080	3080	3080
Chevrier, Andre	1	0			
Claudot, Pierre	1	1	1528	1528	1528
Cocker, Lawrence	2	2	990	2090	1540
Colin, Jean Baptiste	2	2	1760	1870	1815
Conia, Stefano	1	1	2090	2090	2090
Craske, George	1	1	2750	2750	2750
Cuypers, Johannes Theodorus	1	1	16500	16500	16500
Degani, Eugenio	1	0			
Desideri, Pietro Paolo	1	0			
Dieudonne, Amedee	1	1	2111	2111	2111
Duke, Richard	2	2	2420	3300	2860
Enders, F. & R.	1	1	396	396	396
Epeneel, R. V.	1	0			
Esposti, Piergiuseppe	1	1	1980	1980	1980
Fendt, Bernard	1	1	9350	9350	9350
Forster, William	2	1	3850	3850	3850

Item/Maker	*Items Offered*	*Items Sold*	*Lowest £*	*Highest £*	*Average £*
Forster, William (II)	2	1	3620	3620	3620
Gabrielli, Giovanni Battista	1	1	20900	20900	20900
Gadda, Gaetano	1	1	2970	2970	2970
Gadda, Mario	1	1	3080	3080	3080
Gand & Bernardel	1	1	12100	12100	12100
Garonnaire, Christian	1	1	3740	3740	3740
Gibson	1	1	440	440	440
Gilbert, Jeffery J.	1	1	2420	2420	2420
Giraud, Franco	1	0			
Glaesel & Herwig	1	1	858	858	858
Gozalan, Mesut	1	1	506	506	506
Guadagnini, Gaetano (attributed to)	1	1	9350	9350	9350
Guersan, Louis	1	1	14300	14300	14300
Gutter, G. W.	1	1	509	509	509
Haenel, Frederick Ewald	1	1	1515	1515	1515
Hammond, John	1	1	825	825	825
Hill, Lockey (attributed to)	1	1	3520	3520	3520
Hill, W. E. & Sons	1	0			
Hudson, George Wulme	1	1	4950	4950	4950
Hyde, Andrew	1	1	365	365	365
Jais, Johannes (ascribed to)	1	1	6600	6600	6600
Keen, W.	1	1	660	660	660
Kennedy, Thomas	1	1	2640	2640	2640
Kilburn, Wilfred	1	0			
Kloz Family (member of)	2	1	2420	2420	2420
Koberling	1	1	462	462	462
Lazare, Robert	2	1	121	121	121
Le Govic, Alain	2	2	396	704	550
Lee, Percy	1	1	3080	3080	3080
Littlewood, Gerald	1	1	605	605	605
Lucci, Giuseppe	2	2	3960	4180	4070
Luff, William H.	2	1	3740	3740	3740
Martin, Johann Gottlieb	1	0			
Mezzadri, Alessandro (ascribed to)	1	1	14300	14300	14300
Mockel, Oswald	1	0			
Moinel-Cherpitel	1	0			
Morassi, Giovanni Battista	1	1	3850	3850	3850
Morris, Martin	1	0			
Naisby, Thomas Henry	1	1	1760	1760	1760
Neuner & Hornsteiner	1	1	748	748	748
Obbo, Marcus	1	0			
Pacherel, Pierre	1	1	4400	4400	4400
Panormo, Vincenzo	2	1	27500	27500	27500
Pareschi, Gaetano	2	1	1139	1139	1139
Pedrazzini, Giuseppe	1	0			
Perry, James	1	1	4400	4400	4400
Perry, L. A.	1	1	528	528	528
Perry, Thomas	1	1	5060	5060	5060
Resuche, Charles	2	2	1760	3300	2530
Richardson, Arthur	2	1	1650	1650	1650
Rinaldi, Marengo Romanus	1	1	2420	2420	2420
Rocchi, S.	1	1	3093	3093	3093
Rost, Franz George	1	1	3520	3520	3520
Roth, Ernst Heinrich	3	3	605	770	678
Sacchi, Giorgio	1	0			
Saunders, Wilfred G.	1	1	1045	1045	1045
Scheinlein, M. F.	1	1	1078	1078	1078
Schmidt, E. R. & Co.	1	1	770	770	770
Schwarz, Giovanni	2	1	4180	4180	4180
Sgarabotto, Gaetano	3	2	4180	6186	5183
Silvestre, Pierre	1	0			
Simonazzi, Amadeo	1	0			
Solomon, Gimpel	2	1	5830	5830	5830
Storioni, Lorenzo (ascribed to)	1	1	37400	37400	37400
Tenucci, Eugen	1	1	1430	1430	1430
Thibouville-Lamy	1	1	825	825	825
Thibouville-Lamy, J.	1	0			

Item/Maker	*Items Offered*	*Items Sold*	*Lowest £*	*Highest £*	*Average £*
TOPHAM, CARASS	1	1	484	484	484
VETTORI, CARLO	1	1	1100	1100	1100
VICKERS, J. E.	1	1	286	286	286
VOIGT, ARNOLD	1	1	1320	1320	1320
VOIGT, E. & P.	1	0			
VUILLAUME, JEAN BAPTISTE	1	0			
VUILLAUME, NICHOLAS	1	0			
WALTON, R.	1	1	715	715	715
WHITMARSH FAMILY, (MEMBER OF)	1	1	886	886	886
WITHERS, GEORGE	1	1	935	935	935
YOUNGSON, ALEXANDER	1	0			
VIOLA BOW					
BERNARDEL, LEON	1	1	770	770	770
BRISTOW, STEPHEN	2	2	528	990	759
BRYANT, PERCIVAL WILFRED	1	1	1210	1210	1210
COLLIN-MEZIN	1	1	1100	1100	1100
DODD	2	2	352	1650	1001
DODD, JOHN	2	2	1430	1540	1485
DOTSCHKAIL, R.	1	1	430	430	430
DUPUY, PHILIPPE	1	1	1430	1430	1430
FINKEL, JOHANN S.	1	1	660	660	660
FINKEL, JOHANNES	1	1	605	605	605
GEIPEL, RICHARD	2	1	255	255	255
GEROME, ROGER	1	1	1164	1164	1164
GOHDE, GREGORY	1	0			
HILL, W. E. & SONS	6	5	1320	2420	1827
HOYER, OTTO A.	1	0			
HUMS, ALBIN	1	0			
LAMY, ALFRED	1	1	3740	3740	3740
MOINEL, AMEDEE	1	1	886	886	886
MULLER, E. K.	1	1	264	264	264
OUCHARD, EMILE	1	0			
PAJEOT	1	1	1100	1100	1100
PAJEOT, ETIENNE	1	0			
PENZEL	1	1	264	264	264
PENZEL, K. GERHARD	1	0			
PFRETZSCHNER, H. R.	2	2	385	715	550
PFRETZSCHNER, L.	1	1	506	506	506
RAMEAU, J. S.	1	1	531	531	531
SARTORY, EUGENE	1	1	3080	3080	3080
SCHMIDT, C. HANS CARL	1	1	1210	1210	1210
SCHULLER, OTTO	1	1	308	308	308
THIBOUVILLE-LAMY	1	0			
THIBOUVILLE-LAMY, JEROME	2	2	528	605	567
THOMASSIN, CLAUDE	1	1	1045	1045	1045
TUBBS, EDWARD	1	1	6050	6050	6050
TUBBS, JAMES	2	2	2420	3630	3025
TUNNICLIFFE, BRIAN	1	1	770	770	770
VAN DER MEER, KAREL	2	2	561	990	776
WILSON, GARNER	1	1	990	990	990
WITHERS, GEORGE & SONS	1	1	748	748	748
ZOPHEL, ERNST WILLY	1	1	354	354	354
VIOLA D'AMORE					
GUIDANTUS, JOANNES FLORENUS (attributed to)	1	0			
VIOLETTA					
GRANCINO, GIOVANNI (III)	1	1	2420	2420	2420
VIOLIN					
ACHNER, PHILIP	1	1	1320	1320	1320
ACOULON, ALFRED (attributed to)	2	1	1320	1320	1320
ACOULON, ALFRED (FILS) (ascribed to)	1	1	825	825	825
ADAMS, HENRY THOMAS	1	1	1835	1835	1835
ADAMSEN, P. P.	1	1	2200	2200	2200

Item/Maker	*Items Offered*	*Items Sold*	*Lowest £*	*Highest £*	*Average £*
AIRETON, EDMUND	1	0			
AIRETON, EDMUND (ascribed to)	1	1	3740	3740	3740
AITCHISON, FRANK	1	1	286	286	286
ALBANELLI, FRANCO (attributed to)	1	0			
ALBANI, JOSEPH (attributed to)	1	1	3300	3300	3300
ALBERT, CHARLES F.	1	1	841	841	841
ALDRIC, JEAN FRANCOIS	3	2	5458	9900	7679
AMATI, ANTONIO	1	0			
AMATI, ANTONIO & GIROLAMO	1	1	25300	25300	25300
AMATI, ANTONIO & GIROLAMO (ascribed to)	1	0			
AMATI, DOM NICOLO	1	0			
AMATI, NICOLO	1	0			
AMATI, NICOLO (attributed to)	1	1	27500	27500	27500
AMATI FAMILY (MEMBER OF)	1	0			
ANTONIAZZI, ROMEO	1	0			
ANTONIAZZI, ROMEO (ascribed to)	1	1	3300	3300	3300
APPARUT, GEORGES	1	1	1747	1747	1747
ARDERN, JOB	5	4	572	1100	831
ASCHAUER, LEO	1	1	770	770	770
ATKINSON, WILLIAM	2	1	2750	2750	2750
AUBRY, JOSEPH	3	3	1892	2200	2068
AUDINOT, NESTOR	1	1	5095	5095	5095
AYLOR, ALBERT	1	1	168	168	168
AZZOLA, LUIGI (ascribed to)	1	1	3520	3520	3520
BAADER & CO.	2	1	660	660	660
BAILLY, PAUL	5	4	2640	4950	4190
BAILLY, PAUL (ascribed to)	1	1	2090	2090	2090
BAILLY, PAUL (attributed to)	1	1	4950	4950	4950
BAILLY, R.	1	1	946	946	946
BAJONI, LUIGI (ascribed to)	1	1	4400	4400	4400
BALESTRIERI, TOMASO	3	2	25300	93500	59400
BANKS, BENJAMIN	1	1	1760	1760	1760
BANKS, JAMES & HENRY (attributed to)	2	1	715	715	715
BARBE, F.	1	1	764	764	764
BARBE, FRANCOIS	1	1	858	858	858
BARBIERI, ENZO	1	1	1870	1870	1870
BARBIERI, PAOLO (ascribed to)	1	1	1540	1540	1540
BARZONI, FRANCOIS	1	1	209	209	209
BASTA, JAN	1	0			
BAUR, MARTIN	1	1	1650	1650	1650
BAZIN, C.	1	0			
BELLOSIO, ANSELMO (attributed to)	1	1	7150	7150	7150
BERGONZI, LORENZO	1	1	1100	1100	1100
BERNARDEL, AUGUST SEBASTIAN	2	2	4180	5610	4895
BERNARDEL, AUGUST SEBASTIEN PHILIPPE	3	3	10917	15284	13500
BERNARDEL, GUSTAVE	2	1	8800	8800	8800
BERNARDEL, LEON	1	1	2420	2420	2420
BERTELLI ENZO	1	1	1705	1705	1705
BETTS	1	1	484	484	484
BETTS, EDWARD (attributed to)	2	2	1980	3960	2970
BETTS, JOHN	2	2	1430	3960	2695
BETTS, JOHN (ascribed to)	1	1	9900	9900	9900
BETTS, JOHN (attributed to)	1	1	660	660	660
BIGNAMI, OTELLO (ascribed to)	1	0			
BIRD, CHARLES A. EDWARD	1	1	1760	1760	1760
BISIACH, LEANDRO	3	3	9350	13200	11550
BISIACH, LEANDRO (JR.)	1	0			
BLACKBURN, G. B.	1	1	154	154	154
BLANCHARD, PAUL	1	1	5277	5277	5277
BLANCHART (ascribed to)	1	0			
BLANCHI, ALBERT	2	2	4367	4620	4493
BLONDELET, EMILE	1	1	1210	1210	1210
BLONDELET, H. E.	2	2	935	990	963
BLYTH, WILLIAMSON	1	1	329	329	329
BOLLINGER, JOSEPH	1	1	286	286	286
BONNEL, JOSEPH (attributed to)	1	1	605	605	605
BOOSEY & HAWKES	1	1	440	440	440

Item/Maker	Items Offered	Items Sold	Lowest £	Highest £	Average £
Boquay, Jacques (attributed to)	1	0			
Borelli, Andrea	1	1	18195	18195	18195
Borland, Hugh	1	1	582	582	582
Bossi, Giuseppe	1	0			
Boulangeot, Emile	1	1	4950	4950	4950
Boulangeot, Emile (workshop of)	1	1	990	990	990
Boullangier, Charles (attributed to)	1	1	3080	3080	3080
Bourbeau, E. A.	1	1	330	330	330
Bovis, Francois	1	1	6820	6820	6820
Brandini, Jacopo	1	0			
Brandini, Jacopo (attributed to)	1	1	8800	8800	8800
Braund, Frederick T.	1	1	484	484	484
Breton	1	1	550	550	550
Breton, Francois	4	3	278	880	489
Brierley, Joseph	1	1	715	715	715
Briggs, James William	2	2	1870	3080	2475
Briggs, James William (attributed to)	1	0			
Broughton, Leonard W.	2	1	228	228	228
Brown, James (attributed to)	1	1	286	286	286
Browne, John	1	0			
Bruckner, E.	1	1	764	764	764
Brugere, CH.	2	2	2911	3821	3366
Brugere, Charles Georges	2	2	605	4400	2503
Bruni, Mateo	1	1	5095	5095	5095
Bryant, Ole H.	1	1	1459	1459	1459
Buthod	1	1	396	396	396
Buthod, Charles	1	1	1100	1100	1100
Buthod, Charles Louis	2	2	880	990	935
Button & Whitaker	3	2	440	495	468
Byrom, John	1	1	2310	2310	2310
Cabasse	1	1	329	329	329
Cahusac	1	1	660	660	660
Calace, Cavaliere Raffaele	1	1	1739	1739	1739
Calcagni, Bernardo	3	2	25300	28600	26950
Callsen, B.	1	1	655	655	655
Callsen, B. (ascribed to)	1	1	19800	19800	19800
Camilli, Camillus	1	1	44000	44000	44000
Candi, Oreste	1	1	3960	3960	3960
Capellini, Virgilio	1	1	1760	1760	1760
Capicchioni, Marino	1	1	7480	7480	7480
Cappa, Goffredo (ascribed to)	1	0			
Carcassi, Lorenzo (ascribed to)	1	1	4400	4400	4400
Carcassi, Lorenzo & Tomasso	1	0			
Caressa, Albert	1	1	3520	3520	3520
Caressa & Francais (attributed to)	1	1	2640	2640	2640
Carlisle, James Reynold	1	1	126	126	126
Carny, V.	1	1	1456	1456	1456
Castagneri, Andrea (attributed to)	1	0			
Castello, Paolo (ascribed to)	1	1	6600	6600	6600
Cavaceppi, Mario	1	1	1571	1571	1571
Cavalli, Aristide	3	3	949	1320	1079
Cavalli, Aristide (workshop of)	1	1	660	660	660
Cavani, Giovanni	1	1	3639	3639	3639
Cerpi, G.	3	2	605	638	622
Ceruti, Giovanni Maria	1	1	1760	1760	1760
Champion, Rene (ascribed to)	1	1	1066	1066	1066
Chanot, Francis	1	1	1045	1045	1045
Chanot, Frederick William	3	2	1518	4400	2959
Chanot, G. A.	1	0			
Chanot, George	1	1	1100	1100	1100
Chanot, George Adolph	3	2	1485	4180	2833
Chanot, Georges	2	1	8250	8250	8250
Chanot, Joseph Anthony	1	1	784	784	784
Chappuy, A.	2	2	509	3275	1892
Chappuy, N.	1	1	873	873	873
Chappuy, Nicolas Augustin	2	2	1210	1760	1485
Chappuy, Nicolas Augustin (ascribed to)	1	1	660	660	660

Item/Maker	*Items Offered*	*Items Sold*	*Lowest £*	*Highest £*	*Average £*
Chartreux, Eugene	2	1	330	330	330
Chipot, Jean Baptiste	1	0			
Chipot-Vuillaume	4	3	1100	1760	1417
Clark, Samuel	1	1	280	280	280
Claudot, Augustin	1	1	728	728	728
Claudot, Charles	2	1	691	691	691
Claudot, Charles (ascribed to)	1	0			
Claudot, Nicolas	1	1	374	374	374
Clotelle, H.	2	1	550	550	550
Cole, James	1	1	1595	1595	1595
Colin, Claude	2	1	770	770	770
Colin, Jean Baptiste	5	4	495	1392	884
Collenot, Louis	1	1	873	873	873
Collin-Mezin	4	4	715	1650	1224
Collin-Mezin, Ch. J. B.	18	17	341	6550	1922
Collin-Mezin, Ch. J. B. (fils)	2	2	1595	2310	1953
Colton, Walter E.	1	1	1010	1010	1010
Comuni, Antonio	1	1	13100	13100	13100
Conia, Stefano	2	2	3190	3520	3355
Conti Aldo	1	1	2530	2530	2530
Contino, Alfredo	1	1	5890	5890	5890
Cooper, Hugh W.	1	1	770	770	770
Copelli, Maurizio	1	1	1540	1540	1540
Couturieux	2	1	330	330	330
Craske, George	14	13	990	4620	2170
Craske, George (ascribed to)	1	0			
Craske, George (attributed to)	2	2	418	949	684
Dal Canto, Giustino	1	1	954	954	954
dalla Costa, Antonio	1	1	31900	31900	31900
Darche, Hilaire	1	1	5720	5720	5720
Darte, August (attributed to)	1	1	1540	1540	1540
de Rub, Augusto (ascribed to)	1	0			
Dearlove, Mark William	1	1	374	374	374
Deblaye, Albert	1	1	352	352	352
Dechant, G.	1	1	1066	1066	1066
Degani, (workshop of)	1	1	12100	12100	12100
Degani, Eugenio	4	4	6600	13200	9845
Degani, Giulio	5	4	2640	8800	5610
Delanoy, Alexandre	2	2	1638	2178	1908
Delivet, Auguste	1	1	1601	1601	1601
Della Corte, Alfonso (ascribed to)	1	1	8250	8250	8250
Demay	1	1	1237	1237	1237
Derazey, Honore	8	7	1012	6600	2832
Derazey, Honore (attributed to)	1	0			
Derazey, Justin	3	2	1760	1819	1790
Deveau, John G.	1	1	582	582	582
Didier, Marius	2	2	1019	1650	1334
Diehl, A.	1	1	1638	1638	1638
Diehl, M.	2	2	509	2547	1528
Dieudonne, Amedee	5	5	1178	2365	1638
Dixon, Alfred Thomas	1	1	484	484	484
Dollenz, Giovanni (ascribed to)	1	0			
Dolling, Louis (jun)	2	2	605	880	743
Dolling, Robert A.	1	1	421	421	421
Drouin, Charles	1	0			
Duerer, Wilhelm	1	1	190	190	190
Dugade, Aubry	1	1	1155	1155	1155
Dugarde, Aubry	1	1	734	734	734
Duke, Richard	4	3	1430	3520	2750
Dupary, Adolphe	1	1	1320	1320	1320
Eberle, Tomaso	1	1	17600	17600	17600
Eckland, Donald	1	1	1739	1739	1739
Elliot, William	1	1	1430	1430	1430
Enders, F. & R.	1	1	1540	1540	1540
Eyles, Charles	1	0			
Fabricatore, Gennaro	1	1	15648	15648	15648
Fabricatore, Giovanni Battista	1	1	3300	3300	3300

Item/Maker	*Items Offered*	*Items Sold*	*Lowest £*	*Highest £*	*Average £*
FABRICATORE, GIOVANNI BATTISTA (ascribed to)	1	1	6820	6820	6820
FABRIS, LUIGI (ascribed to)	1	0			
FAGNOLA, HANNIBAL	1	1	12736	12736	12736
FALISSE, A.	2	2	1456	2090	1773
FELICI, ENRICO	1	1	1650	1650	1650
FENDT, BERNARD (attributed to)	2	1	1650	1650	1650
FENT, FRANCOIS	1	0			
FERRARI, GIUSEPPE	1	1	1210	1210	1210
FICHTL, M.	1	1	4185	4185	4185
FICHTL, MARTIN MATHIAS	1	0			
FICKER, C. S.	1	1	655	655	655
FICKER, JOHANN CHRISTIAN	3	3	1210	1925	1522
FICKER FAMILY (MEMBER OF)	1	0			
FILLION, G.	1	0			
FIORINI, RAFFAELE (attributed to)	1	1	2420	2420	2420
FISCHER, H. A.	1	1	1980	1980	1980
FLAMBEAU, CHARLES	1	0			
FLEURY, BENOIT	1	1	605	605	605
FORBES-WHITMORE, ANTHONY	1	1	1980	1980	1980
FORCELLINI, F.	1	1	2911	2911	2911
FORD, JACOB (attributed to)	1	1	2860	2860	2860
FORRESTER, ALEXANDER	1	1	462	462	462
FORSTER, WILLIAM	1	1	898	898	898
FORSTER, WILLIAM (II)	3	3	1430	5500	2860
FUCHS, W. K.	1	1	505	505	505
FURBER, JOHN (attributed to)	1	1	1870	1870	1870
FURBER, MATTHEW (attributed to)	1	1	572	572	572
FURBER FAMILY (MEMBER OF) (attributed to)	1	1	2530	2530	2530
GABRIELLI, GIOVANNI BATTISTA	1	1	39600	39600	39600
GADDA, GAETANO	2	2	6600	7642	7121
GADDA, MARIO	2	1	3520	3520	3520
GAGLIANO, FERDINAND	1	1	45100	45100	45100
GAGLIANO, FERDINAND (attributed to)	1	1	16500	16500	16500
GAGLIANO, GENNARO	1	1	33000	33000	33000
GAGLIANO, JOSEPH	3	2	15950	25300	20625
GAGLIANO, JOSEPH & ANTONIO	1	1	6732	6732	6732
GAGLIANO, NICOLO	3	3	13750	54585	35612
GAGLIANO, RAFFAELE & ANTONIO	1	1	17600	17600	17600
GAGLIANO FAMILY (attributed to)	1	1	13200	13200	13200
GAIDA, GIOVANNI	2	2	6820	8800	7810
GALEA, ALFREDO G.	1	1	1100	1100	1100
GALLA, ANTON (attributed to)	1	0			
GAND, CHARLES FRANCOIS (ascribed to)	1	1	15400	15400	15400
GARIMBERTI, F.	1	1	6550	6550	6550
GAVATELLI, ALCIDE	1	1	1113	1113	1113
GAVINIES, FRANCOIS	1	1	3080	3080	3080
GEISSENHOF, FRANZ	1	1	6600	6600	6600
GEISSENHOF, FRANZ (attributed to)	1	1	4400	4400	4400
GEMUNDER, GEORGE	1	1	2300	2300	2300
GERARD, GRAND	1	1	509	509	509
GERMAIN, EMILE	1	1	3300	3300	3300
GIGLI, GIULIO CESARE	1	1	1760	1760	1760
GILBERT, JEFFERY J.	1	1	770	770	770
GILBERT, JEFFERY JAMES	1	1	935	935	935
GILKS, WILLIAM	1	0			
GLASEL, ERNST	1	1	462	462	462
GLASEL, LOUIS	1	1	280	280	280
GLASEL & MOSSNER (attributed to)	1	1	286	286	286
GLASS, JOHANN	1	1	759	759	759
GLENISTER, WILLIAM	2	1	1760	1760	1760
GOBETTI, FRANCESCO	1	1	7920	7920	7920
GOFFRILLER, FRANCESCO	1	1	24200	24200	24200
GOFTON, ROBERT	1	1	715	715	715
GORDON	1	1	352	352	352
GOULDING	1	1	220	220	220
GOULDING (attributed to)	1	1	880	880	880
GOULDING & CO.	1	0			

Item/Maker	Items Offered	Items Sold	Lowest £	Highest £	Average £
JEUNE, LAURENT	1	1	764	764	764
JOHNSON, PETER ANDREAS	1	1	196	196	196
JOHNSTON, THOMAS	1	1	154	154	154
JUZEK, JOHN	2	2	1155	2420	1788
KAUL, PAUL	2	2	1870	4549	3209
KEFFER, JOANNES	1	1	1237	1237	1237
KENNEDY, THOMAS	1	1	3740	3740	3740
KLOZ, AEGIDIUS	4	4	1980	8006	4421
KLOZ, GEORGE	1	1	2729	2729	2729
KLOZ, JOAN CAROL	1	1	1540	1540	1540
KLOZ, JOSEPH	1	1	3520	3520	3520
KLOZ, SEBASTIAN	1	0			
KLOZ, SEBASTIAN (attributed to)	1	1	1980	1980	1980
KLOZ, SEBASTIAN (I)	1	1	3520	3520	3520
KLOZ FAMILY (MEMBER OF)	5	4	421	6050	2422
KLOZ FAMILY (MEMBER OF) (attributed to)	1	1	1100	1100	1100
KNORR, P.	1	1	2402	2402	2402
KNUPFER, ALBERT	1	1	572	572	572
KRAFT, PETER	1	0			
KREUTZINGER, ANTON	1	1	605	605	605
KRUG, J. ADOLPH	1	1	393	393	393
KRUSE WILHELM	1	1	430	430	430
KUDANOWSKI, JAN	1	1	1320	1320	1320
KUNZE, WILHELM PAUL	1	0			
L'ANSON, EDWARD (attributed to)	1	0			
LABERTE-HUMBERT BROS.	1	1	1100	1100	1100
LANCASTER	1	1	242	242	242
LANCINGER, ANTONIN	1	1	1210	1210	1210
LANDOLFI, PIETRO ANTONIO	1	1	48400	48400	48400
LANG, J. S.	1	1	110	110	110
LANGONET, CHARLES	1	1	2183	2183	2183
LANTNER, BOHUSLAV	1	1	1100	1100	1100
LAURENT, EMILE	1	1	3300	3300	3300
LAVEST, J.	1	1	1019	1019	1019
LAZARE, ROBERT	1	1	374	374	374
LE CYR, JAMES FERDINAND	2	1	715	715	715
LECHI, ANTONIO	6	5	440	880	603
LEE, H. W.	1	0			
LEGNANI, LUIGI (ascribed to)	1	1	3520	3520	3520
LEIDOLFF, JOHANN CHRISTOPH	1	1	660	660	660
LOCKE, GEORGE HERBERT	1	1	550	550	550
LONGMAN & BRODERIP	2	2	495	638	567
LONGMAN & LUKEY	1	0			
LONGSON, F. H.	1	0			
LONGSON, J. L.	1	1	990	990	990
LOTT, JOHN	1	1	24200	24200	24200
LOUVET, F.	1	1	509	509	509
LOVERI, CARLO	1	1	1155	1155	1155
LOWENDALL, LOUIS	7	7	143	715	410
LUCCI, GIUSEPPE	2	2	2860	6600	4730
LUFF, WILLIAM H.	3	3	2860	3520	3227
LUPOT, NICOLAS	2	2	30800	44000	37400
LUTSCHG, GUSTAV	1	1	2860	2860	2860
MACPHERSON, H.	1	1	330	330	330
MAGNIERE, GABRIEL	1	1	1375	1375	1375
MALAKOFF, BRUGERE	1	1	3520	3520	3520
MANGENOT, P.	1	1	582	582	582
MANGENOT, PAUL	1	1	1320	1320	1320
MANSUY	1	1	328	328	328
MARAVIGLIA, GUIDO (attributed to)	1	1	1113	1113	1113
MARCHI, GIOVANNI (ascribed to)	1	1	2750	2750	2750
MARIANI, ANTONIO	2	2	1066	14300	7683
MARSHALL, JOHN	2	1	1980	1980	1980
MARTIN, E.	1	1	182	182	182
MARTIN, J.	1	1	619	619	619
MARTIN FAMILY, (MEMBER OF)	1	1	1540	1540	1540
MARTINO, GIUSEPPE	1	1	1122	1122	1122

Item/Maker	*Items Offered*	*Items Sold*	*Lowest £*	*Highest £*	*Average £*
GRAGNANI, ANTONIO	1	1	17600	17600	17600
GRANCINO, FRANCESCO & GIOVANNI	1	1	4207	4207	4207
GRANCINO, GIOVANNI	1	1	41800	41800	41800
GRANCINO, GEBR.	1	1	12736	12736	12736
GRAND-GERARD, JEAN BAPTISTE	3	2	308	3520	1914
GRANDJON, JULES	1	1	1430	1430	1430
GRATER, THOMAS	1	1	968	968	968
GRIBBEN, P. J.	1	1	176	176	176
GRUNER	1	1	346	346	346
GUADAGNINI, ANTONIO (attributed to)	1	1	13100	13100	13100
GUADAGNINI, FRANCESCO	1	1	7700	7700	7700
GUADAGNIN, G. B. & PIETRO	1	0			
GUADAGNINI, GIOVANNI BATTISTA	4	4	27500	176000	98725
GUARNERI, ANDREA	2	2	16500	33000	24750
GUARNERI, GIUSEPPE (FILIUS ANDREA)	1	1	180400	180400	180400
GUARNERI, GIUSEPPE (FILIUS ANDREA) (attributed to)	1	1	35200	35200	35200
GUARNERI, JOSEPH (DEL GESU) (attributed to)	1	1	18700	18700	18700
GUARNERI, PIETRO (OF MANTUA)	1	0			
GUASTALLA, DANTE	1	1	3740	3740	3740
GUASTALLA, DANTE & ALFREDO	2	2	3520	5049	4285
GUERRA, E.	1	1	11281	11281	11281
GUERRA, EVASIO EMILE	1	1	7700	7700	7700
GUERSAN, LOUIS	2	1	1705	1705	1705
GUERSAN, LOUIS (attributed to)	2	1	462	462	462
GUIDANTUS, JOANNES FLORENUS	2	1	15400	15400	15400
GUIDANTUS, JOANNES FLORENUS (ascribed to)	2	1	7150	7150	7150
HAMMA & CO.	1	1	946	946	946
HAMMETT, THOMAS	1	1	638	638	638
HAMMIG, M.	1	1	2620	2620	2620
HAMMIG, WILHELM HERMAN	1	1	2860	2860	2860
HARDIE, JAMES & SONS	2	2	330	455	393
HARDIE, MATTHEW	1	0			
HARDIE, THOMAS	1	0			
HART & SON	2	2	1870	3080	2475
HAWKES & SON	1	1	784	784	784
HEBERLEIN, HEINRICH TH.	1	1	252	252	252
HEBERLEIN, HEINRICH TH. (JUNIOR)	1	1	533	533	533
HECKEL, RUDOLF	1	1	2860	2860	2860
HEINICKE, MATHIAS	1	1	2729	2729	2729
HEINRICH, THEODORE	1	1	533	533	533
HEL, JOSEPH	2	2	8250	10189	9220
HELD, JOHANN JOSEPH	1	1	1815	1815	1815
HERTL, ANTON	1	1	330	330	330
HESKETH, J. EARL	1	1	1045	1045	1045
HESKETH, THOMAS EARLE	2	2	2750	2860	2805
HILL, HENRY LOCKEY	1	0			
HILL, W. E. & SONS	3	3	2970	6050	4107
HILL, W. E. & SONS (workshop of)	1	0			
HOFFMANN, EDUARD	1	1	25300	25300	25300
HOFMANN, JOHANN MARTIN	1	1	1430	1430	1430
HOFMANS, MATHIAS (ascribed to)	1	0			
HOING, CLIFFORD A.	1	1	616	616	616
HOPF	3	3	120	691	331
HOPF, DAVID	1	1	242	242	242
HORNSTEINER, MATHIAS	2	1	3202	3202	3202
HUDSON, GEORGE WULME	3	2	2530	3190	2860
HUTTON, ADAM	1	1	83	83	83
IAROVOI, DENIS	1	0			
JACOBS, HENDRIK	1	1	8580	8580	8580
JACQUOT, ALBERT	1	1	7480	7480	7480
JACQUOT, CHARLES	1	1	8006	8006	8006
JACQUOT, CHARLES (ascribed to)	1	0			
JAIS, ANTON	1	1	418	418	418
JAURA, WILHELM THOMAS	1	0			
JAURA, WILHELM THOMAS (ascribed to)	2	1	2750	2750	2750
JAY, HENRY	2	1	880	880	880
JAY, HENRY (attributed to)	1	1	638	638	638

Item/Maker	*Items Offered*	*Items Sold*	*Lowest £*	*Highest £*	*Average £*
Martirenghi, Marcello	1	1	4180	4180	4180
Masafija, Dimitri	1	1	792	792	792
Mast, J.	1	1	4731	4731	4731
Mast, Joseph Laurent	1	1	990	990	990
Mathieu, Nicolas	1	1	330	330	330
Maucotel, Charles	1	1	3080	3080	3080
Mayson, Walter	7	6	418	1430	759
Mayson, Walter H.	3	3	440	792	667
Mead, L. J.	1	1	308	308	308
Meek, James	1	1	729	729	729
Meinel, Eugen	1	1	2860	2860	2860
Meinel, Oskar	1	1	252	252	252
Melegari, Michele & Pietro	1	1	4180	4180	4180
Mennesson, Emile	1	1	1540	1540	1540
Merling, Pauli	2	2	770	2420	1595
Meurot, L. (attributed to)	2	2	550	1320	935
Millant, R. & M.	1	1	1201	1201	1201
Milton, Louis	1	1	1650	1650	1650
Miremont	1	0			
Mockel, Oswald	1	1	1237	1237	1237
Mockel, Otto	1	1	1155	1155	1155
Moitessier, Louis	1	0			
Monk, John King	1	1	154	154	154
Monnig, Fritz	2	2	1202	1320	1261
Montagnana, Domenico	1	1	88000	88000	88000
Montani, Costante	1	1	2750	2750	2750
Moody, G. T.	1	1	572	572	572
Morizot, Rene	1	1	605	605	605
Mougenot, L.	1	1	3275	3275	3275
Mougenot, Leon	1	1	1760	1760	1760
Mougenot, Leon (attributed to)	1	1	1210	1210	1210
Mougenot, Leon (workshop of)	1	1	880	880	880
Moya, Hidalgo	2	2	825	1760	1293
Mozzani, Luigi	2	2	880	1265	1073
Muller, Joseph	1	1	220	220	220
Nafissi, Carlo	1	0			
Neff, Joseph	2	2	168	238	203
Neuner, Ludwig	1	1	1320	1320	1320
Neuner, Mathias	1	1	286	286	286
Neuner, N.	1	1	273	273	273
Neuner & Hornsteiner	4	3	264	1100	572
Neuner & Hornsteiner (attributed to)	1	1	506	506	506
Nicolas, Didier (l'aine)	11	10	309	2860	1170
Nolli, Marco	1	1	1100	1100	1100
Norman, Barak	1	0			
Oddone, Carlo Giuseppe	2	2	11000	14300	12650
Oldfield, W.	2	1	308	308	308
Olivier, Christian	1	1	814	814	814
Orlandini, A.	1	1	1819	1819	1819
Ornati, Giuseppe	1	0			
Ortega, Asencio (attributed to)	1	0			
Otto,Rudi	1	1	1010	1010	1010
Owen, John W.	1	1	1320	1320	1320
Palzini, Gianbattista	1	1	1010	1010	1010
Panormo, Edward Ferdinand (attributed to)	1	0			
Panormo, George	2	1	6600	6600	6600
Panormo, Vincenzo	4	4	12100	33000	25798
Panormo, Vincenzo (attributed to)	1	1	6160	6160	6160
Papageorgiou, Georges D.	1	1	1540	1540	1540
Parker, Daniel (attributed to)	1	1	5280	5280	5280
Partl, Christian Franz	2	1	1485	1485	1485
Patterson, W. D.	1	1	682	682	682
Pearce, George	1	1	2420	2420	2420
Pedrazzini, Giuseppe	2	1	13750	13750	13750
Pelizon, Antonio	1	0			
Penzl, Ignaz	2	2	484	616	550
Perrin, E. J. (fils)	1	0			

Item/Maker	*Items Offered*	*Items Sold*	*Lowest £*	*Highest £*	*Average £*
Perry, L. A.	2	1	330	330	330
Perry, Stephen	1	1	196	196	196
Perry, Thomas	2	2	841	880	861
Pfretzschner, Carl Friedrich (attributed to)	1	1	880	880	880
Pfretzschner, G. A.	1	1	477	477	477
Phillipson, Edward	2	2	278	286	282
Piccione, Emilio	1	1	4950	4950	4950
Pierray, Claude	2	2	770	3080	1925
Pierray, Claude (attributed to)	3	2	605	2970	1788
Pilat, Paul	1	1	4180	4180	4180
Pillement, Francois	2	2	176	352	264
Piper, W.	1	1	660	660	660
Pique, Francois Louis	2	1	18700	18700	18700
Piretti, Enrico	1	1	2200	2200	2200
Pirot, Claude	1	1	7260	7260	7260
Placht, Johann Franz	1	1	880	880	880
Plumerel, Jean	1	1	440	440	440
Politi, Enrico & Raul	1	0			
Pollastri, Augusto	1	0			
Pollastri, Augusto (attributed to)	1	0			
Pollastri, Gaetano	1	1	9097	9097	9097
Poller, Paul	1	1	218	218	218
Postacchini, Andrea	1	1	12100	12100	12100
Postiglione, Vincenzo	2	2	8250	10189	9220
Praga, Eugenio (ascribed to)	1	0			
Pressenda, Giovanni Francesco	3	2	36300	60500	48400
Preston, John	1	1	176	176	176
Pullar, E. F.	1	1	275	275	275
Pyne, George	3	3	1210	2090	1613
Raffe, E. H.	2	2	880	4400	2640
Rance, J. F.	1	1	1210	1210	1210
Rapoport, Haim	1	0			
Rasura, Vincenzo (ascribed to)	1	1	2750	2750	2750
Rauch, Sebastian	1	1	1092	1092	1092
Rauch, Thomas	1	1	990	990	990
Raymond, Robert John	1	1	242	242	242
Reichel, Johann Friedrich	1	0			
Reiter, Johann	1	1	728	728	728
Remy	2	2	715	770	743
Renisto, Andreas	1	1	1540	1540	1540
Richardson, Arthur	3	2	2076	2200	2138
Richter, Eckart	1	0			
Richter, G.	1	1	983	983	983
Ridge	1	0			
Rinaldi, Marengo Romanus	1	1	10553	10553	10553
Robinson, William	3	3	455	2530	1307
Rocca, Enrico	1	1	9825	9825	9825
Rocca, Giuseppe	1	1	66000	66000	66000
Rocca, Joseph	1	1	94600	94600	94600
Rogeri, Giovanni Battista	1	1	61600	61600	61600
Rogeri, Pietro Giacomo	1	0			
Rost, Franz George	1	1	1320	1320	1320
Roth, Ernst Heinrich	4	4	449	902	648
Roumen, Johannes Arnoldus	1	0			
Rovescalli, T.	1	1	2911	2911	2911
Ruggieri, Francesco	2	1	49500	49500	49500
Ruggieri, Vincenzo	1	0			
Ruggieri, Vincenzo (attributed to)	1	0			
Rushworth & Dreaper	2	1	2090	2090	2090
Salsedo, Luigi	1	1	1870	1870	1870
Salsedo, Luigi (attributed to)	1	1	2860	2860	2860
Salzard, Francois	1	1	286	286	286
Sander, Carl	1	1	550	550	550
Sandner, Edi	1	1	396	396	396
Sannino, Vincenzo	1	0			
Sannino, Vincenzo (attributed to)	1	1	6050	6050	6050
Sarfati, G.	1	1	1019	1019	1019

Item/Maker	*Items Offered*	*Items Sold*	*Lowest £*	*Highest £*	*Average £*
Scarampella, Stefano	1	1	13828	13828	13828
Schaller, Reinhold	1	1	273	273	273
Schau, Carl	1	0			
Scheerer, John	1	1	770	770	770
Scheinlein, M. F.	1	1	1019	1019	1019
Schmidt, E. R. & Co.	3	3	187	935	491
Schmidt, Johann Martin	1	0			
Schmidt, Reinhold	1	1	393	393	393
Schmitt, Lucien	1	1	1980	1980	1980
Schoenfelder, Johann Georg	1	1	3093	3093	3093
Schroeder, John G.	1	1	365	365	365
Schuster, C. J. & Son	1	1	187	187	187
Schwarz, Giovanni	1	1	5720	5720	5720
Schwarz, Heinrich	1	1	385	385	385
Schweitzer, Johann Baptiste (attributed to)	1	1	1705	1705	1705
Scolari, Giorgio	2	2	2530	4620	3575
Sderci, Luciano	1	0			
Sderci, Luciano (attributed to)	1	1	4400	4400	4400
Seidel, Christian Wilhelm	1	1	682	682	682
Seidel, Johann Michael	1	1	242	242	242
Seraphin, Sanctus (attributed to)	1	0			
Sgarabotto, Pietro	1	1	5500	5500	5500
Sgarbi, Antonio	1	0			
Siega, Ettore & Son (ascribed to)	1	1	2090	2090	2090
Silvestre, Pierre	1	1	7920	7920	7920
Silvestre & Maucotel	1	1	7700	7700	7700
Simon, Franz	2	1	990	990	990
Simoutre, Nicholas Eugene	1	1	2530	2530	2530
Simpson, James & John	1	1	2310	2310	2310
Simpson, Thomas	1	1	660	660	660
Smillie, Alexander	2	2	880	2090	1485
Soffritti, Ettore	1	0			
Sorsano, Spirito	1	1	34100	34100	34100
Soubeyran, Marc	1	0			
Stadlmann, Johann Joseph	2	1	1540	1540	1540
Stainer, Jacob	1	1	25806	25806	25806
Stainer, Marcus (attributed to)	1	1	1459	1459	1459
Stanley, Robert A.	1	1	825	825	825
Stirrat, David	2	1	2610	2610	2610
Storioni, Carlo	1	1	935	935	935
Storioni, Lorenzo	1	1	41800	41800	41800
Stradivari, Antonio	2	1	902000	902000	902000
Stradivari, Omobono	1	0			
Straub, Simon	1	1	2729	2729	2729
Suzuki, M.	1	1	253	253	253
Tarasconi, G.	1	1	5095	5095	5095
Tarr, Shelley	1	0			
Tassini, Marco	1	1	1045	1045	1045
Tavegia, Carlo Antonio	2	1	2200	2200	2200
Tecchler, David	1	1	16500	16500	16500
Tecchler, David (attributed to)	1	1	2860	2860	2860
Tenucci, Eugen	1	1	3639	3639	3639
Termanini, Pietro	1	1	7150	7150	7150
Testore, Carlo	1	1	20900	20900	20900
Testore, Carlo (attributed to)	1	1	14850	14850	14850
Testore, Carlo Antonio	1	1	24200	24200	24200
Testore, Carlo Giuseppe	1	0			
Testore Family (member of)	2	2	1980	9680	5830
Thibout, Jacques Pierre	1	1	2750	2750	2750
Thibouville-Lamy	14	13	110	1155	398
Thibouville-Lamy, J.	6	6	143	638	367
Thibouville-Lamy, J. (workshop of)	1	1	2524	2524	2524
Thibouville-Lamy, Jerome	9	8	304	1100	614
Thier, Joseph (attributed to)	1	1	638	638	638
Thir, Mathias	2	1	990	990	990
Thir, Mathias (attributed to)	1	1	2530	2530	2530
Thompson, Charles & Samuel	4	3	528	1430	983

Item/Maker	*Items Offered*	*Items Sold*	*Lowest £*	*Highest £*	*Average £*
Thompson & Son	1	1	2530	2530	2530
Thomson	1	1	176	176	176
Thorburn, S. W.	1	1	209	209	209
Thouvenel, Charles	1	1	1265	1265	1265
Thow, J.	1	1	308	308	308
Tiller, G. W.	1	1	374	374	374
Tim-Geigen	1	1	770	770	770
Tobin, Richard	1	0			
Tobin, Richard (attributed to)	1	1	550	550	550
Tomassini, Domenico (ascribed to)	1	1	2420	2420	2420
Tononi, Carlo	1	1	19800	19800	19800
Tweedale, Charles L.	1	1	396	396	396
Valenzano, Joannes Maria	2	2	16500	35200	25850
Valenzano, Joannes Maria (ascribed to)	1	0			
Vautelint, N. Pierre	1	1	3080	3080	3080
Ventapane, Lorenzo	3	3	4840	20900	13530
Ventapane, Lorenzo (attributed to)	1	0			
Verini, Andrea	1	1	1540	1540	1540
Vickers, J. E.	2	2	582	784	683
Vinaccia Family (member of)	1	0			
Vincent, Alfred	3	3	2640	3740	3043
Vincent, Alfred (attributed to)	1	1	2200	2200	2200
Visconti, Domenico (attributed to)	1	1	1100	1100	1100
Vlummens, Dominic	1	1	2310	2310	2310
Voigt, Arnold	1	1	605	605	605
Voigt, Johann Georg	1	0			
Voigt, Paul	1	1	682	682	682
Voller Brothers	1	1	14300	14300	14300
Von Dolling, (younger)	1	0			
Vuillaume, Jean Baptiste	8	7	10189	33000	19013
Vuillaume, Jean Baptiste (ascribed to)	1	1	10450	10450	10450
Vuillaume, Jean Baptiste (workshop of)	1	1	19800	19800	19800
Vuillaume, Nicholas	2	2	2750	8580	5665
Vuillaume, Sebastian	2	1	2530	2530	2530
Wagner, Benedict (attributed to)	1	1	785	785	785
Walker, William	2	1	1455	1455	1455
Walton, William	1	1	495	495	495
Wamsley, Peter	6	5	546	4950	2243
Wanner, Michael	1	1	528	528	528
Ward, George	1	1	825	825	825
Wassermann, Joseph	1	1	3300	3300	3300
Weigert, Johann Blasius	1	1	1066	1066	1066
Whedbee, William	1	1	785	785	785
Whitbread, W. W.	1	1	190	190	190
White, Asa Warren	1	1	365	365	365
White, H. N. & Co.	1	1	168	168	168
Whitmarsh, Edwin	1	1	770	770	770
Whitmarsh, Emanuel	1	1	605	605	605
Widhalm, Leopold	4	4	660	10553	3927
Wilkanowski, W.	2	2	309	505	407
Wilkinson, John	1	0			
Wilkinson, William & Perry, Thomas	1	1	792	792	792
Wilson, Tom	1	1	209	209	209
Winterling, G.	2	2	3275	5640	4458
Withers, Edward	1	1	1540	1540	1540
Wolff Bros.	5	5	165	418	262
Wouldhave, John	1	0			
Zach, Thomas (attributed to)	1	1	1540	1540	1540
Zanier, Ferruccio	1	1	2365	2365	2365
Zemitis, M.	1	1	691	691	691
Zettwitz, William	1	0			
Zimmerman, Friederich	1	1	374	374	374

VIOLIN BOW

Alvey, Brian	2	1	1210	1210	1210
Apparut, Georges	1	1	582	582	582
Bausch, L.	1	1	165	165	165

Item/Maker	*Items Offered*	*Items Sold*	*Lowest £*	*Highest £*	*Average £*
Bazin	1	1	748	748	748
Bazin, C.	2	2	176	278	227
Bazin, Charles	8	8	176	1155	633
Bazin, Louis	5	5	168	1540	660
Bazin Family (member of)	1	0			
Beare, John & Arthur	1	1	1210	1210	1210
Bernardel, Gustave	4	3	506	1430	997
Bernardel, Leon	2	2	484	990	737
Bernardel, Rene	1	1	1210	1210	1210
Bisch, Paul	1	1	393	393	393
Brand, Karl	1	1	143	143	143
Briggs, James William	1	1	330	330	330
Bristow, Stephen	1	1	418	418	418
Bultitude, A. R.	1	1	1100	1100	1100
Bultitude, Arthur	2	2	660	1760	1210
Buthod, Charles	2	1	143	143	143
Callier, Frank	2	2	309	673	491
Caressa, Albert	1	1	880	880	880
Caressa & Francais	2	1	1705	1705	1705
Carrodus	1	1	455	455	455
Chadwick	1	1	546	546	546
Chanot, Joseph Anthony	1	1	1320	1320	1320
Chardon, Chanot	1	1	237	237	237
Collin-Mezin	2	1	660	660	660
Cuniot-Hury	2	2	152	715	433
Cuniot-Hury, Eugene	1	1	825	825	825
Darche, Hilaire	1	1	462	462	462
Delivet, Auguste	1	0			
Dodd	5	4	241	2111	1083
Dodd, Edward	1	1	1650	1650	1650
Dodd, James	3	2	935	2200	1568
Dodd, John	3	2	715	1430	1073
Dodd, John (ascribed to)	1	0			
Dodd, John (attributed to)	2	2	242	770	506
Dodd Family (member of)	2	1	1430	1430	1430
Dolling, Kurt	1	1	242	242	242
Dorfler, D.	1	1	140	140	140
Dotschkail, R.	1	1	655	655	655
Dugad, Andre	1	1	198	198	198
Dupuy, George	1	0			
Durrschmidt, O.	1	1	218	218	218
Durrschmidt, Otto	6	6	143	462	237
Eulry, Clement	1	1	1980	1980	1980
Eury, Nicolas	2	1	4840	4840	4840
Fetique, Jules	1	1	1122	1122	1122
Fetique, Victor	7	6	770	3190	1870
Finkel, Siegfried	1	1	393	393	393
Francais, Emile	3	2	880	990	935
Gand & Bernardel	1	1	1540	1540	1540
Geipel, Richard	2	1	154	154	154
Gerome, Roger	2	1	473	473	473
Gillet, R.	1	1	1274	1274	1274
Glasel	1	1	655	655	655
Gotz	1	0			
Gotz, Conrad	2	2	396	550	473
Grand Adam	1	1	8250	8250	8250
Guetter, Otto	1	1	354	354	354
Hagemann, F. R.	2	1	110	110	110
Hammig, W. H.	2	1	165	165	165
Hart & Son	1	0			
Hel, Pierre	1	1	660	660	660
Henry, Joseph	1	0			
Hermann, Lothar	1	1	275	275	275
Herrmann, A.	3	3	202	380	311
Herrmann, Edward	1	1	238	238	238
Herrmann, W.	1	1	380	380	380
Hill, W. E. & Sons	45	44	209	3520	1174

Item/Maker	Items Offered	Items Sold	Lowest £	Highest £	Average £
Hoyer, C. A.	1	1	440	440	440
Hoyer, G.	1	1	237	237	237
Hoyer, Otto A.	3	3	477	880	630
Hums, Albin	3	2	484	1045	765
Hums, W.	1	1	121	121	121
Husson, Charles Claude (attributed to)	1	0			
Kessler	1	1	220	220	220
Kittel Family (member of) (ascribed to)	1	1	2860	2860	2860
Knopf, Henry Richard	1	1	280	280	280
Laberte	1	1	328	328	328
Laberte, Marc	1	1	473	473	473
Laberte, Marc (ascribed to)	1	1	198	198	198
Lafleur (ascribed to)	1	0			
Lafleur, Joseph Rene	1	0			
Lafleur, Joseph Rene (ascribed to)	1	1	825	825	825
Lamy, A.	2	1	2729	2729	2729
Lamy, Alfred	9	8	143	4180	2080
Lamy, Alfred Joseph	1	1	2420	2420	2420
Leblanc, P. R.	3	3	255	328	291
Lermetz	1	1	99	99	99
Lotte, Francois	3	3	440	550	506
Lowendall, Louis	1	0			
Lupot, Francois	1	1	7700	7700	7700
Lupot, Francois (attributed to)	1	1	3300	3300	3300
Lupot, Nicolas	1	0			
Maire, Nicolas	3	2	4400	5277	4838
Martin	1	1	198	198	198
Maure, Pierre	1	1	506	506	506
Meauchand	1	1	3080	3080	3080
Meauchand (attributed to)	1	1	3080	3080	3080
Meinel, Eugen	2	2	56	228	142
Millant, B.	1	1	910	910	910
Miquel, E.	1	1	308	308	308
Moller, Max	1	1	770	770	770
Morizot	2	2	617	660	639
Morizot, Louis	5	5	152	715	464
Mougenot, Georges	1	1	550	550	550
Muhl	1	1	462	462	462
Nurnberger, Albert	17	16	127	2475	801
Ouchard, E.	2	2	655	691	673
Ouchard, Emile	3	2	682	1012	847
Paesold, Roderich	3	3	242	330	293
Pajeot	1	0			
Pajeot (attributed to)	1	1	3520	3520	3520
Pajeot, (fils)	2	2	2860	4620	3740
Pajeot, (pere)	1	1	5095	5095	5095
Paquotte Bros.	2	1	990	990	990
Paulus, Johannes O.	1	1	237	237	237
Peccatte, Dominique	2	2	8250	19800	14025
Peccatte, Dominique (attributed to)	1	1	3080	3080	3080
Peccatte, Francois	1	1	6600	6600	6600
Penzel	1	1	582	582	582
Penzel, K.	1	1	91	91	91
Persois (attributed to)	1	1	4950	4950	4950
Pfretzschner, F. C.	1	1	509	509	509
Pfretzschner, H. R.	12	11	91	1100	468
Pfretzschner, T. H.	1	1	228	228	228
Pfretzschner, W. A.	3	2	242	462	352
Pillot	1	0			
Poirson	1	1	1019	1019	1019
Prager, August Edwin	2	2	308	380	344
Prager, Gustav	3	3	330	418	367
Rau, August	4	4	198	660	487
Retford, William C.	1	1	4180	4180	4180
Richaume, Andre	1	1	1870	1870	1870
Rushworth & Dreaper	1	1	330	330	330
Salchow, William	1	1	1430	1430	1430

Item/Maker	*Items Offered*	*Items Sold*	*Lowest £*	*Highest £*	*Average £*
SANDNER, A. E.	1	1	224	224	224
SARTORY, EUGENE	19	18	1092	5500	3354
SAUNDERS, S.	1	1	4950	4950	4950
SCHREIBER & LUGERT	1	1	473	473	473
SCHUBERT PAUL	1	0			
SCHULLER, OTTO	1	1	209	209	209
SCHUSTER, ADOLF	4	3	176	308	257
SCHUSTER, ADOLF C.	2	2	209	582	395
SCHWARZ, B.	2	1	253	253	253
SERDET, PAUL	1	1	1980	1980	1980
SHANTI-DEVA	1	1	76	76	76
SILVESTRE & MAUCOTEL	1	1	1870	1870	1870
SIMON (attributed to)	1	1	1320	1320	1320
SIMON, PAUL	1	0			
SIMON, PAUL (ascribed to)	1	0			
SIMONIN	1	1	691	691	691
STOESS, A.	1	1	200	200	200
SUSS, CHRISTIAN	1	1	286	286	286
TAYLOR, MALCOLM	3	2	440	715	578
THIBOUVILLE-LAMY	4	3	176	352	257
THOMA, MATHIAS	1	0			
THOMASSIN, CLAUDE	5	4	935	1320	1133
THOMASSIN, CLAUDE (attributed to)	1	1	770	770	770
TOURTE, FRANCOIS	4	3	2524	22000	11475
TOURTE, LOUIS	1	1	1980	1980	1980
TOURTE, LOUIS (attributed to)	1	1	2090	2090	2090
TUBBS, EDWARD	2	2	660	3850	2255
TUBBS, JAMES	17	16	329	2970	1708
TUBBS, WILLIAM	2	2	658	1760	1209
TUBBS, WILLIAM (attributed to)	1	1	330	330	330
TUBBS FAMILY, (MEMBER OF)	1	0			
VAN DER MEER, KAREL	4	3	354	1155	705
VIDOUDEZ, FRANCOIS	1	1	660	660	660
VIGNERON, ANDRE	4	4	770	1234	1079
VILLAUME, G.	1	1	218	218	218
VOIGT, ARNOLD	1	1	396	396	396
VOIRIN, FRANCOIS NICOLAS	12	11	1100	8250	3480
VOIRIN, J.	1	1	437	437	437
VOIRIN, JOSEPH	1	1	506	506	506
VUILLAUME, JEAN BAPTISTE	3	2	1066	1234	1150
VUILLAUME, JEAN BAPTISTE (ascribed to)	1	1	1210	1210	1210
VUILLAUME, JEAN BAPTISTE (workshop of)	1	1	3850	3850	3850
WALTON, WILLIAM	1	0			
WEICHOLD, A. R.	1	1	286	286	286
WEICHOLD, R.	5	5	286	440	356
WEICHOLD, RICHARD	5	4	143	880	498
WEIDHAAS, PAUL	5	5	242	1892	690
WERRO, JEAN	1	1	329	329	329
WILSON, GARNER	4	3	242	715	473
WILSON, JAMES J. T.	2	2	374	715	545
WINKLER, FRANZ	2	1	354	354	354
WINTERLING, GEORGE	1	1	237	237	237
WOODFIELD, J. D.	1	0			
WUNDERLICH, F. R.	1	1	825	825	825
ZIMMER, E. W.	1	1	218	218	218

VIOLONCELLO

AIRETON, EDMUND (attributed to)	1	1	1760	1760	1760
BAILLY, PAUL (ascribed to)	1	0			
BANKS, JAMES & HENRY (attributed to)	2	1	2860	2860	2860
BARRETT, JOHN	1	0			
BETTS, JOHN	1	1	17050	17050	17050
BOULANGEOT, EMILE	2	1	4950	4950	4950
CAPPA, GOFFREDO	1	1	19250	19250	19250
CONIA, STEFANO	1	1	8250	8250	8250
CONTINO, ALFREDO (attributed to)	1	1	3080	3080	3080
CORSBY, GEORGE (attributed to)	1	1	1760	1760	1760

Item/Maker	*Items Offered*	*Items Sold*	*Lowest £*	*Highest £*	*Average £*
CRASKE, GEORGE	1	1	4180	4180	4180
CROSS, NATHANIEL	1	1	9900	9900	9900
DE COMBLE, AMBROSE	1	1	2090	2090	2090
DEGANI, EUGENIO	1	1	14850	14850	14850
DERAZEY, HONORE (workshop of)	1	1	4620	4620	4620
DERAZEY, JUSTIN	1	1	792	792	792
DIEHL, JOHANN	1	1	16940	16940	16940
DODD, THOMAS	1	1	9500	9500	9500
DUKE, RICHARD	1	1	1760	1760	1760
FORSTER, WILLIAM	1	0			
FURBER, HENRY	1	1	5060	5060	5060
FURBER, JOHN	1	1	506	506	506
FURBER, JOHN (attributed to)	1	1	4070	4070	4070
GADDA, GAETANO	1	1	9461	9461	9461
GAFFINO, JOSEPH	1	0			
GAGLIANO, GIOVANNI	1	1	16500	16500	16500
GOULDING & CO.	1	1	1265	1265	1265
GRANCINO, GIOVANNI	1	1	41800	41800	41800
GUERSAN, LOUIS	1	0			
GUERSAN, LOUIS (ascribed to)	1	0			
HARRIS, CHARLES	2	1	3960	3960	3960
HART & SON	1	1	2200	2200	2200
HERMANN, LOTHAR	1	0			
HILL, JOSEPH	1	1	13200	13200	13200
HILL, LOCKEY (attributed to)	1	0			
HJORTH, EMIL & SON	1	1	4950	4950	4950
HOFMANS, MATHIAS	1	1	6600	6600	6600
HOYER, JOHANN FRIEDERICH	1	0			
HUBICKA, JULIUS A.	1	1	9900	9900	9900
JAIS, ANDREAS	1	1	1540	1540	1540
JOHNSON, JOHN (attributed to)	1	0			
JORIO, VINCENZO	1	1	9900	9900	9900
KENNEDY, THOMAS	1	1	8250	8250	8250
KENNEDY, THOMAS (ascribed to)	1	1	2750	2750	2750
KREUZINGER, FRIEDRICH	1	1	673	673	673
KRINER, JOSEPH	1	1	2750	2750	2750
LABERTE-HUMBERT BROS.	1	1	2310	2310	2310
LEEB, ANDREAS CARL	1	1	4620	4620	4620
LONGMAN & BRODERIP	1	0			
LONGMAN & LUKEY	2	2	5280	8250	6765
LOWENDALL, LOUIS	1	1	2420	2420	2420
MARCHI, GIOVANNI ANTONIO	1	1	15950	15950	15950
NAMY, JEAN THEODORE	1	0			
NEUNER & HORNSTEINER	2	1	3630	3630	3630
NICOLAS	1	1	9900	9900	9900
OTTO, MAX	1	0			
OWEN, JOHN W.	1	1	4620	4620	4620
PILLEMENT, FRANCOIS	1	0			
PRECUB, FLOREA	1	1	2365	2365	2365
PRESCOTT, GRAHAM	1	1	495	495	495
PRESTON, JAMES	1	1	1705	1705	1705
PURDAY, T. E.	1	1	7150	7150	7150
PYNE, GEORGE	1	1	4620	4620	4620
QUARGNAL, RUDOLFO	1	1	2547	2547	2547
RAMBAUX, CLAUDE VICTOR	1	0			
RAUTMANN, CARL	1	1	3740	3740	3740
RICHARDSON, ARTHUR	2	1	4950	4950	4950
ROCCA, ENRICO	1	0			
ROCCA, ENRICO (attributed to)	1	0			
RODIANI, GIOVITA (attributed to)	1	1	3366	3366	3366
ROGERI, GIOVANNI BATTISTA (ascribed to)	1	0			
ROTH, ERNST HEINRICH	1	1	3850	3850	3850
ROTTENBURGH, JEAN HYACINTHE	1	1	9020	9020	9020
RUGGIERI & GUARNERI, FRANCESCO & P.	1	1	23100	23100	23100
RUSHWORTH & DREAPER	1	0			
SCHUTZ	1	1	1540	1540	1540
SGARBI, GIUSEPPE	1	1	16739	16739	16739

Item/Maker	*Items Offered*	*Items Sold*	*Lowest £*	*Highest £*	*Average £*
Smith, Thomas	1	1	1980	1980	1980
Smith, Thomas (attributed to)	1	1	3289	3289	3289
Sorsano, Spirito (attributed to)	1	1	15400	15400	15400
Stewart, N.	1	1	7620	7620	7620
Symington, George	1	1	770	770	770
Testore Family (member of) (attributed to)	1	1	11550	11550	11550
Thibouville-Lamy	1	1	1650	1650	1650
Thibouville-Lamy, J.	1	1	3300	3300	3300
Tiriot	1	1	509	509	509
Tobin, Richard	1	1	13750	13750	13750
Tobin, Richard (ascribed to)	1	0			
Ventapane, Lorenzo	1	0			
Vuillaume, Jean Baptiste	1	0			
Vuillaume, Jean Baptiste (workshop of)	1	1	16500	16500	16500
Wamsley, Peter	1	0			
Werner, Erich	1	1	990	990	990
Widhalm, Leopold	1	0			
Wolff Bros.	1	1	3080	3080	3080

VIOLONCELLO BOW

Adam, J.	1	1	2183	2183	2183
Alvey, Brian	1	0			
Bausch	2	2	152	176	164
Bausch, L.	1	1	220	220	220
Bausch, L. (attributed to)	1	1	176	176	176
Bazin	1	1	715	715	715
Bazin, Charles	1	1	715	715	715
Bazin, Charles Nicholas	2	2	1045	1100	1073
Bazin, Louis	1	1	770	770	770
Brown, James (attributed to)	2	1	242	242	242
Bryant, Percival Wilfred	2	1	715	715	715
Bultitude, A. R.	1	1	1012	1012	1012
Cuniot-Hury	1	0			
Dodd, John	2	2	275	1980	1128
Dodd Family (member of)	1	1	1045	1045	1045
Dolling, Heinz	2	1	329	329	329
Dorfler, D.	1	1	911	911	911
Dorfler, Egidius	1	1	1210	1210	1210
Dupuy, George	1	1	935	935	935
Durrschmidt, O.	1	1	218	218	218
Eulry, Clement	1	0			
Fetique, Victor	2	1	1540	1540	1540
Fetique, Victor (ascribed to)	1	0			
Finkel, Siegfried	1	1	729	729	729
Forster	1	1	1980	1980	1980
Fritsch, Jean	1	1	462	462	462
Gerome, Roger	1	0			
Glesel, C.	1	0			
Hart	1	1	506	506	506
Hart & Son	1	1	935	935	935
Hermann, Lothar	1	0			
Hill, W. E. & Sons	18	17	165	2640	1043
Hoyer, Hermann Albert	1	1	253	253	253
Hoyer, Otto A.	1	0			
Husson, Charles Claude	2	1	1571	1571	1571
Knopf	1	1	255	255	255
Knopf, W.	1	1	449	449	449
Kun, Joseph	1	1	242	242	242
Lamy, Alfred	3	2	770	2750	1760
Lapierre, Marcel	1	1	550	550	550
Leblanc, P. R.	3	3	400	873	594
Lefin	1	1	266	266	266
Lotte, Francois	1	1	462	462	462
Lupot, Nicolas	1	0			
Malines, Guillaume	1	1	2310	2310	2310
Morizot, Louis	2	1	329	329	329
Neudorfer	1	0			

Item/Maker	*Items Offered*	*Items Sold*	*Lowest £*	*Highest £*	*Average £*
NEUVEVILLE, G. C.	2	2	286	550	418
NURNBERGER, ALBERT	5	5	252	1100	594
PAULUS, JOHANNES O.	1	1	308	308	308
PECCATTE, D.	1	1	6914	6914	6914
PFRETZSCHNER, H. R.	7	6	352	605	499
PFRETZSCHNER, W. A.	2	2	286	352	319
REYNOLDS, J.	1	0			
RIEDL, ALFONS	2	1	455	455	455
SANDNER, B.	1	1	91	91	91
SARTORY, EUGENE	7	6	2420	4400	3263
SCHMIDT, C. HANS CARL	1	1	462	462	462
SEIFERT, LOTHAR	1	1	308	308	308
SILVESTRE & MAUCOTEL	1	0			
THIBOUVILLE-LAMY, J.	1	1	572	572	572
THOMASSIN, C.	2	2	1980	3093	2537
THOMASSIN, CLAUDE	1	1	1320	1320	1320
TOURTE, LOUIS (attributed to)	1	0			
TUBBS, JAMES	2	2	2860	3520	3190
TUBBS, THOMAS (ascribed to)	1	0			
VAN DER MEER, KAREL	1	0			
VIGNERON, ANDRE	2	2	990	2200	1595
VOIRIN, FRANCOIS NICOLAS	5	4	241	3080	2013
VUILLAUME, JEAN BAPTISTE	2	1	2420	2420	2420
WEICHOLD, R.	1	1	682	682	682
WEICHOLD, RICHARD	1	1	660	660	660
WILSON, GARNER	3	2	605	770	688
WITHERS, GEORGE & SONS	1	1	308	308	308
WOODFIELD, J. D.	1	1	275	275	275
WUNDERLICH, F. R.	1	1	352	352	352
WUNDERLICH, FRITZ	1	1	252	252	252

VIOLONCELLO PICCOLO

BOLINK, JAAP	1	0			
WOLFF BROS.	1	1	2200	2200	2200

XYLOPHONE

CULLIFORD ROLFE & BARROW	1	1	88	88	88

Item/Maker	*Items Offered*	*Items Sold*	*Lowest ¥*	*Highest ¥*	*Average ¥*
ACCORDION					
Horne, Edgar	1	1	47835	47835	47835
AEOLA					
Wheatstone & Co., C.	1	1	143286	143286	143286
BAGPIPES					
MacDougall, D.	1	0			
BANJO					
Bacon Banjo Co.	1	1	127710	127710	127710
Fairbanks Co., A. C.	1	1	92235	92235	92235
Fiesta	1	1	26374	26374	26374
Libby Bros.	1	1	39023	39023	39023
BANJO MANDOLIN					
Gibson Co.	1	1	21285	21285	21285
BASS RECORDER					
Goble, Robert	1	0			
BASS VIOL DA GAMBA					
Steber, Ernst	1	0			
BASSOON					
Bilton, Richard	1	1	202664	202664	202664
Bocchia, Bono	1	1	63855	63855	63855
Buffet	1	1	42570	42570	42570
Buffet-Crampon & Co.	1	1	55678	55678	55678
Goulding, Wood & Co.	1	0			
Grenser, Johann Heinrich	1	1	1881880	1881880	1881880
Heckel	2	1	1322640	1322640	1322640
Heckel, Wilhelm	1	0			
Milhouse, William	1	0			
Zimmermann, Julius Heinrich	1	1	46118	46118	46118
BUGLE					
Astor & Co., Gerock	1	1	93773	93773	93773
Pace, Charles	1	1	257875	257875	257875
CITHERN					
Preston	1	1	72387	72387	72387
CLARINET					
Bilton, Richard	2	2	202664	260568	231616
Conn, C. G.	1	1	26374	26374	26374
Cramer	1	1	107468	107468	107468
Darche	1	1	84414	84414	84414
Florio, Pietro Grassi	1	1	173712	173712	173712
Goulding & Co.	1	1	55678	55678	55678
Klemm	1	1	96481	96481	96481
Lot, Isadore	1	1	50114	50114	50114
Martin Bros.	1	1	67531	67531	67531
Metzler	1	1	56760	56760	56760
Otten, John	1	1	41903	41903	41903
Selmer	1	1	32234	32234	32234
Wolf & Co., Robert	1	1	53462	53462	53462
Wood & Ivy	1	1	61904	61904	61904
CLAVICHORD					
Goff, Thomas	1	0			
Lindholm, Pehr	1	0			

Item/Maker	*Items Offered*	*Items Sold*	*Lowest ¥*	*Highest ¥*	*Average ¥*
CONCERTINA					
Crabb, Henry	1	0			
Crabb & Son, H.	1	1	100228	100228	100228
Jeffries, Charles	1	1	46844	46844	46844
Jeffries Bros.	1	1	38977	38977	38977
Lachenal & Co.	3	2	107468	196874	152171
Wheatstone & Co., C.	6	5	67874	202594	124150
CONTRA GUITAR					
Hauser, Hermann	1	0			
CORNOPEAN					
Kohler, John	1	1	607992	607992	607992
CORONET					
Conn, C. G.	1	1	39023	39023	39023
Pepper, J. W.	1	1	49665	49665	49665
DOUBLE BASS					
Cole, James	1	1	1737120	1737120	1737120
Derazey, Justin	1	1	836220	836220	836220
Jacquot Family (member of)	1	1	227040	227040	227040
Panormo, Vincenzo (ascribed to)	1	1	1337952	1337952	1337952
DOUBLE BASS BOW					
Alvey, Brian	1	0			
Bailey, G. E.	1	1	154759	154759	154759
Dotschkail, R.	1	1	89648	89648	89648
Mettal, O.	1	1	70438	70438	70438
Mettal, Walter	1	1	134472	134472	134472
Morizot, Louis	2	1	48165	48165	48165
Paulus, Johannes O.	2	2	121665	128069	124867
Riedl, Alfons	3	3	54568	102455	84358
Vickers, J. E.	3	3	28281	53462	37456
Winkler, Franz	1	1	112552	112552	112552
ENGLISH HORN					
Fornari	1	0			
Loree, Francois	1	1	550861	550861	550861
FLAGEOLET					
Bainbridge	1	1	34791	34791	34791
Hastrick	1	1	61904	61904	61904
Peloubet, C.	1	1	70950	70950	70950
FLUTE					
Boehm & Mendler	1	0			
Cahusac	1	1	77185	77185	77185
Cahusac, Thomas	2	1	84843	84843	84843
Carte, Rudall & Co.	4	3	14847	323587	125510
Clementi & Co.	1	1	58608	58608	58608
Clinton & Co.	1	1	152381	152381	152381
Crosby, W.	1	1	67403	67403	67403
Florio, Pietro Grassi	2	1	926464	926464	926464
Goulding & Co.	1	1	27005	27005	27005
Goulding & D'Almaine	2	1	55678	55678	55678
Graves, Samuel	1	1	49665	49665	49665
Grenser, Auguste	1	1	2342175	2342175	2342175
Hale, John	1	1	38910	38910	38910
Hammig, Philipp	1	1	135749	135749	135749
Haynes Co., William S.	1	1	120615	120615	120615
Holtzapffler	1	0			
Lafleur	1	1	26374	26374	26374
Laurent, Claude	2	1	1516130	1516130	1516130

Item/Maker	*Items Offered*	*Items Sold*	*Lowest ¥*	*Highest ¥*	*Average ¥*
Lot, Louis	3	2	144760	231616	188188
Maker's Guild No. 168	1	0			
Metzler, Valentin	2	1	21595	21595	21595
Milligan	1	0			
Miyazawa & Co.	1	1	190476	190476	190476
Monzani	1	1	413325	413325	413325
Potter, William Henry	2	1	67874	67874	67874
Prowse, Thomas	1	1	154759	154759	154759
Rede, H. W.	1	1	46118	46118	46118
Rudall, George	1	1	231616	231616	231616
FRENCH HORN					
Hawkes & Son	1	1	87912	87912	87912
GUITAR					
Bouchet, Robert	2	2	2479950	4053280	3266615
Contreras, Manuel	1	0			
Gibson Co.	3	3	156090	340560	264880
Guitar Epiphone Co.	1	1	85140	85140	85140
Gutierrez, manuel	1	0			
Hauser, Hermann	1	1	551100	551100	551100
Kohno, Masaru	2	1	347424	347424	347424
Lacote, Rene	1	1	551100	551100	551100
Martin Co., C. F.	1	1	227040	227040	227040
Mauchant Bros.	1	1	434280	434280	434280
Panormo, Louis	2	2	230732	405328	318030
Ramirez, Jose (III)	1	1	247995	247995	247995
Rinaldi, Marengo Romanus	1	0			
Romanillos, Jose	2	2	799095	2460920	1630008
HAND HORN					
Raoux, Marcel-Auguste	1	0			
HARP					
Briggs	1	1	155545	155545	155545
Delveau, J.	1	1	282810	282810	282810
Erard, Sebastian	3	2	231616	694848	463232
Erard, Sebastian & Pierre	1	1	154759	154759	154759
Errard	1	1	154759	154759	154759
Light, Edward	1	1	292331	292331	292331
Nadermann, Henry	1	0			
HARPSICHORD					
de Blaise, William	1	1	318920	318920	318920
Dulken, Johan Daniel	1	1	18954320	18954320	18954320
Kirkman, Jacob & Abraham	1	1	12675300	12675300	12675300
HORN					
White, H. N. & Co.	1	1	14190	14190	14190
HURDY GURDY					
Colson	1	1	222728	222728	222728
LUTE					
Romanillos, Jose	1	0			
Rubio, David	2	1	984368	984368	984368
LUTE-GUITAR					
Barry	1	1	50114	50114	50114
LYRA GUITAR					
Barry	1	1	330792	330792	330792
Mozzani, Luigi	2	1	125285	125285	125285

Item/Maker	*Items Offered*	*Items Sold*	*Lowest ¥*	*Highest ¥*	*Average ¥*
MANDOLA					
Maratea, Michele	1	1	25453	25453	25453
MANDOLIN					
Ceccherini, Umberto	1	0			
Embergher, Luigi	1	1	228296	228296	228296
Vinaccia, Gennaro & Alle	1	1	116932	116932	116932
Gibson Co.	1	1	269610	269610	269610
Salsedo, Luigi	1	1	106924	106924	106924
Vinaccia Family (member of) (attributed to)	1	1	361933	361933	361933
OBOE					
Boosey & Hawkes	1	1	32406	32406	32406
Cabart	1	1	14853	14853	14853
Doelling	1	1	196874	196874	196874
Hanken, Gerhard	1	1	226248	226248	226248
Loree, Francois	2	1	666832	666832	666832
Louis	1	1	463883	463883	463883
Milhouse, William	2	2	260568	405328	332948
Nonon, Jacques	1	0			
OBOE D'AMORE					
Loree, Francois	1	1	463883	463883	463883
Louis	1	1	1101723	1101723	1101723
OPHICLEIDE					
Smith, Henry	1	1	140659	140659	140659
PEDAL HARP					
Erard, Sebastian & Pierre	4	4	234218	385770	306549
PIANO					
Atunes, Manuel	1	1	17084100	17084100	17084100
Ball, Jacob	1	1	261773	261773	261773
Bates & Co.	1	1	153307	153307	153307
Bell, S.	1	0			
Beyer, Adam	1	1	275044	275044	275044
Broadwood, John	1	1	225951	225951	225951
Broadwood, John & Sons	5	4	148797	1873740	685149
Buntlebart, Gabriel	1	1	452496	452496	452496
Clementi, Muzio	1	1	452496	452496	452496
Froschle, George	1	1	696850	696850	696850
Kirkman, Jacob & Abraham	1	1	1198582	1198582	1198582
Mott, J. H. R.	1	1	155545	155545	155545
Rolfe & Co., William	1	1	480777	480777	480777
PICCOLO					
Bonneville	1	1	210989	210989	210989
Lot, Louis	1	1	376376	376376	376376
PIPES					
Burleigh, David	1	1	81180	81180	81180
POCHETTE					
Jay, Henry (attributed to)	1	1	395934	395934	395934
Tobin, Richard	1	1	537339	537339	537339
QUINTON					
Salomon, Jean Baptiste Deshayes	1	1	318472	318472	318472
Wamsley, Peter	1	1	318472	318472	318472
RECORDER					
Dolmetsch, Arnold	1	1	75275	75275	75275
Eichentopf, Johann Heinrich	1	1	318920	318920	318920

Item/Maker	Items Offered	Items Sold	Lowest ¥	Highest ¥	Average ¥
SAXOPHONE					
Guinot, Rene	1	0			
SERPENT					
Metzler	1	1	347424	347424	347424
SMALL PIPES					
Reid, Robert & James	1	0			
SPINET					
Barton, Thomas	1	1	2755500	2755500	2755500
Harris, Baker	1	0			
Slade, Benjamin	2	1	1432860	1432860	1432860
TAROGATO					
Stowasser, Janos	1	1	448756	448756	448756
TENOR VIOL					
Heale, Michael	1	0			
Hintz, Frederick	1	1	1592360	1592360	1592360
TROMBONE					
Courtois, Antoine	1	1	39023	39023	39023
Pepper, J. W.	1	1	4257	4257	4257
TRUMPET					
Gisborne	1	1	395604	395604	395604
VIHUELA					
Romanillos, Jose	1	1	405328	405328	405328
VIOL					
Norman, Barak	1	1	8106560	8106560	8106560
VIOLA					
Albanelli, Franco	1	0			
Atkinson, William	2	1	506484	506484	506484
Barbieri, Bruno	1	1	695825	695825	695825
Bisiach, Leandro (jr.)	1	0			
Booth, William	1	1	393932	393932	393932
Bourguignon, Maurice	1	1	495990	495990	495990
Buchner, Rudolf	1	1	250866	250866	250866
Capela, Antonio	2	1	587399	587399	587399
Carletti, Genuzio	1	0			
Chanot, George Adolph	1	0			
Chanot, George Anthony	1	1	835230	835230	835230
Chappuy, Nicolas Augustin	1	1	537339	537339	537339
Chardon & Fils	1	1	771540	771540	771540
Chevrier, Andre	1	0			
Claudot, Pierre	1	1	397916	397916	397916
Cocker, Lawrence	2	2	260568	529606	395087
Colin, Jean Baptiste	2	2	468864	492184	480524
Conia, Stefano	1	1	550861	550861	550861
Craske, George	1	1	688875	688875	688875
Cuypers, Johannes Theodorus	1	1	4181100	4181100	4181100
Degani, Eugenio	1	0			
Desideri, Pietro Paolo	1	0			
Dieudonne, Amedee	1	1	549502	549502	549502
Duke, Richard	2	2	636944	844140	740542
Enders, F. & R.	1	1	101812	101812	101812
Epeneel, R. V.	1	0			
Esposti, Piergiuseppe	1	1	506484	506484	506484
Fendt, Bernard	1	1	2460920	2460920	2460920
Forster, William	2	1	1014745	1014745	1014745

Item/Maker	*Items Offered*	*Items Sold*	*Lowest ¥*	*Highest ¥*	*Average ¥*
FORSTER, WILLIAM (II)	2	1	917308	917308	917308
GABRIELLI, GIOVANNI BATTISTA	1	1	5373390	5373390	5373390
GADDA, GAETANO	1	1	752598	752598	752598
GADDA, MARIO	1	1	780472	780472	780472
GAND & BERNARDEL	1	1	3032260	3032260	3032260
GARONNAIRE, CHRISTIAN	1	1	956692	956692	956692
GIBSON	1	1	117216	117216	117216
GILBERT, JEFFERY J.	1	1	622182	622182	622182
GIRAUD, FRANCO	1	0			
GLAESEL & HERWIG	1	1	210553	210553	210553
GOZALAN, MESUT	1	1	134798	134798	134798
GUADAGNINI, GAETANO (attributed to)	1	1	2342175	2342175	2342175
GUERSAN, LOUIS	1	1	3583580	3583580	3583580
GUTTER, G. W.	1	1	132639	132639	132639
HAENEL, FREDERICK EWALD	1	1	383130	383130	383130
HAMMOND, JOHN	1	1	206745	206745	206745
HILL, LOCKEY (attributed to)	1	1	904992	904992	904992
HILL, W. E. & SONS	1	0			
HUDSON, GEORGE WULME	1	1	1302840	1302840	1302840
HYDE, ANDREW	1	1	92235	92235	92235
JAIS, JOHANNES (ascribed to)	1	1	1672440	1672440	1672440
KEEN, W.	1	1	169686	169686	169686
KENNEDY, THOMAS	1	1	695825	695825	695825
KILBURN, WILFRED	1	0			
KLOZ FAMILY (MEMBER OF)	2	1	636944	636944	636944
KOBERLING	1	1	125710	125710	125710
LAZARE, ROBERT	2	1	29693	29693	29693
LE GOVIC, ALAIN	2	2	107752	191558	149655
LEE, PERCY	1	1	771848	771848	771848
LITTLEWOOD, GERALD	1	1	151553	151553	151553
LUCCI, GIUSEPPE	2	2	1012968	1069244	1041106
LUFF, WILLIAM H.	2	1	996336	996336	996336
MARTIN, JOHANN GOTTLIEB	1	0			
MEZZADRI, ALESSANDRO (ascribed to)	1	1	3769051	3769051	3769051
MOCKEL, OSWALD	1	0			
MOINEL-CHERPITEL	1	0			
MORASSI, GIOVANNI BATTISTA	1	1	975590	975590	975590
MORRIS, MARTIN	1	0			
NAISBY, THOMAS HENRY	1	1	440880	440880	440880
NEUNER & HORNSTEINER	1	1	199267	199267	199267
OBBO, MARCUS	1	0			
PACHEREL, PIERRE	1	1	1159708	1159708	1159708
PANORMO, VINCENZO	2	1	6888750	6888750	6888750
PARESCHI, GAETANO	2	1	291228	291228	291228
PEDRAZZINI, GIUSEPPE	1	0			
PERRY, JAMES	1	1	1158080	1158080	1158080
PERRY, L. A.	1	1	135062	135062	135062
PERRY, THOMAS	1	1	1280686	1280686	1280686
RESUCHE, CHARLES	2	2	478896	826650	652773
RICHARDSON, ARTHUR	2	1	413490	413490	413490
RINALDI, MARENGO ROMANUS	1	1	613228	613228	613228
ROCCHI, S.	1	1	805305	805305	805305
ROST, FRANZ GEORGE	1	1	926464	926464	926464
ROTH, ERNST HEINRICH	3	3	155545	197967	171848
SACCHI, GIORGIO	1	0			
SAUNDERS, WILFRED G.	1	1	275044	275044	275044
SCHEINLEIN, M. F.	1	1	272842	272842	272842
SCHMIDT, E. R. & CO.	1	1	202949	202949	202949
SCHWARZ, GIOVANNI	2	1	1047090	1047090	1047090
SGARABOTTO, GAETANO	3	2	1100176	1610611	1355393
SILVESTRE, PIERRE	1	0			
SIMONAZZI, AMADEO	1	0			
SOLOMON, GIMPEL	2	1	1534456	1534456	1534456
STORIONI, LORENZO (ascribed to)	1	1	9843680	9843680	9843680
TENUCCI, EUGEN	1	1	362362	362362	362362
THIBOUVILLE-LAMY	1	1	208808	208808	208808
THIBOUVILLE-LAMY, J.	1	0			

Item/Maker	*Items Offered*	*Items Sold*	*Lowest ¥*	*Highest ¥*	*Average ¥*
Topham, Carass	1	1	128938	128938	128938
Vettori, Carlo	1	1	275550	275550	275550
Vickers, J. E.	1	1	72387	72387	72387
Voigt, Arnold	1	1	351648	351648	351648
Voigt, E. & P.	1	0			
Vuillaume, Jean Baptiste	1	0			
Vuillaume, Nicholas	1	0			
Walton, R.	1	1	188453	188453	188453
Whitmarsh Family, (member of)	1	1	235897	235897	235897
Withers, George	1	1	234218	234218	234218
Youngson, Alexander	1	0			

VIOLA BOW

Bernardel, Leon	1	1	192885	192885	192885
Bristow, Stephen	2	2	140659	250866	195763
Bryant, Percival Wilfred	1	1	303105	303105	303105
Collin-Mezin	1	1	289520	289520	289520
Dodd	2	2	90499	434891	262695
Dodd, John	2	2	361933	390236	376085
Dotschkail, R.	1	1	117030	117030	117030
Dupuy, Philippe	1	1	365794	365794	365794
Finkel, Johann S.	1	1	167244	167244	167244
Finkel, Johannes	1	1	159460	159460	159460
Geipel, Richard	2	1	66319	66319	66319
Gerome, Roger	1	1	303174	303174	303174
Gohde, Gregory	1	0			
Hill, W. E. & Sons	6	5	339372	619036	472877
Hoyer, Otto A.	1	0			
Hums, Albin	1	0			
Lamy, Alfred	1	1	984368	984368	984368
Moinel, Amedee	1	1	217302	217302	217302
Muller, E. K.	1	1	66898	66898	66898
Ouchard, Emile	1	0			
Pajeot	1	1	275550	275550	275550
Pajeot, Etienne	1	0			
Penzel	1	1	70330	70330	70330
Penzel, K. Gerhard	1	0			
Pfretzschner, H. R.	2	2	98983	188188	143586
Pfretzschner, L.	1	1	130093	130093	130093
Rameau, J. S.	1	1	134472	134472	134472
Sartory, Eugene	1	1	771848	771848	771848
Schmidt, C. Hans Carl	1	1	322344	322344	322344
Schuller, Otto	1	1	78047	78047	78047
Thibouville-Lamy	1	0			
Thibouville-Lamy, Jerome	2	2	140659	161172	150916
Thomassin, Claude	1	1	275044	275044	275044
Tubbs, Edward	1	1	1533070	1533070	1533070
Tubbs, James	2	2	612502	909315	760909
Tunnicliffe, Brian	1	1	197967	197967	197967
van der Meer, Karel	2	2	141900	247995	194948
Wilson, Garner	1	1	260568	260568	260568
Withers, George & Sons	1	1	187374	187374	187374
Zophel, Ernst Willy	1	1	96378	96378	96378

VIOLA D'AMORE

Guidantus, Joannes Florenus (attributed to)	1	0			

VIOLETTA

Grancino, Giovanni (III)	1	1	606210	606210	606210

VIOLIN

Achner, Philip	1	1	334488	334488	334488
Acoulon, Alfred (attributed to)	2	1	334092	334092	334092
Acoulon, Alfred (fils) (ascribed to)	1	1	209055	209055	209055
Adams, Henry Thomas	1	1	499249	499249	499249
Adamsen, P. P.	1	1	565620	565620	565620

Item/Maker	*Items Offered*	*Items Sold*	*Lowest ¥*	*Highest ¥*	*Average ¥*
Aireton, Edmund	1	0			
Aireton, Edmund (ascribed to)	1	1	936870	936870	936870
Aitchison, Frank	1	1	76190	76190	76190
Albanelli, Franco (attributed to)	1	0			
Albani, Joseph (attributed to)	1	1	868560	868560	868560
Albert, Charles F.	1	1	212850	212850	212850
Aldric, Jean Francois	3	2	1421127	2545290	1983208
Amati, Antonio	1	0			
Amati, Antonio & Girolamo	1	1	6403430	6403430	6403430
Amati, Antonio & Girolamo (ascribed to)	1	0			
Amati, Dom Nicolo	1	0			
Amati, Nicolo	1	0			
Amati, Nicolo (attributed to)	1	1	6968500	6968500	6968500
Amati Family (member of)	1	0			
Antoniazzi, Romeo	1	0			
Antoniazzi, Romeo (ascribed to)	1	1	869781	869781	869781
Apparut, Georges	1	1	454761	454761	454761
Ardern, Job	5	4	144773	293040	216953
Aschauer, Leo	1	1	192962	192962	192962
Atkinson, William	2	1	732600	732600	732600
Aubry, Joseph	3	3	492657	579854	540671
Audinot, Nestor	1	1	1326385	1326385	1326385
Aylor, Albert	1	1	42570	42570	42570
Azzola, Luigi (ascribed to)	1	1	891968	891968	891968
Baader & Co.	2	1	165396	165396	165396
Bailly, Paul	5	4	661320	1240470	1068466
Bailly, Paul (ascribed to)	1	1	523545	523545	523545
Bailly, Paul (attributed to)	1	1	1304672	1304672	1304672
Bailly, R.	1	1	246329	246329	246329
Bajoni, Luigi (ascribed to)	1	1	1158080	1158080	1158080
Balestrieri, Tomaso	3	2	6658960	24038850	15348905
Banks, Benjamin	1	1	445984	445984	445984
Banks, James & Henry (attributed to)	2	1	175461	175461	175461
Barbe, F.	1	1	198958	198958	198958
Barbe, Francois	1	1	233462	233462	233462
Barbieri, Enzo	1	1	492184	492184	492184
Barbieri, Paolo (ascribed to)	1	1	390236	390236	390236
Barzoni, Francois	1	1	53462	53462	53462
Basta, Jan	1	0			
Baur, Martin	1	1	439560	439560	439560
Bazin, C.	1	0			
Bellosio, Anselmo (attributed to)	1	1	1811810	1811810	1811810
Bergonzi, Lorenzo	1	1	275660	275660	275660
Bernardel, August Sebastian	2	2	1047508	1419000	1233254
Bernardel, August Sebastien Philippe	3	3	2842254	3979156	3528390
Bernardel, Gustave	2	1	2319416	2319416	2319416
Bernardel, Leon	1	1	622182	622182	622182
Bertelli Enzo	1	1	432047	432047	432047
Betts	1	1	123807	123807	123807
Betts, Edward (attributed to)	2	2	509058	1012968	761013
Betts, John	2	2	367653	1043737	705695
Betts, John (ascribed to)	1	1	2545290	2545290	2545290
Betts, John (attributed to)	1	1	167046	167046	167046
Bignami, Otello (ascribed to)	1	0			
Bird, Charles A. Edward	1	1	468864	468864	468864
Bisiach, Leandro	3	3	2343110	3306600	2946302
Bisiach, Leandro (jr.)	1	0			
Blackburn, G. B.	1	1	38977	38977	38977
Blanchard, Paul	1	1	1373756	1373756	1373756
Blanchart (ascribed to)	1	0			
Blanchi, Albert	2	2	1136902	1187802	1162352
Blondelet, Emile	1	1	306614	306614	306614
Blondelet, H. E.	2	2	236929	247995	242462
Blyth, Williamson	1	1	84133	84133	84133
Bollinger, Joseph	1	1	70213	70213	70213
Bonnel, Joseph (attributed to)	1	1	154759	154759	154759
Boosey & Hawkes	1	1	113124	113124	113124

Item/Maker	*Items Offered*	*Items Sold*	*Lowest ¥*	*Highest ¥*	*Average ¥*
BOQUAY, JACQUES (attributed to)	1	0			
BORELLI, ANDREA	1	1	4737090	4737090	4737090
BORLAND, HUGH	1	1	148850	148850	148850
BOSSI, GIUSEPPE	1	0			
BOULANGEOT, EMILE	1	1	1239975	1239975	1239975
BOULANGEOT, EMILE (workshop of)	1	1	260934	260934	260934
BOULLANGIER, CHARLES (attributed to)	1	1	787864	787864	787864
BOURBEAU, E. A.	1	1	83523	83523	83523
BOVIS, FRANCOIS	1	1	1726142	1726142	1726142
BRANDINI, JACOPO	1	0			
BRANDINI, JACOPO (attributed to)	1	1	2319416	2319416	2319416
BRAUND, FREDERICK T.	1	1	128938	128938	128938
BRETON	1	1	137775	137775	137775
BRETON, FRANCOIS	4	3	71551	220440	123726
BRIERLEY, JOSEPH	1	1	190476	190476	190476
BRIGGS, JAMES WILLIAM	2	2	473297	810656	641977
BRIGGS, JAMES WILLIAM (attributed to)	1	0			
BROUGHTON, LEONARD W.	2	1	55878	55878	55878
BROWN, JAMES (attributed to)	1	1	76190	76190	76190
BROWNE, JOHN	1	0			
BRUCKNER, E.	1	1	198958	198958	198958
BRUGERE, CH.	2	2	757934	994789	876362
BRUGERE, CHARLES GEORGES	2	2	153307	1131240	642273
BRUNI, MATEO	1	1	1326385	1326385	1326385
BRYANT, OLE H.	1	1	368940	368940	368940
BUTHOD	1	1	101812	101812	101812
BUTHOD, CHARLES	1	1	289927	289927	289927
BUTHOD, CHARLES LOUIS	2	2	222992	250866	236929
BUTTON & WHITAKER	3	2	111496	130284	120890
BYROM, JOHN	1	1	578886	578886	578886
CABASSE	1	1	83245	83245	83245
CAHUSAC	1	1	175824	175824	175824
CALACE, CAVALIERE RAFFAELE	1	1	439890	439890	439890
CALCAGNI, BERNARDO	3	2	6337650	7353060	6845355
CALLSEN, B.	1	1	170535	170535	170535
CALLSEN, B. (ascribed to)	1	1	4961880	4961880	4961880
CAMILLI, CAMILLUS	1	1	11597080	11597080	11597080
CANDI, ORESTE	1	1	1043737	1043737	1043737
CAPELLINI, VIRGILIO	1	1	445984	445984	445984
CAPICCHIONI, MARINO	1	1	1873740	1873740	1873740
CAPPA, GOFFREDO (ascribed to)	1	0			
CARCASSI, LORENZO (ascribed to)	1	1	1102640	1102640	1102640
CARCASSI, LORENZO & TOMASSO	1	0			
CARESSA, ALBERT	1	1	881760	881760	881760
CARESSA & FRANCAIS (attributed to)	1	1	675312	675312	675312
CARLISLE, JAMES REYNOLD	1	1	31928	31928	31928
CARNY, V.	1	1	378967	378967	378967
CASTAGNERI, ANDREA (attributed to)	1	0			
CASTELLO, PAOLO (ascribed to)	1	1	1696860	1696860	1696860
CAVACEPPI, MARIO	1	1	397320	397320	397320
CAVALLI, ARISTIDE	3	3	242831	347424	279709
CAVALLI, ARISTIDE (workshop of)	1	1	169686	169686	169686
CAVANI, GIOVANNI	1	1	947418	947418	947418
CERPI, G.	3	2	153307	173600	163453
CERUTI, GIOVANNI MARIA	1	1	440880	440880	440880
CHAMPION, RENE (ascribed to)	1	1	269610	269610	269610
CHANOT, FRANCIS	1	1	264803	264803	264803
CHANOT, FREDERICK WILLIAM	3	2	384206	1102200	743203
CHANOT, G. A.	1	0			
CHANOT, GEORGE	1	1	282810	282810	282810
CHANOT, GEORGE ADOLPH	4	3	379863	1059212	828722
CHANOT, GEORGES	2	1	2088075	2088075	2088075
CHANOT, JOSEPH ANTHONY	1	1	198506	198506	198506
CHAPPUY, A.	2	2	132639	852676	492657
CHAPPUY, N.	1	1	227380	227380	227380
CHAPPUY, NICOLAS AUGUSTIN	2	2	318472	468864	393668
CHAPPUY, NICOLAS AUGUSTIN (ascribed to)	1	1	173712	173712	173712

Item/Maker	*Items Offered*	*Items Sold*	*Lowest ¥*	*Highest ¥*	*Average ¥*
CHARTREUX, EUGENE	2	1	83523	83523	83523
CHIPOT, JEAN BAPTISTE	1	0			
CHIPOT-VUILLAUME	4	3	293040	468864	371364
CLARK, SAMUEL	1	1	70950	70950	70950
CLAUDOT, AUGUSTIN	1	1	189484	189484	189484
CLAUDOT, CHARLES	2	1	180009	180009	180009
CLAUDOT, CHARLES (ascribed to)	1	0			
CLAUDOT, NICOLAS	1	1	96155	96155	96155
CLOTELLE, H.	2	1	146520	146520	146520
COLE, JAMES	1	1	408001	408001	408001
COLIN, CLAUDE	2	1	205128	205128	205128
COLIN, JEAN BAPTISTE	5	4	134690	370696	229245
COLLENOT, LOUIS	1	1	227380	227380	227380
COLLIN-MEZIN	4	4	181181	418110	311407
COLLIN-MEZIN, CH. J. B.	22	21	85455	1705352	500391
COLLIN-MEZIN, CH. J. B. (FILS)	2	2	434000	615384	524692
COLTON, WALTER E.	1	1	255420	255420	255420
COMUNI, ANTONIO	1	1	3410705	3410705	3410705
CONIA, STEFANO	2	2	839608	900416	870012
CONTI ALDO	1	1	634018	634018	634018
CONTINO, ALFREDO	1	1	1489950	1489950	1489950
COOPER, HUGH W.	1	1	188958	188958	188958
COPELLI, MAURIZIO	1	1	410256	410256	410256
COUTURIEUX	2	1	80982	80982	80982
CRASKE, GEORGE	14	13	250866	1215984	557138
CRASKE, GEORGE (ascribed to)	1	0			
CRASKE, GEORGE (attributed to)	2	2	104751	240268	172509
DAL CANTO, GIUSTINO	1	1	241230	241230	241230
DALLA COSTA, ANTONIO	1	1	7990950	7990950	7990950
DARCHE, HILAIRE	1	1	1433432	1433432	1433432
DARTE, AUGUST (attributed to)	1	1	385924	385924	385924
DE RUB, AUGUSTO (ascribed to)	1	0			
DEARLOVE, MARK WILLIAM	1	1	94659	94659	94659
DEBLAYE, ALBERT	1	1	86416	86416	86416
DECHANT, G.	1	1	269610	269610	269610
DEGANI, (WORKSHOP OF)	1	1	3110910	3110910	3110910
DEGANI, EUGENIO	4	4	1688280	3307920	2517328
DEGANI, GIULIO	5	4	668184	2229920	1427778
DELANOY, ALEXANDRE	2	2	426338	592634	509486
DELIVET, AUGUSTE	1	1	416864	416864	416864
DELLA CORTE, ALFONSO (ascribed to)	1	1	2171400	2171400	2171400
DEMAY	1	1	322122	322122	322122
DERAZEY, HONORE	8	7	258870	1688280	722810
DERAZEY, HONORE (attributed to)	1	0			
DERAZEY, JUSTIN	3	2	452496	473709	463103
DEVEAU, JOHN G.	1	1	142798	142798	142798
DIDIER, MARIUS	2	2	265277	434280	349779
DIEHL, A.	1	1	426338	426338	426338
DIEHL, M.	2	2	132639	663193	397916
DIEUDONNE, AMEDEE	6	6	297990	615822	426508
DIXON, ALFRED THOMAS	1	1	123807	123807	123807
DOLLENZ, GIOVANNI (ascribed to)	1	0			
DOLLING, LOUIS (JUN)	2	2	154759	234432	194596
DOLLING, ROBERT A.	1	1	106425	106425	106425
DROUIN, CHARLES	1	0			
DUERER, WILHELM	1	1	50696	50696	50696
DUGADE, AUBRY	1	1	292677	292677	292677
DUGARDE, AUBRY	1	1	180050	180050	180050
DUKE, RICHARD	4	3	380952	900416	717050
DUPARY, ADOLPHE	1	1	347912	347912	347912
EBERLE, TOMASO	1	1	4410560	4410560	4410560
ECKLAND, DONALD	1	1	439890	439890	439890
ELLIOT, WILLIAM	1	1	380952	380952	380952
ENDERS, F. & R.	1	1	385924	385924	385924
EYLES, CHARLES	1	0			
FABRICATORE, GENNARO	1	1	4073897	4073897	4073897
FABRICATORE, GIOVANNI BATTISTA	1	1	826650	826650	826650

Item/Maker	*Items Offered*	*Items Sold*	*Lowest ¥*	*Highest ¥*	*Average ¥*
Fabricatore, Giovanni Battista (ascribed to)	1	1	1728188	1728188	1728188
Fabris, Luigi (ascribed to)	1	0			
Fagnola, Hannibal	1	1	3315963	3315963	3315963
Falisse, A.	2	2	378967	529606	454287
Felici, Enrico	1	1	439560	439560	439560
Fendt, Bernard (attributed to)	2	1	413490	413490	413490
Fent, Francois	1	0			
Ferrari, Giuseppe	1	1	306614	306614	306614
Fichtl, M.	1	1	1089531	1089531	1089531
Fichtl, Martin Mathias	1	0			
Ficker, C. S.	1	1	170535	170535	170535
Ficker, Johann Christian	3	3	303105	512820	392619
Ficker Family (member of)	1	0			
Fillion, G.	1	0			
Fiorini, Raffaele (attributed to)	1	1	606452	606452	606452
Fischer, H. A.	1	1	501138	501138	501138
Flambeau, Charles	1	0			
Fleury, Benoit	1	1	153307	153307	153307
Forbes-Whitmore, Anthony	1	1	527472	527472	527472
Forcellini, F.	1	1	757934	757934	757934
Ford, Jacob (attributed to)	1	1	761904	761904	761904
Forrester, Alexander	1	1	113421	113421	113421
Forster, William	1	1	227040	227040	227040
Forster, William (II)	3	3	376376	1393700	729395
Fuchs, W. K.	1	1	127710	127710	127710
Furber, John (attributed to)	1	1	478346	478346	478346
Furber, Matthew (attributed to)	1	1	155641	155641	155641
Furber Family (member of) (attributed to)	1	1	673992	673992	673992
Gabrielli, Giovanni Battista	1	1	10422720	10422720	10422720
Gadda, Gaetano	2	2	1739562	1989578	1864570
Gadda, Mario	2	1	927766	927766	927766
Gagliano, Ferdinand	1	1	11297550	11297550	11297550
Gagliano, Ferdinand (attributed to)	1	1	4348905	4348905	4348905
Gagliano, Gennaro	1	1	8697810	8697810	8697810
Gagliano, Joseph	3	2	4041730	6411020	5226375
Gagliano, Joseph & Antonio	1	1	1702800	1702800	1702800
Gagliano, Nicolo	3	3	3484250	14211270	9276240
Gagliano, Raffaele & Antonio	1	1	4688640	4688640	4688640
Gagliano Family (attributed to)	1	1	3393720	3393720	3393720
Gaida, Giovanni	2	2	1744556	2229920	1987238
Galea, Alfredo G.	1	1	281380	281380	281380
Galla, Anton (attributed to)	1	0			
Gand, Charles Francois (ascribed to)	1	1	3902360	3902360	3902360
Garimberti, F.	1	1	1705352	1705352	1705352
Gavatelli, Alcide	1	1	273179	273179	273179
Gavinies, Francois	1	1	780472	780472	780472
Geissenhof, Franz	1	1	1696860	1696860	1696860
Geissenhof, Franz (attributed to)	1	1	1102640	1102640	1102640
Gemunder, George	1	1	581790	581790	581790
Gerard, Grand	1	1	132639	132639	132639
Germain, Emile	1	1	826980	826980	826980
Gigli, Giulio Cesare	1	1	463232	463232	463232
Gilbert, Jeffery J.	1	1	195118	195118	195118
Gilbert, Jeffery James	1	1	236929	236929	236929
Gilks, William	1	0			
Glasel, Ernst	1	1	113421	113421	113421
Glasel, Louis	1	1	70950	70950	70950
Glasel & Mossner (attributed to)	1	1	72387	72387	72387
Glass, Johann	1	1	192103	192103	192103
Glenister, William	2	1	440880	440880	440880
Gobetti, Francesco	1	1	2084544	2084544	2084544
Goffriller, Francesco	1	1	6369440	6369440	6369440
Gofton, Robert	1	1	182897	182897	182897
Gordon	1	1	86381	86381	86381
Goulding	1	1	54010	54010	54010
Goulding (attributed to)	1	1	234432	234432	234432
Goulding & Co.	1	0			

Item/Maker	*Items Offered*	*Items Sold*	*Lowest ¥*	*Highest ¥*	*Average ¥*
Gragnani, Antonio	1	1	4410560	4410560	4410560
Grancino, Francesco & Giovanni	1	1	1064250	1064250	1064250
Grancino, Giovanni	1	1	10592120	10592120	10592120
Grancino, Gebr.	1	1	3315963	3315963	3315963
Grand-Gerard, Jean Baptiste	3	2	75583	891968	483776
Grandjon, Jules	1	1	362362	362362	362362
Grater, Thomas	1	1	237644	237644	237644
Gribben, P. J.	1	1	45021	45021	45021
Gruner	1	1	90005	90005	90005
Guadagnini, Antonio (attributed to)	1	1	3410705	3410705	3410705
Guadagnini, Francesco	1	1	1979670	1979670	1979670
Guadagnin, G. B. & Pietro	1	0			
Guadagnini, Giovanni Battista	4	4	7070250	44088000	25383683
Guarneri, Andrea	2	2	4133250	8484300	6308775
Guarneri, Giuseppe (filius Andrea)	1	1	45190200	45190200	45190200
Guarneri, Giuseppe (filius Andrea) (attributed to)	1	1	8919680	8919680	8919680
Guarneri, Joseph (del Gesu) (attributed to)	1	1	4921840	4921840	4921840
Guarneri, Pietro (of Mantua)	1	0			
Guastalla, Dante	1	1	947716	947716	947716
Guastalla, Dante & Alfredo	2	2	891968	1277100	1084534
Guerra, E.	1	1	2936996	2936996	2936996
Guerra, Evasio Emile	1	1	2026640	2026640	2026640
Guersan, Louis	2	1	438356	438356	438356
Guersan, Louis (attributed to)	2	1	116932	116932	116932
Guidantus, Joannes Florenus	2	1	4053280	4053280	4053280
Guidantus, Joannes Florenus (ascribed to)	2	1	1881880	1881880	1881880
Hamma & Co.	1	1	246329	246329	246329
Hammett, Thomas	1	1	161478	161478	161478
Hammig, M.	1	1	682141	682141	682141
Hammig, Wilhelm Herman	1	1	724724	724724	724724
Hardie, James & Sons	2	2	81015	111801	96408
Hardie, Matthew	1	0			
Hardie, Thomas	1	0			
Hart & Son	2	2	508827	771540	640184
Hawkes & Son	1	1	201644	201644	201644
Heberlein, Heinrich Th.	1	1	63855	63855	63855
Heberlein, Heinrich Th. (Junior)	1	1	134805	134805	134805
Heckel, Rudolf	1	1	735306	735306	735306
Heinicke, Mathias	1	1	710564	710564	710564
Heinrich, Theodore	1	1	134805	134805	134805
Hel, Joseph	2	2	2090550	2652770	2371660
Held, Johann Joseph	1	1	466637	466637	466637
Hertl, Anton	1	1	80982	80982	80982
Hesketh, J. Earl	1	1	261773	261773	261773
Hesketh, Thomas Earle	2	2	723800	731588	727694
Hill, Henry Lockey	1	0			
Hill, W. E. & Sons	4	4	791208	1594599	1026004
Hill, W. E. & Sons (workshop of)	1	0			
Hoffmann, Eduard	1	1	6411020	6411020	6411020
Hofmann, Johann Martin	1	1	362362	362362	362362
Hofmans, Mathias (ascribed to)	1	0			
Hoing, Clifford A.	1	1	164102	164102	164102
Hopf	3	3	29435	180009	85605
Hopf, David	1	1	62218	62218	62218
Hornsteiner, Mathias	2	1	833728	833728	833728
Hudson, George Wulme	3	2	633765	820149	726957
Hutton, Adam	1	1	20246	20246	20246
Iarovoi, Denis	1	0			
Jacobs, Hendrik	1	1	2285712	2285712	2285712
Jacquot, Albert	1	1	1895432	1895432	1895432
Jacquot, Charles	1	1	2084320	2084320	2084320
Jacquot, Charles (ascribed to)	1	0			
Jais, Anton	1	1	102619	102619	102619
Jaura, Wilhelm Thomas	1	0			
Jaura, Wilhelm Thomas (ascribed to)	2	1	688875	688875	688875
Jay, Henry	2	1	220440	220440	220440
Jay, Henry (attributed to)	1	1	164030	164030	164030

Item/Maker	*Items Offered*	*Items Sold*	*Lowest ¥*	*Highest ¥*	*Average ¥*
JEUNE, LAURENT	1	1	198958	198958	198958
JOHNSON, PETER ANDREAS	1	1	49665	49665	49665
JOHNSTON, THOMAS	1	1	41026	41026	41026
JUZEK, JOHN	2	2	283553	644688	464120
KAUL, PAUL	2	2	473858	1184273	829065
KEFFER, JOANNES	1	1	322122	322122	322122
KENNEDY, THOMAS	1	1	984368	984368	984368
KLOZ, AEGIDIUS	4	4	509058	2084320	1133587
KLOZ, GEORGE	1	1	710564	710564	710564
KLOZ, JOAN CAROL	1	1	410256	410256	410256
KLOZ, JOSEPH	1	1	891968	891968	891968
KLOZ, SEBASTIAN	1	0			
KLOZ, SEBASTIAN (attributed to)	1	1	509058	509058	509058
KLOZ, SEBASTIAN (I)	1	1	937728	937728	937728
KLOZ FAMILY (MEMBER OF)	5	4	106425	1592360	626945
KLOZ FAMILY (MEMBER OF) (attributed to)	1	1	289927	289927	289927
KNORR, P.	1	1	625296	625296	625296
KNUPFER, ALBERT	1	1	152381	152381	152381
KRAFT, PETER	1	0			
KREUTZINGER, ANTON	1	1	153307	153307	153307
KRUG, J. ADOLPH	1	1	99330	99330	99330
KRUSE WILHELM	1	1	110020	110020	110020
KUDANOWSKI, JAN	1	1	347912	347912	347912
KUNZE, WILHELM PAUL	1	0			
L'ANSON, EDWARD (attributed to)	1	0			
LABERTE-HUMBERT BROS.	1	1	278740	278740	278740
LANCASTER	1	1	62218	62218	62218
LANCINGER, ANTONIN	1	1	303226	303226	303226
LANDOLFI, PIETRO ANTONIO	1	1	12124200	12124200	12124200
LANG, J. S.	1	1	28138	28138	28138
LANGONET, CHARLES	1	1	568451	568451	568451
LANTNER, BOHUSLAV	1	1	289520	289520	289520
LAURENT, EMILE	1	1	826980	826980	826980
LAVEST, J.	1	1	265277	265277	265277
LAZARE, ROBERT	1	1	95669	95669	95669
LE CYR, JAMES FERDINAND	2	1	194551	194551	194551
LECHI, ANTONIO	6	5	112552	216040	155552
LEE, H. W.	1	0			
LEGNANI, LUIGI (ascribed to)	1	1	926464	926464	926464
LEIDOLFF, JOHANN CHRISTOPH	1	1	168828	168828	168828
LOCKE, GEORGE HERBERT	1	1	140690	140690	140690
LONGMAN & BRODERIP	2	2	124047	164030	144038
LONGMAN & LUKEY	1	0			
LONGSON, F. H.	1	0			
LONGSON, J. L.	1	1	253242	253242	253242
LOTT, JOHN	1	1	6369440	6369440	6369440
LOUVET, F.	1	1	132639	132639	132639
LOVERI, CARLO	1	1	307692	307692	307692
LOWENDALL, LOUIS	8	8	35092	190476	97637
LUCCI, GIUSEPPE	2	2	753810	1696860	1225335
LUFF, WILLIAM H.	3	3	735306	900416	835168
LUPOT, NICOLAS	2	2	8106560	11149600	9628080
LUTSCHG, GUSTAV	1	1	735306	735306	735306
MACPHERSON, H.	1	1	86978	86978	86978
MAGNIERE, GABRIEL	1	1	337425	337425	337425
MALAKOFF, BRUGERE	1	1	891968	891968	891968
MANGENOT, P.	1	1	151587	151587	151587
MANGENOT, PAUL	1	1	347424	347424	347424
MANSUY	1	1	85268	85268	85268
MARAVIGLIA, GUIDO (attributed to)	1	1	273179	273179	273179
MARCHI, GIOVANNI (ascribed to)	1	1	724818	724818	724818
MARIANI, ANTONIO	2	2	269610	3763760	2016685
MARSHALL, JOHN	2	1	501732	501732	501732
MARTIN, E.	1	1	46118	46118	46118
MARTIN, J.	1	1	161061	161061	161061
MARTIN FAMILY, (MEMBER OF)	1	1	390236	390236	390236
MARTINO, GIUSEPPE	1	1	283800	283800	283800

Item/Maker	*Items Offered*	*Items Sold*	*Lowest ¥*	*Highest ¥*	*Average ¥*
MARTIRENGHI, MARCELLO	1	1	1074678	1074678	1074678
MASAFIJA, DIMITRI	1	1	198475	198475	198475
MAST, J.	1	1	1231643	1231643	1231643
MAST, JOSEPH LAURENT	1	1	247995	247995	247995
MATHIEU, NICOLAS	1	1	84843	84843	84843
MAUCOTEL, CHARLES	1	1	780472	780472	780472
MAYSON, WALTER	7	6	106924	362362	192924
MAYSON, WALTER H.	3	3	113124	203623	170545
MEAD, L. J.	1	1	75614	75614	75614
MEEK, JAMES	1	1	184470	184470	184470
MEINEL, EUGEN	1	1	731588	731588	731588
MEINEL, OSKAR	1	1	63855	63855	63855
MELEGARI, MICHELE & PIETRO	1	1	1047090	1047090	1047090
MENNESSON, EMILE	1	1	395934	395934	395934
MERLING, PAULI	2	2	197967	606210	402089
MEUROT, L. (attributed to)	2	2	139205	337656	238431
MILLANT, R. & M.	1	1	312648	312648	312648
MILTON, LOUIS	1	1	413490	413490	413490
MIREMONT	1	0			
MOCKEL, OSWALD	1	1	322122	322122	322122
MOCKEL, OTTO	1	1	283553	283553	283553
MOITESSIER, LOUIS	1	0			
MONK, JOHN KING	1	1	41026	41026	41026
MONNIG, FRITZ	2	2	295165	337656	316410
MONTAGNANA, DOMENICO	1	1	22044000	22044000	22044000
MONTANI, COSTANTE	1	1	696850	696850	696850
MOODY, G. T.	1	1	152381	152381	152381
MORIZOT, RENE	1	1	164620	164620	164620
MOUGENOT, L.	1	1	852676	852676	852676
MOUGENOT, LEON	1	1	463883	463883	463883
MOUGENOT, LEON (attributed to)	1	1	318920	318920	318920
MOUGENOT, LEON (workshop of)	1	1	220440	220440	220440
MOYA, HIDALGO	2	2	217445	452496	334971
MOZZANI, LUIGI	2	2	225104	317009	271057
MULLER, JOSEPH	1	1	54010	54010	54010
NAFISSI, CARLO	1	0			
NEFF, JOSEPH	2	2	42570	60308	51439
NEUNER, LUDWIG	1	1	347424	347424	347424
NEUNER, MATHIAS	1	1	76190	76190	76190
NEUNER, N.	1	1	71056	71056	71056
NEUNER & HORNSTEINER	5	4	64786	289520	132805
NEUNER & HORNSTEINER (attributed to)	1	1	137683	137683	137683
NICOLAS, DIDIER (L'AINE)	12	11	78045	716716	293409
NOLLI, MARCO	1	1	281380	281380	281380
NORMAN, BARAK	1	0			
ODDONE, CARLO GIUSEPPE	3	3	2755500	3676530	3109077
OLDFIELD, W.	2	1	75583	75583	75583
OLIVIER, CHRISTIAN	1	1	221489	221489	221489
ORLANDINI, A.	1	1	473709	473709	473709
ORNATI, GIUSEPPE	1	0			
ORTEGA, ASENCIO (attributed to)	1	0			
OTTO,RUDI	1	1	255420	255420	255420
OWEN, JOHN W.	1	1	339372	339372	339372
PALZINI, GIANBATTISTA	1	1	255420	255420	255420
PANORMO, EDWARD FERDINAND (attributed to)	1	0			
PANORMO, GEORGE	2	1	1653300	1653300	1653300
PANORMO, VINCENZO	4	4	3184720	8266500	6668703
PANORMO, VINCENZO (attributed to)	1	1	1560944	1560944	1560944
PAPAGEORGIOU, GEORGES D.	1	1	385770	385770	385770
PARKER, DANIEL (attributed to)	1	1	1323168	1323168	1323168
PARTL, CHRISTIAN FRANZ	2	1	372141	372141	372141
PATTERSON, W. D.	1	1	174456	174456	174456
PEARCE, GEORGE	1	1	613228	613228	613228
PEDRAZZINI, GIUSEPPE	2	1	3517250	3517250	3517250
PELIZON, ANTONIO	1	0			
PENZL, IGNAZ	2	2	118822	151228	135025
PERRIN, E. J. (FILS)	1	0			

Item/Maker	*Items Offered*	*Items Sold*	*Lowest ¥*	*Highest ¥*	*Average ¥*
PERRY, L. A.	2	1	89793	89793	89793
PERRY, STEPHEN	1	1	49665	49665	49665
PERRY, THOMAS	2	2	212850	222992	217921
PFRETZSCHNER, CARL FRIEDRICH (attributed to)	1	1	225104	225104	225104
PFRETZSCHNER, G. A.	1	1	120615	120615	120615
PHILLIPSON, EDWARD	2	2	68323	76190	72257
PICCIONE, EMILIO	1	1	1272645	1272645	1272645
PIERRAY, CLAUDE	2	2	196966	771540	484253
PIERRAY, CLAUDE (attributed to)	3	2	161172	744282	452727
PILAT, PAUL	1	1	1101723	1101723	1101723
PILLEMENT, FRANCOIS	2	2	47890	95779	71834
PIPER, W.	1	1	165396	165396	165396
PIQUE, FRANCOIS LOUIS	2	1	4684350	4684350	4684350
PIRETTI, ENRICO	1	1	551320	551320	551320
PIROT, CLAUDE	1	1	1818630	1818630	1818630
PLACHT, JOHANN FRANZ	1	1	231616	231616	231616
PLUMEREL, JEAN	1	1	117216	117216	117216
POLITI, ENRICO & RAUL	1	0			
POLLASTRI, AUGUSTO	1	0			
POLLASTRI, AUGUSTO (attributed to)	1	0			
POLLASTRI, GAETANO	1	1	2368545	2368545	2368545
POLLER, PAUL	1	1	56845	56845	56845
POSTACCHINI, ANDREA	1	1	3066140	3066140	3066140
POSTIGLIONE, VINCENZO	2	2	2121075	2652770	2386923
PRAGA, EUGENIO (ascribed to)	1	0			
PRESSENDA, GIOVANNI FRANCESCO	3	2	9670320	15945985	12808153
PRESTON, JOHN	1	1	47890	47890	47890
PULLAR, E. F.	1	1	74827	74827	74827
PYNE, GEORGE	3	3	318920	529606	417951
RAFFE, E. H.	2	2	222992	1114960	668976
RANCE, J. F.	1	1	306614	306614	306614
RAPOPORT, HAIM	1	0			
RASURA, VINCENZO (ascribed to)	1	1	696850	696850	696850
RAUCH, SEBASTIAN	1	1	284225	284225	284225
RAUCH, THOMAS	1	1	260568	260568	260568
RAYMOND, ROBERT JOHN	1	1	62218	62218	62218
REICHEL, JOHANN FRIEDRICH	1	0			
REITER, JOHANN	1	1	189484	189484	189484
REMY	2	2	179179	202949	191064
RENISTO, ANDREAS	1	1	385770	385770	385770
RICHARDSON, ARTHUR	3	2	525030	586080	555555
RICHTER, ECKART	1	0			
RICHTER, G.	1	1	255803	255803	255803
RIDGE	1	0			
RINALDI, MARENGO ROMANUS	1	1	2747512	2747512	2747512
ROBINSON, WILLIAM	3	3	123914	673992	344072
ROCCA, ENRICO	1	1	2558029	2558029	2558029
ROCCA, GIUSEPPE	1	1	17395620	17395620	17395620
ROCCA, JOSEPH	1	1	23971640	23971640	23971640
ROGERI, GIOVANNI BATTISTA	1	1	15430800	15430800	15430800
ROGERI, PIETRO GIACOMO	1	0			
ROST, FRANZ GEORGE	1	1	351648	351648	351648
ROTH, ERNST HEINRICH	4	4	113520	240293	169575
ROUMEN, JOHANNES ARNOLDUS	1	0			
ROVESCALLI, T.	1	1	757934	757934	757934
RUGGIERI, FRANCESCO	2	1	12726450	12726450	12726450
RUGGIERI, VINCENZO	1	0			
RUGGIERI, VINCENZO (attributed to)	1	0			
RUSHWORTH & DREAPER	2	1	550088	550088	550088
SALSEDO, LUIGI	1	1	468435	468435	468435
SALSEDO, LUIGI (attributed to)	1	1	724724	724724	724724
SALZARD, FRANCOIS	1	1	70184	70184	70184
SANDER, CARL	1	1	146520	146520	146520
SANDNER, EDI	1	1	100228	100228	100228
SANNINO, VINCENZO	1	0			
SANNINO, VINCENZO (attributed to)	1	1	1594599	1594599	1594599
SARFATI, G.	1	1	265277	265277	265277

Item/Maker	*Items Offered*	*Items Sold*	*Lowest ¥*	*Highest ¥*	*Average ¥*
SCARAMPELLA, STEFANO	1	1	3600188	3600188	3600188
SCHALLER, REINHOLD	1	1	71056	71056	71056
SCHAU, CARL	1	0			
SCHEERER, JOHN	1	1	195118	195118	195118
SCHEINLEIN, M. F.	1	1	265277	265277	265277
SCHMIDT, E. R. & CO.	3	3	49817	240388	125529
SCHMIDT, JOHANN MARTIN	1	0			
SCHMIDT, REINHOLD	1	1	99330	99330	99330
SCHMITT, LUCIEN	1	1	521869	521869	521869
SCHOENFELDER, JOHANN GEORG	1	1	805305	805305	805305
SCHROEDER, JOHN G.	1	1	92235	92235	92235
SCHUSTER, C. J. & SON	1	1	49817	49817	49817
SCHWARZ, GIOVANNI	1	1	1449448	1449448	1449448
SCHWARZ, HEINRICH	1	1	97444	97444	97444
SCHWEITZER, JOHANN BAPTISTE (attributed to)	1	1	418578	418578	418578
SCOLARI, GIORGIO	2	2	634018	1187802	910910
SDERCI, LUCIANO	1	0			
SDERCI, LUCIANO (attributed to)	1	1	1102640	1102640	1102640
SEIDEL, CHRISTIAN WILHELM	1	1	167431	167431	167431
SEIDEL, JOHANN MICHAEL	1	1	64469	64469	64469
SERAPHIN, SANCTUS (attributed to)	1	0			
SGARABOTTO, PIETRO	1	1	1414050	1414050	1414050
SGARBI, ANTONIO	1	0			
SIEGA, ETTORE & SON (ascribed to)	1	1	523545	523545	523545
SILVESTRE, PIERRE	1	1	1983960	1983960	1983960
SILVESTRE & MAUCOTEL	1	1	1928850	1928850	1928850
SIMON, FRANZ	2	1	254529	254529	254529
SIMOUTRE, NICHOLAS EUGENE	1	1	673992	673992	673992
SIMPSON, JAMES & JOHN	1	1	585354	585354	585354
SIMPSON, THOMAS	1	1	173712	173712	173712
SMILLIE, ALEXANDER	2	2	222992	523754	373373
SOFFRITTI, ETTORE	1	0			
SORSANO, SPIRITO	1	1	8975120	8975120	8975120
SOUBEYRAN, MARC	1	0			
STADLMANN, JOHANN JOSEPH	2	1	390236	390236	390236
STAINER, JACOB	1	1	6527400	6527400	6527400
STAINER, MARCUS (attributed to)	1	1	368940	368940	368940
STANLEY, ROBERT A.	1	1	208808	208808	208808
STIRRAT, DAVID	2	1	686952	686952	686952
STORIONI, CARLO	1	1	236649	236649	236649
STORIONI, LORENZO	1	1	10746780	10746780	10746780
STRADIVARI, ANTONIO	2	1	226041200	226041200	226041200
STRADIVARI, OMOBONO	1	0			
STRAUB, SIMON	1	1	710564	710564	710564
SUZUKI, M.	1	1	62112	62112	62112
TARASCONI, G.	1	1	1326385	1326385	1326385
TARR, SHELLEY	1	0			
TASSINI, MARCO	1	1	261773	261773	261773
TAVEGIA, CARLO ANTONIO	2	1	551100	551100	551100
TECCHLER, DAVID	1	1	4242150	4242150	4242150
TECCHLER, DAVID (attributed to)	1	1	731588	731588	731588
TENUCCI, EUGEN	1	1	947418	947418	947418
TERMANINI, PIETRO	1	1	1811810	1811810	1811810
TESTORE, CARLO	1	1	5237540	5237540	5237540
TESTORE, CARLO (attributed to)	1	1	3719925	3719925	3719925
TESTORE, CARLO ANTONIO	1	1	6064520	6064520	6064520
TESTORE, CARLO GIUSEPPE	1	0			
TESTORE FAMILY (MEMBER OF)	2	2	501732	2452912	1477322
THIBOUT, JACQUES PIERRE	1	1	696850	696850	696850
THIBOUVILLE-LAMY	17	16	29304	307692	101772
THIBOUVILLE-LAMY, J.	6	6	36193	169963	94083
THIBOUVILLE-LAMY, J. (workshop of)	1	1	638550	638550	638550
THIBOUVILLE-LAMY, JEROME	9	8	74503	275550	155039
THIER, JOSEPH (attributed to)	1	1	156629	156629	156629
THIR, MATHIAS	2	1	248094	248094	248094
THIR, MATHIAS (attributed to)	1	1	640343	640343	640343
THOMPSON, CHARLES & SAMUEL	4	3	135062	362362	250222

Item/Maker	*Items Offered*	*Items Sold*	*Lowest ¥*	*Highest ¥*	*Average ¥*
Thompson & Son	1	1	633765	633765	633765
Thomson	1	1	46886	46886	46886
Thorburn, S. W.	1	1	55678	55678	55678
Thouvenel, Charles	1	1	325231	325231	325231
Thow, J.	1	1	83807	83807	83807
Tiller, G. W.	1	1	94659	94659	94659
Tim-Geigen	1	1	209517	209517	209517
Tobin, Richard	1	0			
Tobin, Richard (attributed to)	1	1	140690	140690	140690
Tomassini, Domenico (ascribed to)	1	1	613228	613228	613228
Tononi, Carlo	1	1	4959900	4959900	4959900
Tweedale, Charles L.	1	1	101812	101812	101812
Valenzano, Joannes Maria	2	2	4342800	9264640	6803720
Valenzano, Joannes Maria (ascribed to)	1	0			
Vautelint, N. Pierre	1	1	810656	810656	810656
Ventapane, Lorenzo	3	3	1212420	5500880	3556447
Ventapane, Lorenzo (attributed to)	1	0			
Verini, Andrea	1	1	395934	395934	395934
Vickers, J. E.	2	2	158335	198506	178421
Vinaccia Family (member of)	1	0			
Vincent, Alfred	3	3	703296	996336	810744
Vincent, Alfred (attributed to)	1	1	565620	565620	565620
Visconti, Domenico (attributed to)	1	1	289927	289927	289927
Vlummens, Dominic	1	1	607992	607992	607992
Voigt, Arnold	1	1	155545	155545	155545
Voigt, Johann Georg	1	0			
Voigt, Paul	1	1	167431	167431	167431
Voller Brothers	1	1	3769051	3769051	3769051
Von Dolling, (younger)	1	0			
Vuillaume, Jean Baptiste	8	7	2652770	8352300	4854494
Vuillaume, Jean Baptiste (ascribed to)	1	1	2754307	2754307	2754307
Vuillaume, Jean Baptiste (workshop of)	1	1	4961880	4961880	4961880
Vuillaume, Nicholas	2	2	688875	2261431	1475153
Vuillaume, Sebastian	2	1	673992	673992	673992
Wagner, Benedict (attributed to)	1	1	198660	198660	198660
Walker, William	2	1	368336	368336	368336
Walton, William	1	1	130467	130467	130467
Wamsley, Peter	6	5	142113	1254330	571906
Wanner, Michael	1	1	140659	140659	140659
Ward, George	1	1	217445	217445	217445
Wassermann, Joseph	1	1	836220	836220	836220
Weigert, Johann Blasius	1	1	269610	269610	269610
Whedbee, William	1	1	198660	198660	198660
Whitbread, W. W.	1	1	46719	46719	46719
White, Asa Warren	1	1	92235	92235	92235
White, H. N. & Co.	1	1	42570	42570	42570
Whitmarsh, Edwin	1	1	192962	192962	192962
Whitmarsh, Emanuel	1	1	155545	155545	155545
Widhalm, Leopold	4	4	169686	2747512	1013864
Wilkanowski, W.	2	2	78045	127710	102878
Wilkinson, John	1	0			
Wilkinson, William & Perry, Thomas	1	1	203623	203623	203623
Wilson, Tom	1	1	51310	51310	51310
Winterling, G.	2	2	852676	1468498	1160587
Withers, Edward	1	1	385770	385770	385770
Wolff Bros.	7	7	42207	102577	64870
Wouldhave, John	1	0			
Zach, Thomas (attributed to)	1	1	393932	393932	393932
Zanier, Ferruccio	1	1	615822	615822	615822
Zemitis, M.	1	1	180009	180009	180009
Zettwitz, William	1	0			
Zimmerman, Friederich	1	1	99634	99634	99634

VIOLIN BOW

Alvey, Brian	2	1	311091	311091	311091
Apparut, Georges	1	1	151587	151587	151587
Bausch, L.	2	2	41762	42421	42092

Item/Maker	*Items Offered*	*Items Sold*	*Lowest ¥*	*Highest ¥*	*Average ¥*
Bazin	1	1	189319	189319	189319
Bazin, C.	2	2	43190	75725	59458
Bazin, Charles	9	9	45250	307692	160830
Bazin, Louis	5	5	42570	405898	172322
Bazin Family (member of)	1	0			
Beare, John & Arthur	1	1	303226	303226	303226
Bernardel, Gustave	4	3	130093	362362	255735
Bernardel, Leon	2	2	122500	250866	186683
Bernardel, Rene	1	1	306614	306614	306614
Bisch, Paul	1	1	99330	99330	99330
Brand, Karl	1	1	35107	35107	35107
Briggs, James William	1	1	83622	83622	83622
Bristow, Stephen	1	1	102619	102619	102619
Bultitude, A. R.	1	1	278410	278410	278410
Bultitude, Arthur	2	2	165396	440880	303138
Buthod, Charles	2	1	36193	36193	36193
Callier, Frank	2	2	78045	170280	124163
Caressa, Albert	1	1	220440	220440	220440
Caressa & Francais	2	1	432047	432047	432047
Carrodus	1	1	111755	111755	111755
Chadwick	1	1	142113	142113	142113
Chanot, Joseph Anthony	1	1	330660	330660	330660
Chardon, Chanot	1	1	61582	61582	61582
Collin-Mezin	2	1	165330	165330	165330
Cuniot-Hury	2	2	38421	190476	114448
Cuniot-Hury, Eugene	1	1	209055	209055	209055
Darche, Hilaire	1	1	116932	116932	116932
Delivet, Auguste	1	0			
Dodd	5	4	60972	549502	276633
Dodd, Edward	1	1	434280	434280	434280
Dodd, James	3	2	234311	579040	406676
Dodd, John	3	2	188188	358215	273202
Dodd, John (ascribed to)	1	0			
Dodd, John (attributed to)	2	2	61250	197967	129609
Dodd Family (member of)	2	1	367653	367653	367653
Dolling, Kurt	1	1	62218	62218	62218
Dorfler, D.	1	1	38012	38012	38012
Dotschkail, R.	1	1	170535	170535	170535
Dugad, Andre	1	1	52114	52114	52114
Dupuy, George	1	0			
Durrschmidt, O.	1	1	56845	56845	56845
Durrschmidt, Otto	6	6	38095	123077	62168
Eulry, Clement	1	1	521136	521136	521136
Eury, Nicolas	2	1	1273888	1273888	1273888
Fetique, Jules	1	1	283800	283800	283800
Fetique, Victor	7	6	202664	810656	479963
Finkel, Siegfried	1	1	99330	99330	99330
Francais, Emile	3	2	231616	260568	246092
Gand & Bernardel	1	1	390236	390236	390236
Geipel, Richard	2	1	37792	37792	37792
Gerome, Roger	2	1	123164	123164	123164
Gillet, R.	1	1	331596	331596	331596
Glasel	1	1	170535	170535	170535
Gotz	1	0			
Gotz, Conrad	2	2	101297	139370	120333
Grand Adam	1	1	2067450	2067450	2067450
Guetter, Otto	1	1	96378	96378	96378
Hagemann, F. R.	2	1	29304	29304	29304
Hammig, W. H.	2	1	40491	40491	40491
Hart & Son	1	0			
Hel, Pierre	1	1	167244	167244	167244
Henry, Joseph	1	0			
Hermann, Lothar	1	1	72482	72482	72482
Herrmann, A.	3	3	55073	96051	80389
Herrmann, Edward	1	1	60308	60308	60308
Herrmann, W.	1	1	97076	97076	97076
Hill, W. E. & Sons	66	65	53462	904992	307034

Item/Maker	*Items Offered*	*Items Sold*	*Lowest ¥*	*Highest ¥*	*Average ¥*
HOYER, C. A.	1	1	111364	111364	111364
HOYER, G.	1	1	61582	61582	61582
HOYER, OTTO A.	3	3	120615	220528	158649
HUMS, ALBIN	3	2	128938	268669	198804
HUMS, W.	1	1	30625	30625	30625
HUSSON, CHARLES CLAUDE (attributed to)	1	0			
KESSLER	1	1	53988	53988	53988
KITTEL FAMILY (MEMBER OF) (ascribed to)	1	1	735306	735306	735306
KNOPF, HENRY RICHARD	1	1	70950	70950	70950
LABERTE	1	1	85268	85268	85268
LABERTE, MARC	1	1	123164	123164	123164
LABERTE, MARC (ascribed to)	1	1	52114	52114	52114
LAFLEUR (ascribed to)	1	0			
LAFLEUR, JOSEPH RENE	1	0			
LAFLEUR, JOSEPH RENE (ascribed to)	1	1	206745	206745	206745
LAMY, A.	2	1	710564	710564	710564
LAMY, ALFRED	10	9	36193	1074678	570042
LAMY, ALFRED JOSEPH	1	1	636944	636944	636944
LEBLANC, P. R.	3	3	66319	85268	75793
LERMETZ	1	1	25453	25453	25453
LOTTE, FRANCOIS	3	3	113124	139370	128253
LOWENDALL, LOUIS	1	0			
LUPOT, FRANCOIS	1	1	1951180	1951180	1951180
LUPOT, FRANCOIS (attributed to)	1	1	848430	848430	848430
LUPOT, NICOLAS	1	0			
MAIRE, NICOLAS	3	2	1102200	1373756	1237978
MARTIN	1	1	50906	50906	50906
MAURE, PIERRE	1	1	134798	134798	134798
MEAUCHAND	1	1	771848	771848	771848
MEAUCHAND (attributed to)	1	1	771848	771848	771848
MEINEL, EUGEN	2	2	14190	61957	38074
MILLANT, B.	1	1	236855	236855	236855
MIQUEL, E.	1	1	78047	78047	78047
MOLLER, MAX	1	1	202664	202664	202664
MORIZOT	2	2	156090	173712	164901
MORIZOT, LOUIS	5	5	38421	188188	119416
MOUGENOT, GEORGES	1	1	144760	144760	144760
MUHL	1	1	123077	123077	123077
NURNBERGER, ALBERT	18	17	32017	644244	201266
OUCHARD, E.	2	2	170535	180009	175272
OUCHARD, EMILE	3	2	167431	258870	213150
PAESOLD, RODERICH	3	3	64469	87912	78144
PAJEOT	1	0			
PAJEOT (attributed to)	1	1	882112	882112	882112
PAJEOT, (FILS)	2	2	716430	1157310	936870
PAJEOT, (PERE)	1	1	1326385	1326385	1326385
PAQUOTTE BROS.	2	1	247995	247995	247995
PAULUS, JOHANNES O.	1	1	61582	61582	61582
PECCATTE, DOMINIQUE	2	2	2066625	4961880	3514253
PECCATTE, DOMINIQUE (attributed to)	1	1	771540	771540	771540
PECCATTE, FRANCOIS	1	1	1672440	1672440	1672440
PENZEL	1	1	158335	158335	158335
PENZEL, K.	1	1	23685	23685	23685
PERSOIS (attributed to)	1	1	1240470	1240470	1240470
PFRETZSCHNER, F. C.	1	1	132639	132639	132639
PFRETZSCHNER, H. R.	12	11	23685	289927	122531
PFRETZSCHNER, T. H.	1	1	55878	55878	55878
PFRETZSCHNER, W. A.	3	2	62218	123077	92648
PILLOT	1	0			
POIRSON	1	1	265277	265277	265277
PRAGER, AUGUST EDWIN	2	2	75583	93129	84356
PRAGER, GUSTAV	3	3	86978	107468	94982
RAU, AUGUST	4	4	50648	169686	126140
RETFORD, WILLIAM C.	1	1	1047090	1047090	1047090
RICHAUME, ANDRE	1	1	468622	468622	468622
RUSHWORTH & DREAPER	1	1	89793	89793	89793
SALCHOW, WILLIAM	1	1	358215	358215	358215

Item/Maker	Items Offered	Items Sold	Lowest ¥	Highest ¥	Average ¥
Sandner, A. E.	1	1	56760	56760	56760
Sartory, Eugene	23	22	284225	1406900	871548
Saunders, S.	1	1	1304672	1304672	1304672
Schreiber & Lugert	1	1	123164	123164	123164
Schubert Paul	1	0			
Schuller, Otto	1	1	53734	53734	53734
Schuster, Adolf	4	3	46388	79187	66369
Schuster, Adolf C.	2	2	55678	142798	99238
Schwarz, B.	2	1	64034	64034	64034
Serdet, Paul	1	1	495990	495990	495990
Shanti-Deva	1	1	18633	18633	18633
Silvestre & Maucotel	1	1	468435	468435	468435
Simon (attributed to)	1	1	339372	339372	339372
Simon, Paul	1	0			
Simon, Paul (ascribed to)	1	0			
Simonin	1	1	180009	180009	180009
Stoess, A.	1	1	52108	52108	52108
Suss, Christian	1	1	73531	73531	73531
Taylor, Malcolm	3	2	111496	188188	149842
Thibouville-Lamy	4	3	45250	89091	65520
Thoma, Mathias	1	0			
Thomassin, Claude	5	4	236929	334488	286063
Thomassin, Claude (attributed to)	1	1	197967	197967	197967
Tourte, Francois	4	3	638550	5513200	2919143
Tourte, Louis	1	1	496188	496188	496188
Tourte, Louis (attributed to)	1	1	523754	523754	523754
Tubbs, Edward	2	2	169686	1013320	591503
Tubbs, James	20	19	83245	781704	455505
Tubbs, William	2	2	161424	445984	303704
Tubbs, William (attributed to)	1	1	80982	80982	80982
Tubbs Family, (Member of)	1	0			
van der Meer, Karel	4	3	89648	289328	177428
Vidoudez, Francois	1	1	167244	167244	167244
Vigneron, Andre	4	4	202664	312180	276867
Villaume, G.	1	1	56845	56845	56845
Voigt, Arnold	1	1	101812	101812	101812
Voirin, Francois Nicolas	13	12	278410	2067450	880558
Voirin, J.	1	1	113690	113690	113690
Voirin, Joseph	1	1	129435	129435	129435
Vuillaume, Jean Baptiste	3	2	269610	312180	290895
Vuillaume, Jean Baptiste (ascribed to)	1	1	306614	306614	306614
Vuillaume, Jean Baptiste (workshop of)	1	1	964810	964810	964810
Walton, William	1	0			
Weichold, A. R.	1	1	73159	73159	73159
Weichold, R.	5	5	73531	117216	93053
Weichold, Richard	5	4	35092	226248	127255
Weidhaas, Paul	5	5	62218	492657	178248
Werro, Jean	1	1	80712	80712	80712
Wilson, Garner	4	3	64469	179108	118999
Wilson, James J. T.	2	2	91780	183826	137803
Winkler, Franz	2	1	96378	96378	96378
Winterling, George	1	1	61582	61582	61582
Woodfield, J. D.	1	0			
Wunderlich, F. R.	1	1	217445	217445	217445
Zimmer, E. W.	1	1	56845	56845	56845

VIOLONCELLO

Item/Maker	Items Offered	Items Sold	Lowest ¥	Highest ¥	Average ¥
Aireton, Edmund (attributed to)	1	1	432080	432080	432080
Bailly, Paul (ascribed to)	1	0			
Banks, James & Henry (attributed to)	2	1	735306	735306	735306
Barrett, John	1	0			
Betts, John	1	1	4271025	4271025	4271025
Boulangeot, Emile	2	1	1239975	1239975	1239975
Cappa, Goffredo	1	1	4822125	4822125	4822125
Conia, Stefano	1	1	2090550	2090550	2090550
Contino, Alfredo (attributed to)	1	1	779548	779548	779548
Corsby, George (attributed to)	1	1	441056	441056	441056

Item/Maker	*Items Offered*	*Items Sold*	*Lowest ¥*	*Highest ¥*	*Average ¥*
Craske, George	1	1	1074678	1074678	1074678
Cross, Nathaniel	1	1	2605680	2605680	2605680
De Comble, Ambrose	1	1	523545	523545	523545
Degani, Eugenio	1	1	3956040	3956040	3956040
Derazey, Honore (workshop of)	1	1	1157772	1157772	1157772
Derazey, Justin	1	1	203623	203623	203623
Diehl, Johann	1	1	4292596	4292596	4292596
Dodd, Thomas	1	1	2442450	2442450	2442450
Duke, Richard	1	1	445984	445984	445984
Forster, William	1	0			
Furber, Henry	1	1	1331792	1331792	1331792
Furber, John	1	1	124223	124223	124223
Furber, John (attributed to)	1	1	1107447	1107447	1107447
Gadda, Gaetano	1	1	2463287	2463287	2463287
Gaffino, Joseph	1	0			
Gagliano, Giovanni	1	1	4181100	4181100	4181100
Goulding & Co.	1	1	336996	336996	336996
Grancino, Giovanni	1	1	10470900	10470900	10470900
Guersan, Louis	1	0			
Guersan, Louis (ascribed to)	1	0			
Harris, Charles	2	1	991980	991980	991980
Hart & Son	1	1	557480	557480	557480
Hermann, Lothar	1	0			
Hill, Joseph	1	1	3344880	3344880	3344880
Hill, Lockey (attributed to)	1	0			
Hjorth, Emil & Son	1	1	1254330	1254330	1254330
Hofmans, Mathias	1	1	1653300	1653300	1653300
Hoyer, Johann Friederich	1	0			
Hubicka, Julius A.	1	1	2609343	2609343	2609343
Jais, Andreas	1	1	405328	405328	405328
Johnson, John (attributed to)	1	0			
Jorio, Vincenzo	1	1	2508660	2508660	2508660
Kennedy, Thomas	1	1	2171400	2171400	2171400
Kennedy, Thomas (ascribed to)	1	1	688875	688875	688875
Kreuzinger, Friedrich	1	1	170280	170280	170280
Kriner, Joseph	1	1	696850	696850	696850
Laberte-Humbert Bros.	1	1	584661	584661	584661
Leeb, Andreas Carl	1	1	1215984	1215984	1215984
Longman & Broderip	1	0			
Longman & Lukey	2	2	1357488	2121075	1739281
Lowendall, Louis	1	1	636944	636944	636944
Marchi, Giovanni Antonio	1	1	4198040	4198040	4198040
Namy, Jean Theodore	1	0			
Neuner & Hornsteiner	2	1	909315	909315	909315
Nicolas	1	1	2609343	2609343	2609343
Otto, Max	1	0			
Owen, John W.	1	1	1187802	1187802	1187802
Pillement, Francois	1	0			
Precub, Florea	1	1	615822	615822	615822
Prescott, Graham	1	1	130284	130284	130284
Preston, James	1	1	418578	418578	418578
Purday, T. E.	1	1	1838265	1838265	1838265
Pyne, George	1	1	1215984	1215984	1215984
Quargnal, Rudolfo	1	1	663193	663193	663193
Rambaux, Claude Victor	1	0			
Rautmann, Carl	1	1	984368	984368	984368
Richardson, Arthur	2	1	1240470	1240470	1240470
Rocca, Enrico	1	0			
Rocca, Enrico (attributed to)	1	0			
Rodiani, Giovita (attributed to)	1	1	851400	851400	851400
Rogeri, Giovanni Battista (ascribed to)	1	0			
Roth, Ernst Heinrich	1	1	974435	974435	974435
Rottenburgh, Jean Hyacinthe	1	1	2374064	2374064	2374064
Ruggieri & Guarneri, Francesco & P.	1	1	5786550	5786550	5786550
Rushworth & Dreaper	1	0			
Schutz	1	1	385770	385770	385770
Sgarbi, Giuseppe	1	1	4358123	4358123	4358123

Item/Maker	*Items Offered*	*Items Sold*	*Lowest ¥*	*Highest ¥*	*Average ¥*
Smith, Thomas	1	1	527472	527472	527472
Smith, Thomas (attributed to)	1	1	841326	841326	841326
Sorsano, Spirito (attributed to)	1	1	3857700	3857700	3857700
Stewart, N.	1	1	1930908	1930908	1930908
Symington, George	1	1	205128	205128	205128
Testore Family (member of) (attributed to)	1	1	2926770	2926770	2926770
Thibouville-Lamy	1	1	424215	424215	424215
Thibouville-Lamy, J.	1	1	879120	879120	879120
Tiriot	1	1	132639	132639	132639
Tobin, Richard	1	1	3484250	3484250	3484250
Tobin, Richard (ascribed to)	1	0			
Ventapane, Lorenzo	1	0			
Vuillaume, Jean Baptiste	1	0			
Vuillaume, Jean Baptiste (workshop of)	1	1	4242150	4242150	4242150
Wamsley, Peter	1	0			
Werner, Erich	1	1	243045	243045	243045
Widhalm, Leopold	1	0			
Wolff Bros.	1	1	780472	780472	780472

VIOLONCELLO BOW

Item/Maker	*Items Offered*	*Items Sold*	*Lowest ¥*	*Highest ¥*	*Average ¥*
Adam, J.	1	1	568451	568451	568451
Alvey, Brian	1	0			
Bausch	2	2	38421	45250	41835
Bausch, L.	1	1	56562	56562	56562
Bausch, L. (attributed to)	1	1	45250	45250	45250
Bazin	1	1	183826	183826	183826
Bazin, Charles	1	1	183826	183826	183826
Bazin, Charles Nicholas	2	2	275044	275550	275297
Bazin, Louis	1	1	192885	192885	192885
Brown, James (attributed to)	2	1	61250	61250	61250
Bryant, Percival Wilfred	2	1	188188	188188	188188
Bultitude, A. R.	1	1	256137	256137	256137
Cuniot-Hury	1	0			
Dodd, John	2	2	68888	521136	295012
Dodd Family (member of)	1	1	261773	261773	261773
Dolling, Heinz	2	1	83245	83245	83245
Dorfler, D.	1	1	247829	247829	247829
Dorfler, Egidius	1	1	318472	318472	318472
Dupuy, George	1	1	236929	236929	236929
Durrschmidt, O.	1	1	56845	56845	56845
Eulry, Clement	1	0			
Fetique, Victor	2	1	405898	405898	405898
Fetique, Victor (ascribed to)	1	0			
Finkel, Siegfried	1	1	184470	184470	184470
Forster	1	1	521869	521869	521869
Fritsch, Jean	1	1	123077	123077	123077
Gerome, Roger	1	0			
Glesel, C.	1	0			
Hart	1	1	124172	124172	124172
Hart & Son	1	1	240389	240389	240389
Hermann, Lothar	1	0			
Hill, W. E. & Sons	26	25	41762	694848	272209
Hoyer, Hermann Albert	1	1	62112	62112	62112
Hoyer, Otto A.	1	0			
Husson, Charles Claude	2	1	397320	397320	397320
Knopf	1	1	66319	66319	66319
Knopf, W.	1	1	113520	113520	113520
Kun, Joseph	1	1	63784	63784	63784
Lamy, Alfred	3	2	195118	707025	451071
Lapierre, Marcel	1	1	141405	141405	141405
Leblanc, P. R.	3	3	104216	227380	154745
Lefin	1	1	67403	67403	67403
Lotte, Francois	1	1	113421	113421	113421
Lupot, Nicolas	1	0			
Malines, Guillaume	1	1	578655	578655	578655
Morizot, Louis	2	1	83245	83245	83245
Neudorfer	1	0			

Item/Maker	*Items Offered*	*Items Sold*	*Lowest ¥*	*Highest ¥*	*Average ¥*
Neuveville, G. C.	2	2	73531	134970	104250
Nurnberger, Albert	5	5	63855	289520	152334
Paulus, Johannes O.	1	1	79187	79187	79187
Peccatte, D.	1	1	1800094	1800094	1800094
Pfretzschner, H. R.	7	6	86416	153307	126417
Pfretzschner, W. A.	2	2	73159	90499	81829
Reynolds, J.	1	0			
Riedl, Alfons	2	1	123914	123914	123914
Sandner, B.	1	1	23685	23685	23685
Sartory, Eugene	8	7	613228	1102640	830971
Schmidt, C. Hans Carl	1	1	118780	118780	118780
Seifert, Lothar	1	1	79187	79187	79187
Silvestre & Maucotel	1	0			
Thibouville-Lamy, J.	1	1	140426	140426	140426
Thomassin, C.	2	2	501732	805305	653519
Thomassin, Claude	1	1	334488	334488	334488
Tourte, Louis (attributed to)	1	0			
Tubbs, James	2	2	716430	904992	810711
Tubbs, Thomas (ascribed to)	1	0			
van der Meer, Karel	1	0			
Vigneron, Andre	2	2	260934	551100	406017
Voirin, Francois Nicolas	5	4	60972	810656	522587
Vuillaume, Jean Baptiste	2	1	636944	636944	636944
Weichold, R.	1	1	175342	175342	175342
Weichold, Richard	1	1	169686	169686	169686
Wilson, Garner	3	2	151553	202664	177108
Withers, George & Sons	1	1	78786	78786	78786
Woodfield, J. D.	1	1	74827	74827	74827
Wunderlich, F. R.	1	1	90499	90499	90499
Wunderlich, Fritz	1	1	63855	63855	63855
VIOLONCELLO PICCOLO					
Bolink, Jaap	1	0			
Wolff Bros.	1	1	579040	579040	579040
XYLOPHONE					
Culliford Rolfe & Barrow	1	1	22625	22625	22625

5.9.5